# Abigail E. Weeks
# Memorial Library
# Union College

*presented*
*in memoriam*

Mrs. Pearl May Meyer

# THOREAU'S
# WORLD
# AND
# OURS

*Henry David Thoreau*

*1817–1862*

# THOREAU'S WORLD AND OURS

❖

## A Natural Legacy

Edited by Edmund A. Schofield, former President,
The Thoreau Society
and
Robert C. Baron, Director, The Thoreau Society

Published in cooperation with
The Thoreau Society

North American Press
Golden, Colorado

Library of Congress Cataloging-in-Publication Data

Thoreau's world and ours : a natural legacy / edited by Edmund A.
  Schofield and Robert C. Baron.
      p.    cm.
    "Published in cooperation with the Thoreau Society."
    Includes bibliographical references and index.
    ISBN 1-55591-903-0 (cloth)
    1. Thoreau, Henry David, 1817–1862—Knowledge—Natural history.
  2. Thoreau, Henry David, 1817–1862—Influence.   3. Natural history—
  United States—History.   4. Nature in literature.    I. Schofield,
  Edmund A.     II. Baron, Robert C.    III. Thoreau Society.
  PS3057.N3T48    1993
  818' .309—dc20                                             93-12848
                                                                CIP

Cover design by Sarah Chesnutt
Woodcuts by Ryland Loos

Printed in the United States of America

0  9  8  7  6  5  4  3  2  1

North American Press
a division of
Fulcrum Publishing
350 Indiana Street, Suite 350
Golden, Colorado 80401-5093

*This book is dedicated to*
*Walter G. Harding,*
*Secretary Emeritus of The Thoreau Society.*

# Contents

❖

## Part VII. Thoreau and the Tradition of American Nature Writing

# Preface

## Recollections of the Early Days of
## The Thoreau Society

❖

### Walter Harding

As I wrote in the Spring 1991 *Thoreau Society Bulletin*, my own interest in Henry David Thoreau started as a teenager. Then (in the fall of 1939) as a beginning teacher in a small western Massachusetts town, I was lonely for someone to talk with about Thoreau in this village, where few had even heard of him, let alone were enthusiastic about him. And so I began writing to anyone I could learn of who was interested in Thoreau. In no time I had a large and enthusiastic correspondence, and I began to suggest that we organize ourselves into a society. To my disappointment, no one was enthusiastic, not even Raymond Adams of Chapel Hill, North Carolina, who had been issuing a mimeographed "Thoreau Newsletter" occasionally to about thirty of his friends. They all thought there were too few Thoreauvians in the country to support a society. That is, until I came across the Reverend Roland D. Sawyer, the "barefoot legislator" of Ware, Massachusetts, who in 1917 had published a centennial booklet on Thoreau and who had long wished to organize an annual "Thoreau Birthday Mecca" to Concord. We decided to join forces to organize such a "mecca" to Concord, where I hoped to organize those assembled into a society. Raymond Adams agreed to lend us his mailing list. I added the names of my correspondents. Allen French, the historian, agreed to chair a host committee in Concord of Edward Sherwin, Mrs. Elinor Joslin, and Mrs. Elmer Robinson.

We were to meet at the cairn at Walden at 10 A.M. on July 12, 1941, and then follow it with a luncheon at the Colonial Inn in town. I began to send out notices to every newspaper I could think of in the area. A week ahead of time Allen French, discouraged, called, wanting to cancel the affair because there had been so few reservations for the luncheon. I persuaded him to hold off for a few days.

It was pouring rain when Sawyer and I arrived at the pond on July 12, and the only person in sight was a thoroughly soaked Boy Scout, who told us that the meeting had been moved to the D.A.R. Hall in town. There, to our amazement, we found the hall filled and people peering in the doors and windows because they couldn't crowd in. Raymond Adams, Roland Sawyer, Odell Shepard, and Henry Wadsworth Longfellow Dana, among others, read brief papers. A motion I made to form a society was passed unanimously, and Raymond Adams was elected president, Dr. Fred S. Piper of Lexington, vice-president, and I, secretary–treasurer. The luncheon was followed by a showing of the Herbert Gleason hand-colored slides of Thoreau Country. By that time the rain had ceased and the sun was baking us all, thus starting the tradition of being either soaked or baked—or both—at the Annual Meeting. Approximately a hundred were there, most of whom became members for one dollar apiece. Of those, only two survive as charter members—Fred McGill and I, both of us here today.

In the fall of 1941, from Chapel Hill, where I was a graduate student under Raymond Adams, I issued *Thoreau Society Bulletin* #1 (our latest is #196.) It consisted of a single mimeographed page giving details of the first meeting, printing an unpublished Thoreau letter, and listing some new books and articles by or about Thoreau, thus setting the format we have pretty much followed ever since.

In the summer of 1942 Raymond Adams issued *Thoreau Society Booklet #1*, giving the texts of the papers and poems read at the first meeting. (That series continued almost annually until the 1970s, and included such notables as a reprint of the *Thoreau Annex*, Francis Allen's reminiscences as a Thoreau editor, Thoreau's Minnesota journal, and Mabel Todd's reminiscences of the Thoreau family.)

In the summer of 1942 I was drafted as a conscientious objector to work in hospitals and as a human guinea pig, so I resigned as secretary, but instead the Society voted to put me on leave. In the next several years the war nearly killed the Society. Annual Meetings were canceled and the *Bulletin* appeared only very irregularly. But in 1944 I was able to resume my duties, the *Bulletin* got back on schedule, and Annual Meetings were started again.

Raymond Adams was reelected president over and over again until 1955, when he resigned. His annual president's addresses were high points both in wit and in learning. I recall particularly a hilarious account of Thoreau and Alcott building Emerson's summerhouse and a thoughtful "Thoreau, Imitator Plus" with the thesis that Thoreau had had few original ideas but an ability to write that makes us always associate such ideas as solitude, nature, and civil disobedience with his name.

A new tradition was established then of having a new president every year or two, and a choice collection we have had over the years. They have ranged from the sublime to the ridiculous. The most ridiculous shall remain unnamed. He never joined the Society and never bothered to show up for the Annual Meeting, over which he should have presided; nor did he deliver his presidential address. He was, with relief, dropped from the Society's rolls, but I note he still claims in *Who's Who in America* his presidency of the Society among his "honors."

The good presidents have been too numerous to mention here, but a few in particular really stand out. Edwin Way Teale took the office only after years of urging, but then served notably as president and on our board of directors for the rest of his life. He used to say that The Thoreau Society was the only society to which he belonged whose Annual Meeting was always better than the last, and we all felt much the same way about him. I was privileged for more than twenty years to paddle a canoe with him early on the morning of the Annual Meeting on one of the Concord rivers, and more than once we nearly (but not quite) managed to tumble ourselves into that slow-moving set of rivers. I remember the year he was 80 canoeing to Fairhaven Bay and then taking a long hike in the Adams Woods with the temperature in the 90s. Neither phased him a bit.

I remember also Howard Zahnizer, the executive director of The Wilderness Society, who always spent a week camping in the Adirondacks before coming down to the Annual Meeting, and his magnificent exhortations for the preservation of the wilderness. We all felt a personal triumph when his Wilderness Bill passed Congress and was signed by the President.

Then there was Lewis Leary of Columbia University, who held our only meeting outside of Concord, when in 1962 he planned the commemoration of the hundredth anniversary of Thoreau's death with a series of meetings at the Morgan Library and the dedication of Malvina Hoffman's bust of Thoreau at New York University's Hall of Fame.

Who can forget our first female president, Gladys Hosmer, dressed in her sky-blue garden gown with floppy hat and elbow-length gloves? Seeing her dashing up the aisle shouting "point of order, point of order," was a sight to behold. And those of us who were officers and directors will not forget the dinners she served on her back porch overlooking the Sudbury River. She was a great help to us scholars. I remember her once corraling the Concord town manager to run down an elusive bit of information for me. It was her husband, "Beebe," who gave the magnificent Alfred Hosmer Thoreau Collection to the Concord Free Public Library, and it was Gladys who catalogued it. She was the first one to organize the Concord town archives, after getting a graduate degree at Harvard. I remember her horror when Charlie Dee discovered whole files of town records—including at least one Thoreau signature—being burned in the town dump.

Ruth Wheeler never became president of the Society, but it was not because we did not want her to. Year after year we tried our best to get her to accept the office, but she was always too modest to accept. But I know of no one who did more for the Society. She served as vice president for many years and supervised all the arrangements for the Annual Meeting. It was she as a member of the Concord Free Public Library who saw to it that the Thoreau Society Archives were established and protected there. It was she who acquired Sophia Thoreau's herbarium from the Middlesex School, mounted it, and got it into our Archives. Personally, I would never have written my biography of Thoreau had she not continually needled me to do it and then dug up all sorts of information for it. There is no one of Concord I miss more. As Ed Teale used to say, "She was the salt of the earth."

And then there was Helen Wright, Ruth's sister, who opened up her summer place on Fairhaven Bay for Annual Meeting picnics and housed and fed the Society's officers for the Annual Meeting weekends. It was there that Ed Teale would tell his tale of the three pregnant cats and Carl Bode and Lewis Leary would challenge each other to write sonnets on Mary Sherwood's tales of "worm walks" in the woods at night.

Or remember Leonard Kleinfeld, who as a world traveler recruited new Thoreau Society members on nearly every continent and arranged for a number of them to come to Concord for an Annual Meeting. Assigned to write a term paper in high school on Thoreau's *Cape Cod*, he became an ardent Thoreauvian for the rest of his life. He built up a magnificent collection of Thoreauviana, which sadly has been dispersed since his death. He was one of the most generous men I ever knew and loaded down every visitor to his house with duplicate items from his collection.

It was Charles Ives, the composer of the "Concord Sonata," who inadvertently became the first "life member" of the Society. He became so excited about there being a Thoreau Society that he sent us a check for twenty-five dollars. Dues then were a dollar a year, and we were so excited by his check that we made him the first life member.

Our first big campaign came in 1948 when the Kussin family (descendants of the Alcott family) offered to sell the Thoreau–Alcott House on Main Street, where Thoreau died in 1862, to the Society for $25,000 before putting it on the market at a much higher price. We strove mightily but were able to raise only $13,000 and so had to give it up. We understand that when it sold most recently, a few years ago, it went for more than a million dollars.

Our second big campaign was in 1957, when the Walden Pond State Reservation officials decided to bulldoze a new road down to the pond and create a blacktop parking space there. Unfortunately for their plans, but fortunately for the pond, they started their project only a few days before our Annual Meeting. They did get several acres of trees chopped down, but we quickly got an injunction against them and filed a court suit to force them to adhere to the terms set by the Emerson family when it gave the land to the state: that it was "to be kept as it was when Emerson and Thoreau knew it." It took us two years to fight it through the courts, but we finally won it and also set a legal precedent that even governments must hold to the terms of deeds of gift. The road and parking lot were never made, but one now visiting the pond can still see the scars left by the felling of the trees despite Mary Sherwood's notable efforts to restore it.

It was in 1949 when Mrs. John Buck and Mrs. John Ford came to me at the Annual Meeting and said that in cleaning out the attic of a distant cousin of Thoreau's they had found some letters written by Thoreau's sister Sophia to her cousin Marianne Dunbar. The letters, they said, contained only a very occasional mention of Thoreau and so might as well be thrown away. I quickly persuaded them to throw the letters the way of The Thoreau Society, and so we now have thirty-two Sophia Thoreau letters in our Archives, giving much family history, and including one written on the back of the rare funeral hymn that Ellery Channing wrote to be distributed and sung at Thoreau's funeral services, giving details of the services. The Archives now contain many other treasures, including the papers of Francis Allen, the original editor of Thoreau's *Journal*; Theo. Brown's original copy of the Maxham daguerreotype; and many, many papers of the Ricketson family, Thoreau's New Bedford friends.

The Society has had many colorful members, and so a word or two about some of them. One of our early members was Roger Payne, a graduate of Oxford University who, on coming to this country, happened upon a copy of *Walden* and was quickly converted to the simple life. He wrote a book entitled *Why Work?* and supported himself by peddling copies of it. Each year he would hitchhike up to Concord from New York City. He would notify the police that he was back in town and get their permission to camp out on the old high-school porch in his sleeping bag. In the mid-1940s he came to me and said that he was so pleased with the Thoreau Society that he was going to will it his entire estate. We discovered that in order to be his heir we had to incorporate. (That explains the little "Inc." in our Society's legal name.) A few years later, after Roger's death, his lawyer shipped us his entire estate—twenty-four copies of *Why Work?*

Another individualist was Henry Wadsworth Longfellow Dana, grandson of both Henry Wadsworth Longfellow and Richard Henry Dana. Champion of many liberal causes, he loved to clamber up on to the top of the cairn at Walden Pond at Annual Meetings and orate at length. He won my heart when we were trying to write our by-laws at our second Annual Meeting. Someone proposed that no cranks be permitted to join the Society. Harry killed the motion with laughter when he pointed out that under that regulation Henry Thoreau would have been the first one to be excluded.

Esther Anderson was a lifelong resident of Concord. For years she had roamed the woods and fields of Concord on horseback, photographing the Thoreau sites. If Thoreau mentioned seeing a lady's-slipper in blossom at Brister's Spring on May 30, she went out to Brister's Spring on May 30 and photographed it. She built up a glorious collection of slides of Thoreau

Country and often showed them at our early meetings. It was she who started the custom of decorating our annual meetings with bouquets of wildflowers. Living alone in a house on Garfield Road, she chopped all her own fireplace wood until her mid-80s. At 87, seeing a stray dog in her yard, she enticed it into her empty dog yard and called the police. They immediately identified it as a stray coyote but came back a day later to tell her that it was not a coyote, but a timber wolf. What it was doing loose in Concord no one knows, but she caught it.

Roland Robbins (who, incidentally, was also among our Society's presidents) first attended our 1945 meeting, and when people there began to argue as to whether or not the cairn at Walden actually marked the site of Thoreau's cabin, he got permission to do some digging. Sure enough, he found Thoreau's chimney foundation. We hired him to give a report on his discovery at the 1946 meeting, and that started him off on a lifelong career as archaeologist and lecturer. For many years he and his wife, Gerry, entertained a large portion of those attending the Annual Meetings at picnics in their backyard, and there it was that he built his first replica of the Walden cabin.

Ira Hoover was a Philadelphia postman, who in delivering a letter to Steve Thomas, noticed The Thoreau Society's return address and so joined the Society. Tied down with the care of two elderly invalid sisters, he said he could survive so long as he could get up to Concord for the Annual Meeting. He loved to copy out whole volumes of his favorite quotations from Thoreau and present them to his friends. He willed his residual estate to the Society, and over the years the interest from it has been used on a number of occasions to help purchase choice nature sites in Concord for conservation.

Nor should we forget Anton Kovar, who for years as a hobby searched the bookstores of Boston and built up a tremendous collection of the various editions of *Walden* and then donated it to the Society's Archives. A man of many trades, he taught violin, composed music, invented a star map, did all sorts of things.

And then the prize individualist of them all, Rella Ritchell. She supported herself by operating the Rella Ritchell Culture Clubs, bringing "culture" to the *nouveau riche* of Brooklyn, New York. Every year she ordered a luncheon at the Annual Meeting, ate it, and then refused to pay for it because it was not vegetarian and she was. She was absolutely the world's worst poet, far outshining the Sweet Singer of Michigan, whom Mark Twain denounced. Somehow, she persuaded a disciple to publish a volume of her collected poems. She immediately mailed copies to many of the prominent members of The Thoreau Society, each personally inscribed with great flourishes and followed three weeks later by a bill for the book. When I returned mine, she sent it back with a demand that I pay for it because, since she had written my name in it, she couldn't send it to anyone else! At the next Annual Meeting she rose up to denounce me as a cheat. At one point in the 1950s I issued an invitation for any member to edit an issue of our *Bulletin*. Rella was the only one who responded. Caught in a dilemma, I rewrote the entire thing, tossing about half of it out, expecting her to bring down the wrath of the gods on my head. Instead, she apparently never realized I had rewritten it, and she basked in the glory of her publication. But for all Rella's foibles, she had a tremendous enthusiasm for Thoreau. And she recruited a remarkable number of new members into the Society.

I could go on and on, but there are limits to all things. If you are hurt because I did not mention you, just note that I limited my remarks to those who are no longer living among us. In my files I have a longer history, but since it is a much franker history, some of you will be relieved to know that I am leaving instructions that it not be published until everyone mentioned in it is gone. (Don't you wonder what I have said about you that you will never know?) Now, after that nasty remark, let me close on a different tune.

I wish I knew how to express fully all that this Society and you members have meant to me over this past half-century. You have added immeasurably to the meaning of my life and to the friendships I have enjoyed among you. Each and every year I look upon the Annual Meeting as a high point of the year. Each of the nearly two hundred bulletins I have had the privilege of editing has been a joyful and rewarding experience, thanks in a large part to the support you have steadily given me. Thanks also to you who have so constantly helped me in my searches for new material about Thoreau for the articles and books I have written over the years and am still writing, and for so graciously listening to my findings even when you have not always agreed with them.

It is not without some misgivings that I end my fifty years as secretary. I look forward to continuing to edit the "Additions to the Thoreau Bibliography" column for the *Bulletin*. And I am particularly grateful to see the secretaryship pass on to the able hands of Bradley Dean, who will, I am sure, lead the *Bulletin* to new heights.

# Introduction
## Henry David Thoreau and the 21st Century

❖

### Robert C. Baron

Ecstasies
Let nothing come between you and the light.
—*Letter to H. G. O. Blake*

Henry David Thoreau was born on July 12, 1817. He died on May 6, 1862, two months before his forty-fifth birthday. During his life, less than 2,000 copies of his books were sold. Yet seldom has an American writer had such influence. And as we prepare to enter the 21st century, the thoughts and words of very few writers have as much pertinence.

In *Walden,* Thoreau wrote: "Books are the treasured wealth of the world and the fit inheritance of generations and nations. ... Their authors are a natural and irresistible aristocracy in every society, and, more than kings or emperors, exert an influence on mankind." And also from the same source: "How many a man has dated a new era in his life from the readings of a book."

Where the wisdom of a newspaper lasts a day and a magazine a week, and the wisdom of television, such as it is, lasts but an instant and is forgotten, ideas in books can have permanence. Good writers transcend time and place. They can reach out to many people, some in distant places or not yet born. They can influence people in very significant ways.

Henry David Thoreau's ideas on civil disobedience inspired a young Indian, Mohandas Ghandi, who developed the concept while in South Africa and on his return to India in 1914. "Nonviolence is the first article of my faith," he said in 1922 at his trial before he went to jail. A young American minister, Martin Luther King, followed the same idea. "Nonviolence is the answer to the crucial political and moral questions of our time," he said while accepting the Nobel Peace Prize in 1964.

This idea affected several Russian visitors attending the Thoreau Jubilee in Concord in July 1991, who then returned home and stood in front of the tanks in Moscow, fighting for their freedom. In Beijing, in South Africa, in South America, and throughout the world, the concept of civil disobedience lives and is the basis of the struggle for justice and freedom. At times, Henry David Thoreau is the Voice of our Inner Conscience, a voice that we all need to hear.

Thoreau was not only a naturalist but also a scientist, a musician, a historian, a scholar, a lecturer and traveler, and an ecologist. Essays follow that show his work in each of these fields. His life shows that humans can be more than specialists, can be educated in multiple fields, and can be aware that all ways of discovery and searching for truth are appropriate.

It is in the area of Thoreau and the tradition of American nature writing, however, that I would like to focus.

Once upon a time, for millions of years, all of us were part of nature. We lived in nature, dealt with our fellow inhabitants on this planet, watched the sun and the stars and the seasons.

But then we got this thin veneer of civilization. We believed that we were somehow above nature, that we were sent here by our god to conquer nature. We were the chosen creatures. All other creatures were our slaves to do with as we wanted.

Now the Native American people and other so called "primitive peoples" around the world knew that this was wrong. If we destroyed the buffalo and the deer and the forest and the birds and plants, we were destroying ourselves and leaving our children to starve, if not physically, then emotionally and spiritually.

The love of land in this special place called America has been a common theme throughout American history. It is a major factor in our literature. Nature writing expresses this special love for the land and all that are on it. Thoreau the writer reaches out to such kindred souls. He observed, thought, and cared about nature, and in his writing he encourages us to recognize our proper place in the world and to leave something of value.

In the chapter on "Reading" in *Walden*, Thoreau writes:

> The best books are not read even by those who are called good readers. What does our Concord culture amount to? There is in this town, with a very few exceptions, no taste for the best or for very good books even in English literature, whose words all can read and spell. Even the college-bred and so called liberally educated men here and elsewhere have really little or no acquaintance with the English classics; and as for the recorded wisdom of mankind, the ancient classics and Bibles, which are accessible to all who will know of them, there are the feeblest efforts anywhere made to become acquainted with them.

Thoreau is proof of the theory that writers should be readers and the breadth of reading generally indicates the depth of thought. A writer who is not a reader is like a talker who is not a listener. Thoreau himself was exceptionally well read. A short review of his works show references to the thoughts and writings of:

> Homer, Cato, Marcus Terentius Varro, Virgil, Confucius, the Bible, Geoffrey Chaucer, Francia Bacon, Roger Bacon, Izaak Walton Thomas Gray, Milton, Samuel Johnson, John Donne, Shakespeare, John Bunyan, William Penn, Oliver Cromwell, Sir Walter Raleigh Goethe, Christopher Marlowe, Alexander Pope, Sir Walter Scott, Galileo, Alexander von Humboldt, Louis Agassiz, Charles Darwin, William Bartram and William Bradford, Daniel Webster and Noah Webster, Emerson, George Bancroft, William Channing, Longfellow, Wordsworth and numerous others.

"It would be worth the while to select our reading, for books are the society we keep," he wrote in *A Week on the Concord and Merrimack Rivers*.

A few years ago I had the pleasure of editing *The Garden and Farm Books of Thomas Jefferson*. One is quickly impressed with the number of authors Jefferson was familiar with and how many he read in Greek and Latin and French. After the British burned down Washington, D.C., in the War of 1812, Jefferson's library became the foundation for the Library of Congress.

Another point is that Things Take Time (also called the publishers humility test). It is possible to tell good writing from bad writing. But it may take time to separate great writing from good writing.

Henry David Thoreau only published two books in his lifetime, together with a number of essays and poems published in *The Dial* and *the Atlantic* and other journals. "Civil Disobedience" was published in 1849 in the first and only edition of Elizabeth Peabody's *Aesthetic Papers*.

*A Week on the Concord and Merrimack Rivers* was published on May 30, 1849, by James Munroe and Company of Boston. Thoreau paid the printing cost of the 1,000 copies from his royalties. The book received mixed reviews, the publisher gave away about 75 copies and sold perhaps 200 more. In 1853 Thoreau took back 706 of the original copies and stored them in the family attic, remarking, "I have now a library of nearly nine hundred volumes, over seven hundred of which I wrote myself."

*Walden* was published by Ticknor and Fields of Boston on August 9, 1854. It was the seventh revision of the manuscript. Of the 2,000 copies originally printed, more than 1,700 were sold within the first year. Yet in his lifetime, Henry David Thoreau would in no sense be considered a successful writer.

After his death on May 6, 1862, Thoreau's sister, Sophia, read the seventy handwritten volumes of his journals, containing about two million words. Then she did what most of us would do: She had Emerson look at them.

During the 1860s Alcott, Emerson, and Channing helped Sophia edit five volumes of Thoreau's writings. *The Maine Woods* was published in

1864 and *Cape Cod* in 1865. Harrison Blake, an old friend from Worcester, edited four volumes on the seasons from 1878 to 1892. A 20-volume edition of Thoreau's writings was issued by Houghton Mifflin in 1906, 44 years after his death.

And slowly, but surely, through the work of excellent and caring editors, teachers, and students, Henry David Thoreau's place in the history of American literature and the world of ideas grew. As we enter the 21st century, his reputation, his influence, and the applicability of his ideas are more important than ever.

Let me close with two thoughts: For those of us who are publishers, read every submission. Support your good authors. Things do take time. For those of you who are writers, be nice to your sister.

———————

**ROBERT C. BARON** is the founder and president of Fulcrum Publishing, a Colorado-based book publishing company, specializing in history, biography, nature and the natural sciences, gardening, travel, and the world of ideas. He is a director of The Thoreau Society, the International Wilderness Leadership Foundation, the Denver Public Library Friends Foundation, a trustee of the American Antiquarian Society, and a member of Massachusetts Historical Society and the Organization of American Historians. He is the author of numerous papers and books, including *The Garden and Farm Books of Thomas Jefferson* and *Soul of America: Documenting Our Past, 1492–1974*.

# Part I

❖

# CIVIL DISOBEDIENCE

# Some Thoughts of
# Henry David Thoreau

❖

I think that we should be men first, and subjects afterward. It is not desirable to cultivate a respect for the law, so much as for the right.

*—Civil Disobedience [1849]*

When a sixth of the population of a nation which has undertaken to be the refuge of liberty are slaves, and a whole country [Mexico] is unjustly overrun and conquered by a foreign army, and subjected to military law, I think that it is not too soon for honest men to rebel and revolutionize. What makes this duty the more urgent is the fact that the country so overrun is not our own, but ours is the invading army.

*—Ibid.*

Any man more right than his neighbors constitutes a majority of one.

*—Ibid.*

The frontiers are not east or west, north or south, but wherever a man *fronts* a fact.

*—Ibid.*

We do all stand in the front ranks of the battle every moment of our lives; where there is a brave man there is the thickest of the fight, there is a post of honor.

*—December 2, 1839*

He [John Brown] did not go to the college called Harvard; he was not fed on the pap that is there furnished. As he phrased it, "I know no more of grammar than one of your calves." But he went to the great university of

3

the West, where he sedulously pursued the study of Liberty, for which he had early betrayed a fondness, and, having taken many degrees, he finally commenced the practice of Humanity, as you all know.

—*A Writer's Journal [1859]*

If we are prosecuted for abusing children, others deserve to be prosecuted for maltreating the face of nature committed to their care.

—*September 28, 1857*

# A Sharps Rifle of Infinitely Surer and Longer Range

❖

**Barry Kritzberg**

In John Brown's will, written just three days before he was hanged, he left his rifle—if it could be found—to his son Owen. That rifle was presented to John Brown here in Worcester. And Worcester, of course, was one of the three places that Thoreau delivered his lecture "A Plea for Captain John Brown." There is more to this than mere coincidence, for John Brown's rifle and Henry Thoreau's words are, in my mind, tied together by more than a chance bond. I did not always think so, however. I discovered *Walden* by chance as an adolescent, but I did not read "Civil Disobedience" until it was an assigned reading for a high-school English class. The effect it had on me, in that placid Eisenhower era, was electric. For there, in my textbook—surely the last place I would have thought to look for it—was a magnificent rationale for all of my unarticulated rebelliousness. I eagerly asked my English teacher if this guy *Tha-Row* had written any other stuff, besides *Walden* and this essay in our textbook. "Nah," he said, "nothing worth reading, a couple of nature essays, if you're into that, some journals, and one other nature book that, for good reason, sold only two hundred copies."

In college, my American lit anthology had a bit of *The Maine Woods*, a bit of *A Week*, a couple of paragraphs from *Walden*, all of "Civil Disobedience," but no mention of John Brown. One might read about John Brown in a history book, but not in an anthology of American literature. The image of Henry Thoreau presented in class was that of a great nature writer who, almost by accident, had written a great essay which won him the title the "Apostle of Passive Resistance" by virtue of its profound impact on Tolstoy and Gandhi. (Martin Luther King, Jr., was still virtually unknown.) I dutifully recorded in my notes that Thoreau was the "Apostle of Civil Disobedience," and there the matter rested until

I bought the Modern Library edition of Thoreau's writings for one dollar and ninety-five cents. And there was no tax on books. It was in that volume that I encountered, for the first time "Slavery in Massachusetts," "Life Without Principle," and "A Plea for Captain John Brown." I came away from that experience wondering—as many others no doubt have—what had happened to the "Apostle of Civil Disobedience," wondering what terrible things had happened to compel Thoreau to give up his lofty idealism, to make him say that he could even foresee circumstances in which he could kill or be killed. The biographers and critics I read thereafter suggested that the John Brown episode marked an abrupt departure from the passive-resistance stance Thoreau took earlier in "Civil Disobedience."

I have come to think, however, that there is another way of explaining the matter. The difference between the Thoreau of "Civil Disobedience" and the Thoreau of "A Plea for Captain John Brown" is perhaps no greater than the changing of one's name from David Henry to Henry David. There is, as I see it today, a remarkable consistency of thought and attitude in the life of Henry Thoreau. The Henry Thoreau who rang the bell in 1844—after the sexton and selectmen refused to do so—to call the people of Concord to hear Emerson speak on the tenth anniversary of West Indian Emancipation did so for much the same reasons that Thoreau, himself, in October of 1859, rang the bell to call his townsmen to hear him speak for John Brown. There have been several obstacles in the way of seeing Thoreau's unity of thought on this issue, however. One obstacle is the very title by which his most famous essay has become known: "Civil Disobedience." For all of its witty, Thoreau-like resonance, it was not his title. When it appeared in Elizabeth Peabody's *Aesthetic Papers*, Thoreau called it "Resistance to Civil Government," which has a rather different tone to be sure. Another obstacle is the worldwide reputation of Thoreau—enhanced, of course, by the attention that Gandhi, Tolstoy, and Martin Luther King, Jr., have called to the essay—as the author of the most powerful statement of the moral basis for passive resistance. It is that, without a doubt, but there is more in the essay than merely a call to civil disobedience. Thoreau offers a wide range of alternatives, and some of his words might even be taken to prefigure John Brown:

> A very few, as heroes, patriots, martyrs, reformers in the great sense, and *men*, serve the state with their consciences also, and so necessarily resist it for the most part. (ML, 638)

> And didn't John Brown do just that? Or, again: ... but if it is such a nature that it requires you to be an agent of injustice to another, then, I say, break the law. (643)

And didn't John Brown do just that? Or, again: Action from principle, the perception and performance of the right, changes things and relations; it is essentially revolutionary, and does not consist wholly with anything which was. (643)

It should not surprise us, then, that John Brown was, as Thoreau said in "A Plea for Captain John Brown," "a transcendentalist above all, a man of ideas and principles ... ." (ML, 686) Some fifteen years before the raid on Harpers Ferry, Henry Thoreau had singled out two abolitionists— N. P. Rogers and Wendell Phillips—for high praise. Both men deserved accolades, as Thoreau saw it, because they, like John Brown later, were men who were willing to be guided by their consciences, come what may. Rogers, Phillips, and Brown were men who believed, as Thoreau did, that—as he wrote in *A Week*—"only the absolutely right is expedient for all." This "higher law" doctrine was in the air, of course, and one could hear it invoked from pulpits on any Sunday in the growing tensions of the 1840s and 1850s. For Thoreau, however, it was an old idea, as ancient as Greek tragedy. In *A Week*, for example, Thoreau quotes Antigone's higher-law doctrine as a splendid illustration of the right conduct for a just man in relation to an unjust state. It is that higher-law doctrine, it seems to me, which Thoreau applies consistently, almost as a touchstone, to the events of his day. The principles which Thoreau espouses in "Civil Disobedience," then, are not radically different from those he advocates a decade later in "A Plea for Captain John Brown."

And now we come to the rifle and the word: if Thoreau could conceive of circumstances in which he could kill or be killed, why didn't he act? If it was the nature of heroes to do brave deeds, Thoreau believed, then it was the province of poets to sing their praises. Brave deeds might be ephemeral, but words were not. We would not know of Antigone, if Sophocles did not celebrate her virtues; we would not know of the moral greatness of Socrates, if it were not for the brilliant words of Plato.

The steady power of words could topple institutions, Thoreau believed, and, as he said, "the art of composition is as simple as the discharge of a bullet from a rifle and its masterpieces imply an infinitely greater force behind it." No wonder, then, as Thoreau said, in "A Plea for Captain John Brown," that John Brown could "afford to lose his Sharps rifles, while he retained the faculty of speech—a Sharps rifle of infinitely surer and longer range."

---

**BARRY KRITZBERG** is a teacher at Morgan Park Academy, an independent school in Chicago. His lifelong interest in Thoreau has led to the publication of a number of articles on Thoreau, as well as a grant from the National Endowment for the Humanities for research on reformers of the 1840s.

# Thoreau and Civil Disobedience
## Some Psychological
## and Life-Context Dimensions

❖

### Richard M. Lebeaux

At the outset I want to stress that, in considering the psychological and life-context roots, the private significance and dimensions of Thoreau's "civil disobedience" (in thought, writing, and action), I do not intend to *reduce* Thoreau's deep moral convictions and political beliefs, or the truly great and enormously influential document he wrote, merely to an expression of some private psychic agenda. Considering the psychological roots of, and influences on, political positions and actions certainly does not delegitimize or invalidate them; they need to be evaluated on their own merits, apart from any private motivations that their originators, supporters, or detractors may have. Indeed, I want to make clear my own strong convictions about, and commitment to, civil disobedience as a powerful and ethical way to end oppression and bring about necessary social change, transformation, and justice. I have taught many courses, for instance, on the American 1960s, and I believe the nonviolent civil rights and antiwar movements serve as inspiring models and exemplars for effecting political and social change. My intention here, then, is *not* to cast doubt on the strategy of civil disobedience itself. Having made these crucial acknowledgments, I will embark on my own analysis of some aspects of Thoreau and civil disobedience.

Thoreau ended his first draft of *Walden* by referring to the conclusion of his first year at the pond. It was probably quite significant that one of the most provocative experiences of the Walden period occurred soon after the beginning of his second year at Walden—the night, July 23 or 24, 1846, he spent in jail for refusing to pay his poll tax as a protest against the recently declared Mexican War. This episode was associated with an incipient desire to ward off an incipient sense of stagnation, to remain in touch with "wilderness," to shore up some of the tiny cracks appearing in the Walden life structure and identity. To be sure, he did not choose the exact timing of his arrest by Sam Staples. Thoreau had a history of poll tax resistance—but the jailing nevertheless gave him a providential opportunity to reassert his distance from the townspeople. Soon after this incident, he discussed tax resistance in his journal, accused the society of moral turpitude: "Countless reforms are called for because society is not animated enough or instinct enough with life ... . Better are the physically dead for more lively they rot." (*PJ, II: 262–264) And he observed, "Even virtue is no longer such if it stagnate."[1]

One may justly conclude that he was as concerned about his own potential for "stagnation" at Walden as he was about the undeniable moral lethargy and corruption his country was demonstrating in the Mexican War. But while his act may have provided a temporary pick-me-up, it also served to highlight a flaw his life at Walden. By the evening of his arrest, someone—most likely his proper Aunt Maria—had paid his tax for him, and it was only because Staples wouldn't take the trouble to put his boots back on and inform him that he spent the rest of the night in jail. Staples said that Thoreau was "mad as the devil" at this turn of events and understandably so. It was no doubt deeply embarrassing for him, the supposedly heroic and self-sufficient rebel and sojourner at Walden, to have underscored, for all the community and himself to see, the extent to which he remained linked to, and indebted to, his family (particularly the women) and civilized society. One at least has to wonder whether he anticipated that he would eventually be bailed out. Indeed, Aunt Maria or other family members would continue for years to pay the poll tax for him.[2]

Thus the night in jail, though it would be transmuted into a remarkable and enormously influential political document, did not leave Thoreau with unmixed feelings. The act of passive resistance to civil government was intended to be subversive, but it was itself subverted. As much as it represented an act of courage and conviction, it also left him with questions about the authenticity and viability of the life he was then leading. During the second year, "Walden became ... less of a home and more of a headquarters. He spent more time back in Concord that he had the season before."[3] Thoreau left Walden on September 6, 1847. Emerson's departure for England gave him the opportunity and pretext to become a "sojourner in civilized life again." In Emerson's absence, he would live with Lidian and the children. But Thoreau had difficulties making the transition back to civilized life. He experienced renewed threats to the sense of identity he had achieved at Walden. There were also tensions involved in taking over "head of household" at the Emersons, in becoming a substitute husband and father. And, quite critically, Thoreau's attempts to establish a writing career—one of the important reasons he left Walden—was quite problematic. Emerson had promised to help him with his career (which included getting *A Week* published). But Emerson was gone and Thoreau felt let-down. His feelings toward the absent Emerson became strained and ambivalent—and vice versa—as is revealed in the Emerson-Thoreau correspondence during this period.

Thus, Thoreau was on some level becoming cognizant that his sojourn in civilized life was insidiously contributing to the loss of serenity. "Civil Disobedience," or as it was first entitled, "Resistance to Civil Government," was very much of a piece with the concerns of the period, when Thoreau was again feeling defensive, experiencing blocks to his career, questioning his return to civilized society, and—whether or not he could fully face it on a conscientious level—growing ever more disenchanted with Emerson. He first delivered the lecture, which had been incubating since his one-night stay in jail eighteen months earlier, in public on January 26, 1848, in the same month he completed his troubled essay on "Friendship." A few weeks later, he presented it again at the Lyceum, probably adding another installment or revision.[4]

At the time of his arrest in July 1846, Emerson, according to Bronson Alcott's journal, commented that Thoreau's action was "mean and skulking, and in bad taste."[5] Paul Horihan speculates that "Thoreau would inevitably have received Emerson's precise response, since he and Alcott were in frequent touch during this period and, moreover, Alcott the social crusader not only *disagreed* with Emerson's views on this visceral subject but three years earlier, though escaping a stay in jail, had refused to pay the poll tax himself."[6] Whether or not Alcott passed on Emerson's biting comment is a matter of conjecture (though the Concord rumor-mill was always churning). It is interesting in this light that, in his January 12 letter to Emerson, Thoreau, making an implied comparison with Waldo—praises Alcott as "certainly the youngest man of his age we have seen" (*C,* p. 204).

Emerson's journal entries in July 1846 reveal him to be more ambivalent and—patronizingly—tolerant of his fiery friend's behavior. While he advises, "Don't run amok against the world. ... It is part of a fanatic to fight out a revolution on the shape of a hat or surplice," he also states, "The abolitionists ought to resist & go to prison in multitudes on their known and described disagreements from the state" (*JMN,* IX:446). His mixed attitude is further revealed in his image that the state is a poor good beast who means the best: it means friendly. ... "You are a man walking cleanly on two feet will not pick a quarrel with a poor cow. ... But if you go to hook me when I walk in the fields, the, poor cow, I will cut your throat" (*JMN,* IX:446). It seems less that he disapproves of the dissident's motives and even more the efficacy of such protest: "In the particular it is worth considering that refusing payment of the state tax does not reach the evil so nearly as many other methods within your reach. The state tax does not pay the Mexican War. Your coat, your sugar, your Latin & French & German book, your watch does. ... The prison is one step to suicide" (*JMN,* IX:447). Thus, although Emerson was clearly uncomfortable with Thoreau's behavior (partly, no doubt, because it reflected his own relative inaction), his response may have been more muted and paternalistic—at least to Thoreau's face. At this time, with Emerson still something of a hero and certainly a mentor, Thoreau may have been more willing to accept Waldo's opinion, even if he disagreed with it. Of course, had the "mean and skulking" remark reached Thoreau's ears, he might have been badly shaken. In any event, to a greater or lesser extent, Emerson's less-than-whole-hearted support of the night in jail helped plant the seeds of future hurt and outrage, especially after Emerson had his image of omnipotence and heroism tarnished.[7] If Thoreau had in any way been wounded emotionally by Waldo in the summer of 1846, the wound began to open again by January 1848.

It is difficult to fully understand the intensity and anger of "Civil Disobedience" without reference to the issues that Thoreau was confronting, and the emotions he was drawing on, in the months after leaving Walden. The lecture could perhaps only have been hatched after the return to Concord, when he felt more vulnerable to family, friends, and the demands, expectations, and corruptions of civilized life. In some ways, the lecture was another defiant declaration of independence, as going to Walden had in part been. Once again, he separates himself from his community and society and insists on his heroism, autonomy, and purity. Recreating the night in jail was a means of removing himself imaginatively back to the Walden hut. Once more, he was walled in, insulated from the townspeople, inhabiting pure and pristine territory, cleansing himself in Walden's purgative waters. "It is not a man's duty, as a matter of course," he claims in the lecture, "to devote himself to the eradication of any, even the most enormous wrong; but it is his duty, at least, to wash his hands of it" (*RP*, p. 71). In his prison cell, he "saw that, if there was a wall of stone between me and my townsmen, there was a still more difficult one to climb or break through, before they could get to be as free as I was. I did not for a moment feel confined, and the walls seemed a great waste of stone and mortar. I felt as if I alone of all my townsmen had paid my tax" (*RP*, 80). Rejecting genteel proprieties, he is the one genuine citizen of the country he inhabits.

Thoreau, a "human plant" who in a letter to James Eliot Cabot on March 8, 1848, would express his "sympathy" with the barberry bush (*C*, 210) and who has come to wonder whether he should have transplanted himself in civil society again, introduces his account of the jail experience with this observation: "If a plant cannot live according to nature, it dies; and so a man" (*RP*, 81). The jail cell, like the Walden cabin, is portrayed as a clean and pure setting; it "was the whitest, most simply furnished, and probably the neatest apartment in town" (*RP*, 81). His fellow-prisoner, whom he "presumed to be an honest man" and who in jail "got his board for nothing" (*RP*, 82), claimed that he had been falsely accused of burning a barn. Thoreau, who in 1844 had been convicted without a trial as being a "woodsburner" by many townspeople and who had gone into self-imposed exile at Walden partly in response to the judgment, speculates mildly that "he had probably gone to bed in a barn when drunk and smoked his pipe there; and so a barn was burnt." (At the time of his arrest, Thoreau may have imagined on some level that the jailing was a way for Concordians to get even with him for burning the woods.) Also like Walden, the cell is a place of creative, even poetic, productivity. As Thoreau observes, "Probably the only house in the town where verses are composed, which are afterward put in a circular form, but not published. I was shown quite a long list of verses which were composed by some young men who had been detected in an attempt to escape who had avenged themselves by singing them" (*RP*, 82). Perhaps "Civil Disobedience" was itself in part a form of vengeance written by a young man who felt unjustly imprisoned in civilized society and wanted to escape.

In the second and third versions of *Walden,* worked on in 1849, Thoreau would speak of the necessity for the writer to present a "simple and sincere account of his own life ... some such account as he would send to his kindred from a distant land; for if he has lived sincerely, it must have been a distant land to me."[8] If at Walden he sensed that he had inhabited a "distant land," so being in jail for the night and, though he does not say so, writing about it was "like traveling into a far country, such as I had never expected to behold" (*RP,* 82). He resurrects, too, the Walden-related lessons of economy: "It will be worth the while to accumulate property; that would be sure to go again. You must hire or squat somewhere, and raise but a small crop, and eat that soon. You must live within yourself, and depend upon yourself, always tucked in and ready for a start and not have many affairs" (*RP,* 78).

When he recounts his experience being released from prison, he also appears to be reviewing some of his responses upon reentering civilized life after leaving the pond. He "came out of prison" because "some one interfered, and paid the tax"; somewhat similarly, he had said farewell to Walden because Emerson had "interfered" by deciding to go to England. Lidian's invitation had bailed him out of his Walden hut. Of course, there were many underlying reasons why he bailed out of his life at the pond, and the "interference" was almost surely viewed by him as a blessing at the time. Now, with the passage of several months, there was a temptation to reinterpret the past and view the "interference" as a curse. Since he had changed so much at Walden, he had perhaps expected that Concord, or his feelings about it, would also have changed; but upon taking up residence at the Emersons', he discovered old hostile feelings reemerging. In like manner, he found upon his release from prison "that I did not perceive the great changes that had taken place on the common." Yet his own shift in perspective led him to perceive a change "over the scene—the town, and State, and country—greater than any that mere time could effect." He saw his neighbors as being even more morally bankrupt than he had previously suspected.

Probably the most revealing indictment is his realization of the extent to which "the people among whom I lived could be trusted as good neighbors and friends; that their friendship was for summer weather only" (*RP*, 83). It is likely that Emerson was among the most prominent of these "fair-weather friends." Emerson had been unexpectedly critical of Thoreau's night in jail and after Henry came back from the pond, Waldo had not provided the support, encouragement, or "present-ness" that he had needed, including not enough support for *A Week*. His jail sojourn had not met with general community approval, and, if he had hoped for some sort of welcome or renewed appreciation from his neighbors when he returned to Concord, his hopes had not been realized. "My neighbors did not salute me," he remarks in *Civil Disobedience*, "but first looked at me, and then at one another, as if I had just returned from a long journey" (*RP*, 83). After his release from jail, he picked up the shoe he had left to be mended at the shoemaker's. After leaving Walden, it was imperative that he not lose his soul. His final act in the jailing episode was to join a huckleberry party, where the "State was nowhere to be seen" (*RP*, 83–84)

His recollection, fictionalized or not, about having joined a huckleberry party mirrors, to some degree, his decision to withdraw *A Week* from publication consideration and "sympathize ... with the barberry bush, whose business it is solely to *ripen* its fruit (though that may be not to sweeten it)"—he was adding, among other things, some sour reflections on "Friendship" to *A Week*—"and to protect it from thorns, so that it holds on, all winter even, unless some hungry crows come to pluck it" (*C*, 210). At this point, he suggested, the absent Emerson or his influence was, like the State, "nowhere to be seen."

Early on in the lecture, he contends that "action from principle" is "essentially revolutionary," and that it "not only divides states and churches, it divides families; aye, it divides the *individual,* separating the diabolical in him from the divine" (*RP*, 72). Certainly, Thoreau appears to be drawing on powerful "family feelings" in *Civil Disobedience*. As Raymond Gozzi has argued, the State was, in a crucial sense, the "parental state" for Thoreau.[9] The rebelliousness evident in the lecture is, with its undeniable merits and legitimacy as a response to injustice and oppression, on some level, against parents and quasi parents, people he has looked to and looked up to in the past. In one variant of *Civil Disobedience*, he included a segment of a poem by George Peele, which begins, "We must affect our country as our parents." [10] Often he uses feminine pronouns in reference to the State (as, in *A Week,* he employed feminine pronouns with respect to orthodox religion). Clearly his mother, whose expectations he frequently experienced, at least unconsciously, as "impositions" (*RP*, 64) whose forceful style threatened his sense of autonomy—but whose love and approval he relied upon so heavily—may be regarded as one parent he is bent on resisting. "I was not born to be forced" (*RP*, 80–81), he writes, and he may have been more fearful of coming under her sway now that he was back in Concord. At another juncture he connects his own father directly with his revolt against Church and State, though his mother was generally more involved with the Church:

> Some years ago, the State met me in behalf of the Church, and commanded me to pay a certain sum toward the support of a clergyman whose preaching my father attended, but never I myself. "Pay it," it said, "or be locked up in jail." I declined to pay. But, unfortunately, another man saw fit to pay it ... at the request of the selectmen, I condescended to make some such statement as this in writing:—"know all men by these presents, that I, Henry Thoreau, do not wish to be regarded as a member of any incorporated society which I have not joined" (*RP*, 79).

However, if his father had been an Admetus whom he had served as an Apollo, if he had not been the dynamic male identity model his son had wished him to be, if he evoked unresolved oedipal anxieties and guilt, there was another "father" who was, perhaps more than any other family-figure, the object of wrath and disappointment in the lecture: Emerson. *Civil Disobedience* is an attack, not only on the State itself (which is described in one passage as "pitiable," "foolish," "blundering," "half-witted," and "timid"— *RP*, 80), but also even more harshly, an assault on men who do not go to jail to resist it, and those who condemn those who do. There is a strong undercurrent of being let down by authorities and neighbors. "Oh for a man," he laments, "who is a *man,* and, as my neighbor says, has a bone in his back which you cannot pass your hand through!" (*RP*, 70). If Emerson was indeed critical or condescending with regard to his act of civil disobedience and he knew it, then Thoreau could no longer respect or venerate him as he once had. Waldo's refusal to be one of those "honest men" who withdrew from the State and went to jail constituted moral cowardice for Thoreau. For all his brave talk, Emerson had been but a patron of, and patronizing about, protest. Thoreau comments, "There are nine-hundred and ninety-nine patrons of virtue to one virtuous man" (*RP*, 69). Waldo's mettle was tarnished; he was no longer the "great man" who had been such a radical in the 1830s and early 1840s. "A very few," Thoreau says, "as heroes, patriots, martyrs, reformers in the great sense, and *men,* serve the State with their consciences also; and so necessarily resist it for the most part, and they are commonly treated by it as enemies" (*RP*, 66).

One story, apocryphal perhaps, but nonetheless suggestive, had Thoreau, upon his release from jail, responding to Emerson's inquiries about why he had gone to prison with the rejoinder, "Why did you not?"[11]. In "Civil Disobedience," maybe with Emerson in mind, he restates this point: "Under a government which imprisons any unjustly, the true place for a just man is also prison" (*RP*, 76). Whether or not the two men had had a direct confrontation in 1846, the fact remains that the lecture reflects Thoreau's state of mind in 1848, when his esteem for Emerson was on the wane.

It is indicative, moreover, that at the time Waldo was enraptured with England's manufacturing prowess, Thoreau chose to make prominent in the lecture the image of the unheroic individual and the State as a machine: "The mass of men serve the State, thus, not as men mainly, but as machines, with their bodies" (*RP,* 66). Elsewhere he observes that "all machines have their friction; and possibly this does enough good to counterbalance the evil. At any rate, it is a great evil to make a stir about it. But when the friction comes to have its machine, and oppression and robbery are organized, I say, let us not have such a machine any longer" (*RP,* 67). In a justly famous metaphor, he adds later, "Let your whole life be a counter friction to stop the machine" (*RP,* 73–74). That Emerson was praising civil society in his letters may have spurred Thoreau to be even more contemptuous of it. *Civil Disobedience,* then, represented an indirect way of differentiating himself starkly from and rejecting the mentor he once idolized. It has the tone of a former worshiper disabused of his illusions.

The pent-up aggressive emotions released by, and unleashed in, the lecture, while undeniably cathartic for Thoreau, were also threatening. In challenging the state's authority, and in excoriating the men who refused to take or even countenance bold actions, Thoreau was challenging significant figures—particularly male—in his life. It is wholly in character that he would have hit upon a mode of protest which would combine passiveness and withdrawal with aggressiveness, nonviolence with militant resistance. Elsewhere, I have made the argument that Thoreau and Gandhi not only espoused very similar public strategies had comparable private roots.[12] Both had been "cursed" by a guilt-provoking death, in Gandhi's case the circumstances surrounding the death of his father and in Thoreau's the untimely death of his elder brother. Each developed a style or strategy that permitted them to challenge authority, try to defeat a "superior adversary,[13] but also deny the wish to supersede, hurt, or destroy them. In this way, each could shield himself from the guilt and anxiety aroused by hostile feelings toward, and confrontations with, authority.

Even before the disenchantment with Emerson became pressing, then, Thoreau was oriented to aggressive-passive, militantly nonviolent. Indeed, his dramatic act of civil resistance occurred when Emerson was still perceived as something of an ally and model, even if he already felt stirrings to break away and even though the ally's reaction to his behavior had apparently been one of the wedges that would drive them apart. The strategy of militant nonviolence firmly embodied in the act itself, was even more crucial when he delivered the text of "Resistance to Civil Government," for he now had to deal with the residual and rising guilt regarding his brother and with the inevitable discomfort involved in his shifting emotions toward Emerson. That he was responding to effects associated with his brother's death *and* Emerson (the two "friends" who loomed largest in the "Friendship" essay he was working on at the same time) made passive-aggressive stance of *Civil Disobedience* all the more imperative. For all the rage and defiance evinced in the lecture, toward its end Thoreau seeks to pull back from, even forswear, any monomaniacal destructiveness or murderous intentions. It is simply not rhetorical concession when he remarks, "I do not wish to quarrel with any man or nation. I do not wish to split hairs, to make fine distinctions, or to set myself up with my neighbors. I seek rather, I may say, even an excuse for conforming to the laws of the land. I am but too ready to conform to them." And the final lines of the lecture, with which I conclude, do not express outrage but rather the conciliatory vision of a State which will be a "good father," generative, ripely wise, tolerant, and just:

> There will never be a really free and enlightened State, until the State comes to recognize the individual as a higher and independent power, from which all its own power and authority are derived, and treats him accordingly. I please myself with imagining a State at last which can afford to be just to all men, and to treat the individual with respect as a neighbor; which even then would not think it inconsistent with its own repose, if a few were to live aloof from it, not meddling with it, nor embraced by it, who fulfilled all the duties of neighbors and fellowmen A State which bore this kind of fruit, and suffered it to drop off as fast as it ripen, would prepare the way for a still more perfect and glorious State, which also I have imagined, but not yet anywhere seen (*RP,* 89–90).

# Notes

[1]*Journal II* transcription, provided by the Thoreau Textual Center, Princeton University, Princeton, N.J.

[2]Walter Harding, *The Days of Henry Thoreau* (New York: Alfred A. Knopf, 1965), pp. 199–206

[3]Walter Harding and Carl Bode, eds., in *Correspondence* (New York: New York Univ. Press, 1958), p. 167.

[4]Wendell Glick, "Textual Introduction" to "Resistance to Civil Government," *Reform Papers,* ed. Wendell Glick (Princeton: Princeton Univ. Press, 1973), pp. 313–314.

[5]Harding, *Days,* p. 205.

[6]Paul Horihan in unpublished version of "Crisis in the Thoreau-Emerson Friendship: the Symbolic Function of *Civil Disobedience,*" in *Thoreau's Psychology: Eight Esaays,* ed. Raymond D. Gozzi (Lanham, Md. : University Press of America, 1983).

[7]Cf. Hourihan, "Crisis."

[8]Ronald Clapper, "The Development of *Walden*: A Genetic Text" (Dissertation, University of California at Los Angeles, 1967), p. 45.

[9]Raymond Gozzi, "Tropes and Figures: A Psychological Study of David Henry Thoreau" (Dissertation, New York University, 1957), pp. 251–268.

[10]Glick, "Textual Introduction," p. 325.

[11]Harding, *Days,* pp. 205–206.

[12]Richard LeBeaux, *Young Man Thoreau* (Amherst: Univ. of Massachusetts Press, 1977), pp. 176–178.

[13]Erik Erikson, *Ghandi's Truth* (New York: W.W. Norton & Company, 1969), p. 129.

*PJ refers to the *Journal* of Henry D. Thoreau. Eds. John C. Broderick et al. (Princeton: Princeton Univ. Press, 1981–    ).

*C refers to *The Correspondence of Henry David Thoreau*. Eds. Walter Harding and Carl Bode. New York: New York Univ. Press, 1958.

*JMN refers to *The Journals and Miscellaneous Notebooks of Ralph Waldo Emerson*. Eds. William H. Gilman et. al. Cambridge: Harvard Univ. Press, 1960–    .

*RP refers to *Reform Papers*. Ed. Wendell Glick. Princeton: Princeton Univ. Press, 1973.

———————

**RICHARD M. LEBEAUX** is a professor of English and American Studies at Keene State College, Keene, New Hampshire. He received a B.A. from Middlebury College, an M.A.T from Harvard University, and a Ph.D. from Boston University and taught for nine years at Michigan State University. Currently he teaches courses on transcendentalism, Thoreau and 19th-century American literature. He is the author of *Young Man Thoreau* and *Thoreau's Seasons* (University of Massachusetts Press, 1977 and 1984, respectively).

# Thoreau, Tolstoy, and Civil Disobedience

❖

## Jack Schwartzman

This paper deals with the ideas of Henry David Thoreau (1817–1862) and Leo Nikolayevich Tolstoy (1828–1910) pertaining to the topic of civil disobedience. The writings of the great American sage and the famed Russian author on that subject are here compared and analyzed.

At the end of the nineteenth century, Tolstoy wrote:

> It is now fifty years since a not widely known, but very remarkable, American writer—Thoreau— … in his admirable essay on "Civil Disobedience," … gave a practical example of such disobedience. Not wishing to be an accomplice or supporter of a government which legalized slavery, he declined to pay a tax demanded of him, and went to prison for it. …
>
> Thoreau was, I think, the first to express this view. People paid scant attention to either his refusal or his article fifty years ago—the thing seemed so strange. It was put down to his eccentricity.[1]

Thoreau's own comment about the "prison incident" is that since he paid no poll-tax for six years, he "was put into a jail on this account, for one night."[2] His view was that "under a government which imprisons any unjustly, the true place for a just man is also a prison."[3] Tolstoy, evidently much impressed, once wrote to the Russian governments "Let me be put in prison, or better yet (so good that I dare not hope for such happiness), let me be dressed in a shroud and pushed off a bench so that the weight of my body will tighten the well-soaped slipknot around my old neck."[4]

In another letter, to a friend, he stated: "Indeed, nothing could have satisfied me as fully or given me as much happiness as to be put in prison: a good, proper prison that stinks. Where people suffer from cold and hunger."[5]

18

Concerning his debt to Thoreau and others, Tolstoy, in "A message to the American People" (1901), declared:

> It came to me that if I had to address the American people, I should like to thank them for the writers who flourished about the fifties. I would mention Garrison, Parker, Emerson, Ballou, and Thoreau, not as the greatest, but as those who, I think, specially influenced me. Other names are Channing, Whittier, Lowell, Walt Whitman—a bright constellation, such as is rarely to be found in the literatures of the world.
>
> And I should like to ask the American people why they do not pay more attention to these voices (hardly to be replaced by those of financial and industrial millionaires, or successful generals and admirals), and continue the good work in which they made such hopeful progress.[6]

According to a biographer, Tolstoy, as he became more mature, began to resemble Thoreau in some respects. Tolstoy's "love of nature seemed to grow more and more intense. A description of his walk one June day through the rich, tall grass reminds one of Thoreau. He is intoxicated with the odors of the wood-paths. He watches a bee gathering honey from one after another of a cluster of yellow flowers, and from the thirteenth it flies away, humming, with its load complete."[7]

Toward the end of his life, evidently under the influence of Thoreau's "simplicity" creed, Tolstoy wistfully remarked: "I want to live with the utmost simplicity, spend money parsimoniously."[8]

Concerning the topic of civil disobedience, here, too, Tolstoy followed Thoreau—in his own fashion. The views of both thinkers, according to theme, follow in the succeeding pages.

## The Theme of Government

"Civil disobedience" is disobedience to what one considers to be the unjust decrees of a government. How is "government" defined?

According to Thoreau (who does not differentiate between "government" and "State"), a "government" is a parasitic social body (run by one person or a select group of persons) that "imposes" its will on the people, for its "own advantage." It creates nothing. It merely "takes." "This government," Thoreau observed, "never of itself furthered any enterprise. ... *It* does not keep the country free. *It* does not settle the West. *It* does not educate. The character inherent in the American people has done all that has been accomplished: and it would have done somewhat more if the government had not sometimes got in its way."[9]

Should people be governed? If so, what kind of government should they have? Thoreau had the answer:

> I heartily accept the motto,—"That government is best which governs least," and I should like to see it acted up more rapidly and systematically.

Carried out, it finally amounts to this, which also I believe, "That government is best which governs not at all," and when men are prepared for it, that will be the kind of government which they will have. Government is at best but an expedient, but most governments are usually, and all governments are sometimes, inexpedient.[10]

How do the people serve their government? "The mass of men serve the State," Thoreau replied, "not as men mainly, but as machines, with their bodies ... . In most cases there is no free exercise whatever of the judgment or of the moral senses but they put themselves on a level with wood and earth and stones ... Such command no more respect than men of straw or a lump of dirt."[11]

Why does the government have no concern for its people, asked Thoreau, especially its unique personalities? "Why does it not cherish its wise minority? ... Why does it always crucify Christ, and excommunicate Copernicus and Luther, and pronounce Washington and Franklin rebels?"[12]

Those Americans who believe that their government is "best" because it is a "democracy," are deluding themselves. To Thoreau, to be strictly just, a government must have the consent of the governed.

Is a democracy, such as we know it, the last improvement possible in government? Is it not possible to take a step further towards recognizing and organizing the rights of man? There will never be a really free and enlightened State, until the State comes to recognize the individual as a higher and independent power, from which all its own power and authority are derived, and treats him accordingly. I please myself with imagining a State at last which can afford to be just to all men, and to treat the individual with respect as a neighbor.[13]

The terrible thing about government, as shall be shown, is that it lives by and for war and individual enslavement. Such is "government," as Thoreau saw it.

What were Tolstoy's thoughts on the subject? He equated "government" with force.

Terrible force is lodged in the hands of the authorities, and not merely a material force—a vast amount of money, institutions, riches, submissive functionaries of the clergy, and the army—the mighty spiritual forces of influence are lodged in the hands of the government. It can, unless it is bribed, suppress, annihilate, all those who are opposed to it.[14]

No matter who is in control of a government, the result is the same.

We need only remember that the same kind of oppression and war went on no matter who stood at the head of the governments Nicholas or Alexander, Louis or Napoleon, Frederic or William, Palmerston or Gladstone, McKinley or any one else, in order to see that it is not some definite person who causes the oppression and the ware from which people suffer.[15]

Therefore, it is not the individuals in control but the "order" of things that creates the existing tyranny. People, by their own will, put themselves "in the power" of the rulers.

> The misery of the people is not caused by individuals, but by an order of Society by which they are bound together in a way that puts them in the power of a few, or, more often, of one man: a man so depraved by his unnatural position—having the fate and lives of millions of people in his power—that he is always in an unhealthy state of suffering more or less from a mania of self-aggrandizement, which is not noticed in him only because of his exceptional position.

> Apart from the fact that such men are surrounded, from the cradle to the grave, by the most insane luxury and servility. the whole of their education, and all their occupations, are centered on the one object of murder, the study of murder in the past, the best means of murdering in the present, the best ways of preparing for murder in the future.[16]

Such is "government" as Tolstoy saw it.

## The Theme of Patriotism

Both Thoreau and Tolstoy believed that patriotism (which may be defined as an excessive love for one's own country) perpetuates the iniquity known as the State. In his classic *Walden*, Thoreau proclaimed:

> Every man is the lord of a realm beside which the earthly empire of the Czar is but a petty state, a hummock left by the ice. Yet some can be patriotic who have no *self*-respect, and sacrifice the greater to the less. They love the soil which makes their graves, but have no sympathy with the spirit which may still animate their clay. Patriotism is a maggot in their heads.[17]

Well-meaning people. often the best in their community, Thoreau declared, are the guiltiest when it comes to augmenting the power of government.

> The slight reproach to which the virtue of patriotism is commonly liable, the noble are most likely to incur. Those who, while they disapprove of the character and measures of a government, yield to it their allegiance and support, are undoubtedly its most conscientious supporters, and so frequently the most serious obstacles to reform.[18]

Tolstoy was much more outspoken, and much more vociferous, in his unflagging attacks on patriotism—and what it led to. Calling patriotism "slavery,"[19] Tolstoy wrote:

> Patriotism today is the cruel tradition of an outlived period, which exists not merely by its inertia, but because the governments and ruling

classes, aware that not their power only, but their very existence, depends upon it, persistently excite and maintain it among the people, both by cunning and violence.[20]

A public opinion exists that patriotism is a fine moral sentiment. and that it is right and our duty to regard one's own nation, one's own state, as the best in the world; and ... that it is right and our duty to acquiesce in the control of a government over ourselves, to subordinate ourselves to it, to serve in the army and to submit ourselves to discipline, to give our earnings to the government in the form of taxes, to submit to the decisions of the law-courts, and to consider the edicts of the government as divinely right.[21]

All of these feelings, Tolstoy thought, resulted in jingoism, sword-rattling. and war. Therefore, patriotism had to be opposed and denied. "To destroy war, destroy patriotism. But to destroy patriotism, it is first necessary to produce conviction that it is an evil: and this is difficult to do."[22]

How, then, *can* patriotism be destroyed?

"We must concern ourselves, not about patriotism, but to bring into life that light which is within us: to change the character of life, and approach it to the ideal which stands before us."[23]

## The Theme of War

The State thrives on war. Every war increases the power of government; every war causes destruction, conquest, slavery, and death. The State does not ask permission to wage war; just a few people in control decide the fate of all. "Witness the present Mexican War," Thoreau pointed out, "the work of comparatively a few individuals using the standing government as their tool: for in the outset, the people would not have consented to this measure."[24]

Man-made "law" helps to abolish human freedom and is responsible for the existing militarism.

Law never made men a whit more just; and, by means of their respect for it, even the well-disposed are daily made the agents of injustice. A common and natural result of an undue respect for the law is, that you may see a file of soldiers. colonel, captain, corporal, privates, powder-monkeys and all, marching in admirable order over hill and dale to the wars, against their wills, aye, against their common sense and con-sciences, which makes it very steep marching indeed, and produces a palpitation of the heart. They have no doubt that it is a damnable business in which they are concerned; they are all peaceably inclined. Now, what are they? Men at all? or small moveable forts and magazines, at the service of some unscrupulous man in power?[25]

Tolstoy was equally shocked by the (then-current) Spanish-American War, started by just a few individuals. It was, he cried out, "an old, vain, foolish and cruel war, inopportune, out-of-date, barbarous, which sought by killing one set of people to solve the question as to how and by whom another set of people ought to be governed."[26]

In a passage that reminds one of Thoreau, Tolstoy exclaimed:

When we see trained animals accomplishing things contrary to natures—dogs walking on their forelegs, elephants rolling barrels, tigers playing with lions, and so on, we know that all this has been attained by the torments of hunger, whip, and red-hot iron. And when we see men in uniforms with rifles standing motionless, or performing all together with the same movement—running, jumping, shooting, shouting. and so on—in general, producing those fine reviews and manoeuvers which emperors and kings so admire and show off one before the other, we know the same. One cannot cauterize out of man all that is human and reduce him to the state of a machine without torturing him, and torturing not in a simple way but in the most refined, cruel way—at one and the same time torturing and deceiving him.[27]

The meaning of all the drilling, Tolstoy elucidated, "is very clear and simple. It is preparing for murder. It means the stupefying of men in order to convert them into instruments for murdering."[28]

Watching the behavior of his countrymen, he commented, in a shocked tone:

Our native Russians, men naturally sweet-tempered, good, and kind … spend the best years of their lives in murdering and torturing their brethren, and not only are not remorseful for such deeds, but consider them honorable, or at least indispensable and just as unavoidable as eating or breathing.[29]

Tolstoy gave an example of one such Russians:

I knew such a man, who one evening danced the mazurka with a beautiful girl at a ball, and retired earlier than usual so as to be awake early in the morning to make arrangements to compel a runaway soldier—a Tartar—to be killed in running the gauntlet; and after he had seen this man whipped to death, he returned to his family and ate his dinner![30]

It is commonly stated today (1991) that the invention of weapons which can wipe out a nation in a matter of hours (or less) will make war so terrifying as to (forever) end military conflict on earth. Similar statements were made a century ago, in Tolstoy's time. He responded angrily to these utterances.

It has often been said that the invention of the terrible military instruments of murder will put an end to war, and that war will exhaust itself. This is not true. As it is possible to increase the means of killing men, so it is possible to increase the means for subjecting those who hold the social life-conception. Let them be exterminated by thousands and millions, let them be torn to pieces, men will continue like stupid cattle to go to the slaughter. Some because they are driven thither under the lash. other that they may win the decorations and ribbons which fill their hearts with pride.[31]

Then what is to be done to oppose war, imprisonment, slavery, subjection, and torture? There is but one answer. One must attack these evils by means of "civil disobedience."

## The Theme of Civil Disobedience: Thoreau

In his famed dissertation on "civil disobedience," Thoreau asked rhetorically how an American citizen should behave toward his government. He personally (he said) could not "without disgrace ... recognize that political organization" as his government, "which is the *slave's* government also."[32]

What should one do, therefore, to oppose governmental injustice? Rebel, Thoreau answered; start a revolution. "All men recognize the right of revolution; that is, the right to refuse allegiance to and to resist the government, when its tyranny or its inefficiency are great and unendurable."[33] "I think that it is not too soon for honest men to rebel and revolutionize."[34]

As for Thoreau himself, seeing that injustice prevailed, he made his stand: "I simply wish to refuse alleviance to the State, to withdraw and stand aloof from it effectually ... . In fact, I quietly declare war with the State, after my fashion."[35]

Should this revolution be organized by the formation of factions or revolutionary armies? Not at all. "A wise man will not leave the right to the mercy of chance, nor wish it to prevail through the power of the majority. There is but little virtue in the action of masses of men."[36] Any man who has God on his side. and is "more right than his neighbors, constitutes a majority of one."[37]

When should one commence this revolution? "If the injustice ... is of such a nature that it requires you to be the agent of injustice to another, then, I say, break the law."[38] If one refuses to pay taxes, "that would not be a violent measure, as it would be to pay them, and enable the State to commit violence and shed innocent blood. This is, in fact, the definition of a peaceable revolution."[39]

Should a revolution be in the form of war and the spilling of blood? Not necessarily. "When the subject has refused allegiance, and the officer has resigned his office, then the revolution is accomplished. But even suppose blood should flow, is there not a sort of blood shed when the conscience is wounded?"[40] In any case, "it costs me less in every sense to incur the penalty of disobedience to the State, than it would to obey."[41]

But suppose the State, which has all the power on its side, crushes the individual rebel and destroys him? The State, Thoreau emphasized, can only attack the physical body, not the spirit, not the conscience.

> The State is not armed with superior wit or honesty, but with superior phys-cal strength. I was not born to be forced. I will breathe after my own fashion. Let us see who is the strongest. What force has a multitude? They only can force me who obey a higher law than I.[42]

What happens when there is a confrontation? "When I meet a government which says to me, 'Your money or your life,' why should I be in haste to give it my money? It may be in a great strait, and not know what to do: I cannot help that. It must help itself; do as I do. It is not worth to snivel about it. I am not responsible for the successful working of the machinery of society. I am not the son of the engineer."[43] Since the money may be used to purchase military means of destruction, payment *must* be refused. Civil disobedience, as depicted by Thoreau, is a philosophy of life that has influenced some of the greatest thinkers of the world. It is a doctrine that recognizes the rights of each individual to live according to his nature, and to oppose all attempts to compel him to obey unjust decrees which violate one's own individuality. The individual has a "right" to live according to his own purpose, conscience, and "design of life."

However, concluded Thoreau (and therein lies the essence of his unflinching individualism), "the government does not concern me much, and I shall bestow the fewest possible thoughts on it. It is not many moments that I live under a government, even in this world. If a man is thought-free, fancy-free, imagination-free … unwise rulers or reformers cannot fatally interrupt him."[44]

## The Theme of Civil Disobedience: Tolstoy

Tolstoy, like Thoreau, is the author of a celebrated concept of civil disobedience. Like Thoreau, Tolstoy strongly advocated following one's own conscience. Both men relied on human conscience as the guide to spiritual understanding.

Thoreau had written, "Must the citizen ever for a moment, or in the least degree, resign his conscience to the legislator? Why has every man a conscience then?"[45] And Tolstoy echoed the sentiments: "To man is given another guide, and that an unfailing one—the guide of his conscience, following which he indubitably knows that he is doing what he should do."[46] His conscience will lead the individual to spiritual enlightenment. "If man act in accordance with what is dictated to him by his reason, his conscience, and his God, only the very best can result for himself as well as for the world."[47]

Human conscience, according to Tolstoy, will lead the individual to civil disobedience. The individual (who follows his reason and his heart) will then answer the government: "You wish me to be a murderer, and I cannot do this: both God and my own conscience forbid it. And therefore do with me what you wish, but I will not kill or prepare for murder or assist in it."[48] One should always listen to the "voice" of his conscience.[49]

As for Tolstoy himself, like Thoreau, he made his stand: "I, whilst I live, will not cease from saying what I now say; for I cannot refrain from acting according to my conscience."[50] Like Thoreau, Tolstoy became "civilly disobedient."

What *is* "civil disobedience," as Tolstoy saw it? It is disobedience to the unjust laws of Caesar; it is obedience to the just commandments of God. It is very simple, Tolstoy forcefully declared, for a just man to face Caesar (the State) and say:

> You wish to make me a participator in murder; you demand of me money for the preparation of weapons; and want me to take part in the organized assembly of murderers, ... but I profess that law ... which long ago forbade not murder only, but all hostility, also, and therefore I cannot obey you.[51]

Tolstoy emphasized: "The way to do away with war is for those who do not want war, who regard participation in it a sin, to refrain from fighting.[52]

"And it is just by this simple means," Tolstoy concluded, "and by it alone, that the world is being conquered."[53]

To repeat: "Every man, in refusing to take part in military service or to pay taxes to a government which uses them for military purposes, is, by this refusal, rendering a great service to God and man."[54]

And this is the essence of civil disobedience.

How can one human being (or a few such beings) hope to succeed against the overwhelming might of the Super-State?

> Wonderful to relate, all this vast potential mass of men, armed with all the powers of human authority, trembles, and hides itself, feeling its fault, and shakes in its very being, and is ready to crumble and fly into powder, at the appearance of a single man ... who would not yield to human demands, but obeyed the law of God and was faithful to it.[55]

Civil disobedience taps the "force of freedom" found in each individual.

The most powerful and untrammeled force of freedom is that which asserts itself in the soul of man when he is alone, and in the sole presence of himself reflects on the facts of the universe.[56]

After all, what is civil disobedience but the Golden Rule itself? To counter the vicious demands of the powerful State, one must only follow the Great Tradition expressed in all religious texts:

Tradition—the collective wisdom of my greatest forerunners—tells me that I should do unto others as I would that they should do unto me. My reason shows me that only by all men acting thus is the highest happiness for all men attainable. Only when I yield myself to that intuition of love which demands obedience to this law is my own heart happy and at rest …. I cannot fathom God's whole design, for the sake of which the universe exists and lives; but the divine work which is being accomplished in this world, and in which I participate by living, is comprehensible to me.

This work is the annihilation of discord and strife among men, and among all creatures; and the establishment of the highest unity, concord, and love. It is the fulfilment of the promises of the Hebrew prophets who foretold a time when all men should be taught by truth, when spears should turned into reaping hooks, swords be beaten to plowshares, and the lion lie down with the lamb … Thus the intuitive demands of man's soul coincide with the external aim of life which he sees before him.[57]

The Great Tradition stems from the teachings of the great Prophets and Christs "Moses, in his commandments … laid down the laws *Thou shalt not kill.* The same command has been preached by all the prophets; the same law has been preached by the sages and teachers of the whole world; the same law was preached by Christ."[58]

Tolstoy became lyrical in his impassioned appeal to the world to embrace the philosophy of civil disobediences:

Awake, brethren! Listen neither to those villains who, from your childhood, infest you with the diabolic spirit of patriotism, opposed to righteousness and truth, and only necessary in order to deprive you of your property, your freedom, and your human dignity; nor to those ancient impostors who preach war, in the name of a cruel and vindictive God invented by them, and in the name of perverted and false Christianity … Believe only the consciousness which tells you that you are neither beasts nor slaves, but free men, responsible for your actions, and therefore unable to be murderers either of your own accord or at the will of those who live by these murders.[59]

## The Theme of Truth

Civil disobedience, to both thinkers, had not only its "negative" side (that of opposition to tyranny) but its "positive" side as well (that of living according to purpose). After all, to deny the totality of the State is to assert the individuality of the person—and to seek the meaning of human existence. The individual is not here merely to exist, procreate, and die. He must live in accordance with a "design of life." He possesses certain "innate rights," which only the Beacon of Truth may reveal in the darkness of human ignorance.

To Thoreau, truth is the keynote of life. "Rather than love, than money, than fame, give me truth."[60]

There are people. like lawyers, for instance, who define truth in their own expedient fashion. Such is not truth, in the "eternal" sense. "The lawyer's truth is not truth," wrote Thoreau, "but consistence, or a consistent expediency. Truth is always in harmony with itself."[61]

There are also people who accept truth superficially.

> They who know of no purer sources of truth, who have traced up its stream no higher, stand, and wisely stand, by the Bible and the Constitution, and drink at it there with reverence and humility; but they who behold where it comes trickling into this lake or that pool, gird up their loins once more, and continue their pilgrimage toward its fountain-head.[62]

Man needs the "underpinning" of truth to stand erect before his God.

> We select granite for the underpinning of our houses and barns; we build fences of stone; but we do not ourselves rest on an underpinning of granitic truth, the lowest primitive rock. Our sills are rotten. What stuff is the man made of who is not coexistent in our thought with the purest and subtlest truth?[63]

Unfortunately for us, we mistake the glitter for the gold. "We do not worship truth, but the reflection of truth."[64] Thus, we never come in contact with the precious metal itself.

We must be wary of any "lull" in our continuing and eternal search for truth, or the ritualistic institutions will replace and pervert it. "As a snow-drift is formed where there is a lull in the wind, so, one would say, where there is a lull of truth, an institution springs up. But the truth blows on over it, nevertheless, and at length blows it down."[65]

For Thoreau, therefore, truth, "the lowest primitive rock," was the highest essential virtue. Tolstoy, too, stressed truth above any other concept. He stated:

> As a fire lit on a prairie or in a forest will not die out until it has burned all that is dry and dead, and therefore conbustible, so the truth, once articulated in human utterance, will not cease its work until all falsehood, appointed for destruction, surrounding and hiding the truth on all sides as it does, is destroyed. The fire smolders long; but as soon as it flashes into flame, all that can burn burns quickly.[66]

Religions differ, but truth is the same.

> A man lives, and must, therefore, know why he lives. He has established his relation to God; he knows the very truth of truths, and I know the very truth of truths. Our expression may differ; the essence must be the same—we are both of us men.[67]

The individual must recognize the power of the truth within him. Over and over again, Tolstoy uttered the same thuught. "If only free men would not rely on that which has no power, and is always fettered—upon external aids; but would trust in that which is always powerful and free—the truth and its expression!"[68] "Only let men understand the vast power which is given them in the word which expresses truth ... and their rulers will not dare, as now, to threaten men with universal slaughter."[69] "It is sufficient to believe that truth is not what men talk of but what is told by his own conscience, that is by God—and at once the whole artificially maintained public opinion will disappear, and a new and true one be established in its place."[70]

Tolstoy summarized his philosophy of truth:

> If only the hearts of individuals would not be troubled by the seductions with which they are hourly seduced, nor afraid of those imaginary terrors by which they are intimidated; if people only knew wherein their chiefest, all-conquering power consists—a peace which men have always desired ... the peace attainable by a voluntary profession of the truth by every man, would long ago have been established in our midst.[71]

## The Theme of Living: Human Rights

Man, therefore, must live by obeying the inner voice of his own conscience. Both Thoreau and Tolstoy stressed each person's individuality.

Previously in this paper, there appeared Thoreau's statement:

> Is it not possible to take a step further towards recognizing and organizing the rights of man? There will never be a really free and enlightened State, until the State comes to recognize the individual as a higher and independent power, from which all its own power and please myself with imagining a State at last which can afford to be just to all men, and to treat the individual with respect as a neighbor.[72]

The individualistic philosophy of doing "one's own thing" is true wisdom. Said Thoreau: "The community has no bribe that will tempt a wise man. You may raise money enough to hire a man who is minding his *own business.*"[73]

There is a "higher way" of life; each man must find it.

Wherever a man separates from the multitude, and goes his own way in this mood, there indeed is a fork in the road, though ordinary travellers may see only a gap in the paling. His solitary path across-lots will turn out the *higher way* of the two.[74]

Doing "one's own thing," "minding one's own business," finding one's "higher way,"—these are some of the basic human rights which are "inherent" in each individual by virtue of his existence. These are rights which no government may transgress, trample, or destroy. These rights are the essence of individualism.

Individualism is also uniqueness. "It is for want of a man that there are so many men."[75]

In a comment that is itself a "flash of light," Thoreau brilliantly expounded his doctrine of human existence. Truth and knowledge, Thoreau declared, will not be found in science but in intuition and "light." "Knowledge does not come to us by details, but in flashes of light from heaven."[76]

Those "flashes of light" will guide the individual to wisdom: to live a life of purpose and meaning.

Tolstoy, too, as an apostle of man's inner quest for peace, understanding, and fulfillment of individuality, likewise spoke of intuition and "light." In a previously quoted statement, he commented that it was necessary "to bring into life that light which is within us."[77]

Let the government keep the schools, Church, press, its milliards of money, and millions of armed men transformed into machines; all this ... brute force is as nothing compared to the consciousness of truth, which surges in the soul of one man who knows the power of truth, which is communicated from him to a second and a third, as one candle lights an innumerable quantity of others.[78]

Tolstoy proclaimed the rights of man, the abnegation of government, the search for human understanding, and (again) the inner "light":

The light needs only to be kindled, and, like wax in the face of fire, this organization, which seems so powerful, will melt and be consumed.[79]

"This organization" is the all-powerful government; and the "light" is the conscience in each one of us.

## Conclusion

How should the individual live his life?

Life must be lived to the fullest, urged Thoreau. "However mean your life is, meet it, and live it; do not shun it and call it hard names .... Love your life, poor as it is."[80]

And Tolstoy declared: "Religion is the meaning we give to our lives; it is that which gives strength and direction to our life. Everyone that lives finds such a meaning and lives on the basis of that meaning .... Revelation is what helps man to understand the meaning of life."[81]

Each life must be shaped by *its own design.*

## Notes

All the essays and letters of Leo N. Tolstoy discussed here are translated by different writers, and found in one book, anonymously edited, entitled *Tolstoy and Civil Disobedience and Non-Violence* (New York: Bergman Publishers, (1967). Even though the following notes cite such essays and letters of Tolstoy individually, the page references pertain to the pages of the book which contains these works.

Henry David Thoreau's *Walden* and "Civil Disobedience" are found in one book, edited by Owen Thomas, entitled *Walden and Civil Disobedience* (New York: W. W. Norton & Company, Inc., 1966), Even though the following notes cite either *Walden* or "Civil Disobedience," the page references pertain to the pages of the book which contains both of these works.

Thoreau's "Life without Principle" is found in the book edited by Ronald Gottesman et al, entitled *The Norton Anthology of American Literature*, vol. 1 (New York: W. W. Norton & Company, Inc., 1979). Even though the following notes cite "Life without Principle" individually, the page references pertain to the pages of the book which contains the essay.

[1] Leo N. Tolstoy, "Letter to Dr. Eugen Heinrich Schmitt" (no date), pp. 127–28.

[2] Henry David Thoreau, "Civil Disobedience" (1848), p. 236.

[3] *Ibid.*, p. 232.

[4] Henri Troyat (tr. by Nancy Amphoux), *Tolstoy* (Garden City, New York: Doubleday & Company, Inc., 1967), p. 641.

[5] *Ibid.* p. 642.

[6] Tolstoy, "A Message to the American People" (1901), p. VII.

[7] Nathan Haskell Dole, *The Life of Count Tolstoy* (New York: Thomas Y. Crowell Co., 1911) p. 264.

[8] Troyat, *Tolstoy,* p . 703

[9] Thoreau, "Civil Disobedience," pp. 224–25

[10] *Ibid.*, p. 224.

[11]*Ibid.*, p. 226.

[12]*Ibid* ., p . 231.

[13]*Ibid.*, pp. 242–43.

[14]Tolstoy, "Postscript to the 'Life and Death of Drozhin'"(1895), p. 264.

[15]Tolstoy, "Thou Shalt Not Kill" (1900), p. 158.

[16]*Ibid.*

[17]Thoreau, *Walden* (1854), p. 212.

[18]Thoreau, "Civil Disobedience," p. 230.

[19]Tolstoy, "On Patriotism" (1894), p. 79.

[20]*Ibid.*, p. 77.

[21]*Ibid.*, p. 85.

[22]Tolstoy, "Patriotism or Peace?" (1896), p. 107.

[23]Tolstoy, "A Reply to Criticisms" (1895), p. 134.

[24]Thoreau, "Civil Disobedience," p. 224.

[25]*Ibid.*, pp. 225–26.

[26]Tolstoy, "Two Wars" (1898), p. 18

[27]Tolstoy, "Notes for Officers" (1901), p. 28.

[28]Tolstoy, "Thou Shalt Not Kill, " p. 157.

[29]Tolstoy, "Nikolai Palkin" (no date), p. 195.

[30]*Ibid.*, p. 197.

[31]Tolstoy, "The Kingdom of God Is Within You" (1891), pp. 258–59.

[32]Thoreau, "Civil Disobedience," p. 227.

[33]*Ibid.*

[34]*Ibid.*

[35]*Ibid.*, p. 239.

[36]*Ibid.*, p. 229.

[37]*Ibid.*, p. 232.

[38]*Ibid.*, p. 231.

[39]*Ibid.*, p. 233.

[40]*Ibid.*, p. 233-34.

[41]*Ibid.*, p. 235.

[42]*Ibid.*, p. 236

[43]*Ibid.*, p. 236-37.

[44]*Ibid.*, p. 241.

[45]*Ibid.*, p. 225.

[46]Tolstoy, "*Carthago Delenda Est*" (1899), p. 101.

[47]*Ibid.*, p. 102.

[48]Tolstoy, "Postscript ... ," p. 266.

[49]*Ibid.*, p. 276.

[50]Tolstoy, "The Beginning of the End" (1897), p. 13.

[51]Tolstoy, "Two Wars" (1898), p. 23.

[52]Tolstoy, "*Carthago Delenda Est*," p. 98.

[53]Tolstoy, "Two Wars" (1898) p. 23.

[54]Tolstoy, "*Carthago Delendo Est*." p. 101.

[55]Tolstoy, "Postscript ... ," p. 265.

[56]Tolstoy, "On Patriotism," p. 90.

[57]Tolstoy, "Letter to Ernest Howard Crosby" (no date), pp. 183–84.

[58]Tolstoy, "Postscript ... ," pp. 260–61.

[59]Tolstoy, "*Carthago Delendo Est*." p. 102.

[60]Thoreau, *Walden* p. 219.

[61]Thoreau, "Civil Disobedience," p. 241.

[62]*Ibid.*, p. 242.

[63]Thoreau, "Life without Principle" (1862), p. 1761.

[64]*Ibid.*, p. 1765.

[65]*Ibid.*, p. 1767.

[66]Tolstoy, "The Beginning of the End," p. 14.

[67]Tolstoy, "Church and State" (no date), p. 202.

[68]Tolstoy, "On Patriotism," p. 92.

[69]Tolstoy, *Ibid.*, pp. 93-94.

[70]Tolstoy, *Ibid.*, p. 93.

[71]Tolstoy, *Ibid.*, p. 94.

[72]Thoreau, "Civil Disobedience," pp. 242-43. (see note 13)

[73]Thoreau, "Life without Principle," p. 1755.

[74]*Ibid.*, p. 1758.

[75]*Ibid.*, p. 1762.

[76]*Ibid.*, p. 1764.

[77]Tolstoy, "A Reply to Criticisms," p. 134. (see note 23)

[78]Tolstoy, "On Patriotism," p. 93.

[79]*Ibid.*,

[80]Thoreau, *Walden*, p. 217.

[81]Tolstoy, "Church and State," pp. 211–12.

---

**JACK SCHWARTZMAN** has earned two doctorates, a J.S.D. and Ph.D. He is an attorney in the State of New York, editor-in-chief of *Fragments*, an international "individualistic" magazine, the author of three books and several hundred articles, and professor of English at Nassau Community College, State University of New York, in which capacity he won the New York State Chancellor's Award for Excellence in Teaching. Born in the Soviet Union in 1912, Dr. Schwartzman came to the United States with his family in the 1920s. He is reputed to be the oldest full-time professor in the United States and continues to maintain a heavy schedule of speaking engagements.

# Thoreau Lives
## An Afterward from Moscow

❖

Mr. Edmund Schofield
President
The Thoreau Society
156 Belknap St.
Concord, Mass. 07142

Moscow, USSR
August 16–27, 1991

Dear Mr. President,

We thank you most cordially for a wonderful time in Massachusetts. The Jubilee was a great success, and we will never forget the warmth and hospitality of the members of The Thoreau Society. In our opinion, the conference made a considerable contribution to Thoreau studies, and we hope to see its materials published in the future.

It is true irony of the history that so soon after the Thoreau conference and a great time in Concord, we were compelled to become participants of civil disobedience campaign in Moscow. there was something very symbolic in this. At that time, we were thinking about you all. Your tax message reached us recently.

We are still most willing to invite the delegation of the Thoreau Society to visit us here any time of your convenience. Please keep us informed about your plans.

Please convey our warmest regards to the members of the Thoreau Society and the participants of the Jubilee.

Very truly yours,

Michael Gusev
Nikita Pokrovsky
Piotr Savellev

# Part II

❖

# THOREAU AS SCIENTIST

# Some Thoughts of
# Henry David Thoreau

❖

Every man will be a poet if he can; otherwise a philosopher or man of science. This proves the superiority of the poet.

*—April 11, 1852*

There is no such thing as pure objective observation. Your observation, to be interesting, i.e., to be significant, must be subjective. The sum of what the writer of whatever class has to report is simply some human experience, whether he be poet or philosopher or man of science. The man of most science is the man most alive, whose life is the greatest event. It matters not where or how far you travel,—the farther commonly the worse,—but how much alive you are. If it is possible to conceive of an event outside to humanity, it is not of the slightest significance, though it were the explosion of a planet. Every important worker will report what life there is in him. It makes no odds into what seeming deserts the poet is born. Though all his neighbors pronounce it a Sahara, it will be a paradise to him; for the desert which we see is the result of the barrenness of our experience. No mere willful activity whatever, whether in writing verses or collecting statistics, will produce true poetry or science. ... I look over the report of the doings of a scientific association and am surprised that there is so little life to be reported; I am put off with a parcel of dry technical terms. Anything living is easily and naturally expressed in popular language. I cannot help suspecting that the life of these learned professors has been almost as inhuman and wooden as a rain-gauge or self-registering magnetic machine. They communicate no fact which rises to the temperature of blood heat. It does not all amount to one rhyme.

*—May 6, 1854*

I fear that the character of knowledge is from year to year becoming more distinct and scientific; that, in exchange for views as wide as heaven's cope, I am being narrowed down to the field of a microscope. I see details, not wholes nor the shadow of the whole. I count some parts and say, "I know."

—*August 21, 1851*

I learned today that my ornithology had done me no service. The birds I heard, which fortunately did not come within the scope of my science, sung as freshly as if it had been the first morning of creation, and had for background to their song an untrodden wilderness, stretching through many a Carolina and Mexico of the soul.

—*March 4, 1840*

The secretary of the Association for the Advancement of Science requests me, as he probably has thousands of others, by a printed circular letter from Washington the other day, to fill the blank against certain questions, among which the most important one was what branch of science I was specially interested in, using the term science in the most comprehensive sense possible. Now, though I could state to a select few that department of human inquiry which engages me, and should be rejoiced at an opportunity to do so, I felt that it would be to make myself the laughing-stock of the scientific community to describe or attempt to describe to them that branch of science which specially interests me, inasmuch as they do not believe in a science which deals with the higher law. So I was obliged to speak to their condition and describe to them that poor part of me which alone they can understand. The fact is I am a mystic, a transcendentalist, and a natural philosopher to boot. Now I think of it, I should have told them at once that I was a transcendentalist. That would have been the shortest way of telling them that they would not understand my explanations.

—*March 5, 1853*

The man of science, who is not seeking for expression but for a fact to be expressed merely, studies nature as a dead language. I pray for such inward experience as will make nature significant.

—*May 10, 1853*

It is only when we forget all our learning that we begin to know. I do not get nearer by a hair's breadth to any natural object so long as I presume that I have an introduction to it from some learned man. To conceive of it with a total comprehension I must for the thousandth time approach it as something totally strange. If you would make acquaintance with the ferns you must forget your botany. You must get rid of what is commonly called knowledge of the. Not a single scientific term or distinction is the least to the purpose, for you would fain perceive something, and you must approach the object totally unprejudiced. You must be aware that no thing is what you have taken it to be. In what book is this world and its beauty described? Who has plotted the steps toward the discovery of beauty? You have got to be in a different state from common. Your greatest success will be simply to perceive that such things are, and you will have no communication to make to the Royal Society.

*—October 4, 1859*

The old naturalists were so sensitive and sympathetic to nature that they could be surprised by the ordinary events of life. It was an incessant miracle to them, and therefore gorgons and flying dragons were not incredible to them. The greatest and saddest defect is not credulity, but our habitual forgetfulness that our science is ignorance.

*—March 5, 1860*

# Thoreau as Scientist
## American Science in the 1850s

❖

## A. Hunter Dupree

More than any other decade, the 1850s were a time of testing of the culture of the American people. Literature, economics, politics, religion, philosophy, and science were all responding both to the stimulus of rapid national development and to the moral challenge posed by the continued existence of slavery. American scientists were participating fully in the exploration of Nature and in the building of national institutions for research and education. Science was increasingly separable from other ideals and systems of ideas drawn from religion and philosophy.[1] The transcendentalists of Concord, Massachusetts, were foremost among those who built an overarching structure of transcendent thought on the idea of Nature. Transcendentalism thus itself became a kind of science.

Henry Thoreau received a questionnaire from the American Association for the Advancement of Science when it was only five years old, in 1853. "I felt that it would be to make myself the laughing-stock of the scientific community to describe … that branch of science which specially interests me, inasmuch as they do not believe in a science which deals with the higher law. So I was obliged to speak to their condition and describe to them that poor part of me which alone they can understand. The fact is I am a mystic, a transcendentalist, and a natural philosopher to boot."[2] Emerson took the same line in his 1836 essay "Nature," which impressed Thoreau at Harvard. "All science has one aim, namely, to find a theory of nature … . All the facts of natural history taken by themselves have no value but are barren, like a single sex."[3] Both the independent view of nature and the disdain for academic science that Thoreau bequeathed to posterity are built into the very foundations of transcendental science.

The model of transcendental science in which Thoreau had the most pervasive interest throughout his career was botany. His hero botanist, both as a scientist and a writer, was Johann Wolfgang Goethe.[4] Thoreau had plenty of access to Goethe the literary artist both as an undergraduate studying modern languages at Harvard and slightly later as a young member of Emerson's circle in Concord, which included especially the Goethe enthusiast Margaret Fuller. According to a recent literary critic, Thoreau organized the observations recorded in many years of journal entries into *A Week on the Concord and Merrimack Rivers* on the model of Goethe's *Italian Journey.*[5] Literary narrative of travel and exploration was for Thoreau the preferred form of publication. Goethe's metamorphosis of plants—the insight that all the organs of a plant are transformed leaves—was a process that, in the words of Emerson, suggested the leading idea of modern botany."[6] The idea came to Goethe as a flash of inspiration while in Italy.

Goethe gave some lip service to Linnaeus' nomenclature and informally collected plants to be dried, but botanizing for him was a leisurely social activity. He had little use for organized research or for professional botanists. Thoreau carried on this tradition into the 1850s. In writing about plants, he transforms a perfectly straightforward statement in a botanical textbook into the idea that roots "readily ally themselves to the earth, to the primal womb of things."[7] A better example of transcendental science is hard to find. Thoreau's writings ultimately established their truth by being incorporated into works of literature, often published after his death, and not as natural science in published journals of record. Thoreau's science would go down to posterity through John Muir, John Burroughs, and the myriad nature writers of the 20th century. His writings form a canon, not a contribution to the stream of scientific literature.

The leader of the straight botanists of the 1850s was Asa Gray, who had come to Harvard in 1842. He was the author of the manual and textbook that Thoreau used with impatient contempt. While Thoreau explored the farthest Indies by staying in Concord, Gray also stayed pretty much in Cambridge but explored the American West and the Pacific Ocean area by sponsoring collectors who brought back dried specimens of plants. They were carefully arranged in his herbarium, studied under a microscope, and compared against previous collections and the formal literature of botanical science.

Apparently unknown to Thoreau, Gray by the 1850s was beginning to arrange his empirical data into global patterns. On this base of information he was led to the higher reaches of theory by questions posed by his friend and correspondent Charles Darwin. Gray's leading collector, Charles Wright, had reached Japan on the North Pacific Exploring Expedition of the mid-1850s. By early 1859 Gray was presenting to the American Academy of Arts and Sciences in Boston a series of papers demonstrating that distinct species of plants appearing in East Asia and Eastern North America, until then considered separate creations, were descended from a common ancestor.

The other scientist of world renown who entered the intellectual circles of Concord, Cambridge, and Boston in the 1840s was the Swiss Louis Agassiz. He established at Harvard a museum that did for zoology the kind of straight empirical classification that Gray was doing for botany, and Thoreau was soon sending him turtles. However, he was also the product of many of the same currents of German thought admired by the transcendentalists, and socially he took Boston by storm. In 1852, Emerson wrote in his journal, "I saw in the cars a broad featured, unctuous man, fat and plenteous as some successful politician, and pretty soon divined it must be the foreign professor who has had so marked a success in all our scientific and social circles, having established unquestionable leadership in them all; and it was Agassiz."[8]

Agassiz had a completely idealistic system—"A species is a thought in the mind of the Creator." He believed that each species, including the races of man, had been created in great numbers in the regions they now occupy. Successive geological periods were separated from one another by catastrophes that wiped out all preceding species, and the Creator started all over again. If a naturalist were good enough at observation and classification, he could distinguish these separate creations from one another by straight science. When Southerners were developing a pro slavery argument to prove scientifically the inferiority of the Negro race, Agassiz lent his high authority to Josiah Nott's and George R. Gliddon's *Types of Mankind*, the leading work in this literature.

Thoreau and Emerson seem to have seen no contradiction in their obvious leadership in the antislavery crusade and their forming close intellectual and social ties with Agassiz. He could simultaneously protest antislavery sentiments and insist that the races of man were separate species and that the white race should not hybridize with inferior species. Value-neutral scientific fact had put in its appearance at the heart of transcendental science. So strong was the bond between the transcendentalists' brand of German idealism and that of Agassiz that in 1856 they formed a special club, the Saturday Club, which took Emerson every month to Boston to meet with the professor and a few other choice spirits. Neither Thoreau nor, in these years, Gray was a member.

In 1887 Frederick Douglass, the ex-slave who became the voice of the abolitionists and also of the blacks in the great crusade of the 1850s, contemplating the descendants of the ancient Egyptians, said: "Could I have seen forty years ago what I have now seen, I should have been much better fortified to meet the Notts and the Gliddons ... in their arguments against the Negro as a part of the great African race."[9]

During the 1850s Thoreau maintained his transcendentalism and Goethean botany formally unchanged, but unlike Emerson he exhibited a slow drift toward independent thought in natural history. He became more organized in his observations. In *Walden* he examined in a systematic way the influence of climate on the budding, blooming, and fruiting of plants and on the flight of birds. He also showed a hint of a questioning of Agassiz, culminating in an exchange at dinner at Emerson's over observations of ice crystals in frozen fish and caterpillars.[10]

Thoreau had also discovered Darwin by 1851, not as had Gray though collaboration in science, but by reading the journal of the *Beagle* voyage as travel literature. Thoreau was not under the discipline of straight science, as was Gray or Darwin, in his scientific work. Thoreau could not enter into Gray's Darwinian research program in worldwide plant distribution, nor did he seem aware of Gray's public challenge to Agassiz and his adherence to Darwin in the meetings and the pages of the publications of the American Academy of Arts and Sciences in the spring of 1859.

When Darwin's *Origin of Species* was published in November 1859, a copy immediately came to Gray, who wrote one of the first reviews on either side of the Atlantic for the *American Journal of Science* in the week after Christmas. On January 1, 1860, Gray's copy of the *Origin* traveled to Concord in the hands of Charles Loring Brace, nephew of Mrs. Gray and a lively recurrent visitor to the Gray household. He had had their support in England in 1850 when he had gone to Hungary and been briefly imprisoned as a supporter of Louis Kossuth. Brace, trained as a clergyman, was lecturing on behalf of the Children's Aid movement of New York City. He had dinner that New Year's Day at the home F. B. Sanborn with Bronson Alcott and Thoreau.[11]

Since they discussed Darwin and the *Origin*, it is reasonable to assume that Brace acquainted Thoreau with Gray's review comparing Darwin and Agassiz. Thoreau followed up a few days later, made some extracts in his natural history fact book, and had a discussion with Emerson which shows that both of them had a long way to go to understand the position of Darwin or, surprisingly, Agassiz.[12]

In decade of the 1860s a contest developed between Gray and Agassiz that covered a whole range of issues from a fair hearing for Darwin, to the geographical distribution of plants and animals, to the organization of American scientific institutions, to the structure of the modern university, to the threat to academic freedom at Harvard created by Agassiz's dictatorial ambitions. Thoreau, however, still in his early forties, was already too sick to enter the scientific or general debates of the age of Darwin.

The career of Horace Mann, Jr., serves as a coda to Thoreau's drift toward organized natural history in the 1850s and his approach to the botanist Asa Gray rather than to Louis Agassiz. In 1861, when Thoreau went on a truncated journey in quest of health to Minnesota, he had as his companion the seventeen-year-old son of the great educator of the day and Mary Mann, one of the Peabody sisters and thus a sister-in-law of Nathaniel Hawthorne. Mann had been educated at home, where science had replaced a classical education. At the age of fifteen he had shown his literacy in taxonomic botany by publishing a *Catalogue of the ... Plants Contained in Gray's Manual. ...*[13]

Horace Mann was living in Concord with his mother after the return from Minnesota and had to consider what course to take at Harvard—the classic curriculum of the college or the natural-history curriculum of the Lawrence Scientific School—or whether to go to West Point. A close friend and associate of Mann's wrote:

> Mr. R. W. Emerson, who took much kind interest in him, and who generally councils the College course, said, "If the boy has a vocation thank God for it and let him follow his genius." Mr. Thoreau, with whom he had become intimate on a journey to the West, told him "no teachers ever did him any good in College." The result of the deliberation was what might have been expected, and he rejoicingly pursued the scientific path. In this decision he could have found many supporters among the most advanced thinkers of the age.[14]

Since Agassiz was the absolute dictator of the Lawrence Scientific School, Mann first took up the study of zoology, especially conchology. When the students rebelled against their tyrant, both because he was against Darwin and because he mistreated them in the museum, most had to leave Harvard except Mann, who managed to shift to Asa Gray even though these two senior professors were in a deadlock for more than two years. Mann had found his science in botany and Gray had found a student who could be his successor. Mann, according to his friend, "learned to love the science not only for itself but for the great teacher."[15] Instead of a conventional curriculum Gray arranged for Mann to go collecting to the Hawaiian Islands, one of his primary Darwinian targets of the 1850s. On his return Mann received his Bachelor of Science degree, with Gray's mentor, Dr. John Torrey of New York, and Agassiz joining Gray on the examination committee. The next year Gray went to Europe and left Mann in charge of the garden, the herbarium, and all instruction at Harvard. Within a few months he was struck down by the same disease that had felled Thoreau before his time. Horace Mann was elected to the American Academy of Arts and Sciences on November 11, 1869, at the age of twenty-four. He died the same night.[16]

In the midst of all the transcendental thought that dominated the scientific, philosophical, and religious scene in the 1850s, three people stand out as independent. They used very different literary traditions as instruments, but each in his own way looked through them to Nature. One, of course, was Henry David Thoreau. Another was Asa Gray. The third was Charles Darwin.

# Notes

[1]Paul Forman, "Independence, Not Transcendence, for the Historian of Science, " *Isis* vol. 82/(1991), p. 73

[2]Henry D. Thoreau, "Journal, March 5 [1853]," in Perry Miller, ed., *The American Transcendentalists: Their Prose and Poetry* (Garden City, N.Y.: doubleday, 1957), p. 2.

[3]Ralph Waldo Emerson, "Nature," reprinted in Howard Mumford Jones and Ernest E. Leisy, eds., *Major American Writers* (New York: Harcourt, Brace, 1935), pp. 380, 388.

[4]I am indebted to Lisbet Koerner for the opportunity to see her unpublished paper on this subject.

[5]Robert D. Richardson Jr., *Henry Thoreau: A Life of the Mind* (Berkeley and Los Angeles: Univ. of California Press, 1986), pp. 156–157.

[6]Quoted in Richardson, p. 30.

[7]Quoted in A. Hunter Dupree, *Asa Gray: American Botanist, Friend of Darwin* (Baltimore: John Hopkins Univ. Press, 1988), p. 222.

[8]Quoted in Dupree, p. 225.

[9]Quoted in William S. McFeely, *Frederick Douglass* (New York: W. W. Norton, 1991), p. 330.

[10]Richardson, *Thoreau*, p. 367.

[11]Walter Harding, *The Days of Henry Thoreau: A Biography* (Princeton Univ. Press, 1982), p. 429; Robert Sattelmeyer, *Thoreau's Reading: A Study in Intellectual History* (Princeton, N.J.: Princeton Univ. Press, 1988), pp. 80–92; Richardson, *Thoreau*, pp. 376–379.

[12]See Sattelmeyer, *Thoreau's Reading*, p. 89, for another interpretation.

[13]New York: Ivison and Phinney, 1859.

[14]Friend and Associate, "A Sketch of the Life of the Late Horace Mann," *Bulletin of the Essex Institute* (Salem, Mass.), vol. I (February 1869), No. 2, p. 43.

[15]*Ibid.* p. 44.

[16]Asa Gray, "Horace Mann," in *Proceedings of the American Academy of Arts and Sciences* vol. 8 (June 8, 1869), p. 129.

---

**A. HUNTER DUPREE** is Professor of History, Emeritus, Brown University, Providence, Rhode Island. He is the author of *Asa Gray: American Botanist, Friend of Darwin* (John Hopkins Univ. Press, 1988) and *Science in the Federal Government: A History of Policies and Activities* (John Hopkins Univ. Press, 1986). He has devoted his career to the study of the history of science and technology in American society.

# The Coleridgean Influence on Thoreau's Science

❖

**Robert Sattelmeyer**

When I was invited to discuss Thoreau as a scientist, I was asked specifically to deal with the influence of Samuel Taylor Coleridge's scientific theories on Thoreau, which was the subject of an article that a colleague and I had published in 1985. (The colleague was Richard Hocks, who was more familiar with Coleridge's scientific writings than I was.) I also treated the subject, more briefly, a few years later in an account of Thoreau's reading in 19th-century natural science. But I was happy to agree: there is much more to be said on the subject of Thoreau's scientific sources generally and upon the influence of Coleridge and related authors specifically.

I will briefly recapitulate the argument of the earlier article, which describes Coleridge's principal scientific treatise, *Hints Toward the Formation of a More Comprehensive Theory of Life*, and speculates about its importance in the formation of Thoreau's mature orientation to natural science; describe how this orientation was related to some of the other scientific sources that Thoreau followed during the 1850s; and suggest a few of the ways in which Thoreau diverged from these sources in formulating his own distinctive approach to natural history.

Few students of literature or of the natural sciences are familiar with Coleridge's *Theory of Life*, for it was a posthumously published treatise (first published in 1848, the year Thoreau read it) that has been relatively obscure in the Coleridge canon until fairly recently. Like much of what Coleridge wrote, it is philosophically complex, occasionally to the point of opacity, and these qualities may have had something to do with its obscurity as well. Its importance to a Romantic naturalist such as Thoreau, however, was that it offered him a theoretical framework for natural science that harmonized with his training and orientation in aesthetics and epistemology—a good deal of which was also owing to the influence of Coleridge, who was of course the best known and most influential exponent of German Romantic philosophy in English. What this means in practical terms is that the disharmony between poetry and science, which we tend to assume as a given in our post-Darwinian, post-positivist world, did not yet prevail when Thoreau began his serious scientific study. It was on the horizon, to be sure, but his era—the 1840s and 1850s—was a time of great variety and uncertainty and excitement of competing paradigms and theories, when many of the best scientists subscribed to theories of life and creation profoundly different from the Darwinian model that emerged as the dominant one over the succeeding decades.

## Coleridge's Theory

Briefly, Coleridge, responding to a current debate in British science over the nature of life and distinctions between organic and inorganic matter, proposed that life could only be defined by "the *Law* of the thing, or in such idea of it, as being admitted, all the properties and functions are admitted by implication. It must likewise be so far *causal*, that a full insight having been obtained of the law, we derive from it a progressive insight into the necessity and *generation* of the phenomena of which it is the law." Life, then, for Coleridge, was not immediately dependent upon matter or its organization but upon some higher principle or power that brought it into being. The two key principles for Coleridge in understanding the development of various forms of life are individuation and polarity. Polarity is not merely opposition or contradiction versus identity but a dynamic power of contrary forces (without the other, neither of which could exist) which cause the representations of nature to arise, rather like the way electricity is produced across positive and negative poles. Individuation, as the name implies, is the tendency to individuate, to become detached and independent, but which, in a polar relationship, cannot exist or even be conceived without the opposite tendency to attach and connect.

These principles of polarity and individuation allow Coleridge to perceive the spectrum of nature as a series of dynamic transformations from lower to higher stages of organization and life, all the way from metals to man. Higher forms may be said to evolve from lower ones, although metamorphosis is probably a better word than evolution to describe the transformation. That was the term used by Goethe, who in many respects is the founding figure of the school of German natural science that profoundly influenced both Coleridge and Thoreau. As each stage reaches the epitome of its development, it tends to fall back and give rise to its opposite in a new order of beings at a higher level. Insects, for example, which represent the highest development of an external

49

framework—an exoskeleton—give rise to an order of beings next in complexity, fish, which have their skeletons internalized. Everything in this scheme anticipates the highest order of creation, man.

As Coleridge put it, in a passage from the *Theory of Life* that Thoreau copied in an extract book, "Man possesses the most perfect osseous structure, the least and most insignificant covering. The whole force of organic power has attained an inward and centripetal direction. He has the whole world in counterpoint to him, but he contains an entire world within himself. Now, for the first time at the apex of the living pyramid, it is Man and Nature, but Man himself is a syllepsis, a compendium of Nature—the Microcosm!" But Man too must respect the polar law: "As the ideal genius and originality, in the same proportion must be the resignation to the real world, the sympathy and the inter-communion with nature. In the conciliating mid-point, or equator, does the Man live, and only by its equal presence in both its poles can that life be manifested!"

The other aspect of Coleridge's treatise—implicit in the last sentence quoted—that needs to be stressed, the polar complement to his abstract theory of life, is his insistence on detailed observation and what we might call fieldwork. These laws and their operations were only to be detected and observed by careful study and attention to the particulars of nature.

## *Naturphilosophie* and Louis Agassiz

Encountering this theory and this endorsement of the minute study of nature in 1848, Hocks and I argued, may have played a catalytic role in validating for Thoreau the life's work in natural history that he took up at that time. At the same time, though, it must be stressed, Thoreau was reading and encountering at first hand related ideas and theories about the life sciences. Coleridge's own sources for his scientific thought lay in the *Naturphilosophie* of early 19th-century Germany, especially the writings of Schiller, Schelling, and Lorenz Oken, with whom Thoreau also became acquainted in the late 1840s through both reading and personal acquaintance with a distinguished disciple. The reading was in J. B. Stallo's *General Principles of the Philosophy of Nature*, which contained chapters detailing the views of all the above thinkers organized around the concept of "evolutions," by which Stallo meant the various transformations of form and development observable in nature. The personal acquaintance, of course, was with Louis Agassiz, with whom Thoreau began to correspond and for whom he began to serve as a specimen collector as early as 1847. Agassiz, the most influential and distinguished natural scientist in America during the late 1840s and the 1850s, was a tireless field worker and collector and promoter of natural science; he was also a disciple of *Naturphilosophie* at heart, for he had been educated in the school of Oken and Schelling as a youth. His approach to nature generally was compatible with that outlined in Coleridge's *Theory of Life* and he maintained his essentially idealist and teleological perspective even after the Darwinian revolution, despite the fact that his own work in embryology and other areas had provided much evidence for Darwin and other evolutionists.

The central emphasis of *Naturphilosophie*, according to an article by Evelleen Richards, was the historical understanding of the development of Nature: "*Naturphilosophie* had to demonstrate how the universe originated, and to reconstruct its development or *Entwicklung* from the original Idea thought by God to its highest manifestation as man. "It is certain," affirmed Schelling in 1811, "that whoever could write the history of his own life from its very ground, would have thereby grasped in a brief conspectus the history of the universe." This certainty was based on the fundamental Romantic tenet that man is the prototype and model of all existence—the microcosm. (Remember Coleridge on this point.) There is only one developmental tendency, that of producing man, who is, as Oken put it, the "summit, the crown of nature's development, and must comprehend everything that has preceded him, even as the fruit includes within itself all the earlier developed parts of the plant." Thus man's individual development, or ontogeny, necessarily replicates the development of life on earth, the universal development reflected in that abstraction the Romantics called *Entwicklung*. Man and nature share a common *Entwicklungsgeschichte*—a history of development."

This tendency is most clearly reflected in Agassiz's own almost obsessive preoccupation with embryology and ontogeny as evidence of a progressive development in nature leading up to man. To put the issue in simpler terms: the fact that an embryo revealed earlier stages of development that could also be detected in the fossil record meant to Agassiz and other scientists that the present creation had been prophesied by these earlier stages, not that species currently alive were descended from them. This led Agassiz and others to a theory of life and creation that has been called "progressionism," a less ideal but still teleological view of development that called for repeated instances of divine intervention at successively higher levels of development. Another way of describing this theory, in Evelleen Richards' apt phrase, is "evolution without physical continuity." Earlier stages of life are related to later ones, but in a typological fashion rather than through physical causality. One of the corollaries of this theory was that there must have been not one but a series of special creations, roughly corresponding to the breaks in the fossil record that mark the boundaries between geologic eras. It should be remembered that this theory fit the emerging data much better than the older theory of the divine creation of life at one time with species remaining fixed and immutable, and does, from one perspective, represent a step in the direction of physical evolution. Darwin would make great use of the data Agassiz and his colleagues gathered in support of their theories.

Given this tradition, greatly oversimplified here, what was the general trajectory of Thoreau's own development as a natural scientist? Let me try to answer this question by detailing ways in which he both worked within the tradition I have been describing and diverged from it in important ways. One of the hallmarks of Coleridgean and other *Naturphilosophie*-based science was an attempt to find archetypes or *ur-phenomena*, ideal forms to which all actual life forms may be traced. This was not a search for a primordial ancestor but a primordial form; the development postulated, you will recall, is not one of physical causality but a metamorphosis not necessarily historical. For Goethe, the archetypal plant form was the leaf. All the parts of the plant could be described—flowers, especially—as modified or metamorphosed leaves. In zoology, the archetypal form for transcendental anatomists was an archetypal vertebra, out of which the rest of the skeleton, especially the skull, could be generated.

It is this tradition that Thoreau exploited brilliantly, going far beyond it imaginatively, in what is perhaps the most famous passage of natural description in *Walden*, his account of the thawing sand and clay along the railroad cut in "Spring." After discovering the law of vegetation evident in the flowing sand, which takes the form of leaves and tendrils, he traces the metamorphosis of the leaf form up through various stages of life:

> Thus, also, you pass from the lumpish grub in the earth to the airy and fluttering butterfly. The very globe itself continually transcends and translates itself, and becomes winged in orbit. Even ice begins with delicate crystal leaves, as if it had flowed into moulds which the fronds of water plants have impressed on the watery mirror. The whole tree itself is but one leaf, and rivers are still vaster leaves whose pulp is intervening earth, and towns and cities are the ova of insects in their axils.

His announcement here that "the maker of this earth but patented a leaf" takes a leaf out of the book of *Naturphilosophie*, harking back to Goethe and his *Urpflanze*.

## The Differences Between Thoreau and the *Naturphilosophen*

At the same time, and in the same passage, the way in which Thoreau most differs from this tradition may be seen. Notice that the metamorphoses described do not point, typologically or physically, toward man as the apex of creation or as microcosm. In fact, we are led away from the characteristic anthropocentrism of the *Naturphilosophen*, including Agassiz, toward a valorization of both an earlier stage of creation and a more earth-centered concept of life. The reason the sand foliage excites Thoreau so much is that it evinces a creation that is both ongoing and earlier than the one with which we customarily associate spring. It precedes the regular spring as mythology precedes poetry, and thus is closer—again literally—to the ground of life and being. And it points away from man toward the life of the earth itself, the globe that continually transcends and translates itself. Accordingly, the conclusion of this passage does not point to the glory of man's place but to the glory of the world: the earth is "not a fossil earth but a living earth; compared with whose great central life all animal and vegetable life is merely parasitic." The man is not microcosmic here; he is microscopic.

Thoreau diverged from Agassiz and the other *Naturphilosophen* on more strictly scientific grounds as well, of course. He was much more sympathetic to Darwin's *Origin of Species*, for example, than to Agassiz, and was even explicitly critical of Agassiz on this score. He also rejected Agassiz's theories of special creations at different times in favor of a more uniformitarian theory of adaptation and naturalization suggested to him by his own study of the dispersion of seeds in the late 1850s. "It is more philosophical," he said in 1861 after reading Darwin, to suppose that plants spread and naturalized themselves around the world than to suppose that they were separately created in different places. Likewise, he favored the Darwinian view, which he called the "development theory," because he thought it more compatible with his own view of nature as impelled by an ongoing and dynamic spirit of creation: "The development theory implies a greater vital force in nature, because it is more flexible and accommodating, and equivalent to a sort of constant *new* creation." (10/18/60)

Still, I tend to think that the more important divergence from his Coleridgean orientation lay in his reversal of the anthropocentrism of this entire school. In reading Thoreau's *Journal,* his most important and sustained examination of the nature of nature and the relations between humankind and nature, one simply does not encounter, I think, the sort of sermons in stones pointing toward humanity's privileged place in the universe that one associates with *Naturphilosophie.* Although there are many differences between his practice in *Walden* and in the *Journal,* the attitude toward the earth represented in the "Spring" passage quoted above is I think characteristic of his attitude in the *Journal* as well. His aims, thus, were not to discover in nature evidence of his own or mankind's special place in the universe but rather to understand his own life in all its phases according to the anterior life of nature. What Sharon Cameron has described as the aim of the *Journal,* writing *Nature,*—as opposed to writing *about* Nature—is true at the personal and scientific levels as well as at the literary one; what Thoreau wished to do was to submerge and inscribe himself in the endlessly iterating flow of nature, to participate in the great central life of the earth referred to earlier.

As Emerson said, the maxims "Study Nature" and "Know Thyself" become at last the same. Only one could proceed in two different ways. One could either, as the *Naturphilosophen* would have it, study one's own individual development and see it reflected in the *Entwicklung* of the natural world—which is what Whitman tended to do,—or one could operate the current in the other way, study nature in order to know oneself, to subject oneself to that great central life of the earth as manifested in all its multifaceted phenomena. This is a perspective I would risk calling ecological, one that Thoreau developed without the visual aid that we have had of seeing that great blue-and-white ball spinning in the darkness of space and realizing how dependent we are upon its great central life for our own.

## Bibliography

"'Metaphorical Mystifications': The Romantic Gestation of Nature in British Biology," in *Romanticism and the Sciences*, ed. Andrew Cunningham and Nicholas Jardine (Cambridge: Cambridge University Press, 1990), pages 130–43.

Thoreau and Coleridge's *Theory of Life, Studies in the American Renaissance 1985.* Charlottesville: University Press of Virginia, 1985, pages 269–84.

---

**ROBERT SATTELMEYER** has a Ph.D. in English from the University of Minnesota. Presently, he is an English professor at Georgia State University. He is the general editor for the *Journal of the Writings of Henry David Thoreau* and wrote *Thoreau's Readings* in 1988. He acquired an early interest in Thoreau when he read one of his works in high school.

# Seeing New Worlds
## Thoreau and Humboldtian Science

❖

**Laura Dassow Walls**

The following is a preliminary report on continuing research into possible connections between Henry David Thoreau and an under-represented tradition of natural science. The particularity of Thoreau's approach to nature differentiates him from Emerson—indeed, from all the transcendentalists—and has presented a continuing puzzle for Thoreau scholars. While researching Charles Darwin some years ago, I encountered the work of the scientist-explorer who had inspired him: Alexander von Humboldt. There appeared to be striking similarities of philosophy and method between Humboldt and Thoreau which I have come to believe are anything but accidental, and which may go some way toward explaining not only *what* Thoreau was doing in the last ten to fifteen years of his life, but *why*—that is, why he was doing those particular things, in that particular way.

Thoreau is most often connected to something called "Romantic science," aligned through Goethe to Coleridge and Emerson. Yet their fundamental orientation strikes me as being quite different. All three are concerned with getting through the "facts" of nature, which are often described as a kind of "veil" over a metaphysical reality, to the overarching or underlying system which is believed to be expressed by those facts. Frequently this system is designated as the underlying Divine Law, following Coleridge's central idea of Law as Logos, or the Word of God. Thoreau, on the other hand, is lovingly obsessed with natural facts, and cherishes them in their individuality as if they *mean* something, or are important in themselves. I find one of his most characteristic aphorisms to be: "Let us not underrate the value of a fact; it will one day flower in a truth."

Humboldt positioned himself as a natural scientist and philosopher who, in contradistinction to idealist scientists such as the *Naturphilosophen*, sought to understand the whole, the universe or "cosmos," through interconnected particulars. He taught that only through a study of these interconnected, constituent parts could one appreciate nature and build to a knowledge of the whole. Typical of Humboldt is this statement from the Introduction of *Cosmos*, which Thoreau read in late 1849 or 1850; Humboldt here is discusses how it is that we are so moved by nature, and stressing that what moves us is the impression of the whole, which is given to us, and can only be analyzed by us, through the particular and individual facts:

> The powerful effect exercised by nature springs ... from the connection and unity of the impressions and emotions produced; and we can only trace their different sources by analyzing the individuality of objects and the diversity of forces. (*Cosmos* I; p. 27)

After offering his own experiences in tropical South America as examples, Humboldt continues:

> Thus, in the sphere of natural investigation, as in poetry and painting, the delineation of that which appeals most strongly to the imagination, derives its collective interest from the vivid truthfulness with which the individual features are portrayed. (*Cosmos* I; p. 34)

In other words, facts are not a veil to be pierced or rendered "transparent" (in one of Emerson's favorite metaphors), in order to reveal the underlying truth; they *are* the reality, and it is a reality that can move us powerfully, both aesthetically and emotionally.

In order to clarify the difference between these two positions, imagine two diagrams:

Figure 1                                        Figure 2

Both show ways of connecting facts or observations of the natural world. In the first (Figure 1), facts are illustrations of, and are traced directly to, the underlying Divine Law, in the Coleridgean sense of Law as Logos. One might think of this method of connection as "axial," since it relies on the idea of a central axis or single determining Truth, out of which radiate the different material phenomena which express it. In the second (Figure 2), facts are not connected to preexisting Truth but to each other, and out of the sum total of all the interconnections the observer determines the laws, or inherent properties of matter, that appear to govern the phenomena observed. This method of connection does not rely on a central axis but on an understanding of the "network" of interacting factors. The first approach characterizes Idealist science generally, and in particular both Coleridge and Emerson; I would like to designate it by the term "Rational Holism," after the Coleridgean notion of Reason. The second characterizes the science and philosophy of Humboldt, and I would like to designate it "Empirical Holism." As these terms indicate, both methods arise from a philosophical commitment to holism, but the key difference lies in the method of approaching and studying that "whole."

It is this cherishing of the particulars of nature, whose interconnections can lead us to an understanding of Truth in a philosophy that seeks to connect poetry and science, that I find crucial to Humboldt—and shared by Thoreau. Did Thoreau know Humboldt's work? As early as 1842, Thoreau referred to Humboldt in his essay "A Walk to Wachusett." Thoreau's reading of Charles Lyell's *Principles of Geology* in 1840 would have introduced him to explicitly "Humboldtian" principles, as Lyell himself built on Humboldt's work and methods. Thoreau's extensive reading in the literature of exploration would have introduced him indirectly to Humboldtian methodology; perhaps the best example is the volume Thoreau was reading at Walden Pond, John Charles Frémont's *Report of the Exploring Expedition to the Rocky Mountains in the Year 1842* (1845; Sattelmeyer, p.183); Frémont modeled his expedition and his report after Humboldt's. Finally, in 1849–1850, Thoreau had available in English the key books by Humboldt himself. By 1853 he was steeped in literature by, about, or directly influenced by Humboldt, to the point where he identifies himself with Humboldt in his famous letter to the naturalist Spencer F. Baird, rejecting his offer of membership in the American Association for the Advancement of Science:

> I may add that I am an observer of nature generally, and the character of my observations, so far as they are scientific, may be inferred from the fact that I am especially attracted by such books of science as White's *Selborne* and Humboldt's *Aspects of Nature*. (Thoreau, *Correspondence*, p. 310)

This reference has become obscure to us today. Gilbert White's *Natural History of Selborne* is available, in paperback, in any good bookstore. *Aspects of Nature* has been out of print for 120 years (except in a rare and expensive scientific reprint). Why is this? Although Humboldt initiated and encouraged major developments in a number of scientific fields, and his reputation in the United States rode extremely high from the 1840s through the 1860s, afterward—for a variety of reasons beyond the scope of this paper—his name rapidly fell into obscurity in this country. It is thus difficult, but important, to recapture now the range and scope of his influence in this country, from his 1804 visit with Thomas Jefferson to the 1869 Centennial celebration of his birth, organized and chaired by Louis Agassiz and held, not incidentally, in Boston. All that can be done here is to fill in some high points: Humboldt was a polymathic scientific researcher, especially in plant geography, physical geography, and meteorology, who was also a lifelong friend of Goethe and a direct influence on Goethe's own interests in natural history. From 1799 through 1804 he explored Central and South America, and he spent the rest of his long life publishing the results, and his own meditations, in dozens of scientific and popular books. Through these and through his person he exerted a formative influence on Lyell, on Darwin, and on the scientific explorations of the American West. Finally, in his youth his own philosophy had turned away from the customary vitalism, not to "mechanism" but to a proto-ecological holism; his lifelong interest was therefore not in determining ideal types nor ideal laws of morphological development, but in inquiring into the distribution of plants, animals, and mankind, and the relationship between them all and their environment.

For convenience, Humboldt's global program may be distilled into four diagnostic features or demands: explore, collect, measure, and connect. First, explore: to study nature, one must go, not to the study, the cabinet, the laboratory, the museum, or the botanical garden—but into the field, to nature in its own state, unappropriated by man. Or, more simply, into the *wild.* For ideas, no matter how beautiful, cannot tell us what is actually on the ground and what it might be doing. Second, collect whatever is detachable—plant and animal specimens, rocks and minerals, Indian artifacts, extensive field notes. Third, measure everything that varies over time or distance, accurately and with precision. Finally, connect these multiple observations by comparing them with other places, objects, and measurements. This may be done through writing, but also visually, through maps, diagrams, and charts. Finally, when one had tramped the ground, smelled the air, listened attentively, studied the blue of the sky, the temperature of the water, considered the rocks and handled the plants, one was ready to speculate, to make the intuitive leap to pattern and meaning.

I believe Humboldt's global program can be seen enacted in Thoreau's own local program, which took shape under the direct and indirect influence of Humboldt. First, through Thoreau's own travels. Second, through his massive reading and annotating of others' travels and explorations. Third and most famously, through his travels in Concord, where he put into practice, extensively and rigorously, the Humboldtian methodology: explore, amass, connect. In this way Thoreau was forging what has been called both "a method of higher empiricism" (*Journal* 3:496), and "practical Transcendentalism" (Richardson, p. 248). In 1849

Thoreau, the town surveyor, understood well the method and the intent of this mode of focused observation, or "higher empiricism." In *A Week* he writes:

> The process of discovery is very simple. An unwearied and systematic application of known laws to nature, causes the unknown to reveal themselves. Almost any *mode* of observation will be successful at last, for what is most wanted is method. Only let something be determined and fixed around which observation may rally. How many new relations a foot-rule alone will reveal, and to how many things still this has not been applied! What wonderful discoveries have been, and may still be, made, with a plumb-line, a level, a surveyor's compass, a thermometer, or a barometer! Where there is an observatory and a telescope, we expect that any eyes will see new worlds at once. (*A Week,* p. 363)

I would argue that Humboldt provided Thoreau with what Emerson could not: a method as well as a philosophy, a way to unite the individual and the particular into a comprehension of the Cosmic Whole.

The term "method" suggests extrinsic imitation, while "philosophy" suggests a deeper relationship. These are some of the philosophical assumptions they: First nature is a unified and harmonious whole, "one great whole, animated by the breath of life," in Humboldt's words (*Cosmos* I, p. 24). Second, this whole cannot be known instantly, all at once, nor "in general," but only through its constituent parts, "the individuality of elements" (*Cosmos* I, p. 27). Third, appearance in nature is not merely a veil to be ripped aside nor rendered transparent, but meaningful *in itself,* and thus our bodily senses give us meaningful and important knowledge. Fourth, man is a part of nature, or his environment, affecting it and affected by it; man and nature produce or create each other. This is what makes possible the synthesis of physical nature with moral nature; they are not separate nor dualistically conceived, but continuous and cooperative.

The final question to be addressed here is how we might see all this in Thoreau's writing. Humboldt stressed the need for reciprocal interaction between theory and fact, but he also knew how problematical this balance could be: one risked losing the higher law in a mass of observations. His answer was to insistently remind his readers that their ultimate aim was philosophical, not the mere accumulation of facts. Thoreau, in adopting and adapting Humboldt's standard, is testing and refining the process, leading to some vivid see-sawing in his *Journal.* In 1851, balance is a central concern. For example, in June, he experiments with one way of applying his method: "No one to my knowledge has observed the minute differences in the seasons—Hardly two nights are alike ... ." He would write a "Book of the seasons," each page "out of doors," and capture these subtle moments of change (*Journal* 3: 253) In July, he is indeed attempting to identify the seasons of summer. On July 16: "Methinks this is the first of the dog-days. The air in the distance has a peculiar blue mistiness or furnace-like look—though, as I have said it is not sultry yet—It is not the season for distant views ... ." He analyzes the quality of the air, then catalogues the multitudes of signs, from the drying of the thimbleberries, to the hour haymakers go in to tea (5 o'clock), to the particular stages of blossoms and birdcalls, all told in present tense as if recorded in the instant and order he encounters them (*Journal* 3: 310–11). A week later he writes, "The season of morning fogs has arrived," and is off on another gathering of minute but telling differences (*Journal* 3: 326). Then the next day, he sounds himself a warning:

> But this habit of close observation—In Humboldt—Darwin & others. Is it to be kept up long—this science—. Do not tread on the heels of your experience. Be impressed without making a minute of it. Poetry puts an interval between the impression & the expression—waits until the seed germinates naturally. (*Journal* 3: 331)

And so it goes, as he sorts himself out: fieldwork to synthesis, minute particulars to generalizations: bad science (August 5: "Ah what a poor dry compilation is the Annual of Scientific Discovery" [354]) to good science (August 19: "A meteorological journal of the mind—" [377]).

It is from this perspective that one must consider the famous and often-quoted passage:

> I fear that the character of my knowledge is from year to year becoming more distinct and scientific—That in exchange for views as wide as heaven's cope I am being narrowed down to the field of the micro-scope—I see details not wholes nor the shadow of the whole. I count some parts, & say 'I know'. The cricket's chirp now fills the air in dry fields near pine woods. (*Journal* 3: 380)

As he adds the next day, "I am afraid to be so knowing" (381). He is differentiating his surroundings in new ways, trying to understand how the process is to work, and how not to succumb beneath the weight of the whole, as Humboldt warned; *how*, exactly, he can connect details into wholes, not in theory but on the pulse of his own walking and writing. I think we should read these writings as a dialectic between the practice of close observation and the attainment of higher laws. And something else, too: Thoreau is positioning himself against the Association for the Advancement of Science generally, and in particular the professional, idealist science of Louis Agassiz. In this light it becomes especially telling that when he rejects their membership, it is Humboldt whom he invokes as an ally.

At this point, further speculations may be offered about certain intriguing parallels in the form and organization of Humboldt's and Thoreau's writings. But that is best left for a different forum. Here instead, emphasizing details, are That is, I will leave you with a couple of representative passages from Humboldt's writing, to give you a sense of what it actually was that Thoreau was reading.

First, since Thoreau was extracting from *Cosmos* II, at the end of 1849 or the beginning of 1850, in the second-to-last entry of the Literary Notebook, here is the key passage from Part One of that volume, titled "Incitements to the Study of Nature":

> Descriptions of nature, I would again observe, may be defined with sufficient sharpness and scientific accuracy, without on that account being deprived of the vivifying breath of imagination. The poetic element must emanate from the intuitive perception of the connection between the sensuous and the intellectual, and of the universality and reciprocal limitation and unity of all the vital forces of nature. The more elevated the subject, the more carefully should all external adornments of diction be avoided. The true effect of a picture of nature depends on its composition; every attempt at an artificial appeal from the author must therefore necessarily exert a disturbing influence. He who, familiar with the great works of antiquity, and secure in the possession of the riches of his native language, knows how to represent with the simplicity of individualizing truth that which he has received from his own contemplation, will not fail in producing the impression he seeks to convey; for, in describing the boundlessness of nature, and not the limited circuit of his own mind, he is enabled to leave to others unfettered freedom of feeling. (*Cosmos* II, p. 81)

A simple annotation of this statement may well be another of Thoreau's characteristic aphorisms: "A true account of the actual is the rarest poetry."

Finally, Thoreau was extracting into his *Journal* from the Otto translation of *Ansichten der Natur* in May 1850. Here is one of Humboldt's sketches from that volume, in which he attempts to enact his own ideals. He has just described a night on the banks of the Orinoco in which "the whole animal world [was] in a state of commotion," and he continues:

> A singular contrast to the scenes I have here described, and which I had repeated opportunities of witnessing, is presented by the stillness which reigns within the tropics at the noontide of a day unusually sultry. I borrow from the same journal the description of a scene at the Narrows of Baraguan. Here the Orinoco forms for itself a passage through the western part of the mountains of the Parime. That which is called at this remarkable pass a Narrow (*Angostura del Baraguan*) is, however, a basin almost 5700 feet in breadth. With the exception of an old withered stem of Aubletia (*Apeiba Tiburbu*), and a new Apocinea (*Allamanda Salicifolia*), the barren rocks were only covered with a few silvery croton shrubs. A thermometer observed in the shade, but brought within a few inches of the lofty mass of granite rock, rose to more than 122° Fahr. All distant objects had wavy undulating outlines, the optical effect of the *mirage*. Not a breath of air moved the dust-like sand. The sun stood in the zenith; and the effulgence of light poured upon the river, and which, owing to a gentle ripple of the waters, was brilliantly reflected, gave additional distinctness to the red haze which veiled the distance. All the rocky mounds and naked boulders were covered with large, thick-scaled Iguanas, Gecko-lizards, and spotted Salamanders. Motionless,

with uplifted heads and widely extended mouths, they seemed to inhale the heated air with ecstasy. The larger animals at such times take refuge in the deep recesses of the forest, the birds nestle beneath the foliage of the trees, or in the clefts of the rocks; but if in this apparent stillness of nature we listen closely for the faintest tones, we detect, a dull, muffled sound, a buzzing and humming of insects close to the earth, in the lower strata of the atmosphere. Everything proclaims a world of active organic forces. In every shrub, in the cracked bark of trees, in the perforated ground inhabited by hymenopterous insects, life is everywhere audibly manifest. It is one of the many voices of nature revealed to the pious and susceptible spirit of man. (*Views of Nature*, pp. 200–201)

In conclusion, we need to recognize an alternate Romantic tradition, and thus two forms of "Romantic science." As earlier stated, I have tentatively named the familiar holism of Coleridge, Carlyle, and Emerson, "Rational Holism," from the Coleridgean concept of an all-determining Reason. The alternative, "Empirical Holism," was defined, established, demonstrated, and energetically promoted by Alexander von Humboldt and adopted by, among others, Henry David Thoreau.

# Notes

Humboldt's *Ansichten der Natur* was published in Germany in three editions: 1808, 1826, 1849. There were two translations of the third edition:
1. *Aspects of Nature in Different Lands and Different Climates, with Scientific Elucidations,* tr. Mrs. Elizabeth Juliana Sabine. London: Longman, Brown, Green and Longman's; and John Murray, 1849.
[In America: Philadelphia: Lea and Blanchard, 1850.]
2. *Views of Nature: or Contemplations on the Sublime Phenomena of Creation; with Scientific Illustrations.* tr. E. C. Otto and Henry G. Bohn. London: Henry G. Bohn, [January] 1850.

Humboldt's *Kosmos* was published in Germany in five volumes: 1845, 1847, 1850, 1858, 1862. There were also two English translations, although both were incomplete (the fifth German volume has never been fully translated):
1. *Cosmos: Sketch of a Physical Description of the Universe.* tr. Mrs. Elizabeth Juliana Sabine. 4 vols. London: Longman, Brown, Green, and Longman's, and John Murray, 1849.
2. *Cosmos: A Sketch of a Physical Description of the Universe.* Trans. E. C. Otto. 5 vols. London: Henry G. Bohn, 1849–58. In America, Otto's translation was reprinted by New York: Harper and Brothers, 1850–1869(?).

*Personal Narrative of Travels to the Equinoctial Regions of America* was published in Paris and first translated into English by Helen Maria Williams, London: Longman's, Hurst, Rees, Orme and Brown, 1814–1829. It was retranslated by Thomasina Ross, 3 vols, London: Henry G. Bohn, 1852–1853.

# Bibliography

Humboldt, Alexander von. *Cosmos: A Sketch of a Physical Description of the Universe.* Trans. E. C. Otto. Vol. I: New York: Harper and Brothers, 1850. Vol. II: New York: Harper and Brothers, 1852.

———. *Views of Nature: or Contemplations on the Sublime Phenomena of Creation; with Scientific Illustrations.* Trans. E. C. Otto and Henry G. Bohn. London: Henry G. Bohn, 1850.

Richardson, Robert D., Jr. *Henry David Thoreau: A Life of the Mind.* Berkeley: University of California Press, 1986.

Sattelmeyer, Robert. *Thoreau's Reading, A Study in Intellectual History with Bibliographical Catalogue.* Princeton: Princeton University Press, 1988.

Thoreau, Henry David. *The Correspondence of Henry David Thoreau.* Ed. Walter Harding and Carl Bode. New York: New York University Press, 1958.

Thoreau, Henry David. *Journal, Vol. 3: 1848–1851.* Ed. Robert Sattelmeyer, Mark R. Patterson, William Rossi. Princeton: Princeton University Press, 1990.

Thoreau, Henry David. *A Week on the Concord and Merrimack Rivers.* Princeton: Princeton University Press, 1983.

---

**LAURA DASSOW WALLS** completed her doctorate at Indiana University and is teaching at Lafayette College in Easton, Pennsylvania. Her article, "The Napoleon Scientist: Alexander von Humboldt in Antebellum America" was recently published.

# Thoreau as a Philosophical Naturalist–Writer

❖

## William Rossi

As other essays in this volume show, contrary to the traditional view of Thoreau as a "poet–naturalist" ineffectually critical of "Science" and standing aloof from it, we are gradually coming to see how in his own way Thoreau participated in the natural science of his day. As a result, the work now going forward on Thoreau's scientific knowledge enables us to link his theories and practice to those of other, more professional naturalists. I would like to address an additional dimension of this participation by trying to place Thoreau in relation to an aspect of midcentury discourse on science not yet considered—a discourse not about seed dispersion or species, but about the proper methods of inquiring into such phenomena and thinking scientifically about them.

As the historian and philosopher of science Larry Laudan has pointed out, discussion of scientific methodology intensified as the professionalization of science got under way in the first half of the 19th century. In this period "entire books rather than prefaces or chapters were devoted exclusively to the subject."[1] But discussions of methodological and epistemological matters were not confined to systematic treatises on the philosophy of science such as John Herschel's *Preliminary Discourse on the Study of Natural Philosophy* (1830) (to cite a work in Emerson's library).[2] According to Richard Yeo, who has written extensively on the rhetoric and politics of scientific method, it was not until later in the century that discussion of these questions become almost exclusively the domain of philosophers. In Thoreau's day they were taken up by practicing scientists eager to promote the "advance of science" and "positive knowledge"; to get "the *people* into the right way of thinking about induction," as William Whewell desired; and often to oppose the sort of speculative hypotheses associated in England with German

*Naturphilosophie.* In this enterprise Francis Bacon's name and principles figured prominently. Yeo argues persuasively that there is little sense in trying to determine who actually was a "Baconian" and who was not. Rather, as "Baconianism" was invoked for a host of rhetorical reasons, it served as a framework for wide-ranging discussion of scientific method-ology and philosophy as well as for the public promotion of science.[3] Such discussions of method also appeared "in periodical reviews and in the proceedings and transactions of scientific institutions and societies," with which Thoreau was familiar, where they were raised in connection with specific scientific problems.[4] Thoreau would have encountered these discussions in works such as Sir Charles Lyell's *Principles of Geology* and Edward Tuckerman's treatise on North American lichens, among many others he is now known to have read, and extracts bearing on these issues occasionally appear in his fact books.

I do not intend to suggest that Thoreau was a philosopher of science. He's been called enough names already; and we are still sorting out the names he called himself: "a mystic, a transcendentalist, and a natural philosopher to boot."[5] Instead, I want to claim only that in his reflections in the *Journal* and elsewhere on these issues, and even perhaps in his use of certain phrases associated with the contemporary discourse on method, Thoreau can be shown to have participated in this as well as in the other aspects of contemporary thought and practice of science of his day. Seeing Thoreau in relation to mid-century thought about method can also, I think, bring some light to his persistent identification of himself as a transcendentalist, a habit that has been something of a stumbling block to modern attempts to understand Thoreau as scientist. Finally, I will suggest how Thoreau's reflections on method and epistemology may bear on his representation of discovery in "The Succession of Forest Trees."

In her justly influential article entitled "Thoreau's View of Science," Nina Baym argued that Thoreau became increasingly alienated from both science and the scientific character of his own observations the more he realized that transcendentalism was hopelessly out of touch with the direction of contemporary science.[6] This thesis has begun to lose its hold in light of mounting evidence of Thoreau's real scientific interests and knowledge put forward by William Howarth, Ray Angelo, John Hildebidle, Robert Richardson, Robert Sattelmeyer, and Beth Witherell, among others.[7] Despite Baym's scrupulous attention to all of Thoreau's writing pertinent to the topic and despite her use of the most up-to-date studies in the history of science to place that writing in context, Thoreau is not really allowed to come into contact with science in Baym's account. As a writer, and especially a self-confessed transcendentalist, he is assumed from the beginning to stand apart from real science, which for Baym is Darwinian science. Ultimately, the question to be solved for her reader, then, is *when* this primary truth will become apparent to Thoreau himself and how his resulting "view" or attitude will be reflected in the direction his writing takes.

But while her thesis has become less tenable, Thoreau's ambivalence about science to which she draws attention, and particularly his persistence in identifying himself as a "transcendentalist" in a way that at least partly sets him in opposition to science, can still reveal a great deal about his conception and practice of science and about his position in a culture in which science—and the rhetoric of science—was assuming an increasingly dominant role. I say that Thoreau's self-identification as transcendentalist "partly sets him in opposition to science" because, as Hildebidle points out, Thoreau nevertheless continued to "claim for himself a scientific investigation, and a scientific result."[8] Thoreau never says, that is, that he thinks what he is doing is not science, but rather that it *may not* be seen so by others because of the transcendentalist (or more broadly, the philosophical) component. This is the drift of his explanation in the Journal for declining membership in the Association for the Advancement of Science: "If it had been the secretary of an association of which Plato or Aristotle was the president, I should not have hesitated to describe my studies at once and particularly."[9] And his 1860 letter to Benjamin Austin, a lecture manager for the Young Men's Association in Buffalo, may serve as an even more pertinent and ambiguous example.

> Dear Sir
> I shall be very happy to read to your association three lectures on the evenings named, but the question is about their character. They will not be scientific in the common, nor, perhaps, in any sense. They will be such as you might infer from reading my books. As I have just told Mr. Morse [manager of the Atheneum & Mechanics Association in Rochester], they will be *transcendental*, that is, to the mass of hearers, probably *moonshine*. Do you think that this will do? Or does your audience prefer lamplight, or total darkness these nights? I dare say, however, that they would interest those who are most interested in what is called nature.[10]

The question is: in what does this transcendentalist component consist? It is generally agreed that it involves a claim about knowledge of a spiritual realm, the investigation of a "higher law." But as Hildebidle says, moral and spiritual reflection is common in the genre of natural-history writing as Thoreau received it.[11] And one could add that while not always as explicit as in Agassiz and James Dwight Dana, say, such reflections were plentiful enough in contemporary natural science as well. A few months after Thoreau sent his rejection of membership back to Washington, for instance, the British geologist and president of the Geological Society, Edward Forbes, proposed to the Society a theory of the distribution of organic beings through geological time that was based on the abstract principle of polarity. In summarizing his theory in a published version of the paper, Forbes indicated that, like Thoreau, he too (and doubtless many members of his audience) saw himself as searching for a higher law: "This polarity, or arrangement in opposite directions with a development of intensity toward the extremes of each, is ... , if I am right in my speculations, an attribute or regulating law of the divinely originating scheme of creation."[12]

I suspect, therefore, that Thoreau's sense of heterodoxy in affirming his transcendentalism in this context resulted as much or more from the attendant epistemological and methodological assumptions that "transcendentalism" carried for him and his contemporaries as from the metaphysical ones. Richard Yeo's analysis of the mid-century debate on the value of Bacon's methodology reveals that, at the time, the former (i.e., epistemological) assumptions were much less palatable to Anglo-American scientific authority than the latter. Yet, Yeo's study also reveals that Thoreau was not completely alone within that scientific community in holding such views, anymore than he was in searching for a "higher law."

What then are these views and how do they compare with those of his contemporaries? In defining what he calls Thoreau's "aesthetic of nature," H. Daniel Peck has beautifully demonstrated Thoreau's phenomenological understanding of perception, an understanding that Peck finds epitomized in Thoreau's frequent use of the term "phenomenon." "A phenomenon," says Peck, "is not merely an invention of the [poetic] imagination ... but has an almost empirical status lying halfway between subjective and objective reality. It is, we may say, the meeting place of the perceiver and the perceived."[13] "Phenomenon" was, of course, a common term in the scientific lexicon of Thoreau's day, though not often used with the philological understanding and long Emersonian foreground we can be sure Thoreau brought to it. Thoreau's major preoccupation as a philosophical naturalist–writer involves precisely the interdependence of fact and idea that his usage of "phenomenon" implies—first, in perception, as Peck argues; but inevitably too, for the naturalist, in the *investigation* of nature.

Thus, Thoreau observes in "Autumnal Tints" that all who are trained in a particular field or pursuit (botanists, astronomers, gardeners, and hunters) will see what they look for.[14] Or, as we say now, our assumptions both limit and enable what we know and how we see. It is in this connection that Thoreau affirms that if the sharpshooter is to bag a snipe, he must "*anticipate* it," that is, "know its seasons and haunts, and the color of its wing" and have "dreamed of it" (175). While in this essay he develops the notion with respect to beauty that "there is just as much beauty visible to us in the landscape as we are prepared to appreciate,—not a grain more"—it is clear from his examples that the same goes for other "departments of knowledge" (174). Central to this conception in the essay, and in the mature *Journal,* is the notion that the more familiar one is with one's surroundings the more one is likely to make discoveries, both aesthetic and scientific. This notion, I think, fascinated and delighted Thoreau. He noted with pleasure in the early 1850s, for instance, that farmers are more apt to notice new varieties than are naturalists who come searching for them. His excitement at discovering the roots and leaves analogy in Asa Gray's *Manual* is surely related to it;[15] and it could be said that this idea constitutes the *Journal's* working hypothesis.

Nina Baym interprets Thoreau's conception of the anticipation of nature as a substitute for inference and method, and as denoting an instinctive wisdom acquired by Thoreau's ideal scientist who has learned the "laws of the universe" so well that he can "anticipate ... what comes next."[16] Her understanding of Thoreau's transcendentalist approach to science is, in fact, constructed upon this interpretation. But there is clearly more to it than this. Thoreau does indeed signal by the phrase "anticipation of nature" his faith in the possibility of intuitive knowledge, and, as Baym says, this faith remains a constant in his thinking. But in Thoreau's mature writings (after years of practical experience as a naturalist) this does not seem to me to be advocated as the sole mode of knowing nature. Rather, it emphasizes the importance of the intentional element in perception as one part of the larger dynamic. And this emphasis must be considered, too, in the context of the overwhelmingly empirical character of *Walden*, the *Journal*, and Thoreau's other natural-history writing.

In addition, Thoreau's use of this phrase is particularly interesting as possible evidence of a deeper familiarity with contemporary discourse of science than we are accustomed to expect from a transcendentalist supposed to be hopelessly out of touch with contemporary science. Often repeated by 19th-century reviewers and writers on method, the phrase "anticipation of nature" derives from Francis Bacon's *New Organum*, where it is distinguished, invidiously, as speculative or a priori reason, "rash and premature," from what Bacon calls the "interpretation of nature," that is, the inductive method or "reason which is elicited from facts by a just and methodical process."[17] Thoreau's use of the Baconian phrase signals, then, not the simple dismissal of science for instinct or "sympathy," but a rhetorical stance and a definite opinion about the role of imagination, and possibly hypothesis, in the process of discovery. While it would be rash and premature to claim too much for this usage, it is a telling instance. It matches, moreover, a similar gesture toward Bacon in "Walking," as well as the anti-Baconian slant of some of Thoreau's scientific reading and at least one extract concerning method and epistemology in the Fact Book.[18]

Thoreau would have been stimulated and probably aided in his thinking about the interdependence of fact and idea in the investigation of nature by the writings of Coleridge and Goethe. In *The Friend*, Coleridge argues in his essay on method for the necessity of a prior idea before any fact can be recognized as significant among others, and therefore that laws are "*attributed* to, never derived from" facts. "The utmost we can ever venture to say," Coleridge asserts, "is that the falling of an apple *suggested* the law of gravitation to Sir Isaac Newton."[19] The writings of Coleridge and Goethe, in turn, have been established in recent studies as important resources for several Victorian scientists and thinkers trying in various ways, like Thoreau, to balance the claims of empiricism and idealism in their accounts of the pursuit and construction of knowledge. Goethe's scientific work is now known to have been influential in the circle of British idealist scientists, among them Richard Owen, some of whose acquaintance Emerson made on his trip to England in the late 1840s.[20] And Goethe's work and methods were the subject of a long appreciative essay by George Henry Lewes, which appeared in an 1852 number of the *Westminster Review*.[21]

A sense of the intellectual climate in which Lewes' article appeared can be derived from the running debate at this time on Bacon described by Yeo, and by the anti-Baconian views put forward by the British astronomer and philosopher William Whewell and the Scottish experimental physicist David Brewster. Admittedly, as they were making public arguments their positions were more fully articulated than were Thoreau's home-grown versions. But precisely because they were well articulated, both their criticisms and the response they provoked are instructive.

Whewell's *Philosophy of the Inductive Sciences* (1847) featured an idealist epistemology that "emphasized the unpredictable role of imagination and genius in providing the idea through which inductive discoveries were accomplished."[22] As Thoreau represents it both in the *Journal* and the late natural-history essays, Whewell "stressed the interdependence of ideal and empirical elements in all thought" and "argued that there could be no rigid separation of theory and fact," claiming in 1847 that "a true theory is a Fact; a Fact is a familiar Theory."[23] Similarly, in the *Life of Newton* (which Thoreau was reading in 1856), Brewster aggressively rejected the prevailing opinion that Bacon had founded a method of discovering scientific truth which Newton, among others, had applied. While less radically than Whewell, Brewster nonetheless argued that "nothing even in mathematical science can be more certain than that a collection of scientific facts are of themselves incapable of leading to discovery, or to the determination of general laws, unless they contain the predominating fact or relation in which the discovery mainly resides."[24]

These criticisms of Bacon were regarded as extreme, and Whewell's philosophy of discovery dismayed his scientific colleagues, who believed that his emphasis on the creative contribution of mind threatened the objective status of scientific laws and concepts. "In general," Yeo reports, reviewers and critics of Whewell's book "feared that the idealist aspect of Whewell's work might produce a speculative *Naturphilosophie*" similar to Friedrich Schelling's, and even (quoting a reviewer here) "undermine the 'whole fabric of human knowledge.'"[25] If this reaction to Whewell's extension of idealist epistemology to the philosophy of scientific discovery is an accurate reflection of the Anglo-American climate of scientific opinion, then Thoreau had good reason to hesitate.

That Thoreau conceived his own relation to nature in terms of an intimate interdependence of active, but disciplined imagination and careful observation is no news. It is everywhere evident in his writings. But what I do not think has been sufficiently appreciated is, first, how deliberately and artfully Thoreau represents this interdependence,[26] and second, that his doing so is a productive response to contemporary thought and practice of science.

"The Succession of Forest Trees" is remarkable for being a scientific paper in which Thoreau presents his results and methodology, and at the same time suggestively represents the naturalist's process of discovery. Hildebidle has noted Thoreau's care in emphasizing the experimental character of his observations.[27] Indeed, Thoreau's inspection of the white pine grove where he makes his discovery and begins to elaborate his theory resembles very closely Darwin's similar inspection of a plot of Scotch firs in the third chapter of *On the Origin of Species*, a discovery that functions as one of the central facts for his theory of natural selection.

At the same time, Thoreau as narrator provides enough information that we may see clearly (if we look for it) the importance of prior preparation as a condition for the discovery he makes. By establishing at the beginning his long and intimate familiarity with the back woodlots of his employers as well as numerous conversations with local informants, Thoreau reconstructs for us his own "anticipation of nature." His familiarity and fertile curiosity about natural processes in general and his interest in seed dispersion play a significant role in leading him in the first place to observe the red squirrel burying his pignut—the observation which, he is careful to say with Coleridge, "suggested" his theory (76). This then leads him to look for a place where his theory may be tested, and even then "it was not til my eye had got used to the search" (that is, until he knew what he was looking for) that he discerns the little oaks growing at regular intervals along the pine forest floor. And prior thought plays an equally significant role in the discovery of several rare plants which Thoreau restates later in the essay.

Although the criticisms of Brewster and the philosophy of Whewell were considered extreme in the mid-1850s, Yeo notes that within fifteen years the important role of hypothesis, together with the necessity of mathematical technique, "became orthodoxy within the philosophy of science."[28] In the early 1870s two scientists (whose work Thoreau had read), the physiologist William Carpenter and the geologist John Tyndall, gave presidential addresses to the British Association for the Advancement of Science on the topic of (to quote Tyndall's title) "The Scientific Use of the Imagination."[29] And twenty years after Thoreau's essay, Thomas Henry Huxley wrote,

> No delusion is greater than the notion that method and industry can make up for lack of motherwit either in science or in practical life. ... Bacon's

'via' [i.e., method] has proved hopelessly impracticable; while the 'anticipation of nature' by the invention of hypotheses based on incomplete inductions, which he specially condemns, has proved itself to be a most efficient, indeed an indispensible, instrument of scientific progress.[30]

But by this time, of course, science had become, and already in Thoreau's day was rapidly becoming, securely institutionalized, "an intellectual quest carried out by trained experts beyond the reach of the [lay] public."[31]

# Notes

[1]Quoted in Richard R. Yeo, "Scientific Method and the Rhetoric of Science in Britain, 1830–1917" in J. A. Schuster and R. R. Yeo, eds., *The Politics and Rhetoric of Scientific Method* (Dordrecht, Holland: D. Reidel, 1986), 261.

[2]Walter Harding, *Emerson's Library* (Charlottesville: University Press of Virginia, 1967).

[3]Yeo, "An Idol of the Market-Place: Baconianism in Nineteenth Century Britain," *History of Science* 23 (1985): 251–3 . Whewell is quoted in Yeo, "Scientific Method and the Image of Science, 1831–1891" in *The Parliament of Science: The British Association for the Advancement of Science. 1831–1981*, ed. Roy Macleod and Peter Collins (Northwood, England: Science Reviews Ltd., 1981), 67.

[4]Yeo, "Scientific Method and the Rhetoric of Science," 261–2.

[5]*The Journal of Henry D. Thoreau*, ed. Bradford Torrey and Francis H. Allen (Boston: Houghton Mifflin, 1906), 5:4.

[6]*Journal of the History of Ideas* 26 (1965): 221–34.

[7]William Howarth, *The Book of Concord: Thoreau's Life as a Writer* (New York: Viking, 1982); Ray Angelo, "Thoreau as Botanist," *Thoreau Quarterly* 15 (1983): 15–31; John Hildebidle, *Thoreau: A Naturalist's Liberty* (Cambridge: Harvard University Press, 1983); Robert D. Richardson, Jr., *Henry Thoreau: A Life of the Mind* (Berkeley: University of California Press, 1986); Robert Sattelmeyer, *Thoreau's Reading: A Study in Intellectual History with Bibliographical Catalogue* (Princeton: Princeton University Press, 1988); Elizabeth Hall Witherell, "Assessing the Scope of Thoreau's Broken Task: the Collection and Arrangement of Data in His Phenological Tables," Modern Language Association, Washington, D.C., December 1989.

[8]Hildebidle, 94.

[9]*Journal*, 5: 5.

[10]*The Correspondence of Henry David Thoreau*, ed. Walter Harding and Carl Bode (New York: New York University Press, 1958), 584.

[11]Hildebidle, 67.

[12]Rehbock, 104; Forbes quoted, 107.
     Another, more widespread and important scientific theory associated with
     the search for a higher law was the "philosophical [sometimes called
     "transcendental"] anatomy" of Richard Owen, expounded in his *On the
     Archtype and Homologies of the Vertebrate Skeleton* (1848) and *On the
     Nature of Limbs* (1849), and developed from a concept originally worked
     out by Geoffroy Saint-Hilaire [Toby A. Appel, *The Cuvier-Geoffroy Debate:
     French Biology in the Decades Before Darwin* (New York: Oxford Univer-
     sity Press, 1987), 225–30]. In the United States this theory was developed
     and taught at Harvard by Jeffries Wyman, a colleague and friend of Asa Gray
     and an active member of the Boston Society of Natural History in the 1850s.
     On Wyman and the relation of Asa Gray's work to this doctrine, see Toby
     A. Appel, "Jeffries Wyman, Philosophical Anatomy, and the Scientific
     Reception of Darwin in America," *Journal of the History of Biology* 21
     (1988): 69–94 .

[13]H. Daniel Peck, *Thoreau's Morning Work: Memory and Perception in A Week on
     the Concord and Merrimack Rivers, the Journal, and Walden* (New Haven:
     Yale University Press, 1990), 68.

[14]*The Natural History Essays*, ed. Robert Sattelmeyer (Salt Lake City: Peregrine
     Smith, Inc., 1980), 173–74. All subsequent citations of "Autumnal Tints,"
     "Walking," "Natural History of Massachusetts," and "The Succession of
     Forest Trees" in the text and notes are to this edition and will appear
     parenthetically.

[15]*Journal 3: 1848–1851*, ed. Robert Sattelmeyer, Mark R. Patterson, and William
     Rossi (Princeton: Princeton University Press, 1990), 146–7 and 224–28,
     respectively.

[16]Baym, 226.

[17]Francis Bacon, The New Organon and Related Writings, ed. Fulton H. Anderson
     (New York: Bobbs–Merrill, 1960), 44–5.

[18]I'm referring in "Walking" to Thoreau's oppositional stance toward "positive
     knowledge" and the Baconian conception of knowledge as power (127).
     In the Fact Book Thoreau copied from Edward Tuckerman's *Enumeration of
     North American Lichenes* a classification of three kinds of naturalists,
     ranging from "observers" (who "start simply from nature without philo-
     sophical grounds or ends, and accumulate only and then accommodate
     facts") through "philosophical observers" to true "naturalists." In the work
     of the latter "the divine reason appears . . . and facts are observed not only,
     but eternal laws are prescribed to science" [*Thoreau's Fact Book in the
     Harry Elkins Widener Collection in the Harvard College Library*, ed.
     Kenneth Walter Cameron (Hartford: Transcendental Books, 1966), 1: 58–
     9].

[19]*The Friend*, ed. Barbara Rooke (Princeton: Princeton University Press, 1969), 1,
     467.

[20]For the influence of Coleridge's *Theory of Life* on Victorians, see Diana
     Postlethwaite, *Making It Whole: A Victorian Circle and the Shape of Their*

World(Columbus: Ohio State University Press, 1984); on Goethe's influence, see Rosemary Ashton, *The German Idea: Four English Writers and the Reception of German Thought, 1800-1860*(Cambridge: Cambridge University Press, 1980), and Peter Alan Dale, *In Pursuit of a Scientific Culture: Science, Art, and Society in the Victorian Age* (Madison: University of Wisconsin Press, 1989).

[21][George Henry Lewes,] "Goethe as a Man of Science," *Westminster Review* 58 (1852): 479-506. While Thoreau does not mention ever having read this article, he does mention Lewes' "Life and Doctrine of Geoffroy St. Hilaire," which appeared two years later in the same journal, commenting appreciatively on Geoffroy's doctrine of the "Unity of Plan, Unity of Composition" (*Journal* 6: 179), which formed the cornerstone of transcendental anatomy. Goethe had been a champion of Geoffroy, and in this article Lewes makes frequent mention of Goethe's science, referring the reader to his previous article on "Goethe as a Man of Science." Given Thoreau's reading habits and interests, it's hard to believe he would have neglected to follow this up, if indeed, he had not already read Lewe's essay on Goethe.

[22]Yeo, "An Idol of the Market-Place," 274.

[23]Yeo, "William Whewell, Natural Theology, and the Philosophy of Science in Mid Nineteenth Century Britain," *Annals of Science* 36 (1979): 501.

[24]David Brewster, *The Life of Sir Isaac Newton* (New York: Harper & Brothers, 1831), 298. While Thoreau read this edition, in 1855 Brewster published an expanded version of his biography, *Memoirs of the Life, Writings and Discoveries of Sir Isaac Newton* (in which, however, the section just quoted was retained) which elicited the negative response Yeo describes.

[25]Yeo, "William Whewell," 503–4.

[26]Peck's *Thoreau's Morning Work* excepted.

[27]Hildebidle, 62–3.

[28]Yeo, "An Idol of the Market-Place," 281.

[29]George Basalla, William Coleman, and Robert H. Kargon, eds., *Victorian Science: A Self-Portrait from the Presidential Addresses to the British Association for the Advancement of Science*(Garden City, N. Y.: Doubleday, 1970), 411–35, 438.

[30]Quoted in Yeo, "An Idol of the Market-Place," 281.

[31]Yeo, "Scientific Method and the Rhetoric of Science," 273.

---

**WILLIAM ROSSI** teaches at the University of Oregon and is an editor of the *Journal of the Writings of Henry D. Thoreau*. He is currently at work on a study of Thoreau and other nineteenth century naturalist writers.

# Part III

❖

# CELEBRATING THOREAU THROUGH MUSIC

# Some Thoughts of
# Henry David Thoreau

❖

My profession is to be always on the alert to find God in nature, to know his lurking-places, to attend all the oratorios, the operas, of nature.
—*September 7, 1851*

The bluebird on the apple tree, warbling so innocently to inquire if any of its mates are within call,—the angel of the spring! Fair and innocent, yet the offspring of the earth. The color of the sky above and of the subsoil beneath. Suggesting what sweet and innocent melody (terrestrial melody) may have its birthplace between the sky and the ground.
—*March 10, 1859*

A thrumming of piano-strings beyond the gardens and through the elms. At length the melody steals into my being. I know now when it began to occupy me. By some fortunate coincidence of thought or circumstance I am attuned to the universe, I am fitted to hear, my being moves in a sphere of melody, my fancy and imagination are excited to an inconceivable degree. This is no longer the dull earth on which I stood. It is possible to live a grander life here; already the steed is stamping, the knights are prancing; already our thoughts bid a proud farewell to the so-called actual life and its humble glories. Now this is the verdict of a soul in health. But the soul diseased says that its own vision and life alone is true and sane. What a different aspect will courage put upon the face of things!
—*August 3, 1852*

Listen to music religiously, as if it were the last strain you might hear.
—*June 12, 1851*

I hear one thrumming a guitar below stairs. It reminds me of moments that I have lived. What a comment on our life is the least strain of music! It lifts me up above all the dust and mire of the universe. I soar or hover with clean skirts over the field of my life. It is ever life within life, in concentric spheres. The field wherein I told or rust at any time is at the same time the field for such different kinds of life! The farmer's boy or hired man has an instinct which tells him as much indistinctly, and hence his dreams and his restlessness; hence, even, it is that he wants money to realize his dreams with. The identical field where I am leading my humdrum life, let but a strain of music be heard there, is seen to be the field of some unrecorded crusade or tournament the thought of which excites in us an ecstasy of joy. The way in which I am affected by this faint thrumming advertises me that there is still some health and immortality in the springs of me. What an elixir is this sound! When I *hear* music I fear no danger, I am invulnerable, I see no foe. I am related to the earliest times and to the latest.

There are infinite degrees of life, from that which is next to sleep and death, to that which is forever awake and immortal. We must not confound man with man. We cannot conceive of a greater difference than between the life of one man and that of another. I am constrained to believe that the mass of men are never so lifted above themselves that their destiny is seen to be transcendently beautiful and grand.

—*January 13, 1857*

# A Thoreau Music Sampler

❖

**Walter Harding**

Henry David Thoreau's life was filled with music. Not only did he play the flute throughout his life, but he loved to sing and join others in singing. His choice of music was astonishingly conventional and sentimental for such an iconoclastic individual. He loved romantic ballads such as "Tom Bowline" and the "Canadian Boat Song" and reveled in that atrocious war-horse, "The Battle of Prague," that brought such joy also to Huckleberry Finn when it was one of the Grangerford girls who played it for him.

Of the classical composers—Bach, Beethoven, Mozart, etc.—Thoreau had almost nothing to say, even though their music was enjoyed by many of his transcendentalist friends when it was played in Boston and even in Concord. What he preferred was what he thought of as the music of nature. He made his own aeolian harp—it is now in the Concord Museum. And when telegraph wires were strung through Concord, he rejoiced in the sound of the wind whistling through them, calling them his "telegraph harp." He made many notations on the songs of wild birds, notations that are still considered standard by ornithologists. He loved to meditate on the place of music in our lives and wrote extensively on the subject in his *Journal*. As Charles Ives said, "Thoreau was a great musician, not because he played the flute but because he did not have to go to Boston to hear 'the Symphony.'"

It is thus easily understandable and highly appropriate that many professional musicians have, in their turn, paid their tributes to him. What is surprising is that these tributes are so little known. I venture to say that it would be difficult to find a Thoreau scholar or enthusiast who could off-hand name a half-dozen such tributes. But since beginning this study I have found more than one hundred and sixty, most of them published and many of them recorded, and yet I know my list is far from complete, for old ones that I have missed and new ones continue to turn up, sometimes in the most surprising places. (Since a project such as this is cross-disciplinary, there seems to be no central place to go for information. It tends to fall between music studies and literature studies and is covered adequately by neither. Michael Holand, *Musical Settings of American Poetry: A Bibliography* [New York: Greenwood, 1986] was just about the only cross-discipline reference work that I found to be of any help, and that confined itself to Thoreau's poems that had been set to music.)

There is a wide variety of musical tributes to Thoreau. Among the most common and most obvious are those in which a composer sets a Thoreau poem to music. But since Thoreau's prose is often so poetic, a number of composers have set some of his prose to music, too. More challenging, perhaps, are those cases where a composer has tried to catch in music the spirit of Thoreau. The most notable example of this is Charles Ives's "Concord Sonata" (the final, or "Thoreau," movement), but it is by no means the only one. Off in quite a different direction are ballads, sung to the accompaniment of guitars or rock groups, that were so popular in the late 1960s and 1970s, and that in a gentle way poked fun at "Hank" in his Walden cabin. Then in 1976 there was an upsurge of patriotic cantatas and other choral works featuring Thoreau along with other great American literary figures.

It is astonishing how many types and forms of music have been used to celebrate Thoreau—sonatas, cantatas, orchestral suites, chamber music, oratorios, operas; solos, quartets, choruses, choirs; classical, romantic, jazz, rock, and experimental music. With Thoreau's own emphatic individualism, his own habit of listening to a "different drummer," it is highly appropriate that he should have been widely celebrated by some of our most noted experimental musicians, such as Charles Ives and John Cage.

An amazingly wide variety of musical instruments used, also, ranging from strings to woodwinds, to brass, to percussion (even Orff instruments), and to the various keyboard instruments. Considering Thoreau's obsession with nature, it is not at all surprising that a number of these composers have used tapes of bird songs and other sounds of nature, but the use of a bicycle wheel by the McLeans is a little off the beaten path. It is also (pleasantly) surprising how much of the Thoreau music has been specially commissioned: LaMontaine's "Wilderness Journal," Glickman's "Credos," Abrahamsen's "Walden," Foss's cantata, and so many others. The appeal of Thoreau is wide indeed.

# The Ponds of Thoreau and Charles Ives

❖

## Stuart Feder

After breakfast on one clear November day in 1847, the Danbury poet and historian James W. Nichols set out in an ox-cart on an errand to deliver some tools to the mason "over the backside of Deer Hill"—"no small voyage," as he observed. As he progressed "down Wooster Street, across Main Street" through the town, and across up to Lookaway Hill, the poet, clearly enthralled with his place of birth, paused to "make a stand to look-around indeed upon the beauteous landscape":

> There was a view of the entire length of Wooster Cemetery, the glorious Wooster Monument standing proudly eminent in the picture. The whole of the village swept round in a graceful curve line, thickly sprinkled with buildings, and beyond, the tall ... mountains made up the backing of the picture in the most gorgeous array. ...[1]

When Nichols viewed the Wooster Cemetery, the eye at its center was a pond that was destined to be the first pond of Charles Edward Ives. In time, it would become Ives' last pond as well, the final resting place for himself and his wife, Harmony, as it had been for his father, George Edward Ives, all of *his* generation and that of Charles' grandfather, a contemporary of poet Nichols who had been one of the founders of the cemetery.

In Concord, that autumn of 1847, Henry David Thoreau, age thirty, having just accomplished his two years, two months, and two days at Walden Pond, was living nearby at the home of Emerson (who was lecturing abroad) and looking after his home and family. Walden was the second pond in the life of Charles Ives—the pond of spirit and fantasy. There was a third pond as well, the pond of Ives' maturity, an actual pond that he had constructed near his country home in Redding, Connecticut, at a pivotal point in mid-life.

**Walden Pond**

These then, are the setting and the *dramatis personæ*, as it were, of what is to follow: (1) the Danbury poet will not reappear, but central will be Charles Ives; his father, George; and his wife, Harmony (in that order), as Ives himself put it in his writings[2]; (2) the personal heroes who people his "Second Piano Sonata" (subtitled, "Concord, Mass., 1840–1860"), most notably the Emerson and the Thoreau of memory; and (3) the three ponds—in Danbury, Concord, and West Redding. The fact that our story takes us through nearly 110 years of living history; that the lives of Thoreau and Ives are connected through art; and that the yield of these two lives includes two great works which are related only says something about the power of art to transcend time and to connect mind to mind. I hope to show that the basis and core of such connections lie in fundamental yet ordinary human relationships.

In March of 1845, when Charles' father, George Edward Ives, was born, all four of the heroes who would eventually animate Charles Ives' "Concord Sonata" were living in Concord: Emerson, Hawthorne, Alcott, and Thoreau. Thoreau had only just begun work on the cabin at Walden; it would be almost a decade before the book was published. It is doubtful whether George Ives ever encountered *Walden* in his lifetime. It had not been intended for a mass audience to begin with[3] and was hardly popular at first. The sources of Charles Ives' infatuation with Thoreau—indeed with all four members of his private pantheon—were of a quite different nature: they are to be found in the vicissitudes of the relationship between father and son, George and Charles Ives.

George Ives was the youngest in a family of five in which two brothers, more than ten years his senior, were already following the mercantile and civic path of their father. George's own father, the same who had been a founder of the Wooster Cemetery, also started Danbury's first bank. Along with a cohort of first families, the Iveses were involved in virtually every entrepreneurial venture and civic improvement in 19th-century Danbury. As one descendant put it, "They *were* the town."[4]

George, however, went against the grain of Ives tradition in becoming a musician. Family legend had it that as a child George so much wanted to study music that he once stayed home from a Fourth of July picnic in order to earn money to buy a flute. An increasingly serious interest in music asserted itself in adolescence, and he was permitted to seek out the best teacher he could find, a German in Morrisania, the Bronx, from whom he received rigorous training in the European tradition. The twin roles of maverick and little brother dogged George the rest of his life. Only at one point was George's career synchronous with the strivings of the 19th-century country town and, indeed, the Union itself. This was during the War of the Rebellion, when George enlisted in the Union Army to become what was said to be its youngest bandmaster.

His career as Army Bandmaster was apotheosized by Charles: in a favorite story, Lincoln himself praised the band to General Grant who allowed that it was the best in the army. In fact, George's army career was less than distinguished, and during the decisive final battles of the war he was at home in Danbury on medical leave.[5] Returning to Danbury for good after the war, he felt as though his life was in some sense already over, and reentry into civilian life was awkward. He worked as sometime clerk in his brother's business and as part-time village musician, which rendered him somewhat of a misfit, although, at ceremonial times, a somewhat admired one. The taint of deviance, frivolity, and questionable respectability lay heavily on the roles he chose. Nowhere would this be more apparent than in the ambivalent title so often bestowed on the town musician, "Professor."[6] Further, breaking with the long-standing commercial tradition of the Ives family had practical financial consequences and would place him and his own family somewhere in the range of poor relations.

George's marriage at twenty-nine, as well as the birth of Charlie (as he was called) ten months later, went a long way toward establishing respectability (there was a second son, Moss, as well). But it was not until George was forty-four that he entered the regular, mainstream, conventional business life of Danbury as a clerk, an assistant to a nephew in a business owned by his own older brother. When he did so it was not without a sense of bitterness and resignation.[7]

By then Charlie was fifteen years of age and himself the youngest regular church organist in the state. Going to Yale was already being spoken of; indeed George's shift was motivated in part by the necessity of paying for the boys' educations. Meanwhile, Charlie and George had enjoyed a closeness during Charlie's childhood that became idealized and revered by him. Charlie experienced boyhood as if shared not only by his brother but by his father as well. For much of the boy remained in George Ives the man—much of the curiosity of latency and the heightened narcissism and social thrust of adolescence. Above all, George knew how to play and many of Charlie's early reminiscences of his father were of their playing together in the exciting close-to-real manner of childhood. From early on George was also Charlie's teacher in music and later, when Charlie began to compose, his collaborator as well. George's hand may be found in—and literally on—many of the early manuscripts.

Ives' own account of his childhood is a celebration of boyhood and was experienced with veneration and nostalgia.[8] At its center was George, who he idolized. While he appeared reticent with regard to sensual or romantic love, Ives was always frank and completely unabashed in his love for his father. The sources of the intensity go beyond the genuinely felt conflict-free sphere from which Ives' laudatory prose flows. Feeling of guilt and shame had to be powerfully denied.

Ives himself did not follow in George's footsteps in spite of his becoming a musician. His was a unique solution. He repaired the rent in the Ives tradition created by his father by becoming a businessman and an extraordinarily successful one at that. He became a principal in an extremely successful insurance firm at a time when the industry itself was reorganizing and opportunities were created. At the same time, endowed with a unique musical gift and enormous energy, he became a dedicated evening and weekend composer, ultimately creating a large and distinctive body of work. In both of these endeavors—business, to which George Ives yielded only belatedly and bitterly, and music, to which George was committed, however modest the result—Charles Ives surpassed his father. Thus George not only inspired love in his son but, unwittingly, guilt as well. And, given George's position and history, as well as a boy's experiences in family and community that could not be openly acknowledged, there was also a sense of shame that had to be vigorously disavowed.

An extraordinary creative compromise resulted. Not only did Charles attempt to come to terms with his father within the double professional life of businessman-composer, but the process of composition itself came to involve his father in a singular way. Where George in life was the boy's first teacher and earliest collaborator in composing, after his death composition assumed another meaning. It became, I believe, an intrapsychic collaboration and an intrinsic part of a process of mourning that could never be completely accomplished. Part of this story was articulated by Ives's earliest biographers, the Cowells, Sidney Cowell writing, "The son has written the father's music."[9] Indeed, the very texture of the music is replete with musical quotation of George Ives' music: 19th-century hymn and gospel tunes, Civil War songs, and the like. What Ives made of these was very much something of his own; but intrinsic to the process were the memory and presence of his father.

George Ives died of a stroke at the age of forty-nine, when Charlie (who would live to be nearly eighty) was barely twenty. But as Charles Ives approached the age at which his father died, something in him began to die as well. In the course of his forties he began to pull together his life work in a more or less completed form from the many hastily made sketches in which much of the music existed. A final trilogy started with his "Second Piano Sonata," subtitled "Concord, Mass., 1840–1860," and a book of accompanying prose essays that he called *Essays Before a Sonata.* These Ives had privately printed in 1920, distributing them *sans* copyright to a list of people he compiled and to anyone who asked for them. Two years later, he did the same with the "114 Songs," which he had worked on during his forties, revising and organizing works that spanned his entire career to date. He was forty-eight years of age. Finally, as if it were a part of these culminating efforts and final creative thrust, that spring Ives had built his own pond at Redding. He did little of any creative consequence after he himself turned forty-nine.

George Ives died on Sunday, November 4, 1898. Charlie had been summoned from New Haven, where he had just entered Yale College and also held the post of organist at Centre Church. Given the blow it must have been to him, and his rather elaborate later writings about his father, Ives was curiously silent about the event in any manifest form. Its impact is to be sought in arcane verbal references in various of his works, as well as in the music itself. The deep and complex relationship with his father would determine his choice of personal heroes forever. In this Henry David Thoreau played a special role.

In Ives' Decoration Day (one of the Holidays Symphony), a fictional prose "postface" celebrates the country town's observance of the holiday that commemorated the Civil War dead. He writes nostalgically: "The march to the Wooster Cemetery is a thing a boy never forgets."[10] George, the youngest of his generation, had in actuality been the first to be buried in the family plot in Wooster, on the knoll overlooking the pond. The symbolism of the pond came to be associated with this event and its locale. It was not the first time Charlie had been there, and he already knew that someday he would join George by the pond. It was thus that Thoreau and *his* pond were drawn into the most private circle of the mental life of Charles Ives.

When Ives came to write his "Concord" sonata, along with its Emerson-inspired essays, Thoreau took the place of honor in a manner characteristic of Ives. Just as the music of the Thoreau movement was conceived on an entirely different scale from that of the preceding movements—smaller and more intimate—the prose too was distinctive: elegiac, nostalgic, both passionate and tender at the same time. The essay, reflecting the music, ends with an evocation of Thoreau thoughts "on an autumn day in Indian summer at Walden. ...." In what may be the only manifest reference to the day of George's death, Ives wrote of the solace he found in Thoreau: " ... my Thoreau—that reassuring and true friend, who stood by me one 'low' day, when the sun had gone down, long, long before sunset."[11] By the time Ives wrote this, that autobiographical "'low' day" of autumn might well have referred to other, or additional, events.

It was late in the year 1906, at thirty-two, Ives is said to have sustained his first heart attack. There is no evidence for this, and more likely, he was in a state of depression with somatic symptoms. What more likely may have been a heart attack occurred when he was forty-four, in October, around the time of his birthday. In general, Ives's mood tended toward the melancholy near the end of the year, perhaps an annual revival of the state of November mourning, the observance by his unconscious of an anniversary.

It was in such a mood that Ives, in 1904, wrote a piece called "Autumn Landscape from Pine Mountain." Its manuscript has never been found.[12] Written—if it was ever notated at all—for strings, woodwind, and muted cornet, as if the sound would waft across Pine Mountain in Danbury from Ridgebury, some three miles away, the musical idea was precursor to a group of experimental pieces, among them "The Unanswered Question" and, eventually, the "Universe Symphony." I suggest that "Autumn Landscapes" was an anniversary meditation on the death of the composer's father. The piece most closely realizing its latent personal, musical, and even environmental ideas was called "The Pond," written in 1906. When Ives was compiling his final book of "114 Songs" he included this piece in a revision for voice with piano accompaniment. Only he changed the name of "The Pond" to "Remembrance" and added an epigram from Wordsworth, "The music in my heart I bore/Long after it was heard no more."[13] We will consider the two versions together. "The Pond" is made of memories, and in the changing of its name, Ives rendered it literally, a "remembrance."

"Remembrance" is simplicity itself on the printed page. Only nine measures in length, it is as distinctly an Ives piece as are any of his apparently more complex compositions. It is also characteristic of a group of Ives' works in which the presence of George Ives is somehow made manifest through some reminiscence in music. In "The Pond" and later in "Remembrance" the words are explicit. For the earlier piece for small orchestra was essentially a song and words had been written in as if to be sounded sub-vocally beneath the tune carried by the muted trumpet: "A sound of a distant horn/O'er shadowed lake is borne/—my father's song."

The very "sound of a distant horn" is rendered literally by the hushed trumpet, the closest relative to George Ives' actual instrument, the cornet. Fantasy is expressed in auditory terms as we hear the very sound of the father; he is evoked, re-created in music. Spatial features are further emphasized by the echo of the tune in canon, a round. Thus distance is represented not only in space but in time as the horn's tune is imitated by the flute a measure later, George's first instrument and the instrument of Thoreau. Ives wrote "echo piece" on one of his sketches. And in the echo there are two voices only one of which is living. In his performance notes, Ives suggested that the flute be played offstage: "This, in a way, is to suggest the echo over the pond." Already, in the 1906 "Pond," Ives associated the sound of his father with the music of the Thoreauvian flute echoing across Walden Pond.

*"Rememberance," Charles Ives, 114 Songs, #12 (From The Pond).*
*Copyright © 1954 by Peer International Corp. Used by permission.*

It is this offstage flute that reappears in the last measures of the "Concord Sonata"; we will return to it presently. But first, what of the transcendentalist heroes that make up Ives' private pantheon in his "Piano Sonata No. 2 Concord, Mass., 1840–1860"? The movements are captioned "Emerson," "Hawthorne," "The Alcotts," and "Thoreau." The special role of Thoreau may perhaps be best perceived through a metaphor of mental life. Ives sought to regain and to reexperience his father not only in the persons he encountered in actual life but in the figures of imaginative life as well. In his choice of heroes and ideals, he sought grander and purer, although increasingly distorted, representations of the father he needed to idealize. If one imagines the "Concord" metaphorically as a musical telescope through which Charles Ives endeavored to recreate and reexperience his father, one brings to focus a differently constituted George Ives at four varying focal distances, cloaked in the spiritual garb of Ralph Waldo Emerson, Nathaniel Hawthorne, Bronson Alcott, and Henry David Thoreau. Ives' Emerson is prophet, guide, and explorer; the protean teacher; the first and greatest teacher writ large as if through the eyes of a child:

> ... at the door of the infinite ... peering into the mysteries of life, contemplating the eternities, hurling back whatever he discovers there—now thunderbolts for us to grasp, if we can and translate—now placing quietly, even tenderly, in our hand things that we may see without effort.[14]

Ives' personal "canonization of Emerson" contains within it the private hagiography of his father.

The other Concordians of the "Sonata" fall in some sense under Emerson's shadow, as they had in the Concord of the 1840s. Ives' Hawthorne is the Hawthorne of mystery, imagination, and adventure— an American Grimm or Aesop, "dripping wet with the supernatural, the phantasmal the mystical: surcharged with adventures, from the deeper picturesque to the illusive fantastic."[15] The "wilder, fantastical" side of Hawthorne is invoked in which anything can happen, an atmosphere in which we must not be too surprised to hear in the music an intrusion of Ives' "Country Band March," piercing the jazz-like yet gossamer texture of this American scherzo and pulling the listener away from Hawthorne's fairyland to George Ives leading the Cornet Band in parade down Main Street, Danbury. In "The Alcotts," the very voice of the father is invoked— not so much in the words of the wordy Bronson Alcott as the music of it: " ... an internal grandiloquence made him melodious." Charles' Bronson Alcott, exactly as he wrote elsewhere of his father, left no writings behind, except those enshrined in the hearts of those he influenced. (This was certainly not true in Alcott's case.) And like George, Ives further observed, " ... his idealism had some substantial virtues even if he couldn't make a living."

The thread that is latent in each of the three preceding movements of the "Concord" becomes increasingly clear in the "Thoreau" essay. Its elegiac mood, apotheosis of Thoreau as a great musician, and finally, allusion to the occasion of George's death on some fantasied Indian summer day at Walden Pond, reveals it to be at once a memorial and an artifact of mourning. Both essay and music conspire to evoke in word and tone an mood that is remarkably specific: the traditional blend of commemoration, eulogy and touching sadness that characterizes the elegy. It is past lamentation and redolent of comfort.

The essay starts, "Thoreau was a great musician not because he played the flute but because he did not have to go to Boston to hear the Symphony." Ives' Thoreau is the acoustic Thoreau of *Walden*'s "Sounds." Indeed when Ives completed the movement he wrote on the manuscript: "Walden Sounds—Ch Bells, flute, Harp (Aeolian). ..." When Thoreau's well-known image is quoted by Ives near the end, of "[A]n evening when the whole body is one sense, that "sense" and the sense of Thoreau central to this essay is that of audition. Ives observes, probably correctly, "Thoreau's susceptibility to natural sounds was probably greater than that of many practical musicians." Comparing Thoreau to Beethoven, Ives suggests that it was only because Thoreau could *not* readily expose certain feelings that he failed to employ his musical sensitivity in the act of composing music. These, according to Ives, were feelings of love, for, Ives writes, "a composer may not shrink from having the public hear his 'love letter in tones,' while a poet may feel sensitive about having everyone read his 'letter in words.'"

That great natural musician, who, Ives rationalized, was too sensitive to cast his passionate emotions in Beethovenian form was the enduring, idealized imago of the father of childhood cloaked in the garb of Thoreau. This, I believe, accounts for the curious form of Ives' "Thoreau" essay, as well as some of its disorganized content. For the tone of much of it is less eulogy than apology; polemic soon makes its appearance, and traces of tirade as anger mounts. In fact, Ives undertakes to deal with what some may consider to be Thoreau's least attractive traits—his withdrawal, isolation, cynicism, feistiness, and downright "contrary cussedness," In doing so, he takes on such formidable critics as Henry James, James Russell Lowell, and Mark Van Doren. The excess of Ives' emotion betrays other sources as he defends an idealized maverick: Thoreau a straw man in the image of George Ives. In the end a loss of rational control supervenes, leading Ives to imagine Thoreau's endorsement of some of Ives' own grandiose political schemes: a "People's World Union" and "a policy of a limited personal property right"—distinctly un-Thoreauvian ideals.

But one should bear in mind the interval of the writing of the music and the essays; in the case of "Thoreau" it was about four years, from 1915–1919. It may be a marker for some process of mental deterioration, which led to the rambling, belligerent, disorganized, and illogical trend of thinking that characterized the later Ives. Or, could this tendency have already existed when the music was written?

However, it is in the final section of the essay on Thoreau that Ives manages to capture in words the same elegiac mood that informs the music. It is here that he most authentically recreates Thoreau in his "great musician" mode. If the George Ives of memory emerged from the transcendentalist prism resolved to four bands of light, that band reserved for Thoreau carried the melancholy blue-violet of the end of the day.

I cite the "aeolian harp" of Ives' manuscript "memo," as well as his excerpts from the long musical passage of Thoreau's "Sounds," which starts with the hearing of Concord's Sunday bells (from the inaccuracies of the first part of the passage, one wonders whether Ives quoted from memory):

> a melody as it were, imported into the wilderness. ... At a distance over the woods the sound acquires a certain vibratory hum, as if the pine needles in the horizon were the strings of a harp which it swept ... a vibration of the universal lyre, just as the intervening atmosphere makes a distant ridge of earth interesting to the eyes by the azure it imparts. ... [16]

Here is truly a love-letter to Thoreau as well as to the father-hero he represents—"my Thoreau—that reassuring and true friend, who stood by me one 'low' day when the sun had gone down, long, long before sunset." Addressing their critics and detractors, Ives exclaims,

> You may know something of the affection that heart yearned for but knew it a duty not to grasp—you may know something of the great human passions which stirred in that soul—too deep for animate expression—you may know all of this—all there is to know about Thoreau ... but you know him not—unless you love him.[17]

At the conclusion of the essay, a mood of resignation and comfort pervades:

> And if there shall be a program for our music, let it follow this thought on an autumn day of Indian summer at Walden—a shadow of a thought at first, colored by the mist and haze over the pond.[18]

In the music of the final movement of "Concord," a fused image of Thoreau and George Ives is represented in the musical quotation of Stephen Foster's "Massa's in the Cold, Cold Ground." Fragments from the chorus of the song are heard: "Down in de cornfield. ..." Later, when Ives adapted themes from the "Thoreau" movement for his "114 Songs," he introduced the verbal "cornfield" quotation from Thoreau's "Sounds" as if it were a spoken meditation. The words he chose were:

> He grew in those seasons like corn in the night, rapt in revery, on the Walden shore, amidst the sumach, pines, and hickories, in undisturbed solitude.[19]

This image of Thoreau's cornfield by Walden evokes the same peaceful setting of the pond in Wooster Cemetery, in view of the knoll where George Ives was laid to rest. In "The Pond," the very sound of Ives' father was re-created in the muted trumpet ("A sound of a distant horn,/O'er shadowed lake is borne, my father's song"). At the close of the "Thoreau" movement at the end of the "Concord Sonata," George's instrument is heard once again. But this time, it is his first instrument, the flute of family legend and of Thoreau.

In the final measure of "Thoreau," an optional part for flute is written in the score, the occasion rationalized by the fact that Thoreau had one with him at Walden and played it there. Thus in the last pages of "Concord" it is Thoreau who is virtually brought to life, the "great musician" made audible. It is a curious musical moment. For it would seem strange to expect the flutist to sit on-stage through a lengthy and massive solo composition only to join in the last few seconds; stranger still, perhaps eerie, to have the unanticipated flute waft in from offstage. But in either instance, the actual rendering is of little consequence. It was the *idea* of the flute song that was paramount in Ives' musical thinking.

Indeed, this musical concept may well have been a part of the initial inspiration for the "Concord" in the autumn of 1911. For it was at Elk Lake in the Adirondacks, meditating in the "last mist" over the pond, that Ives said he first had the "idea of a Concord Sonata." If so, the germinal idea that spawned the work is actualized at the end of "Thoreau" in both music and prose. Through it, and through Thoreau, Ives actualized the spirit of his father.

## Notes

"Remembrance" is Copyright © 1954 by Peer International Corporation. Copyright renewed. Used by permission.

[1] Nichols, James W., Log Book of the Barque James W. Nichols Bound to "That bourne whence no traveller returns," MSS in Scott–Fanton Museum, Danbury, Conn.

[2] Charles Ives, *Memos*, ed. John Kirkpatrick. New York: Norton, 1972, "... first, because of my father, and second, because of my wife." p. 114.

[3] Walter Harding and Michael Meyer, *The New Thoreau Handbook*, New York: New York University Press, 1980, p. 53.

[4] Amelia Van Wyck in Vivian Perlis, *Charles Ives Remembered*, New Haven: Yale University Press, 1974.

[5]Stuart Feder, *Charles Ives—My Father's Song: A Psychoanalytic Biography*, New Haven: Yale University Press, 1992.

[6]Frank Rossiter, *Charles Ives and His America*, New York: Liverwright, 1975.

[7]Stuart Feder, "Charles and George Ives: The Veneration of Boyhood," *The Annual of Psychoanalysis*, 9 (1981): 265–316.

[8]Charles Ives, *Memos*, ed. John Kirkpatrick, New York: Norton, 1972.

[9]Henry Cowell and Sidney and Cowell, *Charles Ives and His Music*, Oxford: Oxford University Press, 1955.

[10]Charles Ives, "Holidays in a Connecticut Country Town, Decoration Day," New York, n.d.

[11]Charles Ives, "Essays Before a Sonata," in *Essays Before a Sonata and Other Writings*, by Charles Ives, selected and edited by Howard Boatwright, p.67.

[12]Ives, *Memos*, p.159.

[13]Charles Ives, "114 Songs," #12, p. 27.

[14]Ives, "Essays", p. 67.

[15]*Ibid.*

[16]Thoreau: "Sometimes, on Sundays, I heard the bells, the Lincoln, Acton, Bedford, or Concord bell, when the wind was favorable, a faint, sweet, and, as it were, natural melody, worth importing into the wilderness. At a sufficient distance … " (rest as quoted correctly), *Walden,* in *Henry David Thoreau,* Library of America, n.d., p. 420.

[17]Ives, "Essays," p. 67.

[18]*Ibid.*

[19]Ives, "114 Songs," #48.

---

**STUART FEDER, M.D.**, is a practicing psychoanalyst and a faculty member of the New York Psychoanalytic Institute. He holds an advanced degree in music from Harvard University. He has written extensively in psychoanalysis as applied to the arts, particularly music. Dr. Feder's involvement with Thoreau stems from his interest in Charles Ives. He is the author of a major biography of Ives, *Charles Ives: My Father's Song*, just published by Yale University Press.

# Thoreau Was Somewhere Near
## The Ives–Thoreau Connection

❖

**Stuart Feder**

In 1943 Walter Harding wrote Charles Ives to invite him to renew his membership in the fledgling Thoreau Society and to attend its third meeting in Concord that July. Shortly before the meeting, a reply dated 11 July was received from Ives' adopted daughter, Edith Ives Tyler, who along with Ives' wife, Harmony Twichell Ives now served as amanuensis for the ailing 69-year-old composer. A euphemism used habitually by both was that Ives was "not at all well" and therefore, in this instance, would not be able to attend. But, Edith went on, he sends his greetings:

> Father says—'The grand old seer of Walden will rejoice to be with you all—and his great old friend Emerson will not be far away that afternoon.'[1]

Harding wrote again later that year after hearing John Kirkpatrick's performance of Ives' *Second Piano Sonata*, the *"Concord."* This time it was Mrs. Ives who responded. The letter is reprinted in its entirety.[2]

> Mrs. Charles E. Ives
> West Redding
> Conn
> Dec. 5, 1943
>
> Dear Mr. Harding,
>
> I am writing for Mr. Ives who as you know is not well and it is difficult for him to do so.
> He deeply appreciated your kind letter and most interesting notes about the Kirkpatrick concert. He says "your insight into the hearts and minds of those great Concord people—Olympians as you rightly say— is a great tribute and sincerely deserved." He sends his sincere thanks

for your wonderfully expressed interest in the Sonata and says "There are a few passages in the Thoreau movement which intended to give in a way something of a glimpse of Thoreau's rugged side and perhaps a strain of his occasional perverseness—however these are not prominent in the movement which has more to do with the stronger inner life of Thoreau, as we say, into his calm inner soul."

As to any other Thoreau music which you kindly ask about in some of Mr. Ives's chamber music he had a feeling that Thoreau was *somewhere near*—(sic) in one of these movements called "Tone Roads" Thoreau is definitely there. There are no copies of this here but Mr. Ives will have a copy made later and sent to you.

Do you know the book by Harry Lee "More Day to Dawn" about Thoreau? It was published by Duell Sloan & Pearce about two years ago—we liked it very much.

With our kindest wishes,
I am,
Sincerely yours,
Harmony T. Ives

P.S. Mr. Ives doesn't remember receiving a report of the recent Thoreau meeting in New York but a paper came recently from Chapel Hill which says his name will be taken from the list unless his correct address is given—"West Redding Conn" is the address and he hopes you will see that he is kept on the list.

This letter is a living example of the second most important collaboration in Ives' life. As he put it in his *Memos*, "One thing I am certain of is that, if I have done anything good in music, it was, first, because of my father, and second, because of my wife."[3] During their courtship in 1908 Harmony and Charles elaborated in their correspondence a home-grown romantic aesthetic, which included ideas about the kinds of things that might be represented in music.

Harmony encouraged the putting of things into music "in concrete form" including those emotional experiences that foster inspiration, as she put it, "one's happiest moments."[4] In doing so she exerted some influence in Ives' writing of the great Civil War pieces, which are memorializations of his father, and eventually the "Concord Sonata" with its representations of the four "Olympians" of Ives' personal pantheon. In addition, she widened Ives' literary vistas in fostering a program of home reading, which served as tranquilizer for the sometimes-agitated younger Ives and, at the same time, helped separate him from the circle of young men who had been his prenuptial companions. One result of this was Ives' plan to write a never completed overture series, "Men of Literature," which ultimately proved to be a creative way-station to the "Concord Sonata."

Beyond commonplace romantic notions of program music, Ives himself always retained a magical sense of what music was. This sense stemming from the earliest musical experiences of childhood, informed his adult thinking on a philosophy of music. Many passages in his prose writings reveal a belief in the potential for concrete personification, and even animism, in music. In the Postface to his *114 Songs,* Ives wrote: "A song has a few rights the same as other ordinary citizens," and concluded with the couplet, "—In short, must a song/always be a song!"[5] Similar notions relating to the extramusical may be found in more refined although highly abstract form in portions of his *Essays.*[6]

But beyond this, by the end of Ives' sixth decade a degree of mental deterioration had set in, which was itself of some complexity. This was the circumstance that was responsible, in part, for his family's undertaking such correspondence as the above, which had become something of a cottage industry with the Iveses. (A separate reason was the neurological disorder led to the shaky handwriting Ives called "snaketracks.") The mental condition only served to intensify beliefs about music that had earlier been conventionally romantic; later, colorfully idiosyncratic or highly intellectualized. In short, it seems likely that at times Ives might have believed quite concretely that the individual could be more than represented in the music or evoked by it; that, quite literally, the person could be *there!* As Harmony wrote, "… he had a feeling that Thoreau was *somewhere near*" (her emphasis), in the *Tone Roads* adding as if on further reflection, that "Thoreau is definitely there."

Of the admired "men of literature," a *Robert Browning Overture* was completed and a *Matthew Arnold* sketched; Walt Whitman became a choral song. Beyond these, if Thoreau's "great old friend" Emerson fascinated (Ives continued writing Emerson "Transcriptions" for years after the Emerson Movement of the "Concord") it was Thoreau himself who was the most beloved of the Concord pantheon. In addition to the final, Thoreau movement of the "Concord," and the "Thoreau" song derived from it,[7] Thoreau manifests himself other places in the Ives oeuvre besides the *Tone Roads* noted by Harmony Ives in the letter. Both title and spirit of another of the songs, "Walking," are drawn from Thoreau and what was probably Ives' final creative effort, the song "Sunrise" was written to words which are probably a paraphrase of Thoreau.[8] (We will return to this later.)

Where then, in *Tone Roads*, can Thoreau so definitely be identified? There were three pieces in Ives' *Tone Roads et Al.*, which Ives assembled about 1915.[9] Each was scored for a small chamber orchestra of varying instrumentation. The manuscript of the second has been lost and of the other two it seems likely that Mrs. Ives was referring to the third of the series.[10] There, in a remarkable opening statement (*Andante con moto*) the chimes perform the "tone road"; this is more than Ives' pun for the "tone row" of serial music in which each of the twelve tones of the scale is presented before any is repeated. As Henry Cowell wrote in what remains one of the best descriptions of this little-performed work, the piece "opens with a long solo in slow half-note and whole-note triplets, an atonal melody played by the chimes, which provide the tone quality that is to lie back of the whole piece. The 'tone road' is the tone of the chime, and the whole is a fantasy on the mood of the chime tone." Toward the end of the short work (which takes about three minutes to perform) the chimes pause briefly and "the other parts go wildly every which way, until at the end the chimes reappear as a catalyst to crystallize the sound of the other instruments into sense."[11]

The style of the musical "fantasy" connects Ives with Thoreau. It is aural in mode, philosophical in idea, and poetic in imagery while rooted in the local detail of everyday life. At the same time, a characteristic mood is created. Yet all is integrated into a cogent music.

Toward the end of Ives' essay on Thoreau, in citing a passage from *Walden*, he writes: "His meditations are interrupted only by the faint sound of the Concord bell—'tis prayer-meeting night in the village."[12] Omitted among Ives' elisions is the passage from "Sounds" that informs *Tone Roads* and very likely conveys the Thoreau who was "somewhere near":

> Sometimes, on Sundays, I heard the bells, the Lincoln, Acton, Bedford, or Concord bell, when the wind was favorable, a faint sweet, and, as it were, natural melody, worth importing into the wilderness.[13]

This is the passage partially quoted (and misquoted) by Ives that contains the metaphor of the "universal lyre" evoked by "sound heard at the greatest possible distance":

> There came to me in this case a melody which the air had strained, and which had conversed with every leaf and needle of the wood, that portion of the sound which the elements had taken up and modulated and echoed from vale to vale.[14]

The Harding–Ives correspondence contains two more letters, one each from 1946 and 1948. The first is a reply to a request by Harding to reprint some of the Thoreau music and essay in the *Thoreau Society Bulletin*. In Mrs. Ives' otherwise positive and cordial response, she commented that Ives was not well enough to send the "new comments which you asked for."[15] The final letter, a year later, containing at this point a warm personal greeting, notes the publication of the second edition of the "Concord Sonata," a complimentary copy of which Ives was sending for the Thoreau Society.[16]

Ives, at seventy-three, was by now incapacitated, his composing days long since over. What was probably his last creative effort, the song, "Sunrise," had been written some twenty years earlier. In a sense this final statement in music had been a collaboration with his beloved Thoreau. For the words Ives selected have a distinctly Thoreauvian ring as if paraphrased or stitched together from such sources as "The Pond in Winter" or the final passages of *Walden*.

A light low in the east,—as I lie there!—it shows but does not move—, a light—, a light—as a thought forgotten comes again. Later on as I rise it shows through the trees and lights the dark grey rock and something in the mind, and brings the quiet day. And tomorrow a light as a thought forgotten comes again, and with it ever the hope of a new day.[17]

One may speculate that even at that point Harmony Ives may have been co-author, ever responsive to Ives' relationship with Thoreau. It was she who selected what would be their shared epitaph, a biblical passage that strikingly mirrors the final words of *Walden*: "Awake psaltery and harp: I myself will awake quite early" (Psalm 108).

## Acknowledgment

The author wishes to express his appreciation to Walter Harding.

## Notes

[1]Edith Ives Tyler (Mrs. George G. Tyler) to Walter Harding, 11 July 1943. The Thoreau Library of Walter Harding.

[2]Harmony Twichell Ives to Walter Harding, 5 December 1943. The Thoreau Library of Walter Harding.

[3]Charles E. Ives, *Memos*, ed. John Kirkpatrick, New York: W. W. Norton, 1972, p. 114.

[4]Harmony Twichell to Charles Ives, a Tuesday before 12 March 1908. Ives Collection, Yale Music Library.

[5]Charles Ives, *114 Songs*, Redding, Conn.: Charles Ives, 1922, no page number.

[6]Charles Ives, *Essays Before a Sonata*, ed. Howard Boatwright, New York: W. W. Norton, 1961.

[7]Ives, *114 Songs*, #48.

[8]See Stuart Feder, *Charles Ives and the Unanswered Question,* in *The Psychoanalytic Study of Society*, Hillsdale, N.J., and London: The Analytic Press, Vol. 10, 1984, pp. 321–351.

[9]John Kirkpatrick, *A Temporary Mimeographed Catalogue of the Music Manuscripts and Related Materials of Charles Edward Ives*, New Haven, 1960, p. 50.

[10]Tone Roads No. #3 is scored for flute, clarinet, trumpet, trombone, chimes, piano, violins, viola, cellos, and bass.

[11]Henry Cowell and Sidney Cowell, *Charles Ives and His Music*, London and Oxford: Oxford University Press, 1955, pp.171–172.

[12]Ives, *Essays*, p. 68.

[13]Henry d. Thoreau, *Walden*, in Library of America edition, selected by Robert F. Sayre, New York: Literary Classics of the United States, 1985, p. 420.

[14]*Ibid.*

[15]Harmony Twichell Ives to Walter Harding, 7 December 1946. The Thoreau Library of Walter Harding.

[16]*Ibid.*, 11 January 1948.

[17]Feder, *Op. cit.*, pp. 347–348.

# Thoreau in Music

❖

### Edmund Schofield

1.  Abrahamsen, Hans. "Walden Wind Quintet"
2.  Bacon, Ernest. "Spirits and Elements"
3.  Berger, Jean. "A Different Drummer"
4.  Berry, Chuck. "Henry David Thoreau"
5.  Bob & Jeff Show. "Random Thoreaus"
6.  Brant, Henry. "American Weather"
7.  Briccetti, Thomas. "From Thoreau"
8.  Burleigh, Cecil. "Mist"
9.  Cage, John. Twenty-one pieces
10. Channing, Ellery. "Stanzas"
11. Choset, Charles. "Walden, a New Oratorio"
12. Cines, E. "Thoreau Country"
13. Cochrane, Tom. "Different Drummer"
14. Cone, Edward. Five Thoreau poems set to music
15. Crockett, Donald. "The Pensive Traveller: Six Songs on Poems by Thoreau"
16. Davison, John. "The American Prophet"
17. DiFilippi, Amadeo. "Three Walden Pastoral Portraits"
18. Drake, Ervin. "I Hear a Different Drummer"
19. Erikson, Frank. "Walden"
20. Fennelly, Brian. "In Wildness is the Preservation of the World"
21. Fennelly, Brian. "Thoreau Fantasy No"
22. Ferrazano, Anthony. "The Soul's Dream"
23. Fisher, John. "I Want To Be a More Righteous Man"
24. The Flock. "Dinosaur Swamps"
25. Foley, David. "Smoke"
26. Foss, Lukas. "To Stand Up to One's Chin"

27. Glickman, Eugene. "Credos"
28. Goossen, Frederick. "It Is No Dream of Mine"
29. Hannay, Roger. "Songs from Walden"
30. Hannay, Roger. "New Songs from Walden"
31. Hartway, James. "Impressions of Walden"
32. Hatch, Francis. "Henry Thoreau"
33. Heald, Albert. "A New England Pilgrimage"
34. Healey, Derek. "Mr. Thoreau's Fogscape"
35. Healey, Derek. "The Brown Season"
36. Heim, Norman. "The First Sparrow of Spring"
37. Heiss, John. "From Infinity Full Circle"
38. Heiss, John. "Men Say They Know Many Things"
39. Hockett, Charles. Three Thoreau poems set to music
40. Hovanes, Alan. "The Stars"
41. Husa, Karel. "Every Day"
42. Husa, Karel. "There Are from Time to Time Mornings"
43. Huston, T. Scott. "I Walked by Night Last Moon"
44. Isley, Jasper. "Different Drummer"
45. Ives, Charles. "Concord Sonata"
46. Ives, Charles. "Thoreau"
47. Ives, Charles. "Tone Roads"
48. Jeney, Zoltan. "Solitude"
49. Johnston, Ben. "Five Fragments from Walden"
50. Kasemets, Udo. "Octagonal Ode"
51. Kelly, Robert. "Walden Pond"
52. Kilpatrick, John. "Smoke"
53. Knauff, George. "The Children's Song"
54. Kovar, Anton. "Concord Suite: Thoreau"
55. Kovar, Anton. "Walden Walk"
56. LaMontaine, John. "Wilderness Journal"
57. Ledo, Les. "Walden: A Rock Opera"
58. Lundberg, Harriet. "Journals"
59. Lundergan, Edward. Score for Nicholas Durso's "Huckleberrying with Thoreau"
60. MacBride, David. "Haze"
61. Makara, Steve. "Henry David"
62. Mason, Daniel Gregory. "Chanticleer Festival Overture"
63. McKay, George F. "Summer"
64. McLean, Barton and Priscilla. "In Wilderness is the Preservation of the World"
65. Morgan, Henry. "More Day to Dawn"
66. Nesmith, Mike. "Different Drum"
67. Oliver, Harold. "Walden, a Cantata"
68. Penn, Marilyn. Five Thoreau poems set to music
69. Rich, Buddy. "A Different Drummer"

70. Russell, Stephen. "The Oyster Song"
71. Saminsky, Lazarre. "Newfoundland Air"
72. Schubert, Franz. Thoreau's words set to his music
73. Scibilic, Ed. "The Beauty in the Landscape"
74. Shure, R. Deane. "Silence"
75. Stokes, Eric. "Distant Drummer"
76. Stokes, Eric. "Exposition on Themes by Thoreau"
77. Stokes, Eric. "The Granary of the Birds"
78. Suber, Stephen. "Upon the Bank at Early Dawn"
79. Taylor, James. "Walking Man"
80. VanVactor, David. "Walden"
81. Vigelund, Nils Anton. "Ground"
82. Werner, Fred. "A Different Drummer"
83. Wetzler, Robert. "The Wilderness"
84. Whear, Paul. "From Thoreau"
85. Winter, Paul. "In Wildness is the Preservation of the World"
86. Wise, James W. "What's the Railroad to Me?"

---

**EDMUND A. SCHOFIELD** is the past president of The Thoreau Society.

# Part IV

❖

# A CENTURY OF
# THOREAU SCHOLARSHIP

# Some Thoughts of
# Henry David Thoreau

❖

Why do you flee so soon, sir, to the theaters, lecture-rooms, and museums of the city? If you will stay here awhile I will promise you strange sights. You shall walk on water; all these brooks and rivers and ponds shall be your highway. You shall see the whole earth covered a foot or more deep with purest white crystals, in which you slump or over which you glide, and all the trees and stubble glittering in icy armor.

*—October 18, 1859*

This world is but canvas to our imaginations.

*—Ibid.*

It is never too late to give up our prejudices.

*—Ibid.*

To be a philosopher is not merely to have subtle thoughts, nor even to found a school, but so to love wisdom as to live accordingly to its dictates, a life of simplicity, independence, magnanimity, and trust.

*—Ibid.*

What does education often do? It makes a straight-cut ditch of a free-meandering brook.

*—Undated, 1850*

You might say of a philosopher that he was in this world as a spectator.

*—Undated, 1850*

Of what moment are facts that can be lost,—which need to be commemorated? The monument of death will outlast the memory of the dead. The Pyramids do not tell the tale confided to them. The living fact commemorates itself. Why look in the dark for light? Look in the light rather. Strictly speaking, the Societies have not recovered one fact from oblivion, but they themselves are instead of the fact that is lost. The researcher is more memorable than the researched. The crowd stood admiring the mist and the dim outline of the trees seen through it, and when one of their number advanced to explore the phenomenon, with fresh admiration all eyes were turned on his dimly retreating figure. Critical acumen is exerted in vain to uncover the past; the *past* cannot be *presented*; we cannot know what we are not. But one veil hangs over past, present, and future, and it is the province of the historian to find out, not what was, but what is. Where a battle has been fought, you will find nothing but the bones of men and beasts; where a battle is being fought, there are hearts beating. We will sit on a mound and muse, and not try to make these skeletons stand on their legs again.

*—August 6, 1841*

# The Availability of Thoreau's Texts and Manuscripts from 1862 to the Present

❖

## Elizabeth Hall Witherell

Knowledgeable readers of Thoreau are drawn to the texts of his writings for the impact of his ideas and style. They are looking forward, to the experience of being involved and moved, not backward, to the sources of those texts in the manuscripts he left. But without the manuscripts there would be no texts, and the story of the preservation and transmission of the manuscripts in the first half century or so after Thoreau's death is a fascinating one. Accounts of the production of texts from these manuscripts, and of the fate of the manuscripts in the 20th century, bring the story of the availability of Thoreau's work up to the present.

Parts of this story are familiar to those who know the standard Thoreau biographies, but I have been able to amplify it with information and anecdotes from letters sent to Raymond Adams by Henry Salt, Thoreau's English biographer, and most generously made available to me by Charlotte Garth Adams, Raymond's widow. These letters were written to Salt by Thomas Wentworth Higginson, Daniel Ricketson, Franklin Benjamin Sanborn, Harrison Gray Otis Blake, Alfred Hosmer (born in Concord in 1851 and later a devoted member of the Walden Pond Society and a collector of much of Thoreau's material now in the Concord Free Public Library), and others. I also want to credit Fritz Oehlschlager and George Hendrick, whose *Toward the Making of Thoreau's Modern Reputation* (Urbana: University of Illinois Press, 1979) provides much of the material for understanding the plans and motives of some of the early Thoreauvians. Ray Borst's bibliography of Thoreau's works *Henry David Thoreau: A Descriptive Bibliography* (Pittsburgh: University of Pittsburgh Press, 1982) has also been a great help to me, and for the story of the dispersal of Thoreau's manuscripts after Russell acquired them from Blake, I have summarized the information on pages xxiii–xxviii of William

Howarth's introduction to *The Literary Manuscripts of Henry David Thoreau* (Columbus: Ohio State University Press, 1974). For the account of the circumstances of publication of Thoreau's essays from 1862 to 1866, I have drawn on Thomas Blanding's unpublished introductions to *Excursions* (editing of which is in progress at the Thoreau Edition).

Apart from their importance as sources for the texts, the manuscripts are of particular interest in themselves. They are what we have directly from Thoreau—all the reminiscences and biographies are necessary to help us make a connection with Thoreau as another human being, which is as important for the scholar, whether openly acknowledged or not, as for the devoted reader. But these reminiscences and biographies also give us mediated versions of Thoreau, and the truth of each version is based as much on the extent to which the writer is "impregnated with the [Thoreauvian] ether" (modified from James Atlas, in the *New York Times Magazine* of June 23, 1991, quoting Boswell's biographer, Frank Brody, about Boswell and Johnson) as are the facts the writer has at his or her disposal. It is well to remember that Emerson asked, in *Nature*, "Why should we not also have an original relation to the Universe?"—Thoreau's manuscripts are the means of having an original relation to him, unmediated by either the opinions of his friends or errors of the typesetter.

Even a single manuscript can be a gold mine of evidence about how Thoreau composed, about how his intentions changed as he worked, sometimes even about what was on his desk as he wrote. The Concord Free Public Library has in its rich collection of Thoreau manuscripts a leaf on which he wrote "POKE" with a pokeberry. At the Thoreau Edition, we have tried to collect copies of all of Thoreau's manuscripts, and we work with them to present Thoreau's intention for his works. This is more complicated than savoring the original relation to Thoreau that the manuscript leaf yields, because a single manuscript leaf or draft often does not convey Thoreau's whole intention for a work. Nevertheless, the manuscript is a crucial foundation, and at the outset of the project Walter Harding spent a great deal of time and effort locating and gathering copies of all the Thoreau manuscripts he could find. We now have a collection of photocopies, microfilms, and photographs, at the Textual Center of the Thoreau Edition in Santa Barbara, and without which it would be utterly unable to produce reliable texts.

The availability of manuscripts and thus of texts is crucial to Thoreau's reputation as well. Because Thoreau left so much material in manuscript form, unpublished, the history of the manuscripts' availability parallels the story of the development of his reputation. The material he published during his lifetime did earn him a devoted audience, but it was small. It included several men who were later involved in creating a wider reputation for him by helping to edit his works, by reviewing them, and by publishing a great deal of information about his life: Blake, Ricketson, Higginson, and Sanborn.

Harrison Gray Otis Blake, who played a critical part in making Thoreau's manuscripts available through the end of the century, was prompted to write to Thoreau after reading, in mid-March 1848, "Aulus Persis Flaccus," which was published in the *Dial* of July 1840 (*Correspondence*, pp. 213–214). Blake was a year older than Thoreau, and his letters drew out of Thoreau some of Thoreau's most interesting philosophic statements, as well as encouraging what Hendrick and Oehlschlager call "the prudish vaporous side of Thoreau" (*Thoreau's Modern Reputation*, p. 7). Writing to Henry S. Salt in response to a request for information about his relationship with Thoreau, Blake indicated that they had not been close personally.

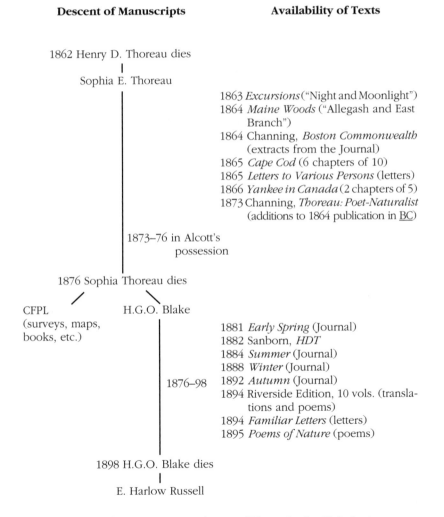

**Descent of Manuscripts**   **Availability of Texts**

1862 Henry D. Thoreau dies

Sophia E. Thoreau

1863 *Excursions* ("Night and Moonlight")
1864 *Maine Woods* ("Allegash and East Branch")
1864 Channing, *Boston Commonwealth* (extracts from the Journal)
1865 *Cape Cod* (6 chapters of 10)
1865 *Letters to Various Persons* (letters)
1866 *Yankee in Canada* (2 chapters of 5)
1873 Channing, *Thoreau: Poet-Naturalist* (additions to 1864 publication in <u>BC</u>)

1873–76 in Alcott's possession

1876 Sophia Thoreau dies

CFPL (surveys, maps, books, etc.)

H.G.O. Blake

1876–98

1881 *Early Spring* (Journal)
1882 Sanborn, *HDT*
1884 *Summer* (Journal)
1888 *Winter* (Journal)
1892 *Autumn* (Journal)
1894 Riverside Edition, 10 vols. (translations and poems)
1894 *Familiar Letters* (letters)
1895 *Poems of Nature* (poems)

1898 H.G.O. Blake dies

E. Harlow Russell

**Figure 1: *Thoreau Manuscripts and Texts in the 19th Century***

Blake encouraged Salt in his plans for a biography, saying he had no such ambition himself (Adams). Blake's obituary in the *Worcester Gazette* for 1898 includes an anecdote that conveys something of his character: on meeting a friend who had been away, Blake remarked that he was very glad to see him again. After the two parted, Blake ran back to say that he was not very glad, actually, he was just glad (Adams). When you think of Thoreau's essay on friendship in *A Week*, you can see why he would appreciate such a man as Blake.

Another early fan was Daniel Ricketson, who wrote Thoreau first in response to reading *Walden* (*Correspondence*, pp. 332–336) and continued to correspond with Thoreau for the rest of Thoreau's life. Ricketson, a perpetual hypochondriac, characteristically reported more of himself and his own condition in his letters to Salt than he said about Thoreau (Adams). Sanborn reports Ricketson's account of a time at Brooklawn when Thoreau cut loose and sang and danced and so embarrassed his host that Ricketson went to hide in his shanty, where Walter Harding has suggested he was more often hiding from his wife (HDT, p. 268; *Thoreau's Modern Reputation*, p. 8). Ricketson's importunate letters inspired or provoked Thoreau to write him in November 1860: "You know that I never promised to correspond with you, and so, when I do, I do more than I promised. ... Not to have written a note for a year is with me a very venial offense" (HDT, pp. 308–309).

Thomas Wentworth Higginson already knew Thoreau when he wrote on August 13, 1854, to "thank [him] heartily" for his paper "Slavery in Massachusetts," read at Framingham on July 4, 1854, and printed in the *Liberator* for July 21, 1854 (*Correspondence*, p. 336; *Reform Papers*, p. 331). Higginson was a Unitarian clergyman who is now best known for being colonel of the first regiment of African-American soldiers in the Civil War and for encouraging and editing, (with Mabel Loomis Todd, Emily Dickinson.) He wrote to Henry Salt in 1889 that he wished Salt had had access to the *Journals* in writing his life of Thoreau. Before Blake had them, he says, there had been talk of publication, and Fields "would gladly have undertaken to publish and I to edit them; but Miss Thoreau could not quite make up her mind to it; & so the plan was dropped" (Adams). (Higginson was also Ellery Channing's cousin and brother-in-law—his wife was Channing's sister—and Ellen Channing had turned to him and his wife when Ellery became impossible to live with.)

Higginson answered questions put by Salt about the possibility that Thoreau's Walden cabin was part of the Underground Railroad: "In one or two conspicuous instances (especially the Shadrach case) fugitives were expressly taken to Concord and they *may* have been in Thoreau's hut, but it must have been quite exceptional" (Adams). Higginson is also the conveyor to Salt of information correcting Sanborn's picture of Thoreau's parents, about which those who knew the Thoreau family were quite indignant. The source of the information was Sarah Storer, Higginson's wife—Sarah Hoar Storer grew up in a house across Main Street and a few houses down from the Thoreaus' house. She says the portrait of John Thoreau is just: there was no more to see of him than Sanborn says. But Cynthia was, she says, "a woman of command and presence, never to be ignored"; she had a keen sense of humor and told funny stories so well and so dramatically that she could hold the attention of an entire group. (I think of some of her son's riotous anecdotes—catching the pig, and Mr. Loring who cut his throat, and what befell at Mrs. Brooks—and have an idea where he got his gift.) Storer also said that Mrs. Thoreau was generous and very fond of children, so that Sarah and the others were always glad to be asked to dine with her (Adams).

Finally, among the early admirers we also find Franklin Benjamin Sanborn, who as a student at Harvard edited the number of the *Harvard Magazine* in which another student had reviewed *Walden* and *A Week*. Thoreau left a copy of *A Week* at Sanborn's room in January 1855 for the author of the review; Sanborn wrote to him rather flippantly later that month ("if anyone should ask me what I think of your philosophy, I should be apt to answer that it is not worth a straw" [HDT, p. 197]) and moved to Concord a couple of months later.

Sanborn came to be almost universally disliked and distrusted by those who edited and published Thoreau material in the later part of the century, including Sophia Thoreau. Among others, Fred Hosmer damned Sanborn soundly in an 1895 letter to Salt, saying that Sanborn had no true love of Thoreau, and that he was out only to fill his own pockets. He expresses his fear that Sanborn will get Blake's Thoreau manuscripts (Adams). Annie J. Ward, whose grandmother and aunt boarded with the Thoreaus, noted to Salt in 1909 that Blake willed the Thoreau manuscripts to E. Harlow Russell because he did not want Sanborn to handle them. Samuel Arthur Jones, a homeopathic physician who, with Fred Hosmer and Salt, "laid the foundation for Thoreau's modern reputation," according to Raymond Adams (*Thoreau's Modern Reputation* pp. 1–2) despised Sanborn. When in 1895 he found out from Salt that Sanborn had not been helpful in work on *Poems of Nature*, he wrote to Fred Hosmer "Drat F. B. S., I'd like to pull his nose!" (*Thoreau's Modern Reputation* p. 243). (When Jones went to Concord, the Concordians all spoke of Emerson, but Jones said, "I don't care a damn about Emerson. What I came here for was to do honor to Thoreau. Emerson is a tallow dip compared with that man!" [Adams—Edwin Hill to Alexander Greene].)

Sanborn's activity as an abolitionist gave him credibility at first with Thoreau and in Thoreau's circle, but he later mangled much of what he edited of Thoreau's. He was known in Concord for "borrowing" Thoreau manuscripts and then stating they were his (Adams—Edwin Hill to Alexander Greene). In addition, he carried on an abortive romance with Edith Emerson, with which he reproached her, causing Ralph Waldo

Emerson to write him an "almost violent" letter in response (George Goodspeed has this letter now—it has never been published).

These four early readers and admirers—Blake, Ricketson, Higginson, and Sanborn—all continued to be involved (though Ricketson least) as Thoreau's work was slowly, a book at a time, revealed in the years after his death.

These and the other characters who helped Sophia edit her "precious brother's" papers and spread the word about him later on make the story of the availability of the manuscripts in the first fifty or sixty years after Thoreau's death a fascinating one. They were players in Thoreau's life, as well—the four mentioned above, and Emerson, Channing, and Alcott—and most were eager to make his work available because of his importance to them personally. Later in the 19th century, individuals added themselves to this group—Henry S. Salt, Samuel Arthur Jones, Alfred Hosmer—and corresponded with or visited those who had known Thoreau, and collected manuscripts, memories, and objects related to him. Several of these men (I found it interesting that so many were men—they outnumbered women admirers who were active and public in their response by more than eight to one) were biographers of Thoreau. The early biographies present much of the manuscript material for the first time, and all were instrumental in collecting and preserving both material associated with Thoreau and recollections of his life.

During the last half of the 20th century, scholars have had access to much of this manuscript material in libraries around the country, but without the efforts of those who edited and presented Thoreau material from 1862 until 1920 or so, we would have nothing to work with now. The story of the dispersal of the manuscripts and their acquisition by the Huntington, Houghton, Morgan, New York Public, and other libraries is also interesting, but it involves dealers and high finance, and takes us away from those who knew and admired Thoreau to those who found a way to make a profit on him.

It is interesting to reflect on what was made available when, and why. The stories of the relationships, in the latter part of the 19th century often carried on in letters, between and among those who admired Thoreau and desired to make his ideas and the story of his life more widely available, have their own attraction. As can be seen from the individuals described above, the cast of characters is every bit as varied and intriguing as those of us who gather in Concord every year for the birthday party. It includes only a few more.

Sophia Thoreau, the youngest and last survivor of the Thoreau children, devoted years to preparing her brother's work for publication. Her relations with the others she worked with were sometimes stormy, and she changed her mind more than once about allowing the *Journal* to be published—at different times, Higginson, Alcott, and Blake were all candidates.

Ralph Waldo Emerson was Thoreau's mentor, friend, and benefactor, with whom he had a continuing but uncomfortable relationship for many reasons. Emerson expressed his disappointment with and misunderstanding of Thoreau's ambition in his eulogy, the document that began to shape Thoreau's reputation as soon as it was published in 1862.

Finally, we have William Ellery Channing, Thoreau's companion, often with his dog, "Professor," on many excursions in and around Concord. Married to and separated from Ellen Fuller, Margaret's sister, he was by Thoreau's own account filled with contradictions: "He is the moodiest person, perhaps, that I ever saw. As naturally whimsical as a cow is brindled, both in his tenderness and his roughness he belies himself. He can be incredibly selfish and unexpectedly generous. He is conceited, and yet there is in him far more than usual to ground conceit upon" (1906, 3: 98–99). Thoreau also records, in January 1854, that "When I was at Channing's the other evening, he punched his cat with the poker because she purred too loud for him" (1906, 6: 75). Emerson notes his response, on a walk to Lincoln in 1853, to Nuttall's description of birds: "On the top of a high tree the bird pours all day the lays of affection. ... "Affection!" snorts Channing, "Why, what is it? a few feathers, with a hole at one end and a point at the other, and a pair of wings: affection! Why just as much affection as there is in that lump of peat'" (JMN 13: 128). In a 1917 letter from Edwin B. Hill, a Thoreau collector and printer, to Alexander Greene, a dealer, Hill notes that Channing was "sexually insane" and says he has a letter about him from Fred Hosmer (Adams)— Thoreau did complain in his *Journal* about Channing's enjoyment of smutty stories, but that hardly qualifies as insanity. Walter Harding told me that many years ago Hill had shared the contents of Hosmer's letter with him, and that Hosmer's characterization arose from a story that Channing, who was estranged from his children when they were very young, had met his daughter when she had grown to be a young woman, and without recognizing her had tried to seduce her.)

Channing was Thoreau's first biographer: *Thoreau: The Poet-Naturalist*, written after Thoreau's death, was published first in the *Boston Commonwealth* in 1863 and 1864, then in book form in 1873, and again after Channing's death in an edition by Sanborn (1902).

Immediately after Thoreau's death, the manuscripts of both his published and unpublished works were available only to his sister and those who worked with her to publish his writings. This diverse group of editors made a number of things accessible to a larger audience. The following is a brief description of the works they prepared and that Ticknor and Fields, who had become Thoreau's publishers, brought out between 1863 and 1866. In each case, I've noted material that was made accessible for the first time. (Figure 1 summarizes the history of the availability of both manuscripts and published texts from 1862 to the end of the 19th century.)

The first of the posthumous volumes was *Excursions,* edited by Sophia Thoreau and Emerson, probably with the help of Channing, and published in 1863. The essays included in the volume were among those Thoreau had been revising during the last months of his life, partly to give his mother and sister the support of whatever income their publication generated. All but one of the essays in the volume had been published in periodicals during Thoreau's lifetime, but they had never been collected. "Night and Moonlight" was the exception; it consisted of material that had never been published—in fact, Thoreau had not completed it as an essay (See William L. Howarth, "Successor to *Walden?*' Thoreau's 'Moonlight—An Intended Course of Lectures,'" in *Proof 2* (1972): 89–115.)

The first publication of any significant portions of Thoreau's journal—Emerson had quoted only a few one- or two-line epithets from it for his eulogy—was by Ellery Channing in the *Boston Commonwealth* in 1863 and 1864. Channing's work was a biography of his friend, and it drew on the journal; it appeared in the paper in several installments.

The next year, Ticknor and Fields brought out *The Maine Woods,* edited by Sophia and Channing. "Ktaadn" and "Chesuncook" had seen periodical publication, but "The Allegash and East Branch" and the "Appendix" were new. In 1865, *Cape Cod* appeared, the product of another collaboration between Sophia and Channing. The first four chapters had been published in *Putnam's Monthly;* Thoreau had reworked them and the 1865 publication included the revised versions as well as six new chapters. In the same year, Emerson's edition of a selection of Thoreau's letters, *Letters to Various Persons,* was published: all of these were new to readers. (Emerson had selected letters and excerpted them in order to present Thoreau as a stoic. Sophia, who exercised control over her brother's material even when she was not herself editing it, saw proofs and objected that Emerson had not conveyed any of Thoreau's human qualities, and insisted that some excised passages be restored. Emerson later complained that Sophia had spoiled his classic portrait.)

Finally, in 1866 *A Yankee in Canada with Anti-Slavery and Reform Papers,* was published, edited by Channing. The first three chapters of the Canada essay had appeared in *Putnam's Monthly,* but the last two were new.

When Sophia moved from Concord to Bangor in 1873, she left her brother's manuscripts with Bronson Alcott in Concord. As his *Journal* reveals, he anticipated owning them if he survived Sophia:

> April 4 P.M. Thoreau's journals, manuscripts and such books as his sister wishes to have in my care come to hand. They are sent in three trunks, the MSS. and the books, with a bookcase made by Thoreau himself. I am to hold them sacred from all but Thoreau's friends, allow none to take them away for perusal, subject to his sister's pleasure during her lifetime, and if I survive her, then they become mine for quotation or publishing.

Many volumes may be compiled from them, and will be when his editor appears. I house them under lock and key safely in my attic. Along with the books are maps and surveys of local value. (*Journals of Alcott*, p. 431)

During a visit to Concord in June 1874, Sophia discussed with Alcott the disposition of some of the manuscripts—the Indian Books to the Concord Free Public Library (they went eventually to the Pierpont Morgan Library in New York) and the *Journal* manuscripts to H. G. O. Blake. The concluding sentence in Alcott's journal entry describing this visit gives a clue as to why Alcott did not finally come into possession of Thoreau's manuscripts: "The 'Diaries' are now at Sanborn's" (*Journals of Alcott*, pp. 450–451). Sophia did not want Sanborn to edit the *Journal,* and she probably saw Alcott's having allowed Sanborn to take the manuscript volumes as an indication of what would occur after her death. In 1876, by the terms of her will, most of the literary manuscripts that Alcott had kept, including the *Journal* volumes, went to Blake. Other material went to the Concord Free Public Library.

For twenty-two years, from 1876 until his death in 1898, Blake determined the availability of what had not been published. During the time he had them, Blake edited four volumes of extracts from the *Journal: Early Spring in Massachusetts* (1881), *Summer* (1884), *Winter* (1887), and *Autumn* (1892). His progress through the manuscript volumes is still evident in the blue pencil marks he made through passages he had chosen for inclusion.) These seasonal volumes represent the first publication of numerous extended *Journal* passages, though the format gives the reader no sense of the daily progression of ideas and observations in the *Journal* as a whole.

The first real collection of Thoreau's works appeared in the autumn of 1893: Horace E. Scudder edited and supervised the production of the ten-volume Riverside Edition. Most of the contents of this edition had been published previously, but several of Thoreau's translations from the Greek were collected for the first time in the volume titled *Miscellanies.*

Sanborn, who had been dissatisfied with Emerson's selection of letters in *Letters to Various Persons,* brought out his own edition in 1894. *Familiar Letters,* which was published as the eleventh volume in the Riverside Edition, made available a number of new letters, but Sanborn exercised such freedom in editing them that in some cases he might more properly be called the author than the editor.

In *Poems of Nature,* the first collection of a large group of Thoreau's poems, and the first publication of several of them, Sanborn's editorial impulses were apparently restrained by his coeditor, Henry Salt. In fact, Salt seems to have prepared the texts, for many of which Sanborn supplied the manuscripts. Blake was the source of some of these, as the introduction to the volume notes. He wrote to Sanborn on June 4, 1895, that Salt had been in touch with him about poems to print. Blake was in favor of publishing excerpts rather than entire poems, but deferred to Sanborn's greater knowledge of poetry. He asked Sanborn to choose material he thought was appropriate and reply to Salt (Adams). *Poems of Nature* was published in 1895, a collaboration of Houghton Mifflin in Boston and John Lane in London.

At Blake's death, the manuscripts passed to Elias Harlow Russell, and he was the agent of their wider distribution, both because he negotiated with Houghton Mifflin to publish the *Journal* in 1906 and because he sold the manuscripts themselves. Annie J. Ward, whose grandmother and great-aunt boarded with the Thoreaus, wrote to Salt in 1909 that she wished he could have had access to the material bought by Bixby of St. Louis and Wakeman of New York. "I think Mr. Russell did a wrong thing when he sold Thoreau's Journals to Wakeman," she writes (Adams). She says Blake willed them to Russell because he didn't want Sanborn to handle them—perhaps the continuing influence of Sophia's animus toward Sanborn—but she thinks that Concord should have them.

Those of us who work with the manuscripts have all at one time or another wished both that they had been kept in their original order and that they were still all together in one place. After a period of inaccessibility, however, during which manuscripts were in the hands of dealers or private collectors, much of the Thoreau material is now available to researchers, though in repositories scattered across the country.

Soon after Russell inherited the manuscripts, Houghton Mifflin approached him about publishing the *Journal.* He eventually agreed, but had to secure the literary rights to the manuscripts before negotiations could be concluded. This he did in court in 1903. Houghton Mifflin paid him for publication rights and for a quantity of manuscript leaves that were to be tipped into the first volume of the planned "Manuscript Edition." Though it involved a relatively small amount of the material, this arrangement has had the most disastrous effect for scholars. At last count, about 165 of the 600 or so sets produced have been located; of those 165 sets, only about 130 still have their manuscripts. [Bradley P. Dean, "A Checklist of 1906 Manuscript Edition Sets," *Thoreau Research Newsletter*, vol. 2, no. 2 (April 1991), pp. 5–7.]

The transaction with Houghton Mifflin took place through George S. Hellman, the New York dealer to whom Russell had sold first the unbound manuscripts and then the bound manuscript volumes of the *Journal* (except for two volumes that somehow did not make their way into the collection that Russell inherited). Hellman found a buyer for the first lot of Thoreau manuscripts in late 1904, soon after he acquired them: William Augustus White bought about 400 leaves. The next year, William Keeney Bixby purchased the rest of the material, except for what had previously been committed to Houghton Mifflin. In 1907, Russell sold the

*Journal* volumes that he had to Hellman, who sold them almost immediately to Stephen H. Wakeman.

In most cases, the next sale of particular Thoreau manuscripts took them into institutional collections, although some of them stayed in private hands. Stephen Wakeman sold his *Journal* manuscripts to J. Pierpont Morgan in 1916, and they can be consulted in his library in New York. (Wakeman bought the two *Journal* volumes that had been missing

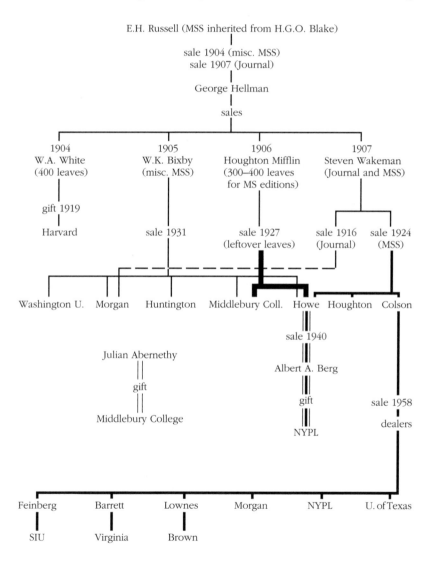

**Figure 2: Thoreau Manuscripts in the 20th Century**

from Russell's inheritance; these next went to Warren H. Colson, who sequestered them for more than thirty years; finally, one went to the Morgan Library and the other to the Berg Collection in the New York Public Library.) In 1919, White gave his Thoreau manuscripts to Harvard, and they are now in the Houghton Library.

Julian Willis Abernethy, who had acquired a sizable collection of Thoreau material through other sources than Hellman, left it to Middlebury College in 1923. The next year, Wakeman's manuscripts were sold; Thoreau material went to Henry Huntington (and thence to the Huntington Library), Warren Colson, and W. T. H. Howe. Houghton Mifflin sold its leftover manuscript fragments in 1927, and Howe and Middlebury College were both buyers. In 1931, Bixby's manuscripts were on the market: after a donation to Washington University, material was sold to the Morgan Library, the Huntington Library, and Middlebury College, along with Howe.

By this time, the largest private collections of Thoreau manuscripts were those of Howe and Colson. Howe's was purchased in 1940 by Dr. Albert A. Berg, who added it to the collection he donated to the New York Public Library that year. Colson's was sold in 1958; material in that sale went ultimately to the Morgan Library, the Berg Collection, the University of Texas, and three private collectors, Charles Feinberg, Albert Lownes, and C. Waller Barrett. Now, Feinberg's collection is at Southern Illinois University, Lownes' at Brown University, and Barrett's at the University of Virginia. (Figure 2 summarizes the transactions described above.)

The other repository of a major collection of Thoreau manuscripts is, of course, the Concord Free Public Library. Much of that material came directly from Sophia Thoreau in 1876, by the terms of her will.

The availability of new Thoreau texts in the 20th century has been influenced by both the publication of the twenty-volume collected edition in 1906, and the period of time during which the manuscripts were in private hands (until the late 1920s and early 1930s for much of the material; until much later for some of it). After the 1906 edition, after the manuscripts had gone into private hands, little new material appeared for some years. The collected edition consumed the market, though *Walden*, *Cape Cod*, and even *A Week* have been almost continuously in print for the past ninety years.

In 1966 a new editorial project, The Writings of Henry D. Thoreau, was established to reedit all of Thoreau's works, including his *Journal* and his correspondence. The goal of the editorial process is to determine and present the works as Thoreau intended them to appear; this requires exhaustive research into the history of composition and publication of each work that is included. It also depends critically on the availability of the manuscripts in research libraries that have the facilities and the authority to make them easily accessible to scholars, both in reading rooms on site and through photoduplicates.

Only one area of Thoreau's work has been almost completely overlooked until the 1980s—probably because the manuscript remains are so daunting. This is his painstakingly detailed study of the natural history of Concord. The manuscripts that represent it are widely scattered, in great disarray, and often in a hand almost impossible to read. I think Emerson had these in mind when he noted, in his eulogy, that "the scale on which Thoreau's studies proceeded was so large as to require longevity," and lamented that Thoreau had left "in the midst his broken task, which none else can finish" (*Studies in the American Renaissance 1979*, pp. 54–55). Thoreau's observations of natural phenomena, usually made in his *Journal,* then transferred first to lists of natural events and then charts, were apparently to be the foundation for a new kind of writing— a transcendental natural history in which Thoreau's skillful classifications and descriptions were not only useful and beautiful in themselves, but also yielded a higher vision of the eternal cycle of life.

Virtually all of Thoreau's manuscripts and texts are available in some form or accessible through some channel. Work on the manuscripts has given some material that was earlier thought to be miscellaneous the shape of texts. It seems unlikely that any great cache of Thoreau manuscripts, hitherto unknown, will come to light and reveal a completely new side of his artistic life or personality—though I say this cautiously. Now we have the task of understanding this material. And of course, new stories of human beings in all their complexity dealing with an exceedingly complex and gifted member of their own tribe.

# Bibliography

For references cited in the text, only short titles and page numbers are given; full bibliographic information follows.

1906: Henry David Thoreau, The Journal of Henry David Thoreau, eds. Bradford Torrey and Francis H. Allen (Boston: Houghton Mifflin, 1906).

Adams: The Thoreau Collection of Raymond Adams, now owned by Charlotte Garth Adams.

Correspondence: Walter Harding and Carl Bode, eds., The Correspondence of Henry Thoreau (New York: New York Univ. Press, 1958).

HDT: Franklin Benjamin Sanborn, Henry D. Thoreau (Boston: Houghton Mifflin, 1882).

JMN: Ralph Waldo Emerson, The Journals and Miscellaneous Notebooks of Ralph Waldo Emerson, eds. William H. Gilman and Alfred R. Ferguson (Cambridge: The Belknap Press of Harvard Univ. Press, 1960–1978).

Journals of Alcott: Odell Shepard, ed., The Journals of Bronson Alcott (Boston: Little, Brown and Company, 1938).

Reform Papers: Henry David Thoreau, Reform Papers, ed. Wendell Glick (Princeton: Princeton Univ. Press, 1974).

Thoreau's Modern Reputation: Fritz Oehlschlager and George Hendrick, eds., Toward the Making of Thoreau's Modern Reputation (Urbana: University of Illinois Press, 1972).

---

**ELIZABETH HALL WITHERELL** is the editor-in-chief of *The Journal of the Writings of Henry D. Thoreau*—an NEH-funded project to produce newly edited texts of Thoreau's works, his *Journal,* and his correspondence. For twenty-five years, this project enjoyed the participation of many individuals and the sponsorship of four institutions. Walter Harding founded the project at the State University College at Geneseo, New York, in 1966; William Howarth took it to Princeton University in 1972; Witherell moved it to the University of California, Santa Barbara, in 1983; and Robert Sattelmeyer, general editor for the *Journal,* set up an office for *Journal* work at Georgia State University in 1989.

# Highlights of the Last Fifty Years of Thoreau Criticism

❖

## Joseph J. Moldenhauer

In the past half-century Thoreau has been recognized increasingly as a great literary artist and a multifaceted, challenging thinker. Published criticism from 1941 through 1990, therefore, dwarfs what preceded it in both bulk and significance. My selective review concerns perhaps forty pieces of scholarship that impress me as especially innovative, penetrating, and influential. I will exclude biographies—Richard Lebeaux's topic—as best I can, but the line between essentially narrative, subject-centered and essentially interpretive, text-centered treatments of Thoreau's career is sometimes difficult to draw.

The primary and secondary bibliographies of Thoreau, records of existing research and textual materials, were in disarray at the beginning of the period. Now these requisite aids to scholarship are in excellent shape. Raymond Borst's *Henry David Thoreau: A Descriptive Bibliography* (1982), the first book-length treatment since Francis Allen's *Bibliography* of 1908, is a complete and reliable record of Thoreau editions and printings, Borst's *Henry David Thoreau: A Reference Guide* (1987) lists all the 19th-century commentaries on our author. Scholarship from 1900 to 1978 is covered in the Jeanetta Boswell and Sarah Crouch compilation, *Henry David Thoreau and the Critics* (1981). Throughout the period of my survey, Walter Harding maintained an exhaustive current bibliography, both primary and secondary, in the *Thoreau Society Bulletin*. We have been well served since 1963 by the authors of the chapter "Emerson, Thoreau, and Transcendentalism" in the annual bibliographical volume, *American Literary Scholarship*. Two guides to scholarship—selective bibliographical essays—have assisted and continue to assist researchers: Lewis Leary's fine chapter on Thoreau in *Eight American Authors* (1956, 1971) and Michael Meyer's excellent and up-to-date section in *The*

*Transcendentalists: A Review of Research and Criticism* (1984), edited by Joel Myerson. The book as a whole is an indispensable bibliographical resource for anyone working in the field of literary transcendentalism; and Meyer's chapter condenses *The New Thoreau Handbook* (1980) by Harding and Meyer, the standard guide to research on Thoreau's life, work, and influence.

William Howarth's *The Literary Manuscripts of Henry David Thoreau* (1974) supplanted all previous censuses locating, identifying, and correlating Thoreau's manuscripts. One of the most fruitful fields of Thoreau scholarship in the past fifty years has been genetic criticism of the books, essays, and poems, that is, studies of construction and development from the initial drafts to the final texts. J. Lyndon Stanley's *The Making of* Walden, *with a Text of the First Version* (1957) is the earliest important instance; others are Ronald Clapper's reconstruction of *Walden* through its seven drafts (1967), Linck Johnson's analysis of the composition of *A Week* (*Thoreau's Complex Weave*, 1986), and Stephen Adams' and Donald Ross' more comprehensive and speculative study, *Revising Mythologies: The Composition of Thoreau's Major Works* (1988). Genetic criticism is often a prerequisite to and by-product of textual editing, as witness the apparatus for established texts in volumes of the Princeton Thoreau Edition.

Great progress has been made in identifying the books that influenced Thoreau's works and provided sources for his quotations and allusions. Harding's work on Thoreau's personal library (1957, revised 1983), Kenneth W. Cameron's lists of Thoreau's institutional library borrowings, John Christie's *Thoreau as World Traveler* (1965), and Robert Sattelmeyer's *Thoreau's Reading* (1988) provide this information, together in the last two instances with extended critical discussion of the growth of Thoreau's thought or the close links between his artistry and his reading. Most volumes of the Princeton Edition, including the *Journal* volumes, trace out Thoreau's sources for the texts at hand and record them in historical essays, bibliographies, and/or textual notes, sometimes deriving emendations from them. Among the intellectual biographies of Thoreau, Robert Richardson's *Henry David Thoreau: A Life of the Mind* (1986) shows how pertinent this work on Thoreau's sources is to the critical understanding of his own rich intelligence.

This golden jubilee of the Thoreau Society is also the fiftieth anniversary of F. O. Matthiessen's *American Renaissance*, the first book fully to credit Thoreau as an artist and to examine his works in the context of transcendental ethics and Romantic aesthetics. A formalist critic as well as a historian of American culture and thought, Matthiessen traced the organic model or metaphor in Thoreau's symbolism and in the structure of his works. He applied the "New Critics'" concern with craftsmanship, artistic form, and linguistic order that affected an entire generation of Thoreau critics. We should remember that he gave the name to the period that we Thoreauvians—and Emersonians, Melvilleans, Hawthornians, and Whitmaniacs—study. Charles Feidelson's *Symbolism and American Literature* (1953) pursued one aspect of Matthiessen's study farther into 19th-century philosophy and theology and, of course, back into the literary practice of our author and his contemporaries. Hard upon Feidelson came Sherman Paul's *The Shores of America* (1958), a sweeping analysis of Thoreau's thinking on all his major subjects except politics, and a fine chronological investigation of the way Thoreau's writings give artistic form to his themes. The last book I want to mention under the head of seminal studies that relate Thoreau's artistry to his ideas, and to the intellectual climate of his time and place, is Lawrence Buell's *Literary Transcendentalism: Style and Vision in the American Renaissance* (1973).

Studies of Thoreau's uses of mythology (Greek, Roman, Eastern, Christian, and Scandinavian), and of his creation of analogous patterns in his own narratives, owed their initial impetus to the "myth-and-symbol" concerns of New Criticism. In my view, the most successful and influential of these essays and books prior to Richardson's historically focused treatment in *Myth and Literature in the American Renaissance* (1978) are those by Stanley Edgar Hyman (1946), Sherman Paul, R.W.B. Lewis (1955), and Charles R. Anderson (1968).

Stylistic and rhetorical analyses of Thoreau's writings, again at first an outgrowth of the New Criticism and of Matthiessen's work, occupied many of the critics of the decades from the 1950s to the 1970s. The best of these analyses studied the relationship of Thoreau's devices of style to his ideas, his conception of his role as writer, and his designs upon his audience. It was into this formalist channel that I first directed my own scholarly efforts. Under newer dispensations, those of Structuralism and Post-Structuralism, Thoreau's rhetoric continues to attract considerable attention, as witness such treatments as Stanley Cavell's *The Senses of Walden* (1972, 1981) and Henry Golemba's *Thoreau's Wild Rhetoric* (1990). Closely related to and overlapping with the foregoing are studies of Thoreau's response to 18th- and 19th-century language theories, such as Philip Gura's in *The Wisdom of Words* (1981) and Michael West's provocative essays (1973, 1974).

Thoreau's conception of and response to the natural world have perennially invited commentary. Especially illuminating or stimulating are James McIntosh, *Thoreau as Romantic Naturalist* (1974), and Frederick Garber, *Thoreau's Redemptive Imagination* (1977), which place Thoreau in the context of English and Continental romanticism while examining his senses of the relationship between the perceiving self and the perceived phenomena of nature. Cavell's book on *Walden* extends these philosophical concerns with great sophistication, and in small compass offers penetrating insights into and poses profound questions. Himself a philosopher, Cavell describes his study as a meditation on a self-reflexive, problematical text. Self-referentiality in

Thoreau's *Journal* is an underlying premise of Sharon Cameron's *Writing Nature* (1985); like Cavell she is interested in Thoreau's interrogative dimension, but is more concerned than he with "gaps," "blanks," "discontinuities," "fragmentations," and "indeterminacies" in Thoreau's prose. This approach reflects Post-Structuralist methods of analysis, notably Deconstruction, with their attendant theoretical assumptions. Like Howarth in *The Book of Concord* (1982), an earlier book-length treatment of the *Journal,* Cameron views it as Thoreau's principal, central creative document, rather than a mere draft-book and literary savings bank. Howarth's critical presuppositions and techniques, however, are those of an ("old") historicist, biographical scholar, and formalist. H. Daniel Peck, in his *Thoreau's Morning Work* (1990), traces the "deep imaginative structures," the psychological and philosophical orderings, that link the *Journal* to *A Week* and *Walden.* Peck's procedures, which seem closer to phenomenological criticism than to the other modern "schools," are considerably more eclectic and traditionally humanistic than those of Thoreau's Post-Structuralist critics; the virtues of Peck's book lie not in theoretical muscle but in its sensitivity to the phenomena of experience, especially memory and perception, rendered in Thoreau's prose.

Virtually ignored by scholars before the 1960s, Thoreau's preoccupation with the American Indians—his actual contacts with them in Massachusetts, Maine, and Minnesota, his shifting conceptions of their character and culture, his treatment of historical and contemporary Indians in his books and essays, and his voluminous reading in New World ethnography as recorded in the eleven-volume Indian Note-books—now generates considerable critical energy. The landmark study to date is Robert Sayre's *Thoreau and the American Indians* (1977).

Thoreau's relation to his own society in its political and economic dimensions was not ignored in the first twenty years of my survey. But it attracted special regard from the 1960s onward, when the sociopolitical positions of many students, academicians, and reform leaders made Thoreau's example and doctrines appear especially relevant as correctives to the perceived materialism, social regimentation, and brutality of modern America. Wendell Glick's dissertation on "Thoreau and Radical Abolitionism" (1950) and Leo Stoller's *After Walden: Thoreau's Views on Economic Man* (1957) are important earlier examinations. Meyer's study of Thoreau's political reputation from the 1920s to the 1960s, *Several More Lives to Live* (1977), is at once wisely informed and wittily written. (Levity is a rare element in treatments of Thoreau's sociopolitical thought and influence.) Michael Gilmore, in his much-admired, "New Historicist" *American Romanticism and the Marketplace* (1985), gives a chapter to "*Walden* and the Curse of Trade," in which he scrutinizes the contradictions in Thoreau's position as an artist and opponent of capitalism. Given the theoretical commitments of the newest generation of scholar-teachers and their students in graduate literature programs, studies that argue for Thoreau's conscious or unconscious complicity in the very institutions he rejected are likely to flourish.

———————

**JOSEPH J. MOLDENHAUER** received his Ph.D. from Columbia University in 1964 and has been teaching at the University of Texas ever since. He is the volume editor of *Maine Woods* (1972), *Early Essays and Miscellaneous* (1975), and *Cape Cod* (1988).

# From Canby to Richardson
## The Last Half-Century of Thoreau Biography

❖

## Richard M. Lebeaux

In Bernard Malamud's novel *Dubin's Lives,* William Dubin was awarded the Medal of Freedom, "presented by Lyndon B. Johnson, President of the United States of America; to William Dubin, for his achievement in the area of biography; at the White House, December 1968." Dubin explains to a young woman: "It was presented to me after the publication of my *H. D. Thoreau*—you've heard of him?—American essayist, 1817–62, author of *Walden* and other works."[1] It's difficult for me to imagine Lyndon Johnson presenting such an award, given Thoreau's advocacy of the civil disobedience that so much characterized the strategies of the antiwar movement (as well as of the earlier civil rights movement). Also, I wonder whether Thoreau is in general "mainstream" enough for such recognition by the establishment, given his challenging and rejection of so many social and cultural assumptions and priorities.

William Dubin has a vision of Thoreau's life and personality that is elaborated on in the novel, but Dubin, whatever his own vision and interpretation, observes with some humility: "No one, certainly no biographer, has the final word. Knowing, as they say, is itself a mystery that weaves itself as one unweaves it. ... The past exudes legend: one can't make pure clay of time's mud. There is no life that can be recaptured wholly; as it was."[2] Thoreau has left a rich legacy to us and he continues to be one whose life and writings stimulate and fascinate us, who challenges each new generation to front *his* essential facts with whatever approaches and new information are available and illuminating. As is noted in Harding and Meyers indispensable *New Thoreau Handbook* (1980), "There will never be a 'definitive' biography of Thoreau to satisfy all times and all people. New factual material about his life continues to turn up with astonishing frequency for one now dead for more than a century. Critical attitudes toward him continue to change, making older biographies seem out-of-date. Someone has once said that major figure needs a new biography for each new generation, and that is undoubtedly true of Henry David Thoreau as of any other."[3]

Thoreau poses his own special problems for would-be biographers. While new factual information on his life and writing does continue to turn up (*The Writings of Henry D. Thoreau* comes to mind immediately for me as a rich source of new information on the texts and the life), Thoreau was in many ways quite reticent about himself, hardly a "confessional" writer, even if his *Journal* is magnificent, formidable, and revealing and even if he sometimes encourages his audience to believe that he is writing in a primarily autobiographical mode. The *Correspondence* also helps greatly. And yet, to attempt to understand Thoreau fully requires much interpretation and interpolation, much intuition as well as tuition (to use Emerson's play on words in "Self-Reliance"). To the extent that biographers seek to come to grips with Thoreau's *inner* life, there will always be some need for educated and sensitive speculation.

There will be no easy consensus on Thoreau; he will remain controversial. However, different biographies do not, I believe, cancel out or fully supplant each other, but rather provide particular emphases, information, and insight that help us further to understand the elusive, complex, and gifted man and writer who was Henry Thoreau. What may appear to be contradictory in different biographies of Thoreau may turn out to be complementary. Biographies are part of a continuing dialogue; they tend to build on, are influenced by, or see to respond to/revise/refine/refute previous biographies. All are valuable, though some more so than others or for different reasons, Some are more reductive or skewed.

Biographical interpretation is subjective and I, too, must be selective and subjective in this discussion. Even a seemingly objective biography cannot fully be without selectivity and subjectivity. It is important for us to be aware of and monitor possible subjectivity as we read (or write) any particular biography and seek to integrate what we learn into a more integrated, holistic understanding of the subject. That we must aspire to, then, is what Erik Erikson calls "disciplined subjectivity."[4]

Michael Meyer's *Several More Lives to Live—Thoreau's Political Reputation in America* (1977) eloquently shows how views and visions of Thoreau's life and writings are influenced by historical, cultural, and political factors.[5] Moreover, it is my assumption that biographies cannot avoid having an implicit, if not explicit, psychology and vision of Thoreau's personality and life.

In *The New Thoreau Handbook,* Harding and Meyer identify some of the difficulties involved in doing biographical work on Thoreau. "Since he was not particularly famous in his own lifetime," they say, "there is a comparative dearth of reminiscences." Also problematic is "the wideness of the range of Thoreau's interests," which led Canby to remark, in his biography of Thoreau, that "there are a half dozen possible biographies of Thoreau, depending on the view the biographer takes of his subject." Moreover, remark Harding and Meyer, due to "the popularity of Emerson's funeral essay on Thoreau and James Russell Lowell's and Robert Louis Stevenson's essays, there is a widespread belief that Thoreau's philosophy was primarily negative."

Although "most twentieth-century biographers disagree with this interpretation, they are almost automatically forced to assume a negative positive and state over and over again, 'Thoreau was not this but that.' The result is that too often his biographers have appeared belligerent," There is, finally, controversy about the "success" of Thoreau's life. Mark Van Doren obviously considers Thoreau's life to have been a failure and Thoreau an embittered man in his last years. Brooks Atkinson, in *Thoreau, the Cosmic Yankee,* was not sure if Thoreau won happiness in the lifestyle he devised. Yet Canby and Harding both maintain that Thoreau was the happiest of the whole Concord group to the very end of his life."[6]

I might add that there continues to be much disagreement concerning the quality and significance of Thoreau's life and work after the publication of *Walden* until his death in 1862. As Michael Meyer points out in his excellent bibliographical essay in *The Transcendentalists: A Review of Research and Criticism* (1984), "Several critics, including Paul, Mark Van Doren, and Perry Miller have argued that Thoreau lost his Transcendental faith in the 1850s, but J. Lyndon Stanley, 'Thoreau: Years of Decay and Disappointment?,' follows Henry Seidel Canby and Joseph Wood Krutch in asserting that Thoreau was essentially happy and satisfied with his life to the end."[7] Such scholars as Leo Marx, William Howarth, Richard Lebeaux, and Robert Richardson have also joined the debate.[8]

Another problem is how difficult it is to separate Thoreau biography from Thoreau criticism. Where does biography leave off and criticism begin as interpretive acts—and vice versa? To an extent biography and criticism are inextricably bound. Thus, many works are hybrids, shedding light on Thoreau's life, personality, and writing to different degrees. Among these works—and I am being quite selective here—are Sherman Paul's *The Shores of America* (1982), Robert Sayre's *Thoreau and the American Indians* (1977), Frederick Garber's *Thoreau's Redemptive Imagination* (1977), William Howarth's *The Book of Concord: Thoreau's Life as a Writer* (1982); James McIntosh's *Thoreau as Romantic Naturalist: His Shifting Stance Toward Nature* (1974), Richard Bridgman's *Dark Thoreau* (1982), Mary Elkins Moller's, *Thoreau and the Human Community* (1980), Linck Johnson's *Thoreau's Complex Weave: The Writing of 'A Week on the Concord and Merrimack Rivers' with the Text of the First Draft* (1985), Robert Sattelmeyer's *Thoreau's Reading* (1988), Adams and Ross' *Revising Mythologies: The Composition of Thoreau's Major Works,* (1988), Robert Richardson's *Henry Thoreau: A Life of the Mind* (1986), and my own two books on Thoreau.

There are also many books that discuss Thoreau among other writers, such as Lawrence Buell's *Literary Transcendentalism: Style and Vision in the American Renaissance* (1973), Leo Marx's *The Machine in the Garden* (1964), Michael Gilmore's *American Romanticism and the Marketplace* (1985), David Reynolds's *Beneath the American Renaissance: The Subversive Vision in the Age of Emerson and Melville* (1988), and David Leverenz's *Manhood in the American Renaissance* (1989), This list of hybrid works is by no means inclusive, and I have not even mentioned the many fine articles that shed light on Thoreau's life and work.

Canby's biography, *Thoreau,* published in 1939 was a landmark in many respects, even if Harding and Meyer find it "disappointing" in some ways:

> Canby was the first to make extensive use of the large and hitherto chiefly unpublished correspondence of the Ward Family, Two members of the Ward family boarded with the Thoreaus for many years. It was they who introduced the Thoreaus to the Sewall family, and they kept up a voluminous, gossipy correspondence filled with intimate details of the Thoreau family life. Canby made extensive and judicious use of this material, printing much of it verbatim. He was also the first biographer of Thoreau to have available such invaluable tools as Wusk's edition of Emerson's letters and Odell Shepard's edition of Alcott's journals, making wise use of both. Canby ... included a more detailed discussion of Thoreau as a writer than had previously appeared. Finally, Canby created a very human portrait by placing greater emphasis on the emotional factors that made Thoreau the man he was.

However, according to Harding and Meyer, the biography "is filled with factual errors (some of which were corrected in later impressions) and the vitally important Harvard period in Thoreau's life is very inadequately covered. ... But the major weakness ... was his handling of the relationship between Thoreau and Emerson's wife."[9]

In my view, Canby's book was the first full-scale biography to probe deeply and with some psychological acuity into the romantic involvement of Henry and John Thoreau with Ellen Sewall and into some of the dynamics of the Emerson-Thoreau relationship, He argues that there *was* what he called a "Transcendental Triangle. It is a family tradition that he did not know John was in love until after his brother's death in '42. This, I am sure, is not true, but he may well not have known it until ... 1840."[10] It seems likely to me that Henry knew, at least indirectly, of John's feelings in the summer and fall of 1839. I argued in *Young Man Thoreau* that no biographer had yet realized the extent to which Thoreau's journal reveals his preoccupation with this rivalry, even in 1939, and the far-reaching implications of that rivalry. With regard to the contention that Henry "loved" Lidian, my belief is that there *was* some attraction between Thoreau and Lidian and that it caused them both-and Mr. Emerson—some discomfort and anxiety. However, though the relationship may have had romantic and oedipal overtones, the overt quality of the relationship hovered between that of elder sister-brother and mother-son. It would, I think, be blowing the matter out of proportion to call it a "romance."

The next significant link in the chain of Thoreau biography was Raymond Gozzi's remarkable, if inevitably controversial, 1957 Freudian doctoral dissertation, "Tropes and Figures: A Psychological Study of David Henry Thoreau." It still remains a mystery to me why Gozzi's important work was not published as a book soon after its completion. One wonders what resistances such a Freudian study might have encountered. In any case, among his findings, based on a meticulous and careful reading of Thoreau's own writings, were that Thoreau's early life left him basically insecure that he emerged. from childhood with an unresolved Oedipus complex; that his unconscious image of his father was of a wild, violent force, that he had a mother-fixation; that Thoreau was a "compulsive, obsessive personality;" that Thoreau's life was "not particularly happy or unhappy" that he associated God with father and mother with nature; that the publication of *Walden* was an "assertion of maturity"; that his "fear of success" after publishing *Walden* led to a physical breakdown in 1855–1857.

Thoreau's hostility toward the state, Gozzi believes, was predominantly an expression of hostility toward his father and, to some extent, his mother. Gozzi speaks of Thoreau's "unconscious homoerotic orientation," Emerson is seen as a "father figure" with whom Thoreau finally competed for success and for women-mother figures. The death of his father in 1859 was deeply guilt provoking, even leading Thoreau to wish himself dead. John Brown's violence toward the state acted as "a projection of Thoreau's seething un-conscious aggression, and his defense of Brown represented his effort to rationalize and justify this aggression to the superego. When Brown was hanged by the state, Thoreau unconsciously experienced the event as a judgment on himself," Thoreau's fatal illness, then, was at least in part psychosomatic—representing retaliation of the superego for the aggressive feelings he had expressed against all his "judges."[11]

Carl Bode's article "The Half-hidden Thoreau" drew extensively on Gozzi's work. The article first appeared in *The Massachusetts Review* in Autumn 1962 and was subsequently republished as part of a collection of essays from the same issue, "A Centenary Gathering for Henry David Thoreau"; the title of the book was *Thoreau in Our Season,* edited by John Hicks. As Michael Meyer points out, *The Portable Thoreau,* which first came out in 1947, included an introduction by Bode, and in 1964, this widely read anthology contained "an epilogue written by Bode," the reprint of his *Massachusetts Review* essay, Thus the Freudian view of Thoreau gained some exposure and currency through Bode's work.[12]

In *Consciousness in Concord* (1958), which included the very important "missing journal volume of 1840–1841, Perry Miller, in his introduction, portrayed Thoreau in a clearly unsympathetic light. There is little compassion or empathy in his account. Thoreau is perceived as a 'Byronic egotist' who rejected the responsibilities of the human community, a person who "strove to transcend not only experience but all potential experience."[13] Miller takes a condescending, moralistic, arrogant view of his subject. Rather than seeking to understand the underlying sources and causes of Thoreau's so-called "perverseness," Miller seems content to condemn the symptoms. He offers penetrating insights into, and insults of, Thoreau, but he neglects to provide corresponding insights into himself, into the reasons he responds to Thoreau as he does. Instead of facing what he might have in common with his subject, Miller presents himself as morally superior to and essentially different from, Thoreau. Miller's denial of common bonds with Thoreau, his "objectification" of his subject, makes his perspective suspect— though not without a pithy richness, Still, Miller did do something that needed to be done: he went beyond worship of a myth and sought to characterize the "historical" Thoreau.

By contrast, Sherman Paul's splendid *The Shores of America: Thoreau's Inward Exploration* (1958) examines Thoreau's "inner life" with sympathy and with painstaking, yet inspired, scholarship. Paul's intention was to "write a spiritual biography or a biography of vocation,"[14] and he does capture Thoreau's spirit and spirituality in a moving way. The book also stressed the diverse ways in which Thoreau's thought developed and changed over the years. As Meyer observes, "Paul's chronological treatment of Thoreau's life covers his minor works as well as the major ones ... and charts his philosophical and artistic development in order to determine 'what it meant to lead a transcendental life.'"[15] However, Paul— although deeply and laudably sensitive to his subject's emotional struggles—stops short of using psychological insights and perhaps seems to intend to portray Thoreau as having resolved his conflicts. Also, as Meyer notes, "The political essays are nearly ignored. ... For Paul, Thoreau was a myth maker but not a troublemaker."[16]

In his 1959 *Thoreau Handbook* Walter Harding argued that until we have a "detailed, factual account of his day-to-day life, we cannot hope for adequate interpretive biographies" of Thoreau.[17] Harding himself answered that need with *The Day of Henry Thoreau* (1965), to this day as definitive a factual biography as we have. His book is a magnificent achievement, not just in its wealth of information but also in its *intended* avoidance of interpretation, His biography continues to be the touchstone for interpretive biographies of Thoreau. The 1982 Dover reprint, moreover, "restores those notes Harding originally had to drop for reasons of space."[18]

In the early 1970s two critics, Leon Edel and Quentin Anderson, commented on what they saw as the shortcomings of previous interpretations and made suggestions for further study. Edel spoke in *Henry D. Thoreau* (1970) of "a crisis of identity so fundamental that Thoreau rescued himself only by an almost superhuman self-organization to keep himself, as it were, from falling apart."[19] In his conclusion, Edel observed, "A much deeper history of Thoreau's psyche may have to be written to explain his tenuous hold on existence in spite of the vigor of his outdoor life: his own quiet desperation, his endless need to keep a journal ... and his early death ... in Concord during the spring of 1862.[20] In his monograph, Edel was intent on debunking myths and stressing certain biographical facts (such as Thoreau's accidental setting on fire one of the Concord woods in 1844). Generally, the monograph is quite reductive and Edel's stance toward his subject is haughty, hostile, and arrogant—somewhat reminiscent of Miller's stance in *Consciousness in Concord.* Nevertheless, Edel's work did encourage, like Miller, a demythified approach to Thoreau. And Quentin Anderson in the July 4, 1971, lead article of the *New York Times Book Review,* spoke forcefully of the need for Thoreau studies liberated from a "cultish" stance:

> We have seized on his "Walden" persona, ignoring (for this purpose) the Journal and the letters, to make a figure who would fulfill our fantasy, answer to our emotional need. On this abstracted persona most current Thoreau scholarship depends. Readers are licensed to do with books what they will, and we may say in defense of those who have used *Walden* for solace that Thoreau invited the reading most have given it. If we haven't accorded it historical meaning, it is in part because, in *Walden* Thoreau offered himself and danced away so that our pursuit of him is a ballet of the American imagination circling about the time when we most nearly possess the whole world, the undifferentiated world of childhood. The passionate attachment to this image of Thoreau substantiates the presence of a cult with roots in the past. But critics, scholars, and historians have a distinct mandate they have failed to carry out in Thoreau's case.[21]

While some of the particulars of his claim may be debated, Anderson did make a convincing "declaration of independence" from mythification.

In *Young Man Thoreau* (1977) I sought to humanize and demythicize Thoreau by tracing his development up to the time he went to Walden Pond in 1845. Making use of Erik Erikson's psychology (an Eriksonian approach seemed appropriate and fruitful in trying to understand Thoreau). I argued that the development of Thoreau's identity was a long, complex, and often painful process—by no means a fully self-assured, stately march to the beat of a different drummer. The Thoreau I portrayed experienced a fatefully prolonged adolescence and delay of adult commitments (a "moratorium," to use Erikson's term) and a troubled young adulthood before coming into his own at Walden Pond. In a society rushing headlong toward commercialism and materialism, the quest for identity could be especially problematic for sensitive, idealistic, gifted young people like Thoreau. And while Concord offered him an unprecedented range of choices, he ultimately found them limiting and limited 'His family experience greatly intensified his identity dilemmas—leading, for instance, to the development of his "militant" independence (partly because he *was* so dependent on his extraordinary, dynamic, sharp-tongued and strong-willed mother and so attached to home and local associations); his aversion to conventional success (due in part to his need not to surpass his less-than-successful, relatively passive father); his need for purity; and his sense of specialness. And though Thoreau deeply loved and respected his elder brother, John (who was more outgoing and popular), he also felt, on some level, a troubling hostility toward him.'

Harvard graduate Thoreau struggled to create and maintain a moratorium for himself while staying in the home and town he was attached to; he quit his first teaching job and avoided conventional success. He would seek to define himself as a "traveler in Concord." Aiding and shaping him was the discovery of a mentor (Emerson) to emulate and a psychologically compatible ideology (Transcendentalism) to embrace. I stress also Thoreau's uncomfortable rivalry with his brother during their courtship of Ellen Sewall (who turned them both down) and in other areas of his life (in the school where they taught together before John's health failed, in the community, and in his own family) John's death from lockjaw in 1842, I show, had a traumatic short-term impact (including an attack of psychosomatic lockjaw from which Thoreau almost died himself) and a more profound long-term influence than other biographers had recognized. The 1842–1845 period was an extended "winter of discontent," but just in the nick of time, Thoreau would move to Walden Pond where he came as close as he ever would to achieving a satisfying identity.[22]

In April 1978, a conference, "Psychology and the Literary Artist: A Case Study of Henry David Thoreau," was held at SUNY-Geneseo, masterfully organized by Walter Harding. The papers from this conference would eventually be published as *Thoreau's Psychology: Eight Essays* (1983), edited by Raymond Gozzi. At this conference a great diversity of psychological approaches was represented—from Freudian to personality testing to good old-fashioned psychological sensitivity and common sense. All approaches yielded fascinating and useful discoveries and hypotheses, making use of our contemporary knowledge about human beings and the latest developments in Thoreau scholarship. The conference represented, I think, an exciting landmark in our willingness to be open-minded, to disregard previous taboos, to engage in educated and sensitive speculation, to tolerate ambiguity. The conference helped serve to demythify Thoreau, yet in my view the Thoreau who emerged as a more fully human being seems even more worthy of our admiration.

Controversies there were, including a dialogue between Raymond Gozzi and me on the relative merits of the Freudian and Eriksonian approach. Perhaps the biggest storm at the conference (aside from a bizarre April snowstorm) was provoked by Walter Harding's courageous effort to present the facts which would suggest that Thoreau had homoerotic inclinations. It is a delicate subject but an important one. Harding's paper asked the reader to join with him in "looking for whatever evidence there may be on the subject, seeing what conclusions we might possibly draw from that evidence, and then looking at the implications of those conclusions." The major areas of evidence cited by Harding are the following: Thoreau's "Gentle Boy" poem which suggests an infatuation with Edmund Sewall, and various *Journal* entries and the essay in *A Week*, which refer to masculine relationships and affection; Thoreau's delight in observing the nude bodies of young men and his tendency to idealize young men; he says almost nothing about the physical attractiveness of young women and makes many negative comments; Thoreau did not appear to be "turned on" by women and was usually attracted to older, married women; Thoreau was openly cynical about marriage, disparaging it regularly; his attitude toward sex, marked by a combination of prudishness, abhorrence, asceticism, and even fear; the "oddness" of the Ellen Sewall affair, its strange lack of fervor—perhaps indicating that Thoreau was trying to conform; and comments by several close friends of Thoreau. Harding observes, "There is enough evidence that I believe we can safely conclude that Thoreau does show a homoerotic inclination that is stronger than that of the so-called 'typical' or 'average' man."

Harding does not think it likely that Thoreau had an active homosexual involvement. Though Thoreau had homoerotic inclinations, Harding says, "he was too conditioned by the society he lived in to accept them, and too conscientious to indulge them. My best guess would be that what he said about his relationship with women—that is, that it was 'virginal'—could also be said about his relationships with men." His homoerotic orientation, Harding speculates, "may have been rooted in his family background of a strong mother and a shy, retiring father and the repressed sexuality of the Thoreau household, which consisted largely of 'old maids' and bachelors. His homoeroticism may have served as a catalyst to rebellion. Society forced him to turn away from his homoerotic inclinations he may well have sublimated them by turning to his love of nature. Harding further speculates that his creativity may have grown out of his feelings of guilt over his homoeroticism and his efforts to combat it," Harding admits that these are "pretty far-ranging speculations"—and oversimplified for purposes of this paper. He challenges someone to provide "foundation" for this "castle in the air"—if it can be done.[23]

In his Afterword to the 1982 Dover edition of *The Days of Henry Thoreau*, Harding observes that "even though I wrote *The Days*, as one reviewer noted, 'as though Sigmund Freud never existed' (that was done intentionally on my part, I might add), I believe that psychology, when carefully handled, can give us a great deal of insight into personality and creativity." He cites *Young Man Thoreau* as "an excellent example of such a work and I look forward. to the sequel that Professor Lebeaux promises us."[24] In 1984 my *Thoreau's Seasons* was published. It picked up essentially where *Young Man Thoreau* left off and dealt with the period from Thoreau's going to Walden in 1845 to his death in 1862.[25] Time and space do not permit me to provide a detailed summary here, nor allow me to begin to do justice to the many fine Thoreau studies published in the 1980s, some of which have been mentioned earlier. Suffice it to say that we have continued to make great strides in our attempts to understand Thoreau more fully. However, given this paper's title, special mention should be made of Robert Richardson's *Henry Thoreau: a Life of the Mind* (1986). Michael Meyer indicates in *The Transcendentalists* (1984), "Nearly twenty years after Harding's *Days*, there is still no comprehensive full-length biography that brings together the accumulated facts of Thoreau's life and the critical insights about his writings that have developed alongside these facts. We need that book."[26] Without going into detail here, I think that Richardson's book meets many of the needs set forth by Meyer. In my view, one of the most significant contributions of Richardson's book is its rich, erudite exploration of how Thoreau's reading—considered in, and interwoven with, the vividly portrayed contexts of his times, life, and writings—influenced and informed his intellectual and creative development. This impressive book establishes beyond any doubt that Thoreau was, virtually to the end of his life, a committed seeker, reader, student, and scholar as well as writer: he *was* an "American Scholar."[27]

Underlying my own views of Thoreau biography is an assumption that Thoreau is strong enough, has such vitality and integrity as a whole person and gifted artist, that he could never be seriously cut up or cut down by psychological analysis, or by any particular biographical approach or bias. Indeed, probably more than most writers, Thoreau makes holistic claims on us—he insists that we finally see him whole. The ongoing work of Thoreau biography may be seen as leading us toward a fresh new synthesis, a humanized, non-reductive, honest, and compassionate understanding of the remarkable human being who was Henry David Thoreau. With respect to Thoreau biography, "The sun is but a morning star."

## Notes

1. Bernard Malamud, *Dubin's Lives* (New York: Avon Books, 1980), p. 29.

2. Malamud, p. 20.

3. Walter Harding and Michael Meyer, *The New Thoreau Handbook* (New York: New York Univ. Press, 1980), pp. 24–25. Other important bibliographical discussions of Thoreau biography were Walter Harding, *A Thoreau Handbook* (New York: New York Univ. Press, 1959); Lewis Leary, "Henry

David Thoreau" in *Eight American Authors, Revised Edition,* ed. James Woodress (New York: W.W. Norton & Company, 1971), pp. 129–171 and Michael Meyer, "Henry David Thoreau" in *The Transcendentalists A Review of Research and Criticism,* ed, Joel Myerson (New York: Modern Language Association of America, 1984), pp. 260–285.

[4]Erik Erikson, "On the Nature of Psycho-Historical Evidence: In Search of Gandhi," *Daedalus* 97, no. 3 (Summer 1968): p. 695.

[5]See Michael Meyer, *Several More Lives to Live: Thoreau's Political Reputation in America* (Westport, Conn.: Greenwood Press, 1977).

[6]Harding and Meyer, p. 24.

[7]Meyer, "Henry David Thoreau," p. 271.

[8]See Leo Marx, "Introduction" to *Excursions* (New York: Corinth Books, 1962), pp. v–xiv; William Howarth, *The Book of Concord: Thoreau's Life as a Writer* (New York: Viking, 1982); Richard Lebeaux, *Thoreau's Seasons* (Amherst: Univ. of Massachusetts Press, 1984) Robert Richardson, *Henry Thoreau: A Life of the Mind* (Berkeley: Univ. of California Press, 1986).

[9]Harding and Meyer, pp. 21–22.

[10]Henry Seidel Canby, *Thoreau* (Boston: Houghton Hifflin Co., 1939), p. 116. See pp. 106–127 for an in-depth discussion of the "Transcendental Triangle."

[11]This summary comes from my unpublished paper, "Recent Psychological Approaches to Thoreau: The Geneseo Conference" and is based on his paper for that conference as well as his "Tropes and Figures: A Psychological Study of Henry David Thoreau" (Dissertation, New York University, 1957).

[12]Meyer, *Several More Lives to Live,* p. 172.

[13]Perry Miller, *Consciousness in Concord* (Boston: Houghton Mifflin Co., 1958, pp, 33–34. Miller apparently had read at least a "digest" of Gozzi's dissertation and may well have been influenced by Gozzi's work.

[14]Sherman Paul, *The Shores of America: Thoreau's Inward Exploration* (Urbana: Univ. of Illinois Press, 1958), p. vii.

[15]Meyer, "Henry David Thoreau," pp. 270–271.

[16]Meyer, *Several More Lives to Live,* p. 121.

[17]Harding, *A Thoreau Handbook,* p. 31.

[18]Meyer, "Henry David Thoreau," p. 265.

[19]Leon Edel, *Henry D. Thoreau* (Minneapolis: Univ. of Minnesota Press, 1970), p. 43.

[20]Edel, p. 43.

[21]Quentin Anderson, "Thoreau on July 4," *The New York Times Book Review,* 4 July 1971, p. 18.

[22]See *Young Man Thoreau* (Amherst: Univ. of Massachusetts Press, 1977).

[23]This summary is from my unpublished paper, "Recent Psychological Approaches to Thoreau: The Geneseo Conference." Harding's paper was published as part of *Thoreau's Psychology: Eight Essays,* ed. Raymond Gozzi (Lanham, Md.: University Press of America, 1983).

[24]Walter Harding, "Afterword to the Dover Edition," *The Days of Henry Thoreau* (New York: Dover Publications, 1982), p. 473.

[25]See *Thoreau's Seasons* (Amherst: Univ. of Massachusetts Press, 1984).

[26]Meyer, "Henry David Thoreau," pp. 265–66.

[27]See Robert Richardson *Henry Thoreau: A Life of the Mind* (Berkeley: Univ. of California Press 1986).

# Part V

❖

# THOREAU IN WORCESTER

# Some Thoughts of
# Henry David Thoreau

❖

As the stars looked to me when I was a shepherd in Assyria, they look to me now, a New-Englander. The higher the mountain on which you stand, the less change in the prospect from year to year, from age to age. Above a certain height there is no change. I am a Switzer on the edge of the glacier, with his advantages and disadvantages, goitre, or what not. ... I have had but one spiritual birth (excuse the word), and now whether it rains or snows, whether I laugh or cry, fall farther below or approach nearer to my standard; whether Pierce or Scott is elected,—not a new scintillation of light flashes on me, but ever and anon, though with longer intervals, the same surprising and everlastingly new light dawns to me, with only such variations as in the coming of the natural day, with which, indeed, it is often coincident.

*—Letter to H.G.O. Blake (February 27, 1853)*

The West of which I speak is but another name for the Wild; and what I have been preparing to say is, that in Wildness is the preservation of the World. Every tree sends its fibres forth in search of the Wild. The cities import it at any price. Men plough and sail for it. From the forest and wilderness come the tonics and barks which brace mankind. Our ancestors were savages. The story of Romulus and Remus being suckled by a wolf is not a meaningless fable. The founders of every State which has risen to eminence have drawn their nourishment and vigor from a similar wild source. It was because the children of the Empire were not suckled by the wolf that they were conquered and displaced by the children of the Northern forests who were.

I believe in the forest, and in the meadow, and in the night in which the corn grows. We require an infusion of hemlock-spruce or arbor-vitæ in our tea.

*— "Walking"*

I am amused to see from my window here how busily man has divided and staked off his domain. God must smile at his puny fences running hither and thither everywhere over the land.

*—February 20, 1842*

After spending four or five days surveying and drawing a plan incessantly, I especially feel the necessity of putting myself in communication with nature again, to recover my tone, to withdraw out of the wearying and unprofitable world of affairs. The things I have been doing have but a fleeting and accidental importance, however much men are immersed in them, and yield very little valuable fruit. I would fain have been wading through the woods and fields and conversing with the sane snow. Having waded in the very shallowest stream of time, I would now bathe my temples in eternity. I wish again to participate in the serenity of nature, to share the happiness of the river and the woods. I thus from time to time break off my connection with eternal truths and go with the shallow stream of human affairs, grinding at the mill of the Philistines; but when my task is done, with never-failing confidence I devote myself to the infinite again. It would be sweet to deal with men more, I can imagine, but where dwell they? Not in the fields which I traverse.

*—January 4, 1857*

And for my afternoon walks I have a garden, larger than any artificial garden that I have read of and far more attractive to me—mile after mile of embowered walks, such as no nobleman's grounds can boast, with animals running free and wild therein as from the first—varied with land and water prospect, and above all, so retired that it is extremely rare that I meet a single wanderer in its mazes. No gardener is seen therein. You may wander away to solitary bowers and brooks and hills.

*—June 20, 1850*

# Worcester in the 1850s

❖

## Albert B. Southwick

When Charles Dickens visited Worcester on February 5, 1842, he was struck by its temporary appearance:

> There was the usual aspect of newness on every object, of course. All the buildings looked as if they had been built and painted that morning, and could be taken down on Monday with very little trouble. In the keen evening air, every sharp outline looked a hundred times sharper than ever. The clean cardboard colonnades had no more perspective than a Chinese bridge on a teacup. ... [1]

To Dickens in 1842, Worcester was a dull, small village of wooden houses. By 1849, when Henry Thoreau made his first visit here, the population had doubled to about 16,000, business activity had tripled, brick factories were humming on Union Street, and the town had adopted a city charter.

It is easy to explain why Worcester was destined to become an industrial colossus. It had long been a community of tradesmen, mechanics, architects, and shops. Card clothing manufacture[2] had begun in nearby Leicester as early as 1790. Factory production in textiles, shoes, farm implements, and many other things were well established by the 1820s. Ichabod Washburn was drawing wire by the 1830s. The Worcester County Mechanics Association was founded in 1842 and flourished so mightily that it was able to build Mechanics Hall only fifteen years later. The Boston–Worcester Railroad began operating in 1835, and by 1850 Worcester was the crossroads of New England, with twenty-four trains a day arriving and departing on six railroads.

It is not so easy to explain why Worcester also become a hotbed of reform ideas and activity. But it did. A whole string of radicals—Abby

Kelley Foster, Stephen Symonds Foster, Lucy Stone, Thomas Wentworth Higginson, John Milton Earle, Eli Thayer—either lived here or made it their base of operations. The weekly *Massachusetts Spy*, and, after 1845, the daily *Worcester Spy* crusaded for Abolition, temperance, women's rights, and other causes. The first and second national Women's Rights Conventions were held here in 1850 and 1851. In 1854 an attempt by a Virginia slave catcher to capture a freed slave here caused a near riot. The lectures presented by the Worcester County Lyceum and the Antislavery Society featured most of the main agitators of the day—Wendell Phillips, Frederick Douglass, William Lloyd Garrison, Thomas Wentworth Higginson, John P. Hale, Salmon P. Chase, Charles Sumner, Lucy Stone, Abby Kelley Foster, Horace Greeley—even John Brown of Osawotamie. In January 1857, Worcester was host to a "Disunion Convention" called to see how the free North could separate from the slave South.

That was one side of Worcester—the city of radical reform and noble dreams. The other side was less attractive. As the immigrant Irish began to pour into Worcester in the 1840s and 1850s, nativist feelings rose, as they did in Boston and other cities. In 1855 and again in 1857, Worcester had a Know-Nothing mayor, George W. Richardson. The Know-Nothings were strong enough to force T. W. Higginson off the School Committee. Although the Know-Nothing tide receded as the new Republican Party took shape, the underlying resentment against immigrants bubbled to the surface periodically for the next half-century.

To understand Worcester and its lively intellectual spirit in those years, we need to look back. Worcester, a typical frontier settlement, got a big break in 1731, when it was designated the seat of the new Worcester County. That meant a courthouse, court sessions, a thriving legal profession, and political activity galore. The first newspaper in the region, the *Massachusetts Spy*, began publishing in Worcester in 1775. The American Antiquarian Society was founded here by Isaiah Thomas in 1812. On one of his visits to Worcester, Thoreau, much impressed, noted that the Society's library was larger than Harvard's.

Josiah Holbrook's Lyceum movement, which did so much to spread ideas across the new nation, began in the adjacent town of Millbury and other nearby towns in the mid 1820s. The Worcester County Lyceum was organized in 1827. It developed steadily and began to assemble a library. By the 1850s, Worcester audiences had heard most of the noted speakers available, including Ralph Waldo Emerson, William Thackeray, Theodore Parker, George Curtis, Thomas Wentworth Higginson and, of course, Thoreau, who sometimes lectured here in private homes.

Something else made Worcester receptive to reform ideas. Quakers, who had settled in the adjacent town of Leicester in the 1730s, began to filter into Worcester by the turn of the century. The Quakers were noted for their business abilities and their social conscience. They were the earliest of Abolitionists and leaders in the women's rights movement.

Abby Kelley Foster was a prime example. Some think that their lack of a male clergy—they had no clergy at all—made it easier for the Quakers to accept the idea of female equality.

The Worcester Quaker settlement—linked to similar settlements down the Blackstone Valley—was small but extraordinarily influential. One family in particular—the Earles—was at the heart of the Worcester establishment.

John Milton Earle was editor and owner of the *Massachusetts Spy* and the *Worcester Spy* from 1820 to 1858, state representative in the 1840s, president of the Horticultural Society, Worcester postmaster, and state commissioner for Indian affairs. Through the *Spy*, he set much of the reform agenda for the community during those crucial years. His wife, Sarah H. Earle, chaired the first Women's Rights Convention in 1851. Thomas Earle was secretary of the Disunion Convention in 1857 and was also secretary of the Lyceum. They all supported Eli Thayer's Emigrant Aid Society, aimed at sending Free Soilers to settle Kansas. Edward and Timothy Earle ran the big T. K. Earle card clothing factory on Grafton Street. Edward Earle served as mayor of the city. Ann B. Earle, his wife, was elected to the Worcester School Committee in 1868, years before Massachusetts women had the vote. Their daughter also was elected to the School Committee. The Earles were friends of Theophilus Brown, T. W. Higginson, and Harrison Blake. John Milton Earle may have met Thoreau at either Blake's or Brown's house, although there is nothing on record to prove it.

A lively account of the 1850s in Worcester can be found in the diary of Stephen C. Earle, a younger cousin who was to become a noted Worcester architect. Growing up in a family at the center of things, and sharing a keen interest in the events of the time, Stephen Earle had a ringside seat. His diary is peppered with references to slavery, the Kansas–Nebraska Act, the Anthony Burns case and the Butman riot, the Disunion Convention, the emigration to Kansas, and the nomination of John C. Frémont as well as family and city matters. Earle rarely missed a Lyceum lecture. He heard Frederick Douglass, Henry Wilson, Charles Sumner, Salmon P. Chase, John P. Hale, Wendell Phillips, T. W. Higginson, Stephen Foster, Theodore Parker, and many others less prominent. On April 3, 1856, he heard the Hutchinson family sing and "was enchanted with the concert." He heard other speakers, too, including one by "Thorough of Concord":

> It was a strange sort of a lecture. The subject was "What shall it profit a man if he shall gain the whole world and lose his own soul," His lecture did not seem to have much to do with his subject. I slept part of the evening—[3]

Despite that, he portrays a lively community, filled with activities ranging from the annual Cattle Show, exhibits at the Horticultural Society,

Lyceum lectures, and the establishment of a literary society. Most lectures were held at Brinley Hall or at the old City Hall on the common. But on September 3, 1855, Earle reported: "A great day for Worcester. the corner stone of the mechanics hall laid with great ceremony." Eighteen months later he was at the grand opening, when 3,000 people jammed into the hall. It now is restricted to 1,600.

The Worcester that Stephen Earle described was a city on the verge of tremendous growth and radical changes in its thinking. It would become a force in Abolition and women's rights as well as an industrial powerhouse. But did any of this lead Henry Thoreau to consider Worcester his second home? Probably not. Neither its manufacturing prowess nor its reform movements were central to his thinking. What attracted Thoreau to Worcester were the two men who became his most dedicated disciples—Theophilus Brown and Harrison Blake. He came here time and again to talk with them, to saunter around Lake Quinsigamond, to hike to Asnebumskit and Mt. Wachusett, and to enjoy the company of people who early on had cherished his unique qualities and considered him a genius.

## Notes

[1]Charles Dickens, *Amercian Notes* in *The Complete Works of Charles Dickens*, vol 3. New York and Boston: Books Inc., 1899(?), p. 63.

[2]Carding is a process used to comb out the fibers of cotton, wool, or flax so that the fibers can be spun into thread or yarn. In the mechanized carding process, belts with steel pins are used. The new material is fed into a machine that presses it onto the belts as they turn, thus carding the fibers. These belts are called "card clothing," and their manufacture was a major industry in Leicester.

[3]The Journals of Stephen C. Earle 1853–1858. Edited by Albert B. Southwick. Worcester: Worcester Bicentennial Commission, 1976, p. 30. This lecture, an early version of Thoreau's "Life without Principle," was delivered in Worcester on January 4, 1855.

---

**ALBERT B. SOUTHWICK** is a graduate of Clark University, Worcester. He is the former editor of the Worcester *Telegram and Evening Gazette*.

# Starting from Home
## A Writer's Reminiscences of Worcester and Thoreau

❖

### Milton Meltzer

When I look back at the schools I went to here in Worcester they seem like some kind of mildly authoritarian society. They meant well, but they didn't allow for democracy in the classroom. The principal ordered teachers around, and they in turn ordered us around. Our sole responsibility was to come to class, to come on time, and to do our assignments. A few students rebelled against the rigid discipline, but in a way that only did harm to themselves and brought about no change for the better.

Ideas? No, there was little said about them. Few teachers at Classical High School made any attempt to get us to think. What they did ask us was to remember—facts, dates, theorems, laws of government or of physics, the succession of kings or presidents, classification of plants or animals, rules of grammar—and only long enough to spew them back on paper at testing time. With few exceptions, they did not ask us to think critically, or give us any hint of how to do that. Such teaching kills the natural curiosity, instead of encouraging it. What too many students learned best was how to con the teacher and beat the system.

The shining exception to those teachers was Anna Shaughnessy, a graduate of Radcliffe. She was Irish and Catholic (like so many of our teachers), young, tall, and very thin. She wore glasses and kept her brown hair in a bun. Her brilliance, her sparkling wit, delighted us. English was her field, but her mind roamed free over all the world of knowledge. Whether it was Hamlet or a poem of Browning's or a novel by George Eliot, in her class it became far more than an assignment to be gotten through dutifully. She paid close attention to the text of the work, but more, she brought in the lives of the writers, the world they lived in, the influences that shaped their ideas, and the language that gave form to them. You could speak up freely in her class, say whatever you felt or thought, without fear of being made to look foolish or ignorant. If she caught you faking, she could be caustic. But so long as you tried honestly to grapple with what you were reading, you were encouraged. She challenged everyone to do better, knowing how little use we made of our capacities And most of us responded.

It was Anna Shaughnessy who introduced me to Henry David Thoreau. His *Walden* was not part of the course of study. (It still isn't, in most schools.) She asked me if I knew of this Massachusetts writer who had lived only some thirty miles away, in Concord. I didn't. Without scaring me off with proclaiming how great he was, she said that he had lived and died in obscurity. But not like some Romantic poet in a dusty garret. He had done all kinds of work for a living—a schoolteacher, surveyor, pencil-maker, gardener, carpenter, mason, lecturer, naturalist, as well as a keeper of a personal journal into which he wrote some two million words.

Living in Concord, not far off, Thoreau often came to Worcester to visit with his two closest friends. One was Harrison Gray Otis Blake, a native of Worcester. Thoreau had known Blake casually for some years. Blake had been two years ahead of him at Harvard, had gone on to Harvard Divinity School to become a preacher, and then had quit the pastorate. He returned to Worcester to teach at a private school for girls.

The closer connection came when Blake read an essay of Thoreau's and, in 1848, wrote him a long letter in praise of it. By this means Thoreau won his first major disciple, and, as Walter Harding said, "began the most important correspondence of his life." During the fourteen years remaining to him, Thoreau wrote some fifty letters to Blake, his devoted friend. The letters were so extraordinary that Blake would invite Worcester friends to come over to his home, at 3 Bowdoin Street, to hear extracts from them.

Theirs was a correspondence given to philosophical issues, not intimate exchanges. But from his Worcester friend, Thoreau got the recognition and encouragement that did so much to sustain him during those long years when fame passed him by.

The other Worcester friend was Theophilus Brown, a tailor whose home was at 10 Chestnut Street and whose shop—elegantly called the "Emporium of Fashion"—was on Main Street. He was known as "the wit of Worcester" and the local intelligentsia enjoyed his company.

Blake and Brown helped to organize lectures for Thoreau, to give before small gatherings at Blake's parlor, or to larger audiences in local halls. Thomas Wentworth Higginson, Worcester's radical minister, and militant abolitionist, spoke of Brown as "the freshest and most original mind in Worcester, by vocation a tailor, and sending out more sparkles of wit and humor, over his measuring tape and scissors, than anyone else would extract from Rabeleis or Montaigne."

When Thoreau began a lecture tour to read chapters from his unpublished Walden, Blake invited him to give a series of three at Brinley

146

Hall in Worcester, to audiences of about a hundred. This was in the spring of 1849. In the years to come Thoreau would lecture more often in Worcester than in any other place but Concord.

In June of 1856, Thoreau came to Worcester to spend a whole week with his friends, giving four nights to the Brown family and to the Blake family. Walter Harding reports that he astonished one of his hostesses when he showed up with neither a valise nor a traveling bag, but with a few of his belongings wrapped up in a red bandanna, or tied up in a sheet of brown wrapping paper. During this week, he walked in the woods, examined the collections in the Natural History Museum, rode around Lake Quinsigamond, studied a man's collection of reptiles and stuffed animals, and took a ride to Sutton where he explored Purgatory Chasm, a spectacular gorge which prehistoric earth movement had filled with house-sized fragments of rock.

While here in town, Thoreau dropped in at Maxham's daguerreo-type studio, on Harrington corner, to have his picture taken at the request of a Michigan correspondent. He paid fifty cents to have three portraits made. He gave one to Blake, and another to Brown. The other he sent to Michigan, writing that "my friends think [it] is pretty good—though better looking than I."

About six months later, in November of 1856, Thoreau was on his way home to Concord from a stay in New Jersey. He had to change trains in Worcester. It was 3:30 A.M. when he got out of the cars at the depot, and he had to kill time until 6:20 A.M. If it had been a reasonable hour, he would have dropped in on Blake or Brown. But not at half past three in the morning! So instead, he said in a letter to Blake,

> I walked up & down the Main Street at half past 5 in the dark, and paused long enough in front of [Theo] Brown's store trying to distinguish its features. ... Meanwhile a watchman seemed to be watching me & I moved off. Took another turn around there, a little later, and had the very earliest offer of the Transcript from an urchin behind, whom I actually could not see, it was so dark. So I withdrew, wondering if you and B[rown] would know that I had been there. You little dream who is occupying Worcester when you are all asleep. Several things occurred to me that night, which I will venture to say were not put in the Transcript A cat caught a mouse at the depot, & gave it to her kitten to play with. So that world-famous tragedy goes on by night, as well as by day. ... Also I saw a young Irishman kneel before his mother, as if in prayer, while she wiped a cinder out of his eye with her tongue; and I found it was never too late (or early?) to learn something. (The Correspondence of Henry David Thoreau, Dec. 6, 1856, Walter Harding and Carl Bode, eds.)

The last time Thoreau spoke in Worcester was on November 3, 1859, at Washburn Hall. It was his "Plea for Captain John Brown," who had been captured during the raid on Harper's Ferry, where he hoped to strike a blow against slavery. Thoreau, long an abolitionist, and whose home was a hideout for fugitive slaves, wanted to explain the meaning of the sensational event and to celebrate John Brown's courage and his devotion to the cause of Black freedom. The Worcester audience responded warmly to the speech.

When Thoreau, two years later, was mortally ill with tuberculosis, his old friends Harry Blake and Theo Brown skated down the river to Framingham, to visit him in January of 1862, and repeated the journey several times until his death in May. Years later Brown recalled:

> We found him pretty low, but well enough to be up in his chair. He seemed glad to see us; said we had not come much too soon. ... There was a beautiful snowstorm going on the while which I fancy inspired him, and his talk was the best I ever heard from him—the same depth of earnestness, and the same infinite depth of fun going on at the same time.

> I wish I could recall some of the things he said. I do remember some few answers he made to questions from Blake. Blake asked him how the future seemed to him. "Just as uninteresting as ever" was his character-istic answer. A little while after he said, "You have been skating on this river, perhaps I am going to skate on some other." And again, "Perhaps I am going up country." He seemed to be in an exalted state of mind for a long time before his death He said it was just as good to be sick as well—just as good to have a poor time as a good time ... (*The Days of Henry Thoreau,* Walter Harding. New York: Alfred A. Knopf, 1965, p. 456.)

Well, I remember Miss Shaughnessy telling me, "Thoreau was born in 1817, about a hundred years before you. But I think, when you read him, you'll find his ideas, his way of looking at life, will mean as much to you as if he were born yesterday."

So I started with a copy of *Walden* that I borrowed from her. I found it hard going at first. But soon he drew me deep into the story of his two-year adventure living in his cabin at Walden Pond. He combined those two years into one, giving the book the rhythm and flow of the changing seasons. It opens with the building of the cabin in the spring, goes on to planting, weeding, and harvesting his bean patch, watching the ice harvesting, and ice-fishing in the winter, and closes with the return of spring.

Out of that pattern came his central symbol—rebirth and renewal, not only in the world of nature around us, but of our own inner development. Many years after my first encounter with Thoreau, I went back to Walden once more. On the last page I read this passage:

> Every one has heard the story which has gone the rounds of New England, of a strong and beautiful bug which came out of the dry leaf of an old table of apple-tree wood, which had stood in a farmer's kitchen for sixty years, first in Connecticut, and afterward in Massachusetts,—from an egg deposited in the living tree many years earlier still, as appeared by counting the annual layers beyond it; which was heard

gnawing out for several weeks, hatched perchance by the heat of an urn. Who does not feel his faith in a resurrection and immortality strengthened by hearing of this? Who knows what beautiful winged life, whose egg has been buried for ages under many concentric layers of woodenness in the dead dry life of society, deposited at first in the alburnum of the green and living tree, which has gradually been converted to the semblance of its well-seasoned tomb,—heard perchance gnawing out now for years by the astonished family of man, as they sat round the festive board,—may unexpectedly come forth from amidst society's most trivial and handselled furniture, to enjoy its perfect summer life at last! (*Portable Thoreau*, rev. ed. Carl Bode. New York: Penguin Press, 1977, p. 571.)

---

**MILTON MELTZER**, biographer and historian, is the author of more than eighty books for young people and adults, including *A Thoreau Profile* (with Walter Harding) and *Thoreau: People, Principles and Politics*. Born in Worcester, Massachusetts, and educated at Columbia University, Meltzer has written or edited for newspapers, magazines, books, radio, television, and films. Among the many honors for his books are five nominations for the National Book Award.

# Part VI

❖

# THE ECOLOGY OF WALDEN WOODS

# Some Thoughts of
# Henry David Thoreau

❖

Our village life would stagnate if it were not for the unexplored forests and meadows which surround it. We need the tonic of wildness,— to wade sometimes in marshes where the bittern and the meadow-hen lurk, and hear the booming of the snipe; to smell the whispering sedge where only some wilder and more solitary fowl builds her nest, and the mink crawls with its belly close to the ground. At the same time that we are earnest to explore and learn all things, we require that all things be mysterious and unexplorable, that land and sea be infinitely wild, unsurveyed and unfathomed by us because unfathomable. We can never have enough of nature. We must be refreshed by the sight of inexhaustible vigor, vast and titanic features, the sea-coast with its wrecks, the wilderness with its living and its decaying trees, the thunder-cloud, and the rain which lasts three weeks and produces freshets. We need to witness our own limits transgressed, and some life pasturing freely where we never wander.

*—Walden ("Spring")*

A man is rich in proportion to the number of things which he can afford to let alone.

*—Walden ("Where I Lived and What I Lived For")*

What shall we do with a man who is afraid of the woods, their solitude and darkness? What salvation is there for him? God is silent and mysterious.

*—November 16, 1850*

I went to the woods because I wished to live deliberately, to front only the essential facts of life, and see if I could not learn what it had to teach, and not, when I came to die, discover that I had not lived.

—*Walden ("Where I Lived and What I Lived For")*

Each town should have a park, or rather a primitive forest, of five hundred or a thousand acres, where a stick would never be cut for fuel, a common possession forever, for instruction and recreation. We hear of cow-commons and ministerial lots, but we want men-commons and lay lots, inalienable forever. Let us keep the New World new, preserve all the advantages of living in the country. There is meadow and pasture and wood-lot for the town's poor. Why not a forest and huckleberry field for the town's rich? All Walden Wood might have been preserved for our park forever, with Walden in its midst, and the Easterbrooks Country, an unoccupied area of some four square miles, might have been our huckleberry-field.

—*October 15, 1859*

It would be worth the while if in each town there were a committee appointed to see that the beauty of the town received no detriment. If we have the largest boulder in the county, then it should not belong to an individual, nor be made into door-steps.

As in many countries precious metals belong to the crown, so here more precious natural objects of rare beauty should belong to the public ...

We cut down the few old oaks which witnessed the transfer of the township from the Indian to the white man, and commence our museum with a cartridge-box taken from a British soldier in 1775!

—*January 3, 1861*

# The Ecology of Walden Woods

❖

### Edmund A. Schofield

## Introduction and
## Historical Perspective

## Location and Physical Description

The "Walden Ecosystem" is a 2,680-acre tract of woodland lying east of the Sudbury River in the towns of Lincoln and Concord, Middlesex County, Massachusetts, at 42°27' north latitude, 71°20' west longitude. It is approximately fifteen miles west northwest of the State House in Boston and is bisected along a southwest–northeast axis by the Lincoln–Concord town line. About 1,500 acres are in Lincoln, 1,180 acres in Concord. Its prevailing elevation is 45 to 90 meters (about 150 to 300 feet) above mean sea level, with extreme elevations of approximately 35 meters (about 110 feet) on its western edge along the Sudbury River and 105 meters (nearly 350 feet) on the summits of Fairhaven Hill and Pine Hill. Several till-covered hills rise above the general terrain, Fairhaven Hill in Concord and the Pine Hill–Bare Hill complex in Lincoln being the largest, and there are a number of wetlands, streams, ponds, and pools within and on the edges of the Ecosystem.

Most of the Walden Ecosystem lies within the Concord River watershed, which in turn is part of the Merrimack River watershed. The rest of the Ecosystem (that portion immediately surrounding Sandy Pond) is part of the Charles River watershed. The surface of Sandy Pond, whose western shoreline marks the eastern boundary of Walden Woods, is 70.5 meters (230 feet) above sea level, while the surface of Walden Pond, located at the center of the Ecosystem, is at approximately 48.5 meters

(160 feet). As noted, the Sudbury River is 35 meters (about 110 feet) above sea level. This east-to-west elevational sequence—Sandy Pond at 70.5 meters elevation, Walden Pond at 48.5 meters, and the Sudbury River at 35 meters—suggests an east-to-west hydrological gradient.

The bulk of the Walden Ecosystem consists of Northern Pine–Oak Forest, a type of biotic community that develops on dry, well-drained sandy soils in many parts of the northeastern United States. The rest of the Walden Ecosystem is divided among several other types of biotic community: wetland, stream, pond, and Transition Forest. While these

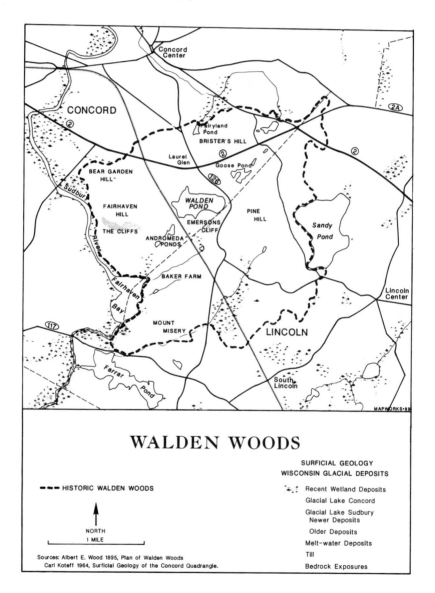

# WALDEN WOODS

◄►► HISTORIC WALDEN WOODS

↑
NORTH
1 MILE

Sources: Albert E. Wood 1895, Plan of Walden Woods
Carl Koteff 1964, Surficial Geology of the Concord Quadrangle.

SURFICIAL GEOLOGY
WISCONSIN GLACIAL DEPOSITS

Recent Wetland Deposits
Glacial Lake Concord
Glacial Lake Sudbury
  Newer Deposits
Older Deposits
Melt–water Deposits
Till
Bedrock Exposures

latter communities differ from the Northern Pine–Oak Forest, they are here considered a part of the Walden Ecosystem because (1) they occur on the same or geologically closely related land forms, and (2) they are regulated by the same or a closely linked hydrologic regime as the Forest. The Northern Pine–Oak Forest is a sub climax community; that is, it is a persistent community that is prevented from succeeding to the climatic climax stage.

The presence of the Walden Ecosystem and its persistence during the three and one-half centuries since European settlement are attributable directly to the area's distinctive surficial geology, which itself is a product of the Pleistocene glaciation. It led to the development of an "island" of Northern Pine–Oak Forest within the surrounding "sea" of Transition Forest. The environmental factors responsible for development of the original pine–oak forest on the site made it difficult for raising crops. Since good agricultural land lay nearby, Walden Woods was farmed much less often and extensively than those nearby areas and has thus remained in woodland for centuries. Even before the advent of the Europeans in Massachusetts, however, Walden Woods was different from the surrounding primeval forest. It was an example of a local, or edaphic, climax community (one strongly influenced by special, localized soil conditions), whereas most of the larger surrounding forest was a regional, or climatic, climax community (one whose character and composition were determined primarily by the regional climate and not by any local peculiarities of the substrate).

Despite marked fluctuations in its borders due to logging and shifting socioeconomic pressures, Walden Woods has retained its ecological integrity and identity virtually from Colonial times. The Ecosystem's principal biotic community is Northern Pine–Oak Forest. Maps dating from the early 19th century and possibly earlier, legal records (e.g., deeds and wills), published and unpublished literary references, drawings, photographs, and other documents attest to its permanence as a dominant feature of the landscape.


## Soils

Even after generations of use by human beings the soil of a site—if it has not been physically disrupted by, say, massive earth-moving operations—retains the telltale imprint of the natural conditions under which the soil developed after the glacier retreated. Even when ditched and drained, for example, a wetland soil is identifiable as a wetland soil. The thick layer of partially decomposed organic matter laid down over millennia in the wetland imparts certain diagnostic characteristics to the wetland's soil and remains after it has been exposed to the air, oxidizing gradually. By the same token, a soil developed in an arid site is recognizable as such long after it has been artificially flooded. It takes decades for a layer of organic matter to accumulate in the new wetland, just as it will take decades for that in the natural wetland to disappear through oxidation; even then a soil scientist probably could distinguish the developing soil from a natural wetland soil.

The same principle applies to farmed woodland soils: even after decades of farming, a woodland soil is identifiable as a woodland soil. Furthermore, one can even make reasonable inferences about the types of trees—deciduous versus evergreen, for example, or a mixture of both—that grew in a woodland soil before it was cleared for farming. Only after decades or centuries under the new environmental conditions do the original "telltale imprints" fade from a soil as the new conditions impose a different profile upon it. Through the process of ecological succession a mature biotic community develops on a site in response to regional climatic and local geological factors. The community continues to occupy the site until some natural or man-made force (e.g., fire, lumbering) intervenes. The soil of a particular site develops in response to the plants that grow in it for centuries or millennia. Thus, the soil reflects its original natural vegetative cover, even after the vegetation has been removed, and it continues to do so for many decades or centuries. (Only the most severe catastrophe could obliterate altogether the vegetation's impact on the soil.) For this reason, perennial ecological factors and relationships, not the chance presence or absence of trees at the time a particular survey, map, or photograph was made, must be used to arrive at a full and accurate delineation of Walden Woods.

Soils consist of (1) an inorganic, mineral component—the "matrix material," or "parent material"—and (2) an organic component consisting of still-living, dead, and partially decomposed organisms (plants, animals, and microorganisms). Under the influence of such climatic factors as temperature and precipitation and such more local and site-specific factors as drainage and topography, soils develop on newly exposed matrix material, whether it be lava, water-laid sediments, or, as in the case of Walden Woods, glacial deposits.

As the Pleistocene glacier retreated from the Concord area about 14,000 years ago, it deposited some of the great load of material it had scraped from the land during its advance, laying down an unsorted mixture of mineral rubble, ranging in size from clay to boulders, known as "till." In the vicinity of Walden Woods till is confined mainly to the uplands, where it covers the hills of the pre glacial terrain. The glacier deposited another kind of glacial drift in Concord, "glaciofluvial" (i.e., glacial-river) and "glaciolacustrine" (i.e., glacial-lake) deposits graded by flowing and pooling meltwater from the ice. Every summer, streams of water ran over the land and were ponded, sometimes in lakes covering many miles, against the ice front and the surrounding hills, and over-flowed through spillways. The streams carried the mixed materials of till but dropped them in a more graded fashion than did the ice itself. These glacial deposits may be broadly sorted into two categories, outwash plains and bottom deposits. Outwash plains consist of gravels and coarse sands, while lower-lying lake-bottom deposits consist of fine sand and silt, and even a little clay (very little in the Concord area).

In the millennia that followed the glacier's retreat, first tundra plants and then forests reclothed the newly exposed landscape. The forests underwent a series of changes as a result of climatic shifts, the immigration of species, natural catastrophes, and (especially since the arrival of Europeans three hundred and fifty years ago) human impact.

## Woodlands

Woodlands were plentiful in Concord at the time of settlement, consisting primarily of pine.[1] The Indians had cut and burned over "sandy fertile locations" for farming on the upland plains along the Musketaquid River (their name for the Sudbury–Concord River system); to attract game, they had cleared paths by burning the underbrush.[2, 3, 4] The first European settlers of Concord had tried to cultivate the uplands, but found them to be of poor quality and unsuitable for sustained agriculture.[5]

By applying modern ecological knowledge to the fragmentary and disparate accounts of Concord's earliest history, one can develop a meaningful and coherent picture of the area as it was when the first Europeans arrived. There can be no doubt that the Indians regularly set fire to the woods there so as to create open space in which to cultivate crops, and to provide open woodlands for game animals, such as deer, which foraged on the tender grasses that came in after the fires. Nor can there can be any doubt that pine and oak were abundant, that the uplands were sandy and poorly suited for farming, or that the forests on the uplands had been burned by the Indians for millennia. Among those upland pine and oak forests, if not principal among them, must have been what came to be called Walden Woods.

The Europeans learned early on—the hard way (by failure)—that such upland soils were unsuitable for farming. They must soon have concluded to leave the uplands in woodland, as a source of fuel and timber, raising their annual crops on the less arid and more fertile lowlands. The forest they encountered on the infertile, sandy uplands (dubbed "sand plains" by geomorphologists about a century ago) would have been Northern Pine–Oak Forest, whether in its earlier or later successional stages of development. Because of the continual burning to which it was subjected, whether the burning was caused by Indians or by lightning, Walden Woods and similar tracts of woodland growing on sand plains seldom if ever attained full maturity as biotic communities—i.e., they never developed into the "climatic climax" forest of the region, the

Transition Forest. After the Europeans arrived fire remained an important influence on Walden Woods. Yet, while subclimactic because of the fires, most of Walden Woods was seldom if ever—and then only temporarily—cultivated for crops.

Some of Walden Woods' soils theoretically were suitable for agriculture (that is, were not stony, shallow, steep, water-logged, etc.), but they were excessively drained and "droughty" and could have been farmed profitably only with the aid of irrigation. Given, first, the presence of much better agricultural soils nearby in Concord, second, the expense of irrigation, third, the primitiveness or even absence of irrigation technology during the first two or three centuries of European occupation, and, fourth, the general exodus of farmers from New England to the Midwest beginning in the mid-nineteenth century, it would have been unnecessary, exorbitantly expensive, foolhardy, or even impossible to squander one's meager resources irrigating the dry soils of the Walden Woods Sand Plain. Those soils were best left in woodland that could be tapped for fuel wood and timber as needed. The evidence presented graphically on maps dating from before 1820 to the present day—namely, the presence of virtually continuous woodland on the Walden Woods Sand Plain—reflects these ecological and economic realities. Any exceptions to the general rule (and there have been a few exceptions) have been sporadic and short-lived.

## Settlement

Concord was settled in 1635 by persons attracted by the abundance of meadow hay along the rivers, by the rich lowland soils derived from a glacial lake (Glacial Lake Concord) that has disappeared slowly, and by its several untilled cornfields, recently abandoned by the sparse Indian population. Added resources were the abundance of virgin pine and hardwood timber: white oak on the flanks of the six or more hills and drumlins, chestnut on the acid gravels of glacial kames and drift, white pine in many stands throughout the town.

Shattuck[6] states (page 9) that the settlers established their farm lots "extending back from the road across the Great Fields and Great Meadows, and in front across the meadows on Mill Brook ... because it contained land of easy tillage ... ," while (page 15) "The uplands, which the first planters selected for cultivation, proved to be of a poor quality. ..."

Concord was predominantly a farming community based on cattle, hay, and grain for over two hundred years, gradually supplemented by sales of cordwood and market-garden produce to the growing Boston market. Thus, Concord became a compact village surrounded by scattered farms, with much arable land, pasture, and many woodlots, the last harvested in rotation without destroying woodland habitat.[7]

Were the preglacial geology, the Pleistocene geology, and the land-use history of the Concord–Lincoln area not what they are, Thoreau would never have been able to write a book like Walden or discover the principles of ecological succession, because the Walden Woods area would not have remained largely in woodland but would have been cleared and exploited for annual crops like those raised in the surrounding parts of Lincoln and (especially) Concord. There is a direct cause-and-effect link between the surficial geology of the Walden Woods area and both the substance and character of Thoreau's writings—his Journal, *Walden,* and "The Succession of Forest Trees," in particular. There is a similar cause-and-effect link between surficial geology and the character of the Walden Woods Northern Pine–Oak Forest ecosystem. Absent Glacial Lake Concord and its bottom deposits and there would have been no prosperous intellectual center like the village of Concord to draw Emerson and the other Transcendentalists. Absent the ice-contact glacial-stream and glacial-lake features of Glacial Lake Sudbury and there would have been no accessible Walden Woods back country for Thoreau and thus neither the book *Walden* nor the essay "Succession of Forest Trees," nor beautiful landscape to inspire him and the other Concord authors. The history of Concord—economic, social, literary, and spiritual—is inextricably linked to the glaciation-created surficial geology of the surrounding countryside. The juxtaposition of rich farmland (bottom deposits of Glacial Lake Concord) and wooded back country (ice-contact deposits of Glacial Lake Sudbury) created a dynamic interplay between the ongoing development of American culture as manifested in Concord's lively political, social, and intellectual life in pre-Civil War America on the one hand, and the nearby still-wild tracts of land on the other. Concord was America in microcosm: it reflected a burgeoning social and economic force on the one hand and the country's wilderness and frontier heritage on the other. Concord's history and geography, related like hand to glove, reflected and influenced development of the larger culture.

In 1841, four years before the Fitchburg Railroad was built, George B. Emerson, author of several works on the trees and forests of Massachusetts, spoke at the Legislature's Tenth Agricultural Meeting, held at the State House, on "The Forest Trees of Massachusetts."[8] Discussing the economic uses of the state's forests, he mentions, among other uses, fuel and timber (for shipbuilding, etc,); but as the railroads were very new at the time and apparently had scarcely yet affected the state's forests, he makes no mention of them. A mere five years later, even as Thoreau was living in Walden Woods, Emerson reported to the Legislature again, mentioning this time the large quantities of wood being consumed to fuel railroad locomotives throughout the state.[9] He does not mention the Fitchburg Railroad, however, perhaps because it was so new, having been built only two years before.

After 1844, the Fitchburg Railroad would transport many cords of wood from Walden Woods and elsewhere to Boston. During the 1850s the railroads of the United States used some 4 million to 5 million cords of wood per year to generate steam in locomotive engines, and after the switch to coal, which itself had powerful environmental effects, the railroads still needed wood for ties. In 1910, one-fourth of the nation's total wood consumption was accounted for by this use.[10]

During the early 1850s Thoreau witnessed with anxiety and sadness the accelerating destruction of Walden Woods, mourning their destruction. He describes in Walden "timber like long battering-rams going twenty miles an hour against the city's walls." In 1853, he complained, "You can walk in the woods in no direction but you hear the sound of the axe."[11]

Expressing alienation at the loss, he records in his Journal (entry for January 24, 1852):

> I see in the woods [in Walden Woods] the woodman's embers, which have melted a circular hole in the snow, where he warms his coffee at noon. ...

> These woods! Why do I not feel their being cut more sorely? Does it not affect me nearly? The axe can deprive me of much. Concord is sheared of its pride. I am certainly the less attached to my native town in consequence. One, and main, link is broken. I shall go to Walden less frequently.[12]

## Effects of Glaciation

New England's forests were shaped by the revegetation of a glaciated landscape over the past 12,000 years. The glacier left behind a wet, poorly drained landscape over much of northern New England; it left thin, 'ledgy' soils and wide areas of sand plain in southeastern Massachusetts, Rhode Island, and Cape Cod. Walden Pond, surrounded by oaks and pines, is an example of the sandy landscapes.[13] By definition, Walden Woods lies east of the Sudbury River (there are similar glacial-lake deposits west of the river). Its soils are acidic, indicating that evergreen trees (viz, pines) played a dominant role in their development. On average, the water table of the Walden Pond Unit of the Walden Ecosystem is deep, lying at least 10 feet below the surface of the ground. The soils are very porous, permeable, rapidly draining (most of them being excessively drained) and are therefore "droughty"—i.e., they are prone to desiccation during the hottest summer months (July, August). The groundwater of the Walden Pond Unit flows outward from Walden Pond in a radial or centrifugal pattern, like the spokes from the hub of a wheel.

In a long passage in the "Spring" chapter of *Walden*, Thoreau describes leaf-like patterns created by the oozing of "sand of every degree of fineness and of various rich colors, commonly mixed with a little clay," from the Deep Cut, a twenty- to forty-foot high bank created a year or two before Thoreau went to live in Walden Woods, when the Fitchburg Railroad was being built. This passage, probably the artistic and philosophical climax of the entire book, owes its existence to the water-laid deposits of Glacial Lake Sudbury.

Thoreau's comments in his Journal and in *Walden* reflect his awareness of the hydrological unity of the Walden Ecosystem. "I have said that Walden has no visible inlet or outlet," he writes in his Journal, but it is on the one hand distantly and indirectly related to Flint's [i.e., Sandy] Pond, which is more elevated [for example, 70.5 meters above sea level in 1987, as opposed to Walden's 48.5 meters], by a chain of small ponds coming from that quarter [Goose Pond, Little Goose Pond, and the smaller nearby kettle ponds], and on the other hand directly and manifestly related to Concord [i.e., Sudbury] River, which is lower [circa 35 meters above sea level], by a similar chain of ponds [the Andromeda Ponds], through which in some other geological period it may have flowed thither [into Fairhaven Bay, an embayment of the Sudbury River], and by a little digging, which God forbid, could probably be made to flow thither again.[14]

In *Walden*, Thoreau states:

The pond [i.e., Walden Pond] rises and falls, but whether regularly or not, and within what period, nobody knows, though, as usual, many pretend to know. It is commonly higher in the winter and lower in the summer, though not corresponding to the general wet and dryness. ... It is remarkable that this fluctuation, whether periodical or not, appears to require many years for its accomplishment. I have observed one rise and a part of two falls, and I expect that a dozen or fifteen years hence the water will again be as low as I have ever known it. Flint's Pond, a mile eastward, allowing for the disturbance occasioned by its inlets and outlets, and the smaller intermediate ponds also, sympathize with Walden, and recently attained their greatest height at the same time with the latter. ...

As for the inlet or outlet of Walden, I have not discovered any but rain and snow and evaporation, though perhaps, with a thermometer and a line, such places may be found, for where the water flows into the pond it will probably be coldest in summer and warmest in winter. ...[15]

Thoreau was acutely aware of the correlation between soils and vegetation. For example, in his Journal entry for October 17, 1860, he states:

It is an interesting inquiry what determines which species of these [trees—viz., white pine, pitch pine, oaks, white birch, and red maple] grow on a given tract. It is evident that the soil determines this to some extent, as of the oaks only the swamp white stands in our meadows, and, so far as these seven trees are concerned, swamps will be composed only of red maples, swamp white oaks, white birch, and white pine. By removing to upland we get rid of the swamp white oak and red maples in masses, and are reduced to white and pitch pine, oaks, and white birches only, i.e., of those that are abundant and important.

Even as early as 1837, when he was only twenty, Thoreau was well aware of the correlation between plants and soils:

Every part of nature teaches that the passing away of one life is the making room for another. The oak dies down to the ground, leaving within its rind a rich virgin mould, which will impart a vigorous life to an infant forest—The pine leaves a sandy and sterile soil—the harder woods a stronger and fruitful mould—

So this constant abrasion and decay makes the soil of my future growth. As I live now so shall I reap. If I grow pines and birches, my virgin mould will not sustain the oak, but pines and birches, or, perchance, weeds and brambles, will constitute my second growth. —[16]

## The Northern Pine–Oak Forest
## in Thoreau's Writing

Huckleberries (Gaylussacia spp.) were important to Henry Thoreau. At his death he left the draft of an essay, "Huckleberries," which was not published until 1970. It derives its character from the nature of huckleberries and therefore from the ecosystems and plant communities of which they were a part. The following quotation shows that Thoreau was aware of their role in ecological succession:

If you look closely you will find blueberry and huckleberry bushes under your feet, though they may be feeble and barren, throughout all our woods, the most persevering Native Americans, ready to shoot up into place and power at the next election among plants, ready to reclothe the hills when man has laid them bare and feed all kinds of pensioners. What though the woods be cut down; it appears that this emergency was long ago anticipated and provided for by Nature, and the interregnum is not allowed to be a barren one. She not only begins instantly to heal that scar, but she compensates us for the loss and refreshes us with fruits such as the forest did not produce. As the sandal wood is said to diffuse a perfume around the woodman who cuts it—so in this case Nature rewards with unexpected fruits the hand that lays her waste.

I have only to remember each year where the woods have been cut just long enough to know where to look for them. It is to refresh us thus once in a century that they bide their time on the forest floor. If the farmer mows and burns over his overgrown pasture for the benefit of the grass, or to keep the children out, the huckleberries spring up there more vigorous than ever. ... All our hills are, or have been, huckleberry hills, the three hills of Boston and no doubt Bunker Hill among the rest. ...

In short all the whortleberry bushes in the Northern States and British America are a sort of miniature forest surviving under the great forest, and reappearing when the latter is cut.[17]

Compare this passage with a statement from Kricher's discussion of the Northern Pine–Oak Forest: "Huckleberries are usually abundant [in the Northern Pine–Oak Forest], along with other heaths [sheep laurel is a heath also], and add to the dense shrub layer. ... "[18]

In *Walden* Thoreau states, "There were scores of pitch-pines around my house, from one to four inches in diameter. ..."[19] In his Journal he speculates on the place of the pitch pine in ecological succession: ... Though the pitch pines are the prevailing trees at the south end [of Hubbard's Wood, a part of Walden Woods], I see no young pitch pines under them. [20]

Perhaps this is the way that a natural succession takes place. Perhaps oak seedlings do not so readily spring up and thrive within a mixed white pine and oak woods as pines do,—in the more open parts,—and thus, as the oaks decay, they are replaced by pines rather than by oaks.

But where did the pitch pines stand originally? Who cleared the land for its seedlings to spring up in? It is commonly referred to very poor and sandy soil, yet I find it growing on the best land also. The expression "a pitch pine plain" is but another name for a poor and sandy level. It grows on both the sand and [in] the swamp, and the fact that it grows on the sand chiefly is not so much evidence that it prefers it as that other trees have excluded it from better soil. If you cut down the pines on the pitch pine plain, oaks will come up there too. Who knows but the fires or clearings of the Indians may have to do with the presence of these trees there? They regularly cleared extensive tracts for cultivation, and these were always level tracts where the soil was light—such as they could turn over with their rude hoes. Such was the land which they are known to have cultivated extensively in this town, as the Great Fields and the rear of Mr. Dennis's,—sandy plains. It is in such places chiefly that you find their relics in any part of the county. They did not cultivate such soil as our maple swamps occupy, or such a succession of hills and dales as this oak wood covers. Other trees will grow where the pitch pine does, but the former will maintain its ground there the best. I know of no tree so likely to spread rapidly over such areas when abandoned by the aborigines as the pitch pine—and next birches and white pines.

Thoreau mentioned a number of the other indicator species of the Northern Pine–Oak Forest, some of them in the book *Walden* itself. For example, he several times mentions the pine warbler (which Walton, page 166, describes as "an uncommon spring migrant and summer resident" in the Sudbury River valley) in his Journal (quoted in Francis H. Allen's *Notes on New England Birds*[21] and in Helen Cruickshank's *Thoreau on Birds*[22], though none of these appear to refer to Walden Woods, but to other sandy plains in Concord, in these cases formed in Glacial Lake Concord. In *Walden*, he mentions the brown thrasher and the bluebird twice each,[23] the chipmunk and towhee once each.[24]

He mentions the whip-poor-will, another indicator bird of the Northern Pine–Oak Forest, several times. For example:

> Regularly at half-past seven, in one part of the summer, after the evening train had gone by, the whip-poor-wills chanted their vespers for half an hour, sitting on a stump by my door, or upon the ridge-pole of the house. They would begin to sing almost with as much precision as a clock, within five minutes of a particular time, referred to the setting of the sun, every evening. I had a rare opportunity to become acquainted with their habits. Sometimes I heard four or five at once in different parts of the wood, by accident one a bar behind the other, and so near that I distinguished not only the cluck after each note, but often that singular buzzing sound like a fly in a spider's web, only proportionally louder. Sometimes one would circle round and round me in the woods a few feet distant as if tethered by a string, when probably I was near its eggs. They sang at intervals throughout the night, and were again as musical as ever just before and about dawn.[25]

The great horned owl,[26] another indicator species of the Northern Pine–Oak Forest, makes at least two long appearances in *Walden*— evidence that it indeed is an indicator species for Walden Woods (and, therefore, that Walden Woods can be characterized as a Northern Pine–Oak Forest). "I was also serenaded by a hooting owl," he says in the chapter "Sounds."[27] "… It reminded me of ghouls and idiots and insane howlings. But now one answers from far woods in a strain made really melancholy by distance.—Hoo hoo hoo, hoorer hoo; and indeed for the most part is suggested only pleasing associations, whether by day or night, summer or winter.

"I rejoice that there are owls," he writes. "Let them do the idiotic and maniacal hooting for me. …"

Thoreau later writes, in the "Winter Animals" chapter of *Walden*:

> For sounds in winter nights, I heard the forlorn but melodious note of the hooting owl indefinitely far; such a sound as the frozen earth would yield if struck with a suitable plectrum, the very lingua vernacula of Walden Wood, and quite familiar to me at last, though I never saw the bird while it was making it. I seldom opened my door in a winter evening without hearing it; Hoo hoo hoo, hooer hoo, sounded sonorously, and the first three syllables accented somewhat like how der do; or sometimes hoo hoo only. One night in the beginning of winter, before the pond froze over, about nine o'clock, I was startled by the loud honking of a goose, and, stepping to the door, heard the sound of their wings like a tempest in the woods as they flew over my house. They

passed over the pond toward Fair Haven, seemingly deterred from settling by my light, their commodore honking all the while with a regular beat. Suddenly an unmistakable cat owl from very near me, with the most harsh and tremendous voice I ever heard from any inhabitant of the woods, responded at regular intervals to the goose, as if determined to expose and disgrace this intruder from Hudson's Bay by exhibiting a greater compass and volume of voice in a native, and boo-hoo him out of Concord horizon. What do you mean by alarming the citadel at this time of night consecrated to me? Do you think I am ever caught napping at such an hour, and that I have not got lungs and a larynx as well as yourself? Boo-hoo, boo-hoo, boo-hoo! It was one of the most thrilling discords I ever heard. And yet, if you had a discriminating ear, there were in it the elements of a concord such as these plains never saw or heard. [28]

In the last paragraph of "Sounds" Thoreau recapitulates, mentioning again several of the indicator species (as well as non-indicator species) of the Northern Pine–Oak Forest:

> ... I kept neither dog, cat, cow, pig, nor hens, so that you would have said there was a deficiency of domestic sounds; ... An old-fashioned man would have lost his senses or died of ennui before this. Not even rats in the wall, for they were starved out, or rather were never baited in,—only squirrels on the roof and under the floor, a whip-poor-will on the ridge-pole, a blue jay screaming beneath the window, a hare or woodchuck under the house, a screech owl or a cat owl behind it, a flock of wild geese or a laughing loon on the pond, and a fox to bark in the night. Not even a lark or an oriole, those mild plantation birds, ever visited my clearing. ... A young forest growing up under your windows, and wild sumachs and blackberry vines breaking through into your cellar; sturdy pitch pines rubbing and creaking against the shingles for want of room, their roots reaching quite under the house. Instead of a scuttle or a blind blown off in the gale,—a pine tree snapped off or torn up by the roots behind your house for fuel. ...[29]

At the end of the "Spring" chapter of *Walden* is a paragraph remarkable for the wealth of ecological insights it supplies about the composition of Walden Woods, its plants and animals. In light of modern ecological knowledge of biotic communities, Thoreau's words, while those of a consummate artist and not designed to fit the constraints of scientific nomenclature, reflect accurately the natural world he saw around his house in Walden Woods.

> Early in May, the oaks, hickories, maples, and other trees, just putting out amidst the pine woods around the pond, imparted a brightness like sunshine to the landscape, especially in cloudy days, as if the sun were breaking through mists and shining faintly on the hillside here and there. On the third or fourth of May I saw a loon in the pond, and during the first week of the month I heard the whip-poor-will, the brown thrasher, the veery, the wood pewee, the chewink, and other birds. I had heard the wood thrush long before. The phœbe had already come once more

and looked in at my door and window, to see if my house was cavern-like enough for her, sustaining herself on humming wings with clinched talons, as if she held by the air, while she surveyed the premises. The sulphur-like pollen of the pitch pine soon covered the pond and the stones and rotten wood along the shore, so that you could have collected a barrel full. ...[30]

In this single paragraph of *Walden*, Thoreau explicitly mentions four indicator species of the Northern Pine–Oak Forest and, by implication, a fifth. Together with the bluebird, chipmunk, and great horned owl and other species mentioned elsewhere in *Walden*, more than seven indicator species of the Northern Pine–Oak Forest are mentioned in this single volume. Thoreau does give short shrift to the indicator herbaceous species and vines, however, mentioning none of them in *Walden*. Even so, it is remarkable that a literary work should contain such an ecologically meaningful catalogue of species for one site. The fact that *Walden* does contain such a catalogue demonstrates the intimate link between *Walden* the book and Walden Woods. *Walden*'s ecological veracity answers, perhaps, to the book's artistic and spiritual veracity.

Had Walden Woods not existed, or had its character been different from what it is, the book *Walden* would have been a very different book—had it been written at all. The Walden Woods Sand Plain provided habitat for a distinct biotic community, the Northern Pine–Oak Forest, as well as a place of resort for Thoreau. Both the existence and character of Walden Woods were crucial prerequisites for the creation of *Walden*. Had the Walden Ecosystem been significantly different from what it is,[31] then Walden would have been significantly different, or nonexistent. If, for example, the Walden Ecosystem had not been the Walden Ecosystem we know, then the following features of the landscape would have been absent from the book *Walden*: Walden Woods, Walden Pond, Brister's Hill, Brister's Spring, the Deep Cut, the Boiling Spring, Baker Farm, Pleasant Meadow. The former human inhabitants of Walden Woods, many of them freed slaves or social outcasts, and Alek Therien, the woodchopper, would not have lived or worked in Walden Woods. Were the hydrological regime of the sand plain (which is a kame and delta complex) not what it is, Thoreau would have had been unable to develop the psychologically powerful symbolism he did around the "sympathic" subterranean relationship of Walden, Goose, and Sandy ponds to each other, their simultaneous rising and falling, and so on.

To be sure, as a master artist he might have used other features of landscape to achieve the same or a similar end, but Walden would have been quite a different book had he been forced to do so. And, of course, had Walden Woods not been a Northern Pine–Oak Forest, many of the animals (whip-poor-will, towhee, great horned owl, thrasher) and plants (pines, shrub oak, huckleberry) would likely not have been found there. Had there been no dry, sandy soil at Walden, but a richer soil, the beanfield might never have existed. Had Walden Pond not been oligotrophic, but eutrophic, its waters would not have been so pure as they are, and Thoreau would have had to resort to other strategies and devices in his art. Were there no sand plain, or kame delta, there would have been no Brister's Spring beside which Thoreau could refresh himself after a hard morning's work in the beanfield, no Deep Cut whose oozing sands and clays provided Thoreau with the perfect symbol of renewal and rebirth.

Clearly, the very substance and character of Walden are linked inextricably, in a cause-and-effect manner, to the characteristics of the Walden Ecosystem. To the humble scenery and unremarkable denizens of this living ecosystem we owe, in large measure, one of the masterpieces of American literature.

# Notes

[1]Charles H. Walcott. *Concord in the Colonial Period* (Boston, 1884), page 17.

[2]Charles H. Walcott. *Concord in the Colonial Period* (Boston, 1884), page 17.

[3]Barbara Robinson. From Musketaquid to Concord: Trading places. Pages 17 to 24 in Shirley Blancke and Barbara Robinson. *From Musketaquid to Concord: The Native and European Experience.* (Concord, Massachusetts, 1985), page 20.

[4]Howard S. Russell. *Indian New England before the Mayflower* (Hanover, New Hampshire, and London, 1980), page 121.

[5]Lemuel Shattuck. *A History of the Town of Concord* (Boston and Concord, 1835), page 15. Jorgensen (*A Sierra Club Naturalist's Guide to Southern New England* [San Francisco, 1978], page 107, says that, "Following the custom of aboriginal people in many parts of the world, the Indians regularly set fire to the woods both to clear it for agriculture and for primitive game management. ... "

[6]Lemuel Shattuck. *A History of the Town of Concord; Middelsex County, Massachusetts, from Its Earliest Settlement to 1832; and of the Adjoing Towns, Bedford, Acton, Lincoln, and Carlisle; Containing Notices of County and State History Not Heretofore Published* (Boston and Concord, 1835), pages 9 and 15.

[7]Richard Jefferson Eaton. *A Flora of Concord* (Cambridge, Massachusetts, 1974), pages.

[8]"Forest Trees of Massachusetts," *Boston Semi-Weekly Advertiser*, March 27, 1841.

[9]George B. Emerson.] *Report on the Trees and Shrubs Growing Naturally in the Forests of Massachusetts* (Boston, 1846), pages 15 and 16.

[10]John H. White, Jr., "Railroads: Wood To Burn," pages 199 to 201, 215 *in:* Brooke Hindle, editor, *Material Culture in the Wooden Age* (Tarrytown, New York, 1981). Quoted in Thomas J. Lyon, editor, *This Incomperable Lande: A Book of American Nature Writing* (Boston, 1989), page 56.

[11]Henry D. Thoreau. *The Journal of Henry D. Thoreau* (New York, 1962), Volume 1, page 521 (28 January 1853).

[12]Henry D. Thoreau. *The Journal of Henry D. Thoreau* (New York, 1962), Volume 1, page 330.

[13]Lloyd C. Irland. *Wildlands and Woodlots: The Story of New England's Forests* (Hanover, New Hampshire, and London, 1982), page 19.

[14]Henry D. Thoreau. *Journal* (Boston, 1906), Volume 4, page 425 (5 December 1852).

[15]Henry D. Thoreau. *Walden* (Princeton, New Jersey, 1971), pages 180, 181, 292.

[16]Entry for October 24, 1837, in: Henry D. Thoreau. *Journal. Volume 1: 1837–1844.* Edited by E. H. Witherell, W. L. Howarth, R. Sattelmeyer, and T. Blanding (Princeton, New Jersey, 1981), page 5.

[17]Henry D. Thoreau, "Huckleberries," edited by Leo Stoller ([Iowa City and New York?], 1970).

[18]John C. Kricher. *A Field Guide to Eastern Forests [of] North America* (Boston, 1988), page 66.

[19]Henry D. Thoreau. *Walden* (Princeton, New Jersey, 1971), page 280.

[20]*Journal*, Volume 14, pages 271 and 272 (26 November 1860).

[21]Francis H. Allen, editor. *Notes on New England Birds by Henry D. Thoreau* (Boston and New York, 1910).

[22]Helen Cruickshank, compiler. *Thoreau on Birds* (New York, Toronto, and London, 1964).

[23]Henry D. Thoreau. *Walden* (Princeton, New Jersey, 1971), pages 158 and 319 and pages 302 and 310, respectively.

[24]Henry D. Thoreau. *Walden* (Princeton, New Jersey, 1971), page 302 (as "striped squirrel") and page 319 (as "chewink"), respectively.

[25]Henry D. Thoreau. *Walden* (Princeton, New Jersey, 1971), pages 127 and 128. Thoreau also mentions whip-poor-wills on pages 86, 128, 129, and 319.

[26]According to Walton (page 140),the great horned owl is "An uncommon permanent resident" of the Sudbury River valley. Its "hooting is noted at dawn or dusk often on the edge of extensive woodlands," he says; the bird is "more often heard than seen." It was encountered every year but two during the annual Concord Christmas Count from 1960 to 1983 (*ibid.*, page 195).

[27]Henry D. Thoreau. *Walden* (Princeton, New Jersey, 1971), page 125. Francis H. Allen (page 183) and Helen Cruickshank (page 111) both identify Thoreau's "hooting owl" as the great horned owl [*Bubo virginianus*], as did Thoreau himself in his *Journal* on November 18, 1851 (where he used the alternative name for that species, "cat owl"). Forbush and May (*Natural History of the Birds of Eastern and Central North America* [Boston, 1939]), page 265) give "cat owl" and "hoot owl" as alternative names for this species. They describe its calls as "a deep-toned hoot, a blood-curdling shriek, and many others."

[28]Henry D. Thoreau. *Walden* (Princeton, New Jersey, 1971), pages 171 to 172. Edward Howe Forbush and John Bichard May (*Natural History of the Birds of Eastern and Central North America* [Boston, 1939], page 265) say that great horned owls "become vocal" in January and February. They are less vocal later in the year, "but now and then, especially in autumn, their hooting may be heard" (page 266). They are nocturnal birds (page 266), "most active in the dark of the evening and on moonlit nights, but . . . may be hooting at times at midnight in the 'dark of the moon.'"

[29]Henry D. Thoreau. *Walden* (Princeton, New Jersey, 1971), pages 127 and 128.

[30]Henry D. Thoreau. *Walden* (Princeton, New Jersey, 1971), pages 318 and 319.

[31]An ecosystem consists of both (1) abiotic and (2) biotic elements, by definition. The Walden Ecosystem thus consists of (1) the Walden Woods Sand Plain (plus the related geological elements of the Sandy Pond Unit) *and* (2) the Northern Pine–Oak Forest. Without the former, the latter would not exist; given the former, the latter *must* be what it is. The sand plain is the *sine qua non* of the latter and completely determines those aspects of its character that are not determined by regional climate. *If* an arid sand plain, *then* a Northern Pine–Oak Forest.

# The Human Impact on
# the New England Landscape

❖

**Charles F. Carroll**

"We find ourselves in a world that is already planted," Henry David Thoreau wrote less than two years before his death, but a world that "is also still being planted as at first." The naturalists of the previous era of the Enlightenment, and the Christian writers before them, had supported the "imperial" view of nature. They believed that God encouraged the human species to lord over the planet aggressively and drastically rearrange the landscape to fulfill a host of needs. The ecologists of the 18th century had argued that a benevolent deity created an extremely resilient and irrepressible natural order that was capable of surviving every one of the vigorous onslaughts of mankind. Thoreau, however, generally adhered to the views of the Romantic or Arcadian naturalists, who believed that there was a flexible, accommodating, and often turbulent vital force in nature. The operations of this animate force could be seriously interrupted, maimed, and even permanently and irreversibly changed by arrogant or even careless human intervention.[1]

Because of his own minute observations of nature, Thoreau also accepted contemporary scientific opinion that the natural order often lacked tidiness, thrift, and efficiency. He theorized that, even before the intervention of large numbers of European colonists, the woodlands of Massachusetts often had been devastated by insects, fires, severe weather, and blight. Young white oaks, sprouting in open woodland hollows and along the Concord plains, he observed in 1860, were "almost annually killed down by frost, they are so tender." In October of the same year he discovered that healthy looking acorns hanging from the white oaks in Hubbard Grove actually were sour, soft, and dead and black within. Such occurrences, he wrote, seemed to reflect "a glaring imperfection in Nature." "The [passenger] pigeons, jays, squirrels, and woodlands are thus impoverished. It is hard to say what great purpose is served by this seeming waste." Such was his ambivalent thinking about the economy of nature.[2]

When Thoreau reflected on the changes in the land brought about by the first English settlers and their descendants in ante-bellum Concord—and in hundreds of other communities in New England—he often displayed a similar sense of ambivalence and bewilderment that often turned to anguish. He had great admiration for the enterprising English settlers and their children who survived and prospered in a harsh wilderness setting. "The race that settles and clears the land," he once said, must be at war with the wilderness, "breaking nature, taming the soil, and feeding it on oats." But he also realized that the hardy pioneers and their descendants, sometimes purposefully, but also out of ignorance of ecological relationships, misused the land.[3]

By 1860 he had sauntered through thousands of miles of field and forest, examined the growth rings on countless tree stumps, and watched the pines disperse their seeds before the winds. He observed peripatetic squirrels burying their nuts, and he dug up hundreds of decaying remains of long-forgotten trees. Through these investigations, he came to realize that the original colonizers had entered a much different environment, a tree-covered landscape of much greater vigor and diversity, one that supported a much broader spectrum of habitats.[4]

Presettlement New England, and indeed the whole Northeastern section of North America, once had been a land unsurpassed in the temperate zone in ecological complexity. When the mass migration of 12,000 Puritans began in 1630, about ninety percent of the land in New England was covered with an enormous variety of trees. The first settlers encountered a vast woodland disturbed only by natural forces and by ground fires, of low intensity, ignited twice a year by Native Americans who engaged in agriculture. The Indians set these fires to destroy brush and underwood to create optimum conditions for the growth of plants with gatherable foods. They also cleared the understory to facilitate travel and to create habitats favorable to wild game. The larger trees were not destroyed by the flames, and in areas where soil, moisture, and proper separation allowed for optimum growth many of them were exceedingly old and very large. There were many white pines over 150 feet, bare of limbs over 100 feet from the ground. White oaks 100 feet tall with trunks 15 to 20 feet in circumference were common, and their horizontal spread could exceed 150 feet. There also was an abundance of wildlife, and ten square miles of these sometimes dense but often park like woodlands could support four or five black bears, two or three mountain lions, the same number of gray wolves, 200 turkeys, 400 white-tailed deer, and possibly 20,000 gray squirrels.[5]

The agricultural Indians of southern New England were a mobile people who followed a subsistence cycle in conformity with the seasons.

In late winter they tapped the maples for syrup. In late spring the women planted a crop of maize, beans, squash, and tobacco in scattered and disorderly fields. Meanwhile, the men used shells and fire to fashion canoes of chestnut wood designed for fishing in fresh and salt water. Early autumn was the time for the collection of acorns and chestnuts, as well as groundnuts and other plants. Later in the season the men broke into small bands to fish, or to stalk or snare the deer, bear, and other wild game. Frequently moving their settlements, and taking care never to overuse a single species, the New England Indians followed a practice of ecological diversity and paid homage to nature for its bounty.[6]

Like Thoreau, the spiritual leaders of the new Puritan community often looked upon this forested environment as metaphor as well as stark reality. But unlike Thoreau who, as champion of the wild, related immersion of self in wilderness to moral perfection and knowledge of God, the Puritan metaphor of wilderness almost always implied evil, barbarism, desolation, and decay. Most Puritans believed that mankind stood alone at the center of the universe and that the subjugation of this wild and savage world was part of a divine decree.[7]

Many have argued that Puritan antipathy toward wilderness on a metaphorical and spiritual level allowed many an inexperienced settler to endure extreme hardship and persist in an extremely hostile environment without reversion to savagery. The Puritans lived in the world, but they always looked beyond the order of nature toward the ultimate goal of a detached, supernatural domain, a celestial realm of everlasting beatific liberation. This dualism strengthened their resolve, and it allowed them to prove their worth in this transitory, material world by conquering its natural forces.[8]

With simple tools such as the ax and mattock, or grub-hoe, the settlers dramatically and quickly altered and even disfigured the landscape. The woodlands and entire natural habitats in New England succumbed very rapidly to those whom Thoreau later was to call the "ax-boys." Change came swiftly for a number of practical reasons. New Englanders were healthy, many children survived childhood illnesses, and longevity was high. Therefore, the English population grew very rapidly, more than doubling every twenty-five years. The colonists and their numerous descendants persisted in the practice of extensive rather than intensive farming, and they continued to do so for almost two hundred years. They also relied on domestic grazing animals for heavy tasks, for a portion of their nutritional needs, and even for some of their durable wearing apparel. Pigs and goats could survive by rooting and scavenging in the woodlands, but imported cattle and sheep fared poorly. These animals required cleared lands, the introduction of English grass and clover, and pastures closed in with mile upon mile of post-and-rail fences. Wooden fences quickly became symbols of a new artificial, humanized, European landscape, symbols of English control and dominance over what soon became a tidy cultivated patchwork set off from a messy, brutish, and chaotic wilderness.[9]

Cattle and sheep raising initially increased the wolf population, but this problem was solved by putting a price on each wolf head and destroying their habitats. Bounties for wolf heads and organized wolf drives successfully exterminated this predator in southern New England by the end of the colonial era. The extermination of the wolf, however, did little to preserve its original prey, the white-tailed deer. Competition from domestic livestock, and uncontrolled hunting, wiped out this herbivore from all but the northern sections of Vermont, New Hampshire, and Maine by the time of the American Revolution. By this time, the beaver, bear, mountain lion, wolverine, lynx, moose, and wild turkey also had vanished from southern New England. Thoreau noted that even some of the pesky insects were gone, including the black fly and the "no-see-em."[10]

By 1700 colonists had cleared over a half million acres in New England for food crops and for forage crops for cattle. Fifty years later, more than three-quarters of all cleared land in Massachusetts was devoted to the grazing of domestic animals or to the growth of hay for winter fodder. For as the land became less productive in the 18th century, especially in the older settlements, much greater acreage was needed for each domestic animal. In the beginning the amount of land had seemed inexhaustible, but by the 18th century, fathers in Concord and other towns in eastern Massachusetts were discovering that they were presiding over an ever-diminishing patrimony. There were too many sons and not enough land. The original land grants in Concord, typical of many other towns, covered 200 or 300 acres. But a small family needed about 50 to 60 acres for survival, and after the original holdings were broken up several times into smaller units, out-migration into the hills of Worcester County and to New Hampshire and Maine by younger sons became the norm. This was happening in Concord as early as 1725. By this time many coppice woods, set aside for the production of cordwood, had been cut over many times. Families used thirty to forty cords of wood a year in their huge fireplaces, burning up a total exceeding 200 million cords by the end of the colonial era. No wonder Concord was so open by 1775 that one historian tells us that "an invading army in the village center could be spotted easily from the northern heights two miles away."[11]

The commercial spirit, the spirit of capitalism, a spirit that prevailed despite—some say because of—the power of religion in the prevailing culture, was another important factor in the transformation of the New England landscape. The entire era, beginning with the initial settlement and extending into the decade following Thoreau's death, has been called "America's Wooden Age." During this period, cordwood and its derivatives furnished almost all energy for home and industry. Brick and glass kilns were fired with wood. Almost all essential products: houses, barns, fences, carts and carriages, containers, ships, and chemicals, such as potash and gunpowder, were made of wood or wood products. The bark of the oak and hemlock was required for the tanning of leather. Hardwoods such as oak and hickory were essential for the manufacture of charcoal, the high-carbon fuel that produced the intense heat required for the manufacture of cast iron, and wrought-iron bars, and a multitude of iron products.[12]

From the very beginning the export of timber and timber products to marketplaces in the West Indies, the Azores, the Canary Islands, Madeira, southern Europe, and England had been a principal means for acquiring English manufactured goods needed for a comfortable life in New England. Sawing wood by hand, either in a pit or on a trestle was extremely difficult labor. Therefore, the reciprocating saw, driven primarily by waterpower, quickly became New England's first large manufacturing machine. The white pine boards cut in the early sawmills reached far-flung markets, together with barrel staves split from the red and white oak, red and white cedar shingles, masts and spars, and ships and ship timbers—always were among the region's leading exports. Thus, the clear-cutting of timber for the oceanic trades also was a major factor in the transformation of the environment.[13]

By the time Thoreau was born in 1817, few commercial timberlands remained in southern New England. All of the white cedar in the swamps had been clear-cut, and the species did not return. By 1820 Maine had become the nation's leading timber- producing state. On his first trip to Maine in 1837 Thoreau estimated that 250 water-driven saws were operating in mills upstream from Bangor. The mission of the men on the Penobscot, he remarked, "seems to be, like so many busy demons, to drive the forest out of the country, from every solitary beaver swamp and mountain-side, as soon as possible." When the white pine was exhausted in Maine the lumbermen turned to the spruce, and the production of spruce timber began to exceed that of the white pine just about the time of Thoreau's death in 1862.[14]

Beginning in the 1850s Thoreau, under the influence of the new science, began an intense examination of forest successions and the regenerative forces of nature, still searching as always for the source of inspiration, the vital force that governed the earth. Under the spell of this holistic urge, believing that nothing is unconnected with the whole, he studied the lives and culture of dispossessed Indians, historical records, and the flora and fauna in the vicinity of Concord. By peeping "under the eyelids of time," and attempting to retrace, in reverse order, the dynamic interaction between man and the landscape that had occurred over more than two centuries, he laid out a record of environmental dismemberment and devastation. Chestnuts and hickories—and to a lesser extent, oaks— once growing in masses in Walden Woods now had become rare. These were the species that lived the longest, but were the first to become extinct under "our present system," for they were "the hardest to reproduce." Oak was the principal framing timber in New England. Hickory was used extensively for firewood, for its wood has the highest caloric value of any tree. After 1845 chestnuts, long used for lumber and fenceposts, were being used up for ties on the new rail lines.[15]

Thoreau filled his *Journal* with lamentations on the inability of farmers to understand the operations of natural forces. For two centuries, he wrote, they had been fighting nature rather than working with it. They had organized countless hunting parties to kill off squirrels when they should have been paying homage to these tree-dwelling rodents for replanting hickories, chestnuts, and oaks. When landowners clear-cut tracts of oak for firewood, they were mystified when the land was renewed, not with this species, but with pine. They often burned off the new pine, or pastured their cows among the saplings, periodically using the bushwhack to fight off the invading trees. The pines suffered terribly for ten or twenty years, but they inevitably prevailed, finally driving out the animals. The result, said Thoreau, was "that we have thus both poor pastures and poor forests." "We are a young people," he wrote, "and have not learned by experience the consequence of cutting off the forest."[16]

"Thank God, men cannot as yet fly," he wrote in one of the last entries in his *Journal* in 1861, for he would "lay waste the sky as well as the earth!" Even in Maine the wild lands were gone. The second- and third-growth forest was receding still in Concord. This is why he was particularly delighted, in November 1860, to discover Inches' Woods, "that grand old oak wood," with little underwood, that extended along both sides of what is now Route 111 in the town of Boxborough, eight miles west of Concord. Here "waving and creaking in the wind" was a seemingly "endless maze of gray oak trunks and boughs stretching far around." "Seeing this," he said, "I can realize how this country appeared when it was discovered. Such were the oak woods which the Indian threaded hereabout."[17]

Although portions of these woods had been cut, cleared, and cultivated by the time of the American Revolution, there still were many massive living trunks, principally white oak, "remarkably straight and round." The largest were ten to fifteen feet in circumference, and Thoreau estimated that some had been growing for 150 years or more. The 400 acres that still belonged to the Inches family was said to be the largest primitive oak forest remaining in Massachusetts. Thoreau did not report seeing much wildlife in these woodlands—although this was the year that he recorded the killing of a lynx in Carlisle. He did encounter "one large [passenger] pigeon-place on the top of the hill" where he first entered the woods.[18]

By 1860 Inches Woods had become a natural, living monument— a tree museum—because over the years farmers had destroyed the capacity of the land for self-renewal. When they first cleared the earth of virgin timber they had enjoyed a transitory gift of fertility given them by the thick compost and the nutrients circulated by the trees. But farming and cattle raising changed the composition and structure of most soils, and these activities drastically disturbed the environment. Void of trees, the soil temperatures in the tidy fields fluctuated greatly with the seasons. In summer the ground dried out much faster and the soil became warmer. In winter, the frost line went far deeper, and the thaws, now occurring later in the season, caused more severe lowland flooding and greater damage to property. Rapid uncontrolled runoff also left less water in the rivers and streams during the summer and fall. "The streams, perchance, are somewhat shrunk," Thoreau once said. Limited discharge in many bodies of water periodically brought mills to a halt, including the very mills that sawed the fallen timber. When the sawmills were operating they polluted the streams with sawdust, and consequently, the fish runs dwindled. In the days of Thoreau there were no longer alewives, salmon, or shad in the Concord River.[19]

Thoreau nor anyone else could devise a way to turn back time and begin the world anew. Most New Englanders still were unaware of the root causes for the changes taking place in the natural order. To prevent further environmental destruction Thoreau did advocate restraint in the use of natural resources, greater sensitivity to our dependence on nature, and more intense self-reflection on the purpose of life and one's place in the environment. To these ends he stressed the need for community-based environmental education, including the preservation of some natural monuments, such as the massive Boxborough oaks, as reminders of the wildness that once existed in every New England town. "Pray, farmers, keep some old woods to match the old deeds. Keep them for history's sake, as specimens of what the township was."[20]

In the heady days of American national consciousness, territorial expansion, sectional controversy, glorification of economic development, and significant achievements in productivity through factory organization and advanced technology, few New Englanders were willing to revert to a simpler life—indeed, the austere and ascetic existence that might be required to restore some of the original harmonies of nature. Unlike Thoreau, they did not believe in an egalitarian brotherhood with woodchucks, hawks, and foxes, nor kinship with the mice and squirrels. They continued to shoot all these so-called "vermin" on sight. Some were even ashamed of uncut woodlands, and few were willing to make the financial sacrifices necessary to keep ancient trees standing, or even beautify their towns.[21]

The woodlands did return again in many sections of New England during the decades after Thoreau's death. But they came back not because of any renewed reverence for life that he had instilled among an enlightened citizenry. Rather, they returned because so many New England farmers, unable to compete with their more productive counterparts of the American West, were forced to abandon their hardscrabble efforts in marginal, sour, and unproductive glacial till. Many trudged off to join that race of mechanical people who were bringing forth even greater and more drastic environmental changes.[22]

# Notes

[1] *The Journal of Henry D. Thoreau*, ed. Bradford Torrey and Francis H. Allen (1906; reprint ed., Dover Publishing, New York, 1962), XIV: 146; hereafter cited as JHT. For an analysis of changes in ecological thought see Donald Worster, *Nature's Economy: The Roots of Ecology* (Sierra Club, San Francisco, 1977).

[2] JHT, XIV: 148–149.

[3] JHT, III: 269–270; VIII: 149–150, 220–222.

[4] JHT, VIII: 150, 220–222; XIV: 142–143, 197, 200.

[5] William Cronon, *Changes in the Land: Indians, Colonists, and the Ecology of New England* (New York, 1983), pp. 49–51; Charles F. Carroll, *The Timber Economy of Puritan New England* (Providence, R.I., 1971), pp. 35–37; Worster, *Nature's Economy*, p. 67.

[6] Cronon, *Changes in the Land*, pp. 35–48.

[7] Peter N. Carroll, *Puritanism and the Wilderness: The Intellectual Significance of the New England Frontier, 1629–1700* (New York, 1969), pp. 86, 110, 119, 140–147. Alan Heimert, "Puritanism, the Wilderness and the Frontier," *The New England Quarterly*, 26 (1953): 361–82; Roderick Nash, *Wilderness and the American Mind* (New Haven, 1967), pp. 23–43, 84–87.

[8] Charles Lloyd Cohen, *God's Caress: The Psychology of Puritan Religious Experience* (New York, 1986), pp. 12–13, 123–133, 211, 250.

[9] JHT, VIII: 130–132; Charles F. Carroll, "The Forest Society of New England," in Brooke Hindle, ed., *America's Wooden Age: Aspects of its Early Technology* (Tarrytown, N. Y., 1975), pp. 13–36.

[10] Cronon, *Changes in the Land*, pp. 23–24, 34–35, 51, 99–101, 132–134, 159, 162; JHT, VIII: 149–150, 220–221.

[11] David Grayson Allen, *In English Ways* (New York, 1982). pp. 100, 223–36; Worster, *Nature's Economy*, p. 67; Cronon, *Changes in the Land*, p. 121; Robert A. Gross, *The Minutemen and their World* (New York, 1976), pp. 3–4, 15–16, 77–80, 86–87, 210 note 21, 213–214 note 35, 214 note 37; Thomas R. Cox, et al., *This Well-Wooded Land: Americans and Their Forests from Colonial Times to the Present* (Lincoln, Neb., 1985), pp. 62–64

[12] For the uses of wood see the articles in: Hindle, ed., *America's Wooden Age*, and Brooke Hindle, ed., *Material Culture of the Wooden Age* (Tarrytown, N.Y., 1981).

[13]Carroll, *Timber Economy*, pp. 74–97; Cox, *This Well-Wooded Land*, pp. 64–68

[14]Cox, *This Well-Wooded Land*, pp. 74–78, 89; Henry David Thoreau, *The Maine Woods*, ed. Joseph J. Moldenhauer (Princeton, N.J., 1972), p. 5.

[15]Sherman Paul, *The Shores of America: Thoreau's Inward Exploration* (Urbana, Ill., 1958), pp. 174, 182–185, 197, 358, 392–393; JHT, XIV: 133, 135, 137–138.

[16]JHT, II: 461–462; XIV: 129–131, 150–151.

[17]JHT, XIV: 141–142, 224–231, 241–249, 275, 304, 306–307.

[18]JHT, XIV: 78–81, 83–87, 230.

[19]Cox, *This Well-Wooded Land*, pp. 38–41; Cronon, *Changes in the Land*, pp. 115–116, 121–126, 155; JHT, VIII: 121–122, 149; IX: 327.

[20]JHT, XI: 299–300; XII: 387; XIV: 125–127, 304–306.

[21]JHT, I: 470; V: 246; VI: 310–311, 452; IX: 289, 343; XIII: 104.

[22]"I thought I heard the hum of a bee," Thoreau wrote in March 1856, "but perhaps it was a railroad whistle on the Lowell Railroad." JHT, VIII: 220; Carroll, *Timber Economy*, pp. 25–30.

---

**CHARLES F. CARROLL** is a professor and department chairperson at the University of Massachusetts–Lowell. He received his doctorate at Brown. His interest in the environment led him to the writings of Thoreau.

# Henry David Thoreau and
# the Environment of Concord

❖

**Brian Donahue**

If Henry Thoreau is known for anything, it is probably for his declaration "that in Wildness is the preservation of the World." Thoreau is popularly remembered as an antisocial idealist who withdrew from the civilized streets of Concord to commune with Nature in the wilderness of Walden Pond. Every few years we hear someone triumphantly denounce Thoreau as a fraud, having recently discovered that the Hermit of Concord sometimes spent the night at his mother's house in town instead of toughing it out in the woods—reducing his life to a kind of prolonged adolescent misadventure.

But if this is a gross oversimplification of Thoreau, it is perhaps an even greater distortion of Nature, in Concord in Thoreau's time. Thoreau lived in the mid-19th century, when our industrial development was still in its infancy. Consequently, many readers of *Walden* presume that the Nature he sought at Walden Pond and throughout the backwoods of Concord was wilder than the Nature that is left to us today. That is, less polluted and degraded and diminished by deliberate exploitation and inadvertent "economic externalities" than now. Thoreau stands, in our imagination, at the ever-receding ecotone between two worlds: the simple, natural world of the past, and the overdeveloped world of the future that is now upon us—a solitary figure at the edge of the woods, warning of the spiritual, and as it turned out, very real dangers inherent in man's total domination of nature.

But oddly enough, there was arguably less wildness in Concord in Thoreau's time than there is today. By 1845 Walden Woods was hardly the edge of the great American forest. It was one of the few patches of woods remaining in Concord. In the farm towns of the Sudbury River valley, forest cover reached its all-time low point of about ten percent around 1850. Two-thirds of the land in these towns was abandoned or very scrubby, run-down pasture. Thoreau's Concord was a deforested, farmed-out, environmentally degraded landscape. It had been degraded by the rapid expansion of a system of commercial agricultural that severely depleted the forest, soil, and water resources of the region.

This was the environment to which Thoreau reacted. He was not just looking into the future, foreseeing the negative consequences of unbridled economic development. He was already seeing those consequences all around him.

Since Thoreau's time, the Concord forest has made a dramatic recovery. I think it is fair to say that Nature has shown a recuperative power that would have delighted and gratified Henry Thoreau. Forest cover in the Sudbury River valley today is around sixty-five percent—in fact, if the impact of Indian burning on the landscape was as dramatic and extensive as many environmental historians believe (or at least suspect), it may well be that there is more forest out there now than there has been at any time in the past thousand years. Deer have returned, and coyotes. It would not surprise me to see healthy populations of beaver, otter, turkeys, osprey, and even eagles in the environs of Concord in my lifetime.

Henry Thoreau was concerned about the loss of wildness, or as we would say today, of natural ecosystems. And wildness has to some extent returned to Concord. The farmland has been largely overgrown by forest. Unfortunately, this does not signal that the residents of Concord have learned to live in better balance with their immediate environment. It merely signals that we have learned to live without relying on the local natural world for anything. Having no practical need to generate our vital heat from this land, we have abandoned it to nature—at least until we reclaim it to underlie our residences, office parks, and shopping malls.

Repeated over the entire surface of the globe, the conversion of natural ecosystems to farmland, which concerned Thoreau, is lamentable and even dangerous. But it is possible for people to create farming systems that have their own kind of ecological integrity and beauty, within limits. My concern here is with the failure of the farmers of Concord to achieve even this kind of sustainable "agroecological" relationship with their environment—a failure that reached its moment of truth during Thoreau's lifetime. The farmers of Concord cut the land out from under themselves. They used up local resources faster than Nature could resupply them. The story I want to review concerns the long-term failure of a community to establish an enduring relationship with its land. It is a very American story. And I think it helps put the thinking of Henry Thoreau into its proper context.

For convenience in presenting this environmental history of Concord, I am dividing it into a series of periods, based on what I take to be the key agricultural commodity—that is, whatever was being fed to the cows. Thus we have the "Meadow hay" period, which lasted from 1635 to about

1790; the "English hay" period until 1850; the "Western grain" period until about 1920; and the "What cows?" period since then. When Steve Verrill over in Nine Acre Corner got out of the dairy business in 1990, he essentially returned the cow population of Concord to zero.

Of course, this periodization of a complex history is a gross oversimplification. I have dropped the Native Americans completely out of the story, because my business here is not to contrast the Europeans with the Indians, but to follow the development of Yankee farming. I want to provide a feeling for the ecological dynamics of life in Concord during each era, and to try to identify the external and internal forces of change. Just hitting the high points.

Or the low points. Concord was settled early because of its low-lying meadows. It is important to remember that 17th-century English farmers grew very little hay. The grazing season in England is very long, almost year round in places. Hay as a deliberately planted and cultivated crop was virtually unknown there at that time. Hay was cut from the edges of fields, and from waste places, and especially from meadows along streams.

In New England the colonists quickly discovered that the grazing season is much shorter, and that stock need to be provided with fodder nearly half the year, from November into May. The first two centuries of farming in New England revolved around finding and improving adequate supplies of hay to support the growth of the country. Providentially, when these Puritans arrived they found a great deal of God-given grass, salt-marsh hay along the coast, and fresh meadow hay along watercourses inland. This was familiar, and they knew how to deal with it. In towns like Concord and Sudbury, they found tremendous supplies of such hay in the great river meadows and smaller brook meadows extending back into the country, and that is why these inland towns were settled so soon.

Concord and Sudbury were both originally laid out as common field towns. All the proprietors resided in the village, and received strips to cultivate in several large tillage fields that had been inherited from the Indians. The farmers also apportioned themselves strips for cutting hay in the Great Meadows nearby. The rest—that is to say the great bulk—of the landscape was left for several decades as common grazing and woods. However, meadows that were found in every corner of town were also parceled out among the village farmers, who were willing to go great distances over the waste to bring in more hay. Later all the common upland was divided, and gradually consolidated into distinct individual farms, but even into the 19th century the meadows remained subdivided into strips. It was still common for a farmer in Thoreau's time to own four acres in Fair Haven meadow, and two acres in Nut meadow, and five acres in Dunge Hole meadow, and to cart his meadow hay home several miles from various points of the compass.

To give you a feeling for this landscape, try to imagine that originally much of the farmland we now call Nine Acre Corner was still meadow, or even black ash and willow swamp. Only gradually, over generations were portions of it sufficiently drained to become tilled land. The southern and eastern parts, stretching out to the river, were known as Fair Haven meadow. Then there were more meadows stretching south into Sudbury on the west side of what is now the Nawshawtuc Golf Club: World's End meadow, and Little Gulf meadow, and Gulf meadow, and Weir meadow. What we now call Pantry Brook was known as "the Gulf." The upland, where golf is played now, was known as "Haynes' Island"—it would not occur to us today, driving over this landscape, that this is an island, but to the farmers cutting meadow hay in August, standing down in the landscape, it was an island in a sea of meadow.

This fresh meadow hay drove the entire agricultural system, because it fed the cattle, and this was definitely a cattle economy. Cattle, as oxen, provided locomotion. Cattle driven to market were the main wealth of the country. Above all, cattle provided subsistence in the form of butter and cheese, salt beef, and salt pork that was fed on whey. And cattle also provided manure for the light, sandy tilled fields that grew the principal bread crops of corn and rye. So, in simplified agroecological terms, the meadows supplied nutrients to the tilled fields via the livestock. As the New England proverb had it, "No grass—no cattle, no cattle—no manure, no manure—no crop." And the meadows were essentially inexhaustible, for, as the farmers observed, they flooded and were recharged every winter like the Nile.

It took over a century for this farming system to get fully elaborated—that is, for successive generations to clear and establish farms across the available land, to get the meadows well ditched so that they were reliably accessible, to make the switch from beer to cider as the primary beverage, which was a far more efficient use of land and labor. But by the mid-18th century, the system began to show signs of stress. Robert Gross has described this crisis in Concord, and it is documented in other New England towns as well. In essence, it was a Malthusian crisis—as population increased, farms became fragmented and too small to support families, yields declined, and people were marginalized off the land. Clearly, the farm population was outrunning what its agroecological system could provide.

But not all the available land was yet in production. There was still plenty of forestland, covering forty percent or so of these towns about the time of the Revolution, and indeed a lot of this land was subsequently cleared during the 19th century. So why not just clear more land? The answer is that it was not doing much good to clear more pasture or tillage land, given the farming methods of the time. There was already way too much tilled land in production for the supply of manure that could be spread over it. The real bottleneck in the system was the supply of meadow hay, and all the available natural hay meadows were in production—there was a natural limit to that crucial resource. So without more meadow hay, they could not keep more cattle, they could not provide more manure to grow more subsistence grain crops, and the entire system hit a snag. Out of this crisis came a new agricultural system—a much more productive system, at least in the short run.

This new system involved an agroecological change in cropping patterns, and an economic change away from subsistence and toward marketing. The transformation began in the 1780s or 1790s, and climaxed around 1850. This marked the high point for farming in the Sudbury River valley, at least in terms of acres in cultivation. It was a point beyond which the land could not be driven.

The key element in the new farming system was the expansion of cultivated, or "English," hay. Farmers attacked the hay shortage directly by learning to plant red clover, timothy, and redtop in upland fields. English hay acreage climbed from 700 acres in 1791 to 2,200 acres in 1850. The farmers did not abandon their natural meadows, but English hay supplanted meadow hay as the main crop by 1840. This expanded hay supply allowed more livestock to be kept, it boosted the manure supply, and it also provided a valuable new market crop.

This breakthrough led to a period of vigorous agricultural expansion during the first half of the 19th century. Stone walls delineating hay fields and pastures ran over the hills and down around the swamps, and most of the remaining forest was cleared off. At the same time, many more swamps and meadows were thoroughly drained. Swamp drainage was all the rage between 1830 and 1860. Ditches and buried stone or tile drains lowered the water table at least two feet, creating improved land for English hay and other crops. Thus cultivation was pushed into every corner of the landscape. Behind this expansion were strong markets and a new commercial drive to supply them. The first step taken by farmers in this direction was to stop growing their own bread. Farmers and their neighbors in the villages ate less johnnycake, or "rye 'n' Injun," and began purchasing wheat flour from Pennsylvania, New York, and the West. At the same time, farmers began specializing their own production and marketing more of what they grew. This was tied into the commercial and industrial growth of the region, as mill towns like Waltham, Lowell, Maynard, and Framingham sprang up, providing an excellent market for provisions and fodder. Instead of growing rye for subsistence, for example, Concord farmers began to grow oats to sell for horse feed, fueling the transportation system of the time.

The key commercial crops of this era were hay, dairy products, and firewood. English hay itself was in very high demand for town cows and horses, and many farmers strove to feed their meadow hay and market their best stuff. Butter and cheese, and then fluid milk after the railroad reached Concord, were the commercial mainstay for many farmers. And there was a very strong market for firewood as well, which lubricated the labor of clearing land—firewood was going for about four dollars a cord out here in 1840, but it fetched six dollars in Boston. Of course, a trip to Boston by oxcart was an all-day affair—set off at four o'clock in the morning, get home about midnight. A substantial amount of firewood also went in on the Middlesex Canal during the early decades of the century. And again, the coming of the railroad in the 1840s stepped up the demand on the forests even further.

In brief, the commercialization of agriculture effectively channeled the energy of farmers into more productive exploitation of the resources at hand. Of course, this response of the farm sector to the rise of markets in the manufacturing towns is a familiar staple of New England agricultural history. In recent years, economic historians have pushed the date of this transformation back into the late eighteenth century, and have given farmers themselves more credit for stimulating New England's economic takeoff, rather than being dragged into the hurly-burly of the 19th century kicking and screaming. But what has not been examined as closely as it should be is the simplistic equation of a progressive, commercial outlook with agricultural "improvement." Taken as a whole, the new farm system did not improve the land. It just wore it out faster and more efficiently.

By the middle of the 19th century this expanding commercial system had reached its ecological limits. The central problem was that upland hay fields and pastures were steadily exhausted by the extraction of nutrients. Nowhere near enough manure was ever returned to hay fields, let alone to pastures—after the hay was consumed by the stock, the manure was mainly consigned to the tilled fields. Or worse, the hay was sold off the farm, the cardinal sin of virtuous farming. So yields on older hay fields constantly declined, and exhausted pastures began growing up to huckleberries and pine—a delight to Henry Thoreau, but no way to run a farm in the long run.

It worked all right as long as there was more fresh land to clear, but along about mid-century the available land finally began to run out. The result was the nearly complete deforestation of the valley, and the accumulation of great stretches of what was classified as "unimproved" land. In 1801 Concord had 3,600 acres of woodland, and 1,300 "unimproved." By 1850 the situation was reversed—only 1,500 acres of woods in the entire town, and 3,700 acres of unimproved land—most of which was exhausted, abandoned pasture. So it appears that "improved" farming progressively unimproved the land.

This deforestation had an unforeseen impact. By 1850 only about ten percent of the Sudbury River watershed was still forested. When land is converted from forest to farmland or scrub, there is a big increase in run-off, because trees transpire much more moisture in the course of the growing season than does a scrubby pasture, a hay field, or even a corn field. This dumped a lot more water into the river in the summer. The farmers were already having problems with worsened flooding of their meadows during the haying season because of the Billerica dam, which backed the river up all the way to Wayland and Sudbury. What they did not know was that their own mismanagement of the watershed was bringing the water up too. As a result, the river meadows gradually ceased to be of any agricultural importance, after two centuries at the very heart of farming in the valley.

The upshot was that this commercial farming system pushed the land beyond the limits of what it could sustainably provide, and caused ecological disturbance in the watershed. This should go a long way toward explaining why Henry Thoreau was so down on his farming neighbors, when one considers the scrubby, exhausted, denuded state of the landscape they stuck him with. But, as Thoreau pointed out, not many of the farmers in town felt they were making a great financial go of it, either. What was to become the paradigm of American agriculture had been discovered: agricultural production was going great guns, while farmers and farmland were losing out.

So what happened next? Here things took an interesting twist. The usual story is that when New England was connected to the Midwest by rail in 1850, agriculture in this region disintegrated, because it couldn't compete. This story is wrong, and should be forgotten. What really happened is much more instructive.

There is no question that the advent of cheap Western meat and grain had a dramatic impact on farming in New England. However, continued urban growth and the completion of a rail network within the region also meant that there continued to be a strong home market for commodities that were too perishable or too bulky to bear transport from outside the region. Late 19th-century New England farmers specialized in milk, hay, and produce, the "big three." The results were startling: between 1880 and 1910, the value of Massachusetts agricultural production, in constant dollars, doubled.

Concord farmers epitomized the new, thoroughly commercial approach to farming. By the late 1800s Concord was one of the top ten farming towns in the state. The key to it was cheap western grain. Western corn was a boon, not a bane to New England agriculture. Farmers began to run tons of purchased feed through their cows, and increased their milk production by several times. By 1910 about six times more feed grain was being imported than grown in Massachusetts. This also increased the manure supply, allowing some Concord farmers to dress their best hay fields and treat hay strictly as a cash crop. The demand for hay was strong, because there were more horses than ever on the roads. And back from the livery stables in the cities came more manure, which farmers in Concord used to feed a booming market-garden industry.

This new system, relying on imported nutrients, allowed farmers to simply dump the more troublesome parts of the old farm system that had been breaking down. The river meadows grew up to a brushy wilderness visited only by a few naturalists. All that scrubby pasture simply was not needed anymore, so it was allowed to grow up to pine, which provided another cash crop a few decades later. Coal by now had relegated wood to a secondary fuel source, so forests made a dramatic recovery. Across the state as a whole between 1880 and 1910, during the same years when agricultural production was doubling, land in agriculture fell in half. They just let it go.

So it is clear what was going on:—there was no economic decline in farming in the region during the second half of the 19th century, but there was a pronounced agroecological decline. That is, farmers gave up trying to farm a large portion of their own land. Having greatly exhausted local resources, they turned to another, fresh source of nutrients, which was the Midwest. Farming was transformed from a circular process that had to look for its own, internal means of renewal, to a nice linear reprocessing of purchased inputs—the industrial agricultural model. Beginning to sound familiar? Welcome, at last, to the 20th century.

With the advent of the age of oil after about 1920, local agriculture finally did collapse. First of all, the automobile and the tractor wiped out the hay market at a stroke. Then, high-yielding milk cows and milking machines led to the consolidation of the dairy industry into far fewer operations, most of them farther from the city on cheaper land, as in Vermont. Improved transportation and refrigeration of produce from Florida and California and Washington knocked most Massachusetts truck farms and orchards out of the fruit-and-vegetable business. And finally, especially after World War II, the automobile brought suburban development and pushed the value of land out of the range of farming.

So we are left today with a situation where forest has recovered virtually all of the land that hasn't yet been developed. Although it is a very fragmented forest, changes the forest itself has undergone over the past few centuries, provide a very interesting part of this story. In any case, the people of the Concord area today have almost no functional connection to the land they inhabit; to the vanished farmland, or to returned forest, or to the nearly invisible river. We are completely reliant on resources from other regions, brought to us by the abundance of a single resource, which is cheap oil. This is not an abrupt departure from our past, but the logical result of a step-by-step process of development that goes deep into our history.

In Henry Thoreau's time, the farmers of Concord faced the challenge of learning to live within their means. But they did not actually solve this problem; they just displaced it into other regions, which made great economic sense at the time. Through steps like that, we have now elaborated a global system of resource extraction, which may not be any more sustainable on that scale than was farming in Concord in 1850.

Presumably we want to go on living here. We might not all fully endorse Henry Thoreau's solution, as much as we may admire it, but at least he did front the essential question of what it means to live here, in this place. And he did it at a moment when his community and American society at large were setting foot decisively in another direction.

# Bibliography

This paper is taken from work in progress on the author's dissertation. These are preliminary findings that will be subject to modification from further research. For documented accounts, see:

Donahue, Brian, "'Dammed at Both Ends and Cursed in the Middle' The 'Flowage' of the Concord River Meadows, 1798–1862," Environmental Review, vol. 13, 1989.

Donahue, Brian, "The Forests and Fields of Concord: An Ecological History," in David Hackett Fischer, ed., *Concord: The Social History of a New England Town, 1750—1850* (Waltham, Mass., Low, 1983).

Donahue, Brian, "Skinning the Land: Economic Growth and the Ecology of Farming in Nineteenth Century Massachusetts" (Unpub., 1984).

Gross, Robert A., The *Minutemen and Their World* (New York, Hill & Wang, 1976).

Gross, Robert A., "Culture and Cultivation: Agriculture and Society in Thoreau's Concord," Journal of American History, vol. 69, 1982.

Kimenker, James, "The Concord Farmer: An Economic History, 1750–1850," in Fischer, Concord, Brandeis Univ.: Social History, 1983

MacMahon, Sarah F., "A Comfortable Subsistence: A History of Diet in New England, 1630–1850" (Ph.D. Dissertation, Brandeis University, 1982)

Rothenberg, Winifred B., "A Price Index for Rural Massachusetts, 1750–1855," Journal of Economic History, vol. 39, 1979.

Rothenberg, Winifred B., "The Emergence of Farm Labor Markets and the Transformation of the Rural Economy: Massachusetts, 1750–1855," *Journal of Economic History*, vol. 48, 1988.

**BRIAN DONAHUE** is co-founder and former director of Land's Sake, a community land stewardship organization in Weston that operates ecologically sustainable farm and forest projects involving young people with the environment; his central concern is the relationship of communities to the local environment. He is currently completing a doctoral dissertation in environmental history at Brandeis University.

# A History of
# Concord's Flora

❖

## Mary M. Walker

## Introduction

Anyone discussing the history of the flora of Concord, Massachusetts, owes a great debt to Richard Eaton, author of *A Flora of Concord*. He gathered all the pertinent facts about the geology, soils, climate, settlement history, special habitats, students of the flora, and finally an annotated catalogue of the 1,100 species in the town that can be verified by an herbarium specimen.

Eaton's *Flora* was published in 1974 based on his fieldwork, begun in the late 1930s, but done mainly in the 1950s and early 1960s, a thirty-year labor of love. Most of the information is still pertinent, but more habitats and their plants disappear because of real estate development, and a few new plants have been added to the flora. Some new studies and books throw new light on the history of the development of Concord's vegetation. This article is an expansion of my notes accompanying a slide talk which aimed to present visually the information in Eaton's *A Flora of Concord* and later publications. Readers will find a full discussion of this information I present in the references listed at the end of this paper.

## History

Concord, Massachusetts, covers an area of twenty-seven square miles. Its varied topography is largely due to the Pleistocene Wisconsin glaciation. Wisconsin ice was at its maximum thickness 18,000 years ago. Retreat, mainly by melting in place, was completed between 12,000 to

10,000 years ago. The wide flat lowlands had been glacial lake beds. Here soils are good for farming. Fronting the glacial lake bed areas are higher (by 70 to 100 feet) relatively level areas of delta deposits, water-laid sands and gravels, such as underlie the Walden Woods ecosystem. There are three hills over 300 feet and several lesser ones, most with the oval shape of drumlins, a few with steep cliffs on the south side created by ice-plucking as the glacier moved over them.

Imposed upon this topography are the Sudbury, Assabet, and Concord rivers with their extensive meadows, and ponds, such as Walden, which occupy kettle holes formed by late melting of ice blocks in the sheets of glacial outwash, after the local area was ice-free. There is considerable swampy ground. Eaton lists some thirteen meadows and swamps and six sphagnous bogs. Concord's soils, acidic in nature, are derived from glacial till, glacial lake deposits, and the few exposures of bedrock, mostly metamorphic gneiss and schist. A few thin beds of marble give rise locally to neutral or alkaline soils which support a characteristic flora.

This variety of habitats and types of soil enabled many kinds of plants to colonize and become established in Concord. In 12,000 years the climate and kinds of plants have changed several times, but the modern flora consists of 1,100 species, one-fifth of all the species in Gray's *Manual* which covers the entire northeastern United States, and one-third of all the species in New England. No wonder botanists have studied this intriguing flora for nearly 200 years.

Before the glaciation, perhaps 1.5 million years ago, the vegetation of the Concord area resembled closely our modern types. We would have recognized oaks, maples, pines, and spruces, for example. As the climate cooled, plants either died out or retreated to refugia, along the central and southern Appalachians, or along the Atlantic Coastal Plain.

The melting back and disappearance of the Wisconsin Ice Sheet took place over 2,000 or 3,000 years in southern New England. The ground was bare at first, but not for long. Tundra lay to the south of the ice front, and these plants, sedges, grasses, and dwarf shrubs were the first to recolonize the land. Remnants of this tundra vegetation are still found in our bogs, like Gowing Swamp, leatherleaf, cranberry, Labrador tea, pitcherplant, sundews, cotton-grass, and species of *Carex*. As the climate began to moderate, where seed sources were nearby, spruce–fir forest rapidly invaded the tundra and became dominant.

Numerous pollen diagrams from bog core samples show that around 10,000 years ago the spruce–fir forest declined rather abruptly. New tree species appeared in Concord, same migrating inland from the Atlantic Coastal Plain, others migrating west to east from the Pennsylvania Appalachians, and some coming from much farther south. Advancing a few hundred meters a year, generation after generation, some species took 4,000 years, some took 6,000 years, some only arrived 2,000 years ago. But the oaks, maples, white pine, followed by hemlock, beech, hickory, and chestnut arrived in ever increasing numbers, into New England. In *After the Ice Age*, E. C. Pielou sums up a wealth of research on plant and animal migrations in a readable and fascinating book.

Around 6,000 years ago there was a significant warming of the climate shown by the marked increase in white pine pollen here in New England, and by other indications elsewhere in the country. This is known as the hypsithermal interval or climatic optimum. Since that time the climate has become slightly cooler, warmed again, and in the past 2,000 years the increase in spruce–fir pollen especially in northern bogs indicates that we are in a cooling trend.

Presently, in New England, there are four major forest communities according to John C. Kricher in *Eastern Forests*. They are Northern Hardwood, Oak–Hickory, Northern Pine–Oak, and the Ecotone Forest between Northern Hardwood and Boreal in Canada. Concord lies in the Oak–Hickory Forest Zone. However, where soils and microclimate are right, trees such as yellow birch, paper birch, beech, sugar maple, and hemlock grow, relics of an age 9,000 to 7,000 years ago when all of Concord was covered with trees of the Northern Hardwood Forest. Black spruce growing with the bog plants in Gowing Swamp reminds us of an even earlier period when tundra was followed by boreal spruce–fir forest as the ice age receded, in Concord, Massachusetts!

The Oak–Hickory Forest Community in the Concord area consists of such trees and shrubs as red, black, and white oaks, the hickories, sassafras, hornbeam and hop hornbeam, highbush and lowbush blueberries, and viburnums. Among the herbaceous plants are wintergreen, partridgeberry, spotted and common pipsissewa, wild sarsaparilla, rue-anemone, Jack-in-the-pulpit, false Solomon's seal, Canada mayflower, pink ladyslipper, bracken, hay-scented and other ferns, and clubmosses. Gray squirrels, chipmunks, and blue jays are abundant. Where abandoned pastures are reverting to woodland plants indicating this oldfield succession are daisies, goldenrods, and asters, sumac, red cedar, gray birch, and aspen. Along our rivers are plants of the Northern Floodplain Forest elm (now disappearing due to disease), silver maple, sycamore, elder, silky dogwood, nettles, and grapes. In our many red maple swamps are plants of the Northern Swamp Community such as sweet pepperbush, skunk cabbage, jewelweed, goldthread, marsh marigold, among these our earliest spring flowers.

The vegetation growing in that part of Concord long known as Walden Woods is characteristic of the Northern Pine–Oak Forest Community. It is a community typical of the coastal plain and occurs here on the sandy soils of the delta outwash deposits: pitch pine, scrub, red and black oak, low bush blueberry and huckleberry, sweet fern, and the like. This community depends on occasional fires and since fires seldom occur now in Concord, it is becoming more typically an Oak–Hickory Forest. Readers will find Neil Jorgensen's book most helpful in explaining and documenting the vegetation of the various plant communities encountered in southern New England.

Concord, founded in 1635, was one of the earliest inland settlements, primarily because of the abundant meadow hay along the rivers, the rich lowland soils derived from the former glacial lake bed, and several fields of corn abandoned by the Indians. On the low hills were good stands of timber: white oak, chestnut and white pine. Concord was a farming community for two hundred years with woodlots cut in a rotation sequence. All this favored the native plants, allowing many to expand their habitats. Because Concord was a farming community, many of our wildflowers are naturalized plants that escaped from the gardens of the early settlers, plants that had been brought here from overseas for medicinal, and practical use, plants such as chicory, tansy, and oyster plant.

During Concord's three hundred years of settlement, its landscape changed several times from largely wooded, to largely cleared (only ten percent wooded) by Thoreau's time. Since then steadily abandoned pastures have reverted to woods again. Thus plant habitats have expanded, contracted, and expanded again. In these last three decades Concord plant habitats are losing out to development. A pasture will revert to woodland, but when a house and lawn, or a condominium, or a mall are built the plants disappear forever. Some of Concord's plants are now endangered because of this loss of habitat. Others are rare because they have always grown in small populations, such as those on Conantum's neutral soils. Or they are perhaps northern plants which reaching the southern limits of their range in this area, grow under stress and tend to die off more readily than plants in the middle of their ranges.

Since most of Concord's citizens worked the land or lived close to it, and since Concord had a rather remarkable number of intellectuals residing here in the 1800s and 1900s, botanical activities in Concord have a long history. The first botanists that we know of were the Jarvis brothers, Charles (1800–1826) and particularly Edward (1803–1884) who was a doctor in this town from 1827 to 1833. One of their herbarium collections was given to the University of Massachusetts at Amherst and included 97 plants from Concord. Another collection is mentioned in an autobiography but has not been located. The Concord Free Public Library fortunately has Jarvis' copy of Bigelow's *Florula Bostoniensis*, the field botany in use in those days, and in it Jarvis records some 300 plants he had seen in Concord.

Henry David Thoreau (1817–1862) also used Bigelow from his college years on, but he did not take a serious interest in botany until about 1850. His journals, all fourteen volumes, 1848–1862, are increasingly full of references to plants. Ray Angelo's index to these references is 144 pages long! Thoreau's herbarium collection of some 900 specimens, many from Concord, is at Harvard University.

Sophia Thoreau (1819–1876), Henry's sister, also pursued botanical interests and found such unusual plants as the whorled pogonia, the painted trillium, and the perfoliate bellwort. Her small herbarium collection is at the Concord Library.

Edward Sherman Hoar (1823–1893) was a frequent walking trip companion of Thoreau's and took a great interest in botany. He was a lawyer, but out in the field often. His collection of 356 specimens is at the New England Botanical Club Herbarium.

Minot Pratt (1805–1878), a horticulturist and nurseryman, joined Thoreau on many a walk about town. He introduced many outside plants into the Concord flora, to see if they would naturalize. Fortunately he left a record of his introductions, which is at the Concord Library. He made an annotated list of the native plants of Concord, also at the Library.

Alfred W. Hosmer (1851–1903), a storekeeper in Concord, carried on the botanical studies of Concord's flora, and made and published a record of Pratt's introductions and their fate. He developed a large herbarium collection, but more interestingly he made a ten-year record of flowering dates of the town's plants.

Richard Eaton (1890–1976) was born in Concord, later lived in Lincoln, but studied Concord plants for thirty years, finally publishing his *Flora* in 1974. His local herbarium collection is at the Concord Field Station of the Museum of Comparative Zoology, in Bedford. Three volunteers continued to develop the local flora herbarium there, and it is available to the public by appointment. One of these curators, Ray Angelo, lived in Concord for seven years and continued botanical studies in the tradition of these earlier men. He found a number of new species for the town's flora, discovered new locations of rare plants, and relocated several "lost" plants.

There are more botanical discoveries to be made in Concord. In 1990 Edmund A. Schofield wrote a detailed ecological history of the Walden Woods Ecosystem, part of which appears in this volume. There is room for more work of this kind, for the greatest need now is for the identification and protection of good examples of each of Concord's typical habitats, as well as those of rare plants, for future botanists to study and for all of Concord's citizens to enjoy.

# Bibliography

Angelo, Ray, "Botanical Index to the Journal of Henry David Thoreau." *The Thoreau Quarterly*, vol. 15: 32–203, 1983.

Angelo, Ray, "Thoreau as a Botanist." *The Thoreau Quarterly*, vol. 15: 15–31, 1983.

Eaton, Richard, *A Flora of Concord*, Special Publication, no. 4, The Museum of Comparative Zoology, Harvard University, Cambridge, MA, 1974, 236 pp.

Hosmer, Alfred W. "Plants Introduced by Minot Pratt at Concord, Massachusetts." *Rhodora*, vol. 1: 168–170, 1899.

Jorgensen, Neil. *A Sierra Club Naturalist's Guide to Southern New England,* Sierra Club Books, San Francisco, Q, 1978, 417 pp.

Kricher, John C. *A Field Guide to Eastern Forests North America*, Houghton Mifflin, Boston, MA, 1988, 368 pp.

Pielou, E. C. *After the Ice Age: The Return of Life to Glaciated North America,* The University of Chicago Press, Chicago, IL, 1991, 366 pp.

Schofield, Edmund A. *The Walden Ecosystem*, working draft manuscript, July 1990, 82 pp.

---

**MARY M. WALKER** is a past president of the New England Botanical Club. She is co-curator of the Concord Field Station (Museum of Comparative Zoology) Herbarium in Bedford, and has been a member of the hut naturalist program of the Appalachian Mountain Club since 1973. She has recently retired after 18 years as librarian for the New England Wild Flower Society in Framingham, but continues to do research there.

# Underwater Walden

❖

## Kristina A. Joyce

Many people come to Walden Pond in Concord, Massachusetts, to see where Henry David Thoreau lived and wrote his American classic *Walden*. The site of Thoreau's cabin was discovered and first excavated by Roland Wells Robbins in 1945.

Walden Pond was formed about 12,000 years ago, when the Wisconsin glacier was melting. Actually, it does not fit the common definition of a pond, which is a quiet body of water so shallow that rooted plants grow completely across it. It is really a lake where water is too deep for plants to grow except around the shore. In summer the upper layer of Walden's water is 65–70°F; the middle layer is 45–65°F; and the bottom layer is cold at 39–45°F. The water warmed by the sun is less dense and floats on the top. At the bottom, organic matter decays and increases carbon dioxide. Since there is little oxygen, most fish live above the thermocline.

In autumn the water overturns. The upper layer cools until it approaches the temperature of the middle and bottom layers. Aided by winds, the surface water sinks causing circulation from top to bottom. In winter the cold surface water continues to sink until, near the freezing-point, it is less dense. The near freezing water eventually turns to ice, which is lighter than water and floats. During this time, thick ice screens out light and photosynthesis stops. Plants and animals may die due to lack of oxygen, which one cause of "winterkill." In spring the ice melts and the surface water warms above 39°F. Aided by winds, another mixing occurs which is called "spring overturn."

Although I may be the first to have photographed Walden from underwater, I am not the first to dive there. In the fall of 1968 the New England Chapter of the Marine Technological Society held its fall meeting at Walden. Researchers probed the depths of Walden and tested for unknown characteristics of the pond. At that time Thoreau's soundings with a line and weight were confirmed as accurate. The maximum depth of the pond is 102 feet. Surface temperature was 76°F and bottom 41°F. No underground river was feeding the pond as rumored. Walden is a water-table pond. Reclamation of the pond was done a week before. All living organisms were killed by Rotenone. People gathered the fish and ate them. The fish died by chemical action on the exchange of oxygen in the gills. The purpose of this reclamation was to introduce species good for sport fishing.

During this survey, "grass" was found growing at depths of 35-40 feet. In January of 1986, Bruce Sorrie of the Massachusetts Division of Fisheries and Wildlife discovered lake quillwort washed up on the bathing beach after a storm. He believed it to be a rare plant last seen in 1967—the species *Isoëtes macrospora*. This is where my expertise came into the picture.

Knowing the above, I made a proposal to the State to hunt for the location of the *Isoëtes*. Since the State had no funds to pay me, I assumed all expenses and risks personally. The State initially granted me a one-day permit. Later, this was extended. The agreement was that I would make copies of my slides available to the Department of Wildlife and Fisheries. Generally, scuba diving is not permitted in Walden Pond.

My first dive was made in October of 1985. My dive buddy was Chris Michel, owner of Ultramarine Divers in West Concord. I was not accustomed to freshwater diving and Chris was my teacher.

The first plant that we found we hoped would be the rare quillwort, so we took a lot of pictures of it. We used a black plastic notebook cover as the background in some photographs. The plant was not the quillwort; it is *Nitella flexilis*, which Thoreau observed in his writings. He would pull it up on weighted lines.

On some of the plants we saw small hydra which are coelenterata—this includes corals, jellyfishes, and sea anemones in the ocean. Hydra are less than an inch long; they eat one-celled animals; and they move by inching along or by turning somersaults. The variety we observed is the green hydra or *Chlorohydra viridissima*. It is common in North America.

In 15-20 feet of water off the bathing beach, we found the lake quillwort. It is small in size—like a tuff of grass. I was very happy to find this plant because I thought it was an endangered species—*Isoëtes macrospora*. However, when my specimens were examined under a microscope by Laima Kott at the Ontario Agricultural College, the spores were characteristic of *Isoëtes tuckermanii*.

At the bottom in the long cove area at 40 feet, the only green things we saw were about the same size and shape as Brussels sprouts. Underwater currents may roll the plant *Cladophora* into these shapes. They decay from the inside and then rise to the surface.

The most predominant fish I saw was the small-mouth bass. As a juvenile, it may be recognized by its characteristic black on the tail. The mature bass are much larger—over a foot long. Their black lateral stripe indicates that they are largemouth bass. I also saw blue gills, recognizable by their distinctive dark gill and reddish fin color.

Crayfish are not indigenous to Walden. They were introduced from the Midwest—presumably via the stocking of fish. One was identified by Doug Smith at the University of Massachusetts. It was a good-sized specimen of *Orconetes virilis*. Fish love to eat crayfish. If I held one, I would attract a lot of small-mouth bass. When I tossed one out, it would be swallowed whole.

My last and favorite subjects are the shells of Walden. Most freshwater mollusks burrow into the bottom of bodies of water. The *Compeloma decisa* is a freshwater snail about three-quarters of an inch in size. The freshwater shells are fragile because minerals are not as plentiful in freshwater as in salt water. Some shells actually eat each other. A radula is a drill-like appendage with which the mollusks attack the shell of other mollusks. Sometimes poisons are injected into the hole by the attacker to finish off the victim.

Snail shells can be left- and right-handed like people. If the shell opening is on the right, it is right handed. If a shell is generally right-handed, once in a while a left-handed form may turn up and it will be considered rare. Thoreau was intrigued by the brassy quality that he saw in these shells.

Freshwater shells are partly identified by their shapes, colors, and hinge structure. The *Anodonta cataracta* has a green shell that later, as it matures, darkens to deep brown. The shell is paper thin. Commonly, it is known as the "floater." Thoreau observed it "floating" like a pearly skiff. The *Anodonta* has no hinge structure. Its habitat is sand.

Thoreau observed the brassy spots in freshwater shells before they were named scientifically as "Tullberg layers." Finally, Thoreau especially loved freshwater shells because though they grew in dark depths, they showed tints of the sky inside. Let me end with a quote from Thoreau on this subject:

> It is a somewhat saddening reflection that the beautiful colors of this shell for want of light cannot be said to exist until its inhabitant has fallen a prey to the spoiler and it is thus left a wreck upon the strand.

---

**KRISTINA A. JOYCE** is a freelance artist living in Concord.

# Changes at Walden Pond During the Last 600 Years
## Microfossil Analyses of Walden Pond Sediments

❖

**Marjorie Green Winkler**

Walden Pond was given by Henry Thoreau to all of us. Without his book describing its natural wonder and the sense of solitude it provided him (Thoreau, 1854), we would be seeing a different landscape—one lined with homes and dotted with "no trespassing" signs. Instead, today, Walden Pond is here for everyone.

Walden Pond is not only important as a literary or philosophical landmark. Thoreau was the first North American scientist to study a lake ecosystem. Lakes and bogs are very important to the study of past environments because the remains of the past are preserved in anoxic, water-logged lake muds and bog peats. I analyze the remnants of past biota to determine how the climate changed in the past; to determine the rates of climate change, and how these changes affected the soils, the vegetation, and the water, and to attempt to predict future environmental changes from knowledge of the past.

The history of this planet reveals that there were great differences in the world long ago in contrast to the world as it is today. A few examples of these differences are:

(1) A billion years ago the composition of the atmosphere and the number and kind of organisms growing were different from today.

(2) The global map over the past several hundred million years was not as we know it today. There is evidence in the fossil record, some of it in Concord, for several land-sea configurations—each one with a unique climate.

(3) Over the past two million years, there is evidence of periodic glaciations, possibly triggered by variations in the orbital parameters of the earth. During the last glaciation, ice covered a large part of eastern North America (south to about 40° north latitude, Figure 1), sea ice

connected the continents, global sea level was 130 meters lower than at present, and the Atlantic Coastal Plain to the southeast of Walden Pond was much larger than present. That means that the Concord area was covered by ice and was then farther inland for many millennia when the ice receded (Figure 1).

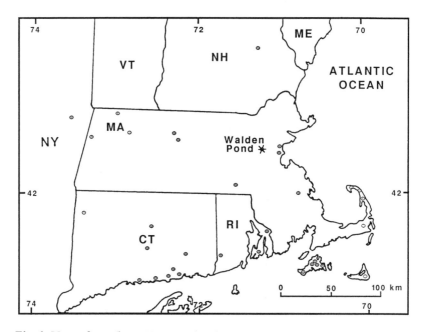

**Fig. 1. Map of southern New England. Walden Pond is shown in relation to late-glacial and Holocene pollen sites (gray dots) from which the regional vegetation history of the Concord area since deglaciation has been derived.**

(4) Deglaciation, the shrinking of ice masses due to a warming climate, began about 18,000 years before the present and produced an ever-changing environment. The time periods referred to here are the *Last Glacial Maximum* (the 18,000 year date), the *Late Glacial*—a cold period characterized by tundra or spruce parklands in a large portion of eastern North America between 18,000 and 10,500 years ago; and the *Holocene,*—the relatively warm period since the decline of the spruce forests, which extends from about 10,500 years ago up to today. During the Late-Glacial and the Holocene, global climate and vegetation changed and lake levels rose and fell (COHMAP, 1988). On the New England coast—and at Walden Pond as well—there were great changes in the climate, the landscape, and the vegetation between 18,000 years ago and now (Winkler, 1985a).

## Geological Setting: Modern Upland Vegetation and Limnology

Walden Pond is a kettle pond 25 hectares in area with 2 deep basins—one about 18 meters deep and one more than 31 meters in depth (Thoreau, 1854; Figure 2). It was formed probably between 14,000 and 12,000 years ago when an ice block left by the receding glacier melted in glacial outwash.

Thoreau was the first person to study Walden Pond (Figure 2)—for its unique attributes: the transparency of the water, the organisms which lived in the pond, the depth and bathymetry of the pond, and the differences in the temperature of the shallow and deep waters and how the thermal stratification affected the biology of the pond. He drew a map of the pond from his measurements of depth taken by compass and chain while lying on the ice during the winter of 1846 (Thoreau, 1854). About 80 years later, a second limnologist—Ed Deevey—also constructed a bathymetric map of Walden Pond (Deevey, 1942), and the two maps are in most ways comparable.

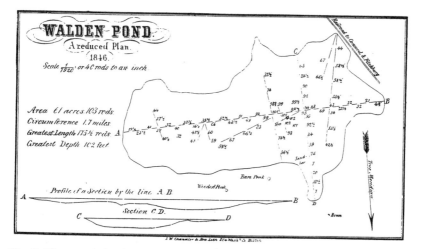

*Fig. 2. Thoreau's bathymetric map of Walden Pond (Thoreau, 1854).*

In August of 1979, I obtained a sediment core from Walden Pond—taken from the deepest basin in 28.8 meters of water using a freeze-coring technique.

I was interested in Walden Pond for three reasons:
(1) From Thoreau's bathymetry (Figure 2), I thought the pond might have annually layered sediments. These layers, called varves, are sometimes formed in small, deep lakes when lake mixing does not disturb the bottom

sediments. The annual deposits can be separated because of seasonal color differences. Varves would provide excellent time control with which to date vegetation and climate changes in southern New England since deglaciation.

(2) I wanted to compare Thoreau's account of the changing woodlands and land use in the Concord area to the evidence for these changes preserved in the lake sediments.

(3) Walden Pond is interesting paleobotanically because it is on the edge of three major vegetation regions: It is at the western edge of the Atlantic Coastal plain pitch pine and oak forests; it is on the northeastern edge of the oak-chestnut/oak-hickory forests of the Appalachians; and it is on the southeastern edge of the great hemlock-white pine northern hardwood forest.

Because of these ecotones, slight changes in climate can effect relatively large vegetation changes.

Preserved in anoxic, water-logged sediments are pollen, leaves, twigs, and seeds from regional upland vegetation, as well as from local vegetation and aquatic plants. Also deposited layer upon layer are algal cysts and scales, pieces of invertebrates, as well as pieces of charcoal windborne from forest fires, and sand and gravel lenses from erosional events. All are there to be dated, identified, and interpreted.

The core recovered was 83 centimeters long and contained 600 years of sediment—enough to contrast the pre- and post-European settlement environment in the Concord area, but still requiring the extrapolation of history from sites nearby.

## Deglaciation Vegetation and Climate History from Pollen and Charcoal

There are several Late-Glacial and Holocene pollen sites near to Walden Pond from which the regional vegetation and climate changes of the past 18,000 years in southern New England can be derived (Figure 1).

Pollen, the male gamete of plants, is one of the most abundant plant fossils in lake sediments. The coat is resistant to decay. The changes in the pollen types at different times tells us what is happening in the forests and grasslands and to the climate at a specific time.

Pollen are microscopic grains ranging from about 12 to over 100 microns in size. Most pollen can be identified to genus and some to species.

The regional pollen stratigraphy for all of the lowland southern New England sites is similar and synchronous during the Late-Glacial and the Early Holocene. By examination of the pollen frequencies in my Walden Pond core and the abundance of pine pollen in the sediments, I think that the Middle and Late Holocene Walden pollen stratigraphy would be most like stratigraphies from Massachusetts ponds to the east: Houghton Pond in Blue Hills Reservation, Boston from P. Newby by personal communication; to the southeast: Winneconnet Pond near Taunton (Suter, 1985); and on Cape Cod: Duck Pond in Wellfleet (Winkler, 1985a). Therefore, I have extrapolated from these a history of the vegetation and climate changes in the Concord area since deglaciation.

To summarize these changes briefly, the earliest pollen assemblages suggest tundra and spruce parklands, a cold, open, and windy environment more than 12,000 years before the present. *Hudsonia* was abundant and spruce and arctic willow grew in protected places. After 12,000 years there was a boreal forest of spruce, jack pine, and green alder. By 10,500 years before the present, spruce disappeared from southern New England forests and there was a northern conifer forest of white and jack pines. By about 9,500 years ago—during a warm and dry climatic period—pitch pine replaced jack pine and the oak and pine barrens vegetation was established on the Atlantic Coastal Plain and probably on the dry sandy soils in Walden Woods. The warm and dry climate lasted until about 5,000 years before present but, even before this time, in wetter habitats conifers such as hemlock and white cedar, and hardwoods such as beech, maple ironwood, ash, chestnut, and hickory, became established in southern New England.

After 5,000 years there were alternating periods of dominant pine-oak forests and expanded white pine-hemlock-hardwood forests. A cooler

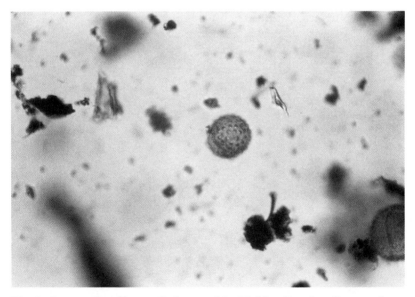

**Fig. 3. Ragweed pollen and charcoal in Walden Pond sediments from about the time that Thoreau lived at Walden Pond. The photo was taken through the microscope. The ragweed pollen grain is 19um in diameter.**

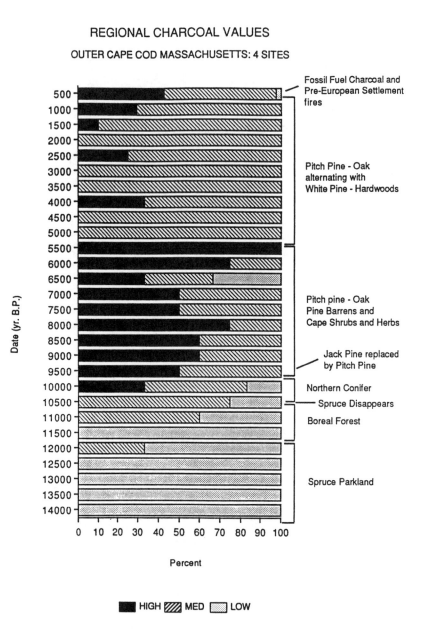

**REGIONAL CHARCOAL VALUES**

**OUTER CAPE COD MASSACHUSETTS: 4 SITES**

*Fig. 4. Summary diagram of regional charcoal values and regional vegetation changes for southeastern Massachusetts. The highest charcoal values (the dark bars) are most abundant between 9000 and 5000 yrs. B.P. (from Winkler, 1989; and ms. in prep.).*

period after 3,000 years ago is evidenced by increased spruce and birch pollen and a systematic decrease of both hemlock and beech in southern

New England. These Late Holocene changes are also seen in the Walden Pond sediments. European settlement changes are indicated by increased pollen from herbs, mostly ragweed (Figure 3), and grass in the top sediments of the cores.

Another index I use is charcoal—microscopic pieces of burned plants that are windborne to the lakes during forest fires and provide a record of the fire history of the region, which is also related to climatic change (Winkler, 1985b). The high charcoal abundances signify a hot and dry climate. The regional charcoal stratigraphy for southern Massachusetts (Figure 4) supports the vegetation and climate interpretations since deglaciation interpreted from the pollen (Winkler, 1989; and in preparation). High charcoal concentrations are most evident between 9,000 and 5,000 years ago when pitch pine and oak became established.

In my Walden Pond pollen percentage diagram, there is a pronounced increase in herb and grass pollen after European settlement of the Concord area, which provides time control for the pollen stratigraphy (Figure 5). The ragweed pollen rise is used as *the* time marker of European

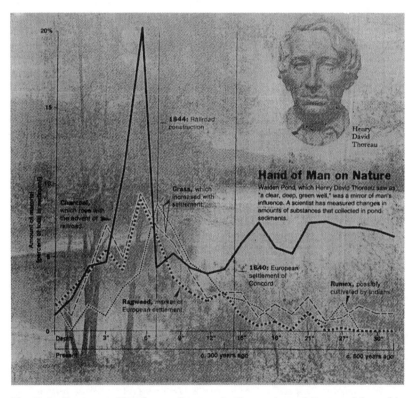

**Fig. 5. Indicators of land use changes in the region of Concord found in the Walden Pond sediments. Graphics from New York Times Science Times, Oct. 8, 1991. Data from M.G. Winkler.**

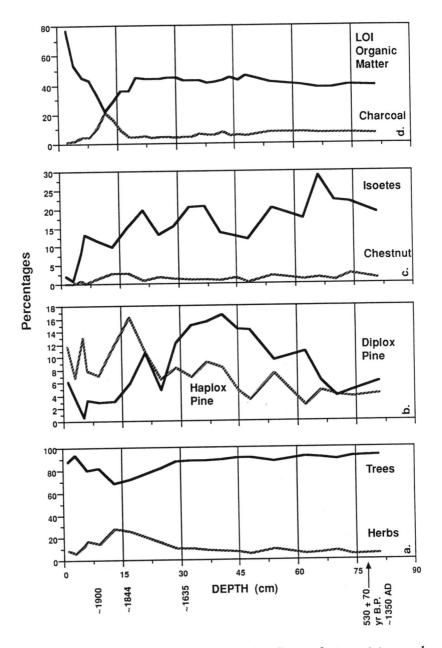

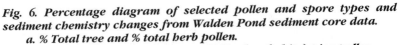

*Fig. 6. Percentage diagram of selected pollen and spore types and sediment chemistry changes from Walden Pond sediment core data.*
 *a. % Total tree and % total herb pollen.*
 *b. % Diplox (pitch/red)pine and % Haplox (white) pine pollen.*
 *c. Chestnut pollen and* Isoetes *spores.*
 *d. % Organic matter (as represented by loss-on-ignition analysis) and % charcoal (Winkler, 1985b) in Walden Pond sediments.*

206

settlement, and at Walden Pond it increases, along with grass and *Rumex* pollen, as tree pollen decreases (Figures 5, 6a). These changes indicate the clearing of land for homes and farms and the demand for wood for heating and building. The striking European settlement changes are at about 30 centimeters depth in the Walden Pond core. The basal 53 centimeters of the core therefore documents pre-European settlement vegetation. There is a radiocarbon date of 530 plus or minus 70 years before the present (WIS-1832, Steventon and Kutzbach, 1987) for the 75-81 centimeter level of the core.

At European settlement there is also a switch in the pine species present around Walden Pond when white pine became more abundant than pitch pine (Figure 6b). This change in pine types documented by the changes in the pollen record had previously been interpreted from surveyor's records of the forest vegetation in Concord at settlement (Whitney and Davis, 1986). The change in pine species may have been due to several factors: (1) fire suppression by the colonists—white pine is less tolerant of frequent large fires; (2) a cooler climate—suggested by the increased spruce pollen and the systematic decrease of hemlock and beech that had begun before European settlement; (3) the "King's trees" policy—which forbade colonists to cut down white pine, reserving those trees for the masts of British ships; and (4) the reforestation policy of the colonists—white pine being a more valuable tree than pitch pine.

At the time Henry Thoreau was living at Walden Pond white pine, oak, and birch were the most abundant trees. Charcoal (Figures 3,5), which was slightly more abundant in the lake sediments before European settlement when pitch pine was dominant, decreased immediately after settlement. However, a large charcoal peak identifies the time of Thoreau's residence at Walden Pond (Figure 5). In 1844 the railroad was built near the southwestern end of the pond. Sparks from the trains as well as the railroad policy of burning brush adjacent to the tracks—coupled with Thoreau's own practice of throwing burning logs from his campfires into the pond, his actual accidental setting of a fire in the western part of Walden Woods in 1844, and the fire that destroyed part of Thoreau's pine plantation in 1870—all contribute to the high charcoal concentrations in the sediments that could be seen by eye and be measured chemically.

Another time marker in the pond sediments is the disappearance of the chestnut pollen (Figure 7) in about 1913 in southern New England. There was about 2 percent chestnut pollen at almost every level in the sediments until the top centimeters (Figure 6c). There was a small but definite presence of chestnut trees in the Concord area in the centuries before 1913. Thoreau writes of chestnutting in Walden Woods (Thoreau, 1853) and while walking near Sandy Pond—gathering the nuts floating at the shoreline (Thoreau, 1854). By 1913 the chestnut trees in the Eastern states were decimated by the chestnut blight fungus, and the decline in chestnut pollen is a definite time marker at New England sites (Brugam,

1978). No chestnut pollen was found in the top few samples of the Walden Pond core (Figure 6c).

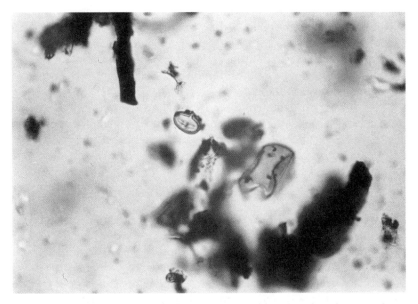

***Fig. 7. Chestnut pollen and charcoal in Walden Pond sediments from about the time that Thoreau lived at Walden Pond and gathered chestnuts in Walden Woods. The photo was taken through the microscope. The chestnut pollen grain is 13.5um in length.***

## Limnology of Walden Pond
## and Land Use Changes in the Walden Watershed

Changes within the drainage basin of Walden Pond large enough to alter the chemistry of the pondwater or the composition of the sediments, and hence result in a change in the pond biota, are documented in the stratigraphy. I have several lines of evidence of dramatic within-lake changes during the past 600 years.

The first evidence is changes in the aquatic pollen and spore profile. *Isoëtes*, a rosette-forming aquatic plant most often found in very clear, nutrient-poor ponds such as Walden where it can grow under as much as 14 meters of water, has microspores which are seen in the sediments. *Isoëtes* remains a constant presence in Walden Pond even throughout the European settlement changes, railroad construction, and Thoreau's residence (Figure 6c). However, *Isoëtes* spores decreased dramatically in the recent sediments after the beach, bathhouse, and amusement park were built and Walden Pond became a place of recreation for the metropolitan area. Decreased

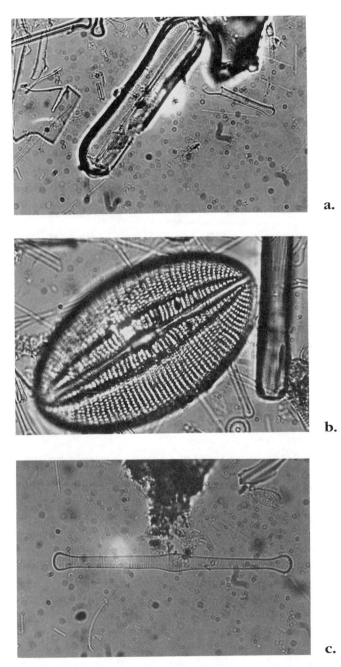

*Fig. 8. Diatoms from Walden Pond sediments. Microscope photo taken under oil at 1000 to 1250X magnification, from 28–29cm core depth.*
  *a.* Neidium *62um long.*
  *b.* Diploneis *40um long.*
  *c.* Tabellaria flocculosa v linearis *70um long.*

209

water transparency and increased nutrients were the results of the popular-
ization of the pond by the railroad company.

A decrease in the percentage of organic matter in the pond
sediments is another bit of evidence for railroad construction and
subsequent land-use changes which increased shoreline erosion and
deposited large quantities of sand and gravel into the pond (Figure 6d).
Organic matter increased again after the turn of the century and in fact
doubled in the recent sediments (Figure 6d)—a striking indication of
increased nutrient-rich runoff reaching the pond.

I have also analyzed the remains of plankton, the mostly microscopic floating organisms that are the foundation of the food web. There
have been many changes in these organisms in the pond due to European
settlement changes.

Diatoms are microscopic algae with silica cell walls that are well
preserved in the lake sediment (Figure 8). Something is known of the
chemical and environmental tolerances of diatom taxa, many of which
can be identified to species and even variety. The diatoms from Walden
Pond represent taxa from a low nutrient environment which has
increasingly become more eutrophic and more acidic. Some of the major
changes are at 30 centimeters in the core—concurrent with European
settlement changes—and some have taken place more recently, concurrent with the decline of the aquatic plant—*Isoëtes*—presented earlier.

There is some evidence of the disappearance of some algal taxa from
Walden Pond immediately after European settlement. A possibly "new"
diatom taxon—a *Neidium* which I like to refer to as *Neidium thoreauii*, was
abundant in most of the pre-European settlement sediments (Figure 8a).
This diatom was not present in the top 28 centimeters of the core. Dr. John
Smol of Queens College in Kingston, Ontario, observed a similar phenomenon when he analyzed the scales of other chrysophyte algae in the Walden
Pond sediments that I had sent him. He found an unusually great abundance
of two Mallamonads in the pre-European settlement sediments. He said that
the Walden abundances of these species were greater than any he had seen
anywhere—but they had become extinct in recent years, being replaced by
more cosmopolitan and nutrient-tolerant species.

The analysis of zooplankton—water fleas—*Cladocera*—show similar
changes with species changes from smaller-bodied *Eubosmina* to large-
bodied *Daphnia* in the topmost sediments (S. Barta, personal communication).

All these changes show that there has been a decline in the water
quality at Walden Pond due to modifications of the drainage basin by
people. These results are interesting, but they could also be frightening or
forewarning if we knew more about the importance of these microorganisms to our lives and could interpret these changes more clearly.

The sedimentation rates today are very high in Walden Pond
compared with most other clear kettle ponds. But Walden is very deep
and should be able to reverse eutrophication processes if shoreline and

watershed modifications cease and sewage is adequately treated and removed from the beach area.


# Bibliography

Brugam, R. B. (1978). "Pollen Indicators of Land-Use Change in Southern Connecticut". *Quaternary Research,* vol. 9, pp. 349–362.

COHMAP Members. (1988). "Climatic Changes of the Last 18,000 Years: Observations and Model Simulations," *Science,* vol. 241, pp. 1043–1052.

Deevey, E. S. (1942). "A Re-Examination of Thoreau's 'Walden'," *The Quarterly Review of Biology,* vol. 17: pp. 1–11.

Steventon, R. L. and J. E. Kutzbach (1987). University of Wisconsin Radiocarbon Dates XXIV. *Radiocarbon* 29 (3): 397–415.

Suter, S. (1985). "Late-Glacial and Holocene Vegetation History in Southeastern Massachusetts: A 14,000 year pollen record. *Current Research in the Pleistocene,* vol.2: pp. 87–88.

Thoreau, H. D. (1854). *Walden; or, Life in the Woods.* Boston: Ticknor and Fields Publishers. Reprinted in 1960 by Dolphin Books, Doubleday and Co., Inc., Garden City, New York.

Thoreau, H. D. (1853). *The Journal of Henry D. Thoreau.* Journal IV (1852–1853). B. Torrey and F. H. Allen, editors. Boston: Houghton Mifflin Company, 1906.

Whitney, G. G. and W. C. Davis (1986). "Thoreau and the Forest History of Concord, Massachusetts." *Journal of Forest History ,* vol. 30, no. 2: pp. 70–81.

Winkler, M. G. (1985a). "A 12,000–Year History of Vegetation and Climate for Cape Cod, Massachusetts. *Quaternary Research* vol. 23: pp. 301–312.

Winkler, M. G. (1985b). Charcoal Analysis for Paleoenvironmental Interpretation: A Chemical Assay. *Quaternary Research* vol. 23: pp. 313–326.

Winkler, M. G. (1989). *Geologic, Chronologic, Biologic, and Chemical Evolution of the Acid Kettle Ponds within the Cape Cod National Seashore.* Report to the National Park Service, North Atlantic Region. 145 pp.

---

**MARJORIE GREEN WINKLER** is an associate scientist for the Center of Climatic Research at the University of Wisconsin. She holds a Ph.D. in Environmental Science from the University of Wisconsin Institute of Environmental Studies. She has studied the environment in many parts of New England as well as in the Midwest and has used *Cape Cod* as a comparison to current work she has done.

# Bedrock Geology of the Walden Woods

❖

### Patrick J. Barosh

## Introduction

The geology around Walden Woods records an ancient continental collision that took place along the southeast edge at the present Appalachian Mountains. It was under way before any higher forms of plant or animal life evolved, and continued for a considerable time. Marine sediments in the areas were squeezed, broken, baked, and intruded by granitic rock between two converging continental plates. The features formed then controlled the present shape of the bedrock topography. The topography, in turn, guided the deposition of the overlying Late Pleistocene glacial sands and gravels, and these determined the position of Walden Pond.

Almost all that has been learned this century on the bedrock geologic history of the area is due to the work of the U.S. Geological Survey. Cupples (1964) and Bell and Alvord (1976) located a major fault zone to the southeast of Walden Pond and subdivided the rock type in the area. The work by Koteff (1964) on the surficial geology of the area provided additional clues to the bedrock structure. These and other, unpublished data were used later to prepare a detailed map of Concord (Barosh, 1979). The compilation and analysis of this and other work in eastern Massachusetts showed the Walden area to lie in a zone of faulting that separates two continental plates (Barosh and others, 1977, Alvord and others, 1976). The dating of many rock samples by the degree of decay of radioactive elements done by Robert Zartman and others provided the information on the timing of the events and enabled the history to be told (Barosh, 1984). These data provide the basis for this report.

# The Geologic Setting

Walden Woods lies on the southeastern edge of the Nashoba Thrust Belt, which is the greatest zone of faults known in North America. The belt snakes across southeast New England and extends out to sea north of Cape Ann (Figure 1). This belt separates two totally different geologic provinces. The region to the southeast consists mainly of Precambrian granite, about 630 million years old, with a few down-dropped blocks of younger rock, such as the Boston Basin, and some younger granite. The region to the northwest is an equally ancient terrain made up of an enormously thick pile of marine siltstone, sandstone, and shale that has been metamorphosed under high temperature and pressure. This terrain formed offshore of an earlier "North American" continent that lay farther to the northwest, whereas the terrain to the southeast was apparently once attached to what is now northwest Africa.

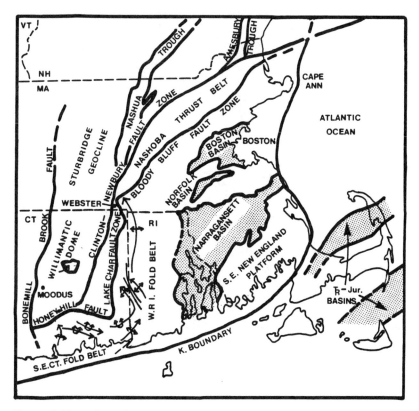

***Figure 1. Map of southern New England showing major geologic provinces***

The Nashoba Thrust Belt formed as terrain to the southeast collided and slid beneath one on the northwest. The belt now forms a zone of steeply northwest-dipping thrust faults that varies in width. It is widest northwest of Boston, where Walden lies, and thins abruptly to the southwest (Figure 2). The belt contains a variety of sandstone and shale that appears to be mainly derived from volcanic debris, and some limestone. These strata have been metamorphosed into many kinds of gneiss, schist and marble as the area was squeezed and intruded by granite. The granite invaded along many of the fault zones and interdigitates with the metamorphic rock.

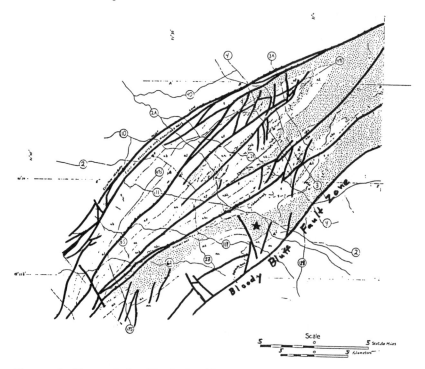

**Figure 2. Map of the Nashoba Thrush Belt northwest of Boston, Massachusetts. Walden Pond shown by star. Andover Granite shown by stipple.**

Walden Woods is underlain mainly by granite and is situated adjacent to the Bloody Bluff fault zone, which is one of the great faults marking the boundary of the Nashoba Thrust Belt. Walden's geologic history is that of this great zone of movement.

## Rock Types

Few rocks crop out in the Walden Woods, but the kinds present are well known from adjacent areas. Most of the Walden area lies over granitic rock with some gabbro and remnants of the metamorphosed sedimentary strata (Figure 3). These form a series of irregular northeast-trending zones across the area. The metamorphosed strata comprise the Marlboro Formation and the overlying Shawsheen Gneiss. The granitic rock is the Andover granite that invades the older Assabet Quartz Diorite to the northwest. Some quartz diorite and gabbrodiorite are present to the southwest and may be younger. These rocks are described briefly below, starting with the oldest:

## Marlboro Formation

The Marlboro is a dark gray to nearly black thinly layered rock. It is fine-grained, almost laminated in appearance. It forms a northeast zone through Lincoln, and good examples may be seen on Mount Misery, around the DeCordova Museum and along Route 2 at and just east of Bedford Road. Small remnants of Marlboro may also be seen in the intrusive rock.

## Shawsheen Gneiss

The Shawsheen Gneiss consists of light- to medium-gray, medium-bedded, medium-grained gneiss that may weather to a yellowish, rusty or dark-brown surface. Parts of it are schistose. It originally formed much of the Walden area but has been largely eaten away by the Andover Granite. Remnants occur scattered in the Andover, and one is well displayed along the north side of Route 2 at a slight knoll a little east of the Concord town line.

## Assabet Quartz Diorite

The Assabet is a medium-gray, medium- to coarse-grained variable granitic rock with equant to stretched-out mineral grains. Abundant dark-gray mica (biotite) and hornblende minerals are present. It forms much of central Concord and can be seen around the visitors' center near the North Bridge and on Lowell Road just west of the Concord River.

## Andover Granite

The granite is a light-gray variable rock that weathers buff and generally is present in three phases. The main phase is medium- to coarse-grain with noticeable silver mica (muscovite) and commonly has enclosed pieces of Shawsheen Gneiss and Assabet Quartz Diorite. It grades locally

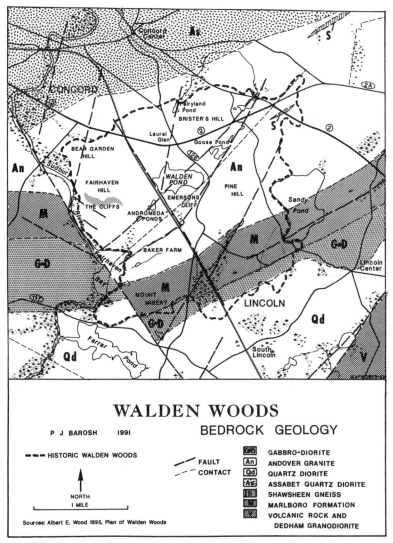

**WALDEN WOODS**

P J BAROSH      1991

**BEDROCK GEOLOGY**

- - - HISTORIC WALDEN WOODS

⟋ FAULT
⟋ CONTACT

NORTH
1 MILE

Sources: Albert E. Wood 1895, Plan of Walden Woods

GABBRO-DIORITE
ANDOVER GRANITE
QUARTZ DIORITE
ASSABET QUARTZ DIORITE
SHAWSHEEN GNEISS
MARLBORO FORMATION
VOLCANIC ROCK AND
DEDHAM GRANODIORITE

*Figure 3. Bedrock geologic map of Walden Woods*

into a very coarse-grained phase known as pegmatite. A slightly later phase, which is generally fine-grained and uniform, occurs as tabular dikes in the former. The Andover forms the bulk of the bedrock of Walden Woods. It is very well exposed along the east and south sides of Emerson's Cliff, south of Walden, and in scattered outcrops on Pine Hill to the east.

## Quartz Diorite

The quartz diorite is a generally medium-gray, medium-grained rock that is similar to, but usually less variable than, the Assabet Quartz

Diorite and may be slightly younger. It forms a zone across the area, just south of Walden Woods. Scattered outcrops occur near Route 117 in southern Lincoln east of Hathaway Hill.

## GabbroDiorite

Dark gray to very dark gray fine-grained gabbro, which locally grades to medium-grained diorite, appears to be the youngest intrusive body in the area. The gabbrodiorite forms an irregular belt along the south edge of Walden Woods and southwest of it. It can be seen easily in small outcrops along the roads just west of Fairhaven Bay.

All of these rocks are very old. The Shawsheen Gneiss and Marlboro Formations are not well dated, but they are probably similar in age to the volcanic rock, southeast of the Bloody Bluff fault zone (Figure 3), which are older than 630 million years as they are intruded by the Dedham Granodiorite of that age. The intrusive rocks near Walden Woods may range from 630 to 380 million years in age (Late Precambrian to Lower Paleozoic). In addition, there are probably a few small dark-gray diabase dikes of about 200 million years (Jurassic) age in the area, but they have not been located thus far.

## Structural Geology

The geologic structure of Walden Woods is revealed by the orientation and offset of rock units and interpretation of the landscape. The latter is especially important in this area where the rock surface is generally deeply buried by glacial deposits.

During the repeated passage of glaciers across the area, ice scoured away the soil and softer and loose rock. This brought out differences in resistance between rock types and etched out the broken rock in fault zones. The ice then proceeded to lay down varying thicknesses of clayey silt and rock fragments called till and sand and gravel, as the glaciers melted back. This covered much of what had been scraped clean. The shape of the etched rock, however, exerted considerable control as to where these deposits were laid down and the shape of this buried surface can be largely surmised. Faults can be interpreted from this shape in many places. Thus, although little rock is exposed, it can be ascertained that the position of Walden and its neighboring ponds and the Sudbury River are fault controlled. In fact, all the rivers in the region are generally fault controlled.

The regional trend of the rock units and principal faults is to the northeast in this portion of the Nashoba Thrust Belt. The major Bloody Bluff fault zone, which forms the southeast border of the belt, lies but a short distance southeast of Walden Pond. It forms the boundary of the volcanic rock and Dedham Granodiorite (Figure 3). The fault forms a distinctive narrow topographic trough that extends from the junction of Lincoln, Wayland, and Weston northeastward to Route 2A just west of Route 128. The latter spot is alongside Bloody Bluff, the site of a skirmish in the Revolutionary War site, from which the fault was named. Many other roughly parallel faults lie to the northwest of this fault zone, and some pass through Walden Woods. The initial position of these faults was influenced by the layering of the strata. Some of the early faults were invaded by granitic material when the rocks were deeply buried in ancient time, thus giving the bodies an elongation to the northeast. Many faults continued to move and later broke these rocks. The result of all this produced a northeast trend of the metasedimentary strata, faults, and granitic rocks across the area.

The faults dip very steeply northwestward near the surface, but bend and are more gently dipping at depth. Hundreds of miles of displacement has occurred along the Bloody Bluff fault zone and significant amounts along many of the others also. The southeast sides of these faults moved relatively under and to the southwest of the northwest sides. This movement occurred over a long period of time. A few of these faults probably also moved in a different manner at a much later time when the region was being stretched.

A zone of faults apparently extends northeastward of Fairhaven Bay along a buried valley that passes beneath Walden Pond and bisects Walden Woods. This Andromeda fault zone, named after ponds along it, parallels the Bloody Bluff fault and would have a closely related history.

A northwest-trending fault lies beneath the nearby Sudbury River. This accounts for the unusual trend of this reach in the otherwise northeasterly flow of the river. Offset rock units show the northeast side of the fault, referred to as the Sudbury River fault, has moved relatively southeastward approximately one mile, with respect to the southwest side. The railroad in Walden Woods may follow another northwest-trending fault. Some such northwest-trending faults formed early, but as a group they, along with north-trending ones, are the youngest in New England. A few are apparently still moving today.

## Topographic Development

The topography of the Walden Woods results from many factors: the bedrock surface, which is controlled by rock types, faults and some ice carving; the mantle of glacial till and deltaic sand and gravel deposits; and the subsequent swamp and Sudbury River floodplain deposits.

The two quartz diorite bodies form lowlands, whereas the Marlboro Formation and gabbrodiorite stand up as does the rock southeast of the

Bloody Bluff fault. The Andover Granite generally forms a lowland, but it supports a number of hills, such as Fairhaven Hill, Emerson Cliff, and Pine Hill, along its southeastern part. More would have stood up if it were not broken by faults.

Northeast-trending faults cut through Walden Woods to help form a buried valley and give shape to these hills. A buried valley of over 100 feet deep extends from Fairhaven Bay through Andromeda Ponds, Walden Pond, Goose Pond, Little Goose Pond, and Crosby Pond. The faults in this valley, along with another nearer Sandy Pond give Pine Hill its northeasterly elongation. If it were shaped primarily by the southeasterly flowing glacial ice, it would be elongated in that direction. Both Fairhaven Hill and Emerson's Cliff are also fault controlled, but have in addition a

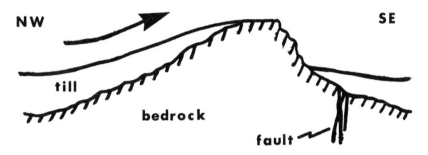

**Figure 4. Diagrammatic cross-section of a rock-cored drumlin such as Fairhaven Hill or Emersons Cliff with arrow showing direction of ice flow.**

buildup of ice-smoothed glacial till on their northwest sides. They could be called fault-controlled rock-cored drumlins (Figure 4). The faults controlling the direction of the main cliffs on these hills are of different directions. Emerson's Cliff is part of a fault sliver on the side of the northeast-trending buried valley, and its cliff faces a small northeast-trending valley. The cliff at Fairhaven Hill mainly faces toward the northwest-trending Sudbury River fault.

The buried valley beneath Walden is responsible for its and the other ponds' being formed where they are. Some of the relatively thicker ice in the valley remained as the last glacier front retreated to north of the present nearby Route 2. Sand and gravel carried by streams issuing forth from beneath the glacier were diverted into this valley and buried these remnants. Their melting produced the series of kettle-hole depressions forming the ponds and Fairhaven Bay.

Walden Woods is formed of an upland of relatively more resistant Andover Granite and strata of the Marlboro Formation capped by sand and gravel. Its southwest edge is formed by the fault controlled Sudbury River valley and its northeast edge mainly by the border of the sand and gravel.

## Summary History

The geologic history of Walden Woods began long before the present Atlantic Ocean existed. Another earlier ocean had previously separated a version of the present northwest Africa from a smaller continent where the current North America lies. This northwest Africa extended farther to sea and included much of what became eastern Massachusetts and Rhode Island. The shore of North America, on the other hand, may have stood in central New York and had volcanic islands, surrounded by thick sediments, offshore to the east. These sediments extended across most of the present Connecticut and western and central Massachusetts and beyond. These continental masses moved toward one another in fits and starts over a great period of time to gradually squeeze out the ocean between. The major part of this collision was about 630 million years ago, but it was not over until approximately 380 million years ago when all of New England rose from the sea. Walden Woods lies at the eastern edge of this great zone of collision took place. Its major geologic features formed then as the continent to the southeast smashed into and slid under that to the northwest.

Great northeast-trending faults were formed and intruded by various types of granite and gabbro to metamorphose the marine sediments. This process was repeated several times to produce what we see today in the rocks around Walden. A few northwest-trending faults also formed in adjusting local stress, to interrupt this general pattern in places. Some of these faults undoubtedly moved again in a different fashion a little over 200 million years ago (at the time of the dinosaurs) during the initial formation of the present Atlantic Ocean. But this later movement does not appear to have made any significant change to the area of Walden Woods. This new oceanic break, which formed as the present continents moved apart, has a slightly different position from the older one. The region around Boston that was east of the earlier ocean was left behind to dangle into the western North Atlantic. Walden Woods, thus, continued to remain high and dry. It probably remained so until it was submerged by a series of great ice sheets during the last million or so years.

The ice scoured out the relatively weaker rock, especially the fault zones, and shaped the bedrock topography beneath Walden Woods. The Andover Granite and the Marlboro Formation were left as a slight upland crossed by a fault-controlled valley extending northeastward from Fairhaven Bay. The ice sheet was thicker over this valley than in the area adjacent to it, and when the glacier melted back to the edge of the upland north of Route 2, remnants of ice remained in it. These remnants were buried by sand and gravel in a delta that built out southward from the ice front into a lake. Their melting later produced the kettle holes forming Walden Pond, Fairhaven Bay, and other ponds.

The bedrock geology thus reveals a long, complex history and has been directly and indirectly instrumental in forming the upland of Walden Woods and its famous ponds, despite the rarity of its exposures.

# Bibliography

Alvord, D.C., K. G. Bell, M. H. Pease, Jr., and P. J. Barosh, 1976, The Aeromagnetic Expression of Bedrock Geology Between the Clinton-Newbury and Bloody Bluff Fault Zones, Northeastern Massachusetts: U.S. Geological Survey, *Journal of Research*, vol. 4, pp. 601–604.

Barosh, P. J., 1979. Bedrock Geology Town of Concord, Massachusetts: Concord Department of Natural Resources, scale 1:12,000.

Barosh, P. J., 1984. Regional Geology and Tectonic History of Southeastern New England, in L. S. Hanson., ed., *Geology of the Coastal Lowlands from Boston, MA to Kennebunk, ME:* New England Intercollegiate Geologic Conference, 76th annual meeting, Salem State College, Salem, Massachusetts, pp. 1–35.

Barosh, P. J., Fahey, R. J., and Pease, M. H., Jr., 1977. Preliminary Compilation of the Bedrock Geology of the Land Area of the Boston 2 Degree Sheet, Massachusetts, Connecticut, Rhode Island, Maine and New Hampshire: U.S. Geological Survey Open-File Report 77-285, 142 pp., map scale 1:125,000.

Bell, K. G., and D. C. Alvord, 1976. Pre-Silurian Stratigraphy of Northeastern Massachusetts, in L.R. Page, ed., *Contributions to the Stratigraphy of New England: Geological Society of America,* Memoir 148. pp. 149–216.

Cuppels, N. P., 1964. The Marlboro Formation in the Concord Quadrangle, in *Guidebook to Field Trips in the Boston Area and Vicinity.* New England Intercollegiate Geologic Conference, 56th annual meeting, Boston College, Newton, Massachusetts, pp. 81–89.

Koteff, C., 1964. Surficial Geology of the Concord Quadrangle, Massachusetts: U.S. Geological Survey, Geologic Quadrangle Map GQ-331, scale 1:24,000.

---

**PATRICK J. BAROSH** has a doctorate in geology and has been working in eastern Massachusetts for over twenty years. He lives within a mile of Walden Pond.

# Walden Pond
## Its Geological Setting
## and the Africa Connection

❖

### James W. Skehan, S.J.

White Pond and Walden are great crystals on the surface of the earth,
Lakes of Light. If they were permanently congealed, and small enough
to be clutched, they would, perchance, be carried off by slaves, like
precious stones, to adorn the heads of emperors; but being liquid, and
ample, and secured to us and our successors forever, we disregard them,
and run after the diamond of Kohinoor. (*Walden*, 1899, page 210)

## I. Geological and Scientific Setting

Thoreau sang the praises of Walden, Goose, White's, and Sandy
(Flint's) ponds (Figure 1) loudly and poetically on many occasions. These
bodies of water and related sands and gravels of the area near Walden and
Concord were all spawned by processes active at the southeastern margin
of the Pleistocene continental ice cap. That a continental glacier had
covered the northern part of North America for a lengthy period until
approximately 10,000 to 15,000 years ago and, indeed, was responsible
for the many aspects of Nature that enthralled the "Bard of Walden," was
hardly suspected by Thoreau or most geologists of his time.

In this paper I will first outline a summary of the glacial and
postglacial geology in the vicinity of Walden Pond (Figures 1 and 2).
Then, I will briefly discuss the ancient and prolonged evolution of the
bedrock foundation (Figure 3) upon which the glacial soils were
deposited prior to reforestation and repopulation in the intervening
10,000 years.

Events relating to the evolution of the bedrock will be summarized
in a plate-tectonic model (Figure 4) that will propose that this Nashoba

terrane, on which Walden is located, together with its geological neighbor to the east, the Boston Avalon terrane, were a part of St. Botolph's volcanic arc, which formed on the western margin of the West African continent (Figure 5). The events of this prolonged evolution from continental margin about 1 billion years ago led to the formation of this volcanic arc about 630 to 540 million years ago, and to subsequent involvement in several mountain building collisions from about 450 to 275 million years ago. The last date is the approximate time of the last major continental collision that culminated in the formation of the Appalachian Mountains of eastern North America, which, in turn, gave way to later continental rifting in Mesozoic time, beginning about 225 million years ago. It was approximately at that time that North America, Africa, and other pieces in the Pangean continental jigsaw puzzle started rifting apart in a separation that continued throughout the Pleistocene glaciation and is still going on.

Thoreau's scientific interests were mainly concerned with characteristics of Walden's water, its plants and animals, and those of the surrounding landscape. His writings, however, reflect an interest in the origin and history of what we now refer to as glacial soils. However, in the absence of a theory of glaciation and a lack of interest in or belief in a worldwide Noah's Flood, he paid scant attention to questions about the origin of the soils or the bedrock. Thoreau was intensely concerned with various aspects of Walden Pond and the other water bodies of the region (*Walden*, 1899, pages 182–210), with a view to discovering why the level, quality, depth, and other characteristics of their water varied.

In discussing the puzzle of how Walden's shore became "so regularly paved with stones" (*Walden*, 1899, page 191), Thoreau recounts the Indian legend that spoke of "a hill here, which rose as high into the heavens as the pond now sinks deep into the earth." The story tells that "the hill shook and suddenly sank, and only one old squaw, named Walden, escaped, and from her the pond was named." Thoreau, convinced that the narrative contained some element of history, concluded as to Walden Pond's origin: "It is very certain, at any rate, that once there was no pond here, and now there is one" (page 192).

This legend, so puzzling yet convincing for Thoreau, is quite consistent with an interpretation of the origin of Walden Pond based on the following data from the glacial deposits presented by Koteff (1964). Walden Pond occupies a steep-sided kettle hole, "formed as glacial sands and gravels washed into Glacial Lake Sudbury from the front of the glacier and built up layer upon layer around a stagnant iceberg. The melting of the ice left a depression, or kettle hole, which contains water because the groundwater level is high enough and the kettle hole deep enough to expose the water table (Skehan, 1979, page 47). Thoreau cites the "Indian legend which tells how a hill formerly occupied the present site of the pond. It is plausible that the Indians did actually see the gravel-covered 'ice hill' melt and finally disappear" (*Walden*, 1897). Similar situations are known today under conditions in which "stagnant ice covered with sediment are observed in Alaska supporting trees and other vegetation" (Skehan, 1979, page 47).

Emerson's Cliff south of Walden Pond, rising some 115 feet above its surface, exposes glacial till and outcrops of the Andover Granite. Emerson's Cliff forms a buttress, to the north of which lay the deep depression in the bedrock that stranded the large block of glacial ice (Figures 2 and 3) about which were deposited the sands and gravels of Glacial Lake Sudbury. When the iceberg melted it left a deep depression filled with a renewable supply of groundwater, Walden Pond (Skehan, 1979, page 47).

The fact that Thoreau does not allude to a theory of glacial origins for the formation of Walden Pond should not surprise us if we remember that Thoreau graduated from Harvard College in 1837. Louis Agassiz, who developed and popularized his theory of continental glaciation, had arrived in Britain from his native Switzerland only in 1840, and in North America in 1846 where, right from the beginning he had found overwhelming evidence for the former presence and activity of an ice cap that covered large parts of North America. Nevertheless, Agassiz found that it was difficult to have a new, revolutionary theory accepted by other scientists—"some of the greatest names in science were arrayed against the novel glacial theory" said Agassiz decades later (Louis Agassiz, *Geological Sketches*. J. R. Osgood & Co. Boston, 1876, page 1).

Thoreau, although intensely interested in, and a keen observer of, the products of earth processes, seems to have had no formal acquaintance with the geological branch of natural history. Studies of the bedrock geology of eastern Massachusetts were just beginning (Dana and Dana, 1818). Although this geological map of Boston and vicinity extended as far west as Weston, Lincoln, and Bedford, Thoreau would have gained little insight from it concerning the bedrock geology of the Concord area because the rock west of the Charles River was mapped under the generalized category of "greenstone" (see Skehan, 1976, 1979, map decorating the cover). Thoreau's intense interest, however, in all other aspects of science suggest that, had the door to geological insight been open to him, he would have entered enthusiastically.

## Pleistocene Glacial History

Walden Pond, Goose Pond, and White's Pond (but not Sandy—or Flint's—Pond), so much a part of Thoreau's life, are known as "kettles" (Figure 1). The American Geological Institute's *Glossary of Geology* defines a kettle as "a steep-sided, usually basin- or bowl-shaped hole or depression, commonly without surface drainage, in glacial-drift deposits ... often

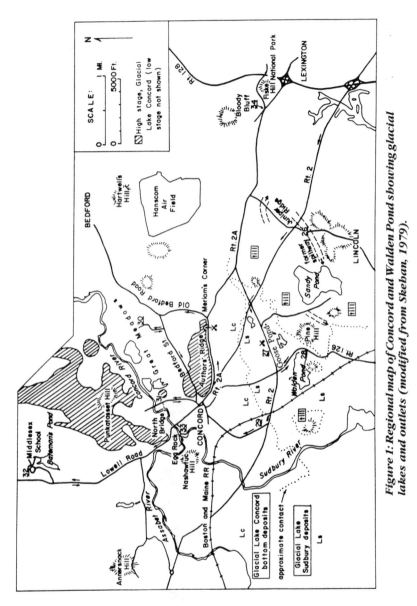

*Figure 1: Regional map of Concord and Walden Pond showing glacial lakes and outlets (modified from Skehan, 1979).*

containing a lake or swamp; formed by the melting of a large, detached block of stagnant ice (left behind by a retreating glacier) that had been wholly or partly buried in the glacial drift. Kettles range in depth from about a meter to tens of meters, and in diameter to as much as 13 km. Thoreau's Walden Pond is an example" (Bates and Jackson, eds., 1980).

Sometimes such features as kettle lakes are distinguished from kettle holes by whether the water table rises high enough in the glacial soils to form a body of water in the depression. In walking through the Walden

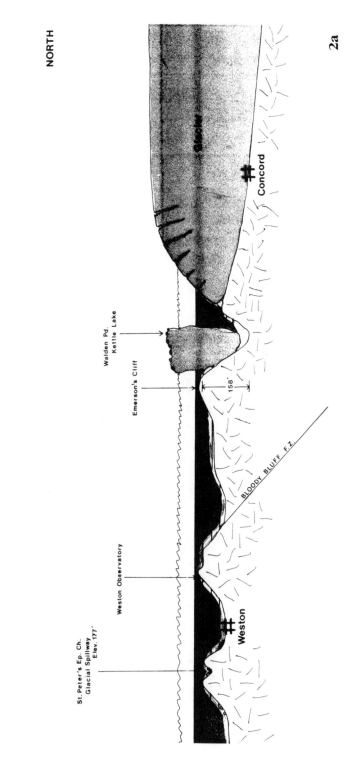

GLACIAL LAKE SUDBURY

High Water Stage

NORTH

2a

Glacier

Concord

Walden Pd.
Kettle Lake

Emerson's Cliff

158'

BLOODY BLUFF F.Z.

Weston Observatory

Weston

St. Peter's Ep. Ch.
Glacial Spillway
Elev. 177'

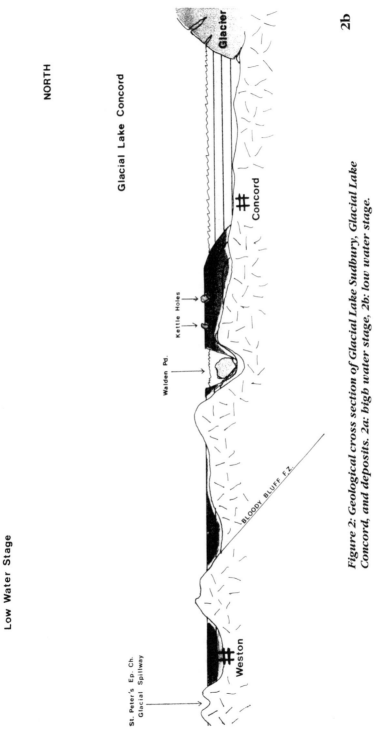

*Figure 2: Geological cross section of Glacial Lake Sudbury, Glacial Lake Concord, and deposits. 2a: high water stage, 2b: low water stage.*

Pond State Reservation south of Route 2, and Hapgood Wright Town Forest north of Route 2, one may observe numerous kettle holes that pockmark the otherwise relatively flat surface of the northern part of Glacial Lake Sudbury. Several kettle ponds adorn the surface of deposits laid down in Glacial Lake Sudbury within a few hundred feet to a half-mile of its junction with the deposits of Glacial Lake Concord to the north. Such kettles include Goose Pond and Little Goose Pond south of Route 2 (Figure 1).

The glacial deposits near Walden Pond, in the vicinity of Concord, have been described by Koteff (1964) as composed of poorly to well sorted sand, gravel, and cobble deposits of considerable variety. Some of these deposits (referred to as "till") were laid down directly on the underlying bedrock from the melting ice. Other, more abundant and thicker deposits, commonly laid down in turn on the till, consist of stratified sand and gravel deposits with small amounts of silt and clay. These materials consist of rock particles carried by streams of water melted from the ice-cap when it was located in the vicinity of Concord, north of Walden (Figure 2). The rock fragments making up the sand and gravel are pieces of the weathered bedrock that were carried by streams of glacial meltwater flowing into a lake impounded in front of, that is to the south of, the glacier. Geologists have given those lakes that dominated the Pleistocene landscape and its weather the names, "Glacial Lake Sudbury" and "Glacial Lake Concord" (Koteff, 1964).

Walden Pond is located within the bowl-shaped deposits that were laid down in Glacial Lake Sudbury (Figure 2), near a drainage divide. South of the divide modern streams, such as Stony Brook in Weston, drain to the Charles River and thence to the Atlantic at Boston; north of the divide the Sudbury and Assabet rivers join to form the Concord River, which empties into the Merrimack River, which in turn empties into the Atlantic near the New Hampshire border.

Glacial Lake Sudbury was prevented from flowing northward by the glacier itself (Figures 1 and 2). The glacial meltwater was impounded by a series of bedrock ridges southeast of Walden Pond, as well as by previously deposited glacial soils that prevented the lake from draining out of the basin in which the meltwater was accumulating. Glacial Lake Sudbury continued in existence long enough for the glacier to form stratified deposits hundreds of feet thick in places over the lake's bottom.

Eventually, the glacier melted back, north of Concord, giving rise to Glacial Lake Concord, which formed in stages (described by Skehan, 1979, pages 44–45). Glacial Lake Concord itself drained to the northeast once the glacier had melted northward, beyond the present location of the Concord River. The Shawsheen River valley became exposed, allowing drainage of Glacial Lake Concord to the northeast, toward Bedford and Billerica. The most obvious changes that have taken place around Walden and Concord in the 10,000 years since these glacial lakes disappeared have been caused by the generations of plants and animals that have flourished here, forming lake-bottom and swamp deposits, organic soils, and a vegetation cover.

## Bedrock Geology of Walden Pond and Vicinity

To place the geology of the Concord area in a regional context, it should be noted that the bedrock formations of Walden Pond and vicinity are part of a larger block of rock units, the Nashoba belt, Nashoba terrane, or Nashoba Thrust Belt, as geologists have variously referred to it in recent years, depending on what aspect of the geology is being considered (Hill and others, 1984; Barosh, 1984). To its north and west, the Nashoba terrane is bounded by the Merrimack trough and the Kearsarge–Central Maine synclinorium, respectively (Figure 3; see also Zen, 1983), which I will refer to simply as the central Massachusetts terrane.

The glacial deposits that form a veneer of soils over the landscape were laid down on a foundation of bedrock, the nearest outcrops of which may be observed in Emerson's Cliff, the hill just south of Walden Pond. Walden, Concord, and surrounding elements of the landscape are located on the Nashoba block, named for the nearby Nashoba River Valley, that Thoreau knew well from his excursions into the neighboring countryside.

Southern New England is divisible into several terranes each having its own distinctive geological evolution and rock formations, and separated from each other by large-scale faults, suggesting that the evolution of each was not linked to that of its neighbor since the time of formation of the fault. The boundary between the Nashoba and the Avalon terranes is a major zone of geologically ancient faulting (at least 275 Ma, and more probably about 350 Million years ago), the Bloody Bluff fault zone, named for the historic Revolutionary battle site, near Fiske Hill, Lexington (Skehan, 1979, page 51). The bedrock of the Nashoba terrane consists mainly of gneisses and schists of Neoproterozoic or Late Precambrian age (between 900 and about 540 million years) and of intrusive pulses of molten granite magma, the Andover Granite and related igneous rocks, that crystallized during Ordovician and Silurian time (450 to 415 million years ago). The Fish Brook Gneiss, for example, has been interpreted to be of volcanic origin and its age has been determined to be about 730 Million years ago (Olszewski, 1980).

The amateur geologist can readily recognize the difference between the dominant rock units that make up the Nashoba block and those of the Boston Avalon block to the southeast of the bounding Bloody Bluff fault zone. The major, easily recognized differences consist of contrasts in the dominant color of the rocks and by the relative degree of discernible deformation such as folds. The field guides by Hill and others (1984) and Skehan (1979) will assist in this quest. Such an observer may, with perhaps

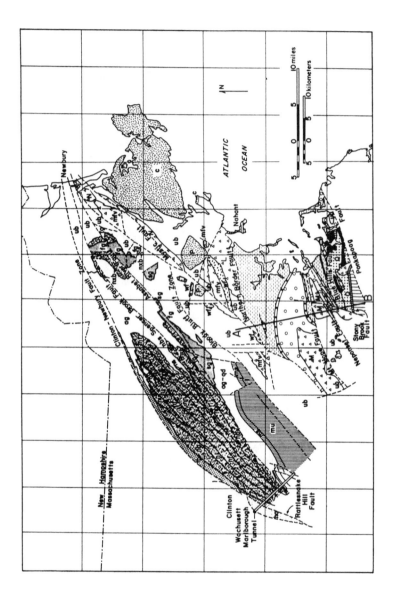

3a

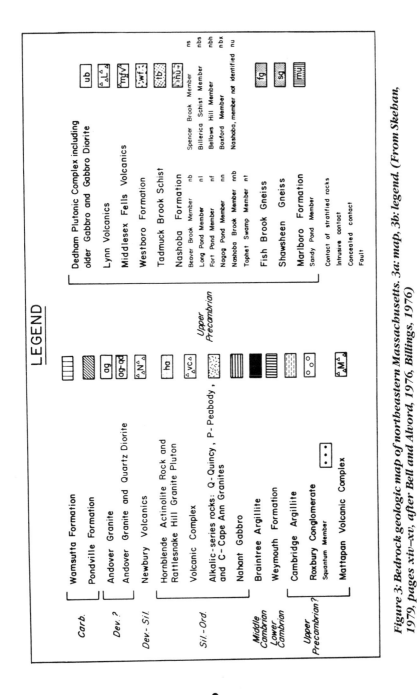

*Figure 3: Bedrock geologic map of northeastern Massachusetts. 3a: map, 3b: legend. (From Skehan, 1979, pages xiv–xv, after Bell and Alvord, 1976, Billings, 1976)*

greater difficulty, also recognize distinctive differences between the rocks of the Nashoba terrane and those of central Massachusetts, to the west and northwest of the bounding Clinton–Newbury fault zone, named by Skehan (1968) for two towns along the extent of the fault zone. The Clinton–Newbury fault zone, consisting of highly fractured rock, commonly is located in prominent valleys such as that of the Wachusett Reservoir in Clinton and Lake Quinsigamond in Worcester because the broken rock is rendered less resistant to erosion in as much as it is weathered and leached.

In spite of these pronounced differences, some fragments of the oldest rock units in the Avalon zone (quartzites, carbonates and calc-silicate rocks, and volcanic units) have similarities to some rock units in the Nashoba belt. These similarities have suggested to Skehan and Rast (1983) that rocks similar to those of the Nashoba belt may compose the foundation underlying the Avalon terrane (see the foundation rocks shown in Figure 4.) Thus I conclude that the Nashoba terrane rocks now exposed in the Walden area are part of a group of rock formations that have had a history of evolution that, at least in part, is the same as that of the deeper and older part of the Avalon terrane. Although in the field one can readily observe rocks in the Avalon terrane that are very different from those in the Nashoba terrane, their early histories may have been linked and similar, but with time their deformational histories varied as each block evolved separately as it experienced its own distinctive geological environment.

## Rock Formations of the Nashoba Terrane

The rocks of the Nashoba terrane are some of the most complex, and in many respects are the least understood sequence of the exotic terranes noted abovenamely the Avalon, the Nashoba, and the Merrimack trough. The major rock units of Neoproterozoic age from oldest to youngest consist of the following: the Fish Brook Gneiss, the Shawsheen Gneiss, and the Nashoba Formation. The age of the Marlboro Formation is not yet established with certainty but is thought to be of Cambrian age (Hill and others, 1984). All of these rock formations are intruded by Silurian–Ordovician plutons, collectively referred to as the Andover Granite and the Sharpners Pond Gabbro.

The distribution of the rock units named above is shown in Figure 3. A number of professional geologists over the years have contributed to the mapping, analysis, and description of these rock units. The amateur geologist may have some difficulty in identifying some of these formations in the field and in distinguishing some units from others, as the differences may be subtle. As aids for further study of these rock formations are the paper by Hill and others (1984) that describes a road log that points out localities where distinctive features of each may be seen. Also in the same paper are a brief description of the major rocks that compose each formation is presented in the same paper by Hon and others, and lengthier descriptions by Goldsmith (1991), Bell and Alvord (1976), Skehan and Abu-moustafa (1976), and Abu-moustafa and Skehan (1976).

The rock formations and major faults in the vicinity of Walden Pond and Concord include the following and localities where they may be observed or inferred are indicated:

## Bloody Bluff Fault Zone

Figures 2 and 3 show the Bloody Bluff fault zone, which separates the Nashoba terrane from the Avalon terrane. The fault is crossed by Route 117 in Lincoln, in the lowland near the Railroad Crossing just east of Drumlin Farm and just west of Tower Road. Evidence of the fault may be found at its type locality, Bloody Bluff, the Revolutionary War battle site, near Fiske Hill National Park where the cliffs of rock at Bloody Bluff consist of highly fractured and weathered granite.

## Marlboro Formation

Northwest of the Bloody Bluff fault is the Marlboro Formation (Figure 3), named by Emerson (1917) for ledges in Marlboro, consisting dominantly of metaigneous and metasedimentary rocks. These consist of interlayered, dark green to black biotite-amphibolite schist, amphibolite gneiss (banded), light colored quartzo-feldspathic gneiss, and rusty weathering sillimanite schist with minor amounts of quartzite, pink, and green, very fine-grained cherty layers of coticule and epicule, respectively, and marble (Goldsmith, 1991, pages F3–F5; DiNitto, 1984; Skehan and Abu-moustafa, 1976; Skehan, 1973). The upper part of the Marlboro Formation is called the Sandy Pond Member of the Marlboro Formation, named for outcrops in the hills near the glacial lake frequented by Thoreau. Hill and others (1984) have carried out neodymium isotope studies on amphibolites of the Marlboro Formation that suggest that they formed in the interval from 450 to 550 million years ago.

## Andover Granite

The Andover Granite (Figure 3) intrudes the adjacent rock formations and is exposed more broadly in the area around Walden Pond and Concord than any other rock unit. In strong contrast to the dominantly dark-green to black amphibolite schists of the Marlboro Formation are outcrops of the light-colored, commonly pink, muscovite- and garnet-bearing, generally gneissic Andover Granite with its associated pink pegmatites and gray to pink fine-grained granite and aplite. The strong alignment of muscovite defines a strong foliation. The Andover so pervasively intrudes the rocks of the Nashoba Formation that it is commonly referred to as a migmatitic or "mixed metamorphic–igneous" rock (Figure 3). The "gneissic Andover Granite is about 445–450 million years ago, and the younger phase of granite and pegmatite is 410–415 million years ago" (Wones and Goldsmith, 1991, pages 147–148). The rocks of this great body of igneous rock are readily recognized since they consist of pink intrusive masses of granite and pegmatite (coarsely crystalline) ranging from large elongate masses tens of miles long to very small lens-shaped masses a fraction of an inch long. The most reliable age for the oldest part of the Andover Granite is Ordovician (450 ± 23 million years ago, Zartman and Marvin, 1991, Ch. J, Table 1).

## Shawsheen Gneiss

The Shawsheen Gneiss (Figure 3), named by Bell and Alvord (1976), lies north of the Andover Granite and associated plutonic rocks and underlies much of the northeastern part of the Concord quadrangle southeast of the Assabet River fault. The Shawsheen consists of light-gray to dark-gray, micaceous sillimanite schist and gneiss, rusty weathering and sulfidic near its eastern margin, it contains some fine-grained, dark-green to black amphibolite lenses (Goldsmith, 1991, pages F5–F6). The Shawsheen has been interpreted by Bell and Alvord (1976) as being stratigraphically above the Marlboro Formation and in fault contact with the Fish Brook Gneiss along the Assabet River fault (Figure 3).

## Fish Brook Gneiss

The Fish Brook Gneiss (Figure 3), named by Castle (1965), forms a very narrow band of rock in the Concord to Maynard area but is much more broadly exposed to the northeast as far as Georgetown near the type locality at Fish Brook. The Fish Brook Gneiss, is a "pearly white to very light gray, distinctly foliated but generally unlayered biotite–quartz–plagioclase (feldspar) rock" (Castle, 1965, page C81). A light-colored gneiss, it contains fragments of amphibolite, biotite gneiss, and other kinds of rocks and is interpreted to have been a tuffaceous volcanic rock (Hill and others, 1984). It is nearly everywhere in fault contact with the Shawsheen Gneiss and is intruded by the Andover and related granites (Goldsmith, 1991, page F6). The 730 million years ago age date obtained by Olszewski (1980) on zircons of volcanic type indicates that the Fish Brook Gneiss is the oldest igneous rock unit thus far documented in the Nashoba terrane (Hill and others, 1984).

## Nashoba Formation

The northwestern corner of the Concord quadrangle, north and northeast of Concord Center, is underlain by rocks of the Nashoba Formation (Figure 3), named by Hansen (1956). Some of the high hills east of Lowell Road are held up by the abundant outcrops that are relatively resistant to erosion. The Nashoba Formation outcrops broadly for about 6.5 miles to the northwest of the Concord quadrangle. It consists dominantly of interlaminated light to dark gray, silver-tinted mica–garnet–sillimanite schist, and light- to dark-gray micaceous, sillimanite gneiss, with lesser amounts of quartzite, marble, and amphibolite. The presence of abundant mica and sillimanite indicates that the rock is rich in alumina. The boundary between the dominantly schist and gneiss units is marked by the Spencer Brook fault (Bell and Alvord, 1976; DiNitto and others, 1984).

## Tadmuck Brook Schist

Tadmuck Brook Schist (Figure 3), named by Bell and Alvord (1976), consists of interlaminated dark-gray slaty rocks and gray quartzite originally interpreted by Skehan and Abu-moustafa (1976) as resting unconformably on Nashoba Formation rocks. The chief basis for this interpretation was the presence of granule conglomerate, calc-silicate and quartzite at the contact of these units resting on the migmatitic and, in part, granoblastic mylonitized gneisses of the Nashoba Formation. The Tadmuck Brook is most distinctive, consisting of sillimanite schist, coaly dark-gray graphitic staurolite phyllite with crystals and fragments of sillimanite overgrowths on pink andalusite up to 18 inches long. Its western margin is marked by the Clinton–Newbury fault zone. I now reinterpret the Tadmuck Brook Schist as a phyllonite, a dominantly metamorphosed "phyllitic" rock containing coarse fragments and crystals of minerals indicating high metamorphic conditions that have been intensely sheared— a mylonite. Thus it is likely that the contact between the Nashoba Formation and the Tadmuck Brook Schist is a fault, and possibly a faulted unconformity.

# II. The African Connection

The Avalon terrane of southeastern New England consists of a sequence of rock units very similar to that of the Anti Atlas Mountains of Morocco and in turn similar to other parts of the circum-Atlantic region (Skehan, 1988; Rast and Skehan, 1983; Skehan and Rast, 1983). Certain rock units of the Nashoba terrane also are plausibly correlatives of older Neoproterozoic rocks of the Avalon terrane of coastal Maine and New Brunswick (Rast and Skehan, 1991). Additionally I interpret the rocks of the Merrimack trough to the west of the Nashoba terrane as having affinities more closely related to the Avalon than to terranes of central and western New England. Thus it seems reasonable to interpret the Avalon, the Nashoba, and the Merrimack terranes as having originated off the west coast of West Africa (Figure 5) since the rock sequences on both sides of the Atlantic bear a striking relationship of similarity to each other. The landmass, Armorica, was a part of West Africa and western Europe, and also includes the landmasses that became attached to Laurentia, the name for ancient North America. These western landmasses (Avalon) include the southern British Isles, Ireland, Newfoundland, the Maritime Provinces, southeastern New England, and the eastern part of the southern Appalachians.

These rock sequences consist of two distinct kinds. The older consists of metamorphosed sandstones, limestones, shales, volcanic rocks, and mafic plutonic rocks of southeastern New England (Nashoba and the older rocks of Avalon) that are interpreted as having originated mainly on continental crust. The younger sequence consists of Neoproterozoic granitic rocks, such as the Dedham Granite (630 Million years ago), and mid-Paleozoic mafic plutons and volcanic rocks. These rocks are interpreted as having originated as a part of the West African continental crust that evolved in such a way (Figure 4) that the crust became faulted, a subduction zone generated volcanic and plutonic rocks (the Dedham) that rose up to form an offshore volcanic–plutonic arc with a back-of-the-arc sea basin separating the arc from the continental mainland (Bailey and others, 1989; Skehan, 1988).

The situation that prevailed along the margin of West Africa is envisioned as a mirror image of what prevails today in Japan as a volcanic–plutonic arc, the Sea of Japan being a behind-the-arc, that is, a back-arc or rift basin, and the mainland of Asia being the counterpart of West Africa. West Africa is interpreted as having collided at least twice with eastern North America. The first collision is interpreted as having produced a very high, Himalayan-size mountain chain in central and western New England. There is evidence that the Nashoba block rose up subsequent to the Acadian mountain building episode (Hepburn and Hon, 1991) in the Devonian (about 380 Million years ago).

A second collision of West Africa with eastern North America (along the western margin of the shaded area of Figure 5) left behind rock masses

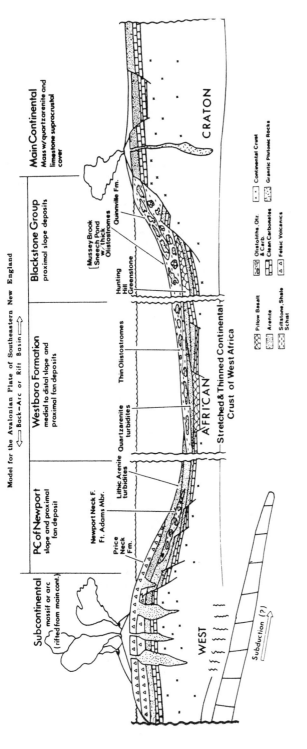

*Figure 4: Tectonic model for the evolution of the Avalonian terrane of southeastern New England suggesting that the older rocks of the West African continental shelf consisted of limestone (brick pattern: carbonates) and sandstones (dotted pattern: arenite), with the later volcanic-plutonic arc on the left, the behind-the-arc-basin in the center, and the African continent on the right (from Bailey and others, 1989).*

that are referred to as Meguma terrane attached to the mainland of North America (Skehan and Rast, 1990) in southern Nova Scotia, and New Brunswick, and in southeastern Massachusetts and Rhode Island (Figure 5). Following that collision about 275 Million years ago near the end of the Pennsylvanian and the beginning of Permian time, an episode of rifting took place. That rifting produced the dinosaur-bearing Mesozoic

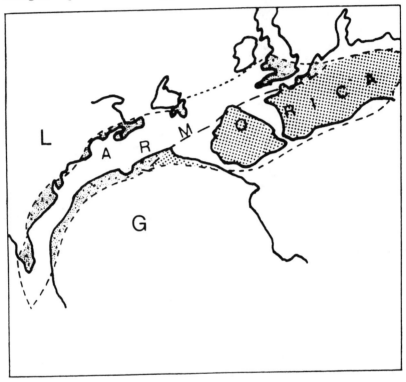

***Figure 5: Map showing the Armorican microcontinent as part of North America, West Africa, and parts of western Europe. L = Laurentia, the pre-collision part of North America; G = Gondwana, the ancient southern continent of which West Africa was a part. The shaded portion represents all land masses of eastern North America, West Africa, and Europe that are interpreted to have been part of Armorica, a land mass most closely linked to the Avalon and related terranes of eastern North America and West Africa.***

basins of eastern North America and Africa as the megacontinent Pangea began to split apart. That episode of rifting and separation of Africa and Europe from North America and South America still continues to this day. This interpretation is based on data gathered from the rock formations that comprise the terranes in the circum-Atlantic region, and by comparison of the evolutionary history of these terranes relative to each other (Skehan, 1988).

# Acknowledgments

I thank Edmund A. Schofield for the invitation to participate in the Thoreau Symposium held in Concord. I appreciate the help of Edward M. Myskowski and Patricia C. Tassia who assisted in the preparation of the manuscript, and I am grateful to the leadership of the Jesuit Community of Boston College who subsidized the preparation of this paper.

# Bibliography

Abu-moustafa, A., and Skehan, S.J., J. W., 1976. Petrography and geochemistry of the nashoba formation, East-Central Massachusetts, in Lyons, P. C., and Brownlow, A. H., eds., *Studies in New England Geology:* Geological Society of America Memoir 146, pages 31–70.

Bailey, R. H., Skehan, J. W., Dreier, R. B., and Webster, M. J., 1989. Olistostromes of the Avalonian terrane of southeastern New England, in Horton, J. W. Jr., and Rast, N., eds., *Melanges and Olistostromes of the U.S. Appalachians:* Geological Society of America Special Paper 228, pp. 93–112.

Barosh, P., 1984, Regional geology and tectonic history of southeastern New England, in Hanson, L. S., ed., *Geology of the Coastal Lowlands, Boston, MA, to Kennebunk, ME:* New England Intercollegiate Geologic Conference, Salem State College, Salem, Mass., pp. 136–146.

Bates, R. L., and Jackson, J. A., eds., 1980, *Glossary of Geology:* Falls Church, Va., American Geological Institute, 749 pp.

Bell, K. G., and Alvord, D. C., 1976, Pre-Silurian stratigraphy of northeastern Massachusetts, in Page, L. R., ed., *Contributions to the Stratigraphy of New England:* Geological Society of America Memoir 148, pp. 179–216.

Billings, M. P., 1976, Geology of the Boston basin, in Lyons, P. C., and Brownlow, A. H., eds., *Studies in New England Geology: Geological Society of America Memoir 146*, pp. 5–30.

Castle, R. O., 1965. Gneissic rocks in the South Groveland quadrangle, Essex County, Massachusetts: *U.S. Geological Survey Professional Paper 525–C.* pp. C81–C86.

Dana, J. F., and Dana, S. L., 1818, *Outlines of the Mineralogy and Geology of Boston and Its Vicinity, with a Geological Map:* Boston, Cummings and Hilliard.

Dinitto, R., Hepburn, J. C, Cardoza, K. D., and Hill, M., 1984, The Marlboro Formation in its type area and associated rocks just west of the Bloody Bluff fault zone, Marlborough area, Massachusetts, in Hanson, L. S., ed., *Geology of the Coastal Lowlands, Boston, MA to Kennebunk, ME:* New England Intercollegiate Geologic Conference, Salem State College, Salem, Mass., p. 186–206.

Emerson, B. K., 1917, The geology of Massachusetts and Rhode Island: *U.S. Geological Survey Bulletin 597*, 289 p.

Goldsmith, R., 1991, Stratigraphy of the Nashoba Zone, eastern Massachusetts; an enigmatic terrane, and Structural and metamorphic history of eastern Massachusetts, in Hatch, N. L. Jr., ed., *The Bedrock Geology of Massachusetts*: U.S. Geological Survey Professional Paper 1366-E-J, p. F1–F22, H1–H63.

Hansen, W. R., 1956, Geology and mineral resources of the Hudson and Maynard quadrangles, Massachusetts: *U.S. Geological Survey Bulletin 1038*, 104 p.

Hepburn, J. C., and Hon, R., 1991, The Avalon terrane boundary in east-central New England: *Geological Society of America, Abstracts with Programs* 23 (1): 44.

Hepburn, J. C., Hill, M., and Hon, R., 1987, The Avalonian and Nashoba terranes, eastern Massachusetts, U.S.A.; an overview: *Maritime Sediments and Atlantic Geology* 23: 1–12.

Hill, M., Hepburn, J. C., Collins, R., and Hon, R., Igneous rocks of the Nashoba block, eastern Massachusetts, in Hanson, L. S., ed., *Geology of the Coastal Lowlands, Boston, MA to Kennebunk, ME*: New England Intercollegiate Geologic Conference, Salem State College, Salem, MA, p. 61–80.

Koteff, C., 1964, *Surficial Geology of the Concord Quadrangle*: U.S. Geological Survey, Map GQ-331, scale 1:24,000.

Olzewski, W. J., 1980, The geochronology of some stratified metamorphic rocks in northeastern Massachusetts. *Canadian Journal of Earth Sciences* 47: 1407–1416.

Rast, N., and Skehan, J. W., 1983, The evolution of the Avalonian plate, in Friedman, M., and Toksoz, M. N., eds., *Continental Tectonics: Structure, Kinematics, and Dynamics: Tectonophysics* 100: p. 257–286.

Rast, N., and Skehan, J. W., 1991, Tectonic relationships of Carboniferous and Precambrian rocks in southwestern New Brunswick, in Ludman, A., ed., *Geology of the Coastal Lithotectonic Block and Neighboring Terranes, Eastern Maine and Southern New Brunswick*: New England Intercollegiate Geologic Conference.

Skehan, S.J., J. W., 1968, Fracture tectonics of southeastern New England as illustrated by the Wachusett–Marlborough Tunnel, east-central Massachusetts, in Zen, E-an, White, W. S., Hadley, J. B., and Thompson, J. B. Jr., eds., *Studies of Appalachian Geology: Northern and Maritime*: New York, Wiley Interscience, p. 281–290.

Skehan, S.J., J. W., 1973, Subduction zone between the Paleo-American and Paleo-African plates in New England: *Geofisca International* 13: 291–308.

Skehan, S.J., J. W., 1979, *Puddingstone, Drumlins, and Ancient Volcanoes; a Geologic Field Guide along Historic Trails of Greater Boston*: Weston, Massachusetts, WesStone Press, 63 p.

Skehan, S.J., J. W., 1985, *Correlation of Stratigraphic Units of North America (COSUNA) Chart, New England Region*: American Association of Petroleum Geologists.

Skehan, S.J., J. W., 1988, Evolution of the Iapetus Ocean and its borders in pre-Arenig times: A synthesis, in Harris, A. L., and Fettes, D. J., eds., *The*

*Caledonian–Appalachian Orogen*; Geological Society of London Special Publication 38: Oxford, Blackwell Scientific Publications, p. 185–229.

Skehan, S.J., J. W., and Abu-moustafa, A. A., 1976, Stratigraphic analysis of rocks exposed in the Wachusett–Marlborough Tunnel, east-central Massachusetts, in Page, L. R., ed., *Contributions to the Stratigraphy of New England*: Geological Society of America Memoir 148, p. 217–240.

Skehan, J. W., and Rast, N., 1983, Relationship between Precambrian and Paleozoic rocks of southeastern New England and other North Atlantic Avalonian terranes, in Schenk, P. E., ed., *Regional Trends in the Geology of the Appalachian–Caledonian–Hercynian–Mauritanide Orogen*: Dordrecht, Reidel, pages 131–162.

Skehan, J. W., and Rast, N., 1990, Pre-Mesozoic evolution of Avalon terranes of southern New England, in Socci, A. D., Skehan, J. W., and Smith, G. W., eds., *Geology of the Composite Avalon Terrane of Southern New England*: Geological Society of America Special Paper 245, p. 13–54.

Thoreau, H. D., 1897, *Walden, or, Life in the Woods*: Boston, Houghton Mifflin.

Thoreau, H. D., 1899, *Walden, or, Life in the Woods*: New York, T. Y. Crowell and Co., 350 p.

Wones, D. R., and Goldsmith, R., 1991, Intrusive rocks of eastern Massachusetts, in Hatch, N. L. Jr., ed., *The Bedrock Geology of Massachusetts*: U.S. Geological Survey Professional Paper 1366-E-J, p. 111–161

Zartman, R. E., and Marvin, 1991, Radiometric ages of rocks in Massachusetts, in Hatch, N. L. Jr., ed., *The Bedrock Geology of Massachusetts*: U.S. Geological Survey Professional Paper 1366-E-J, p. J1–J19.

Zartman, R. E., and Naylor, R. S., 1984, Structural implications of some radiometric ages of igneous rocks in southeastern New England: *Geological Society of America Bulletin*, v. 95, p. 522–539.

Zen, E-an, ed., 1983, *Bedrock Geologic Map of Massachusetts*: U. S. Geological Survey, scale 1:250,000.

---

**JAMES W. SKEHAN, S.J.**, Professor of Geology and Director of Weston Observatory, Department of Geology and Geophysics, Boston College, is a Jesuit priest with advanced degrees in philosophy from Boston College and in theology from Weston College. He has a Ph.D. in Geology from Harvard University and is the author or editor of approximately 100 papers and books on popular geology, emphasizing the origin of the Circum-Atlantic region due to plate movements. His interest in Thoreau was kindled by an interest in the environment and by geological studies of the areas that Thoreau described.

# The Archaeology of
# Walden Woods

❖

## Shirley Blancke

Within the boundaries of Walden Woods are nine archeological sites which indicate that the known human occupation of the woods covers 8,000 years. Two more sites lie close to its borders. These locations are known primarily from the collections of stone artifacts made by local people for more than a hundred years, and in recent years two have been surveyed and excavated by professional archeologists.

The habit of collecting "Indian" artifacts in the town of Concord appears to have been started by Henry David Thoreau whose collection is in the Fruitlands Museum, Harvard, Massachusetts. Thoreau made many references to arrowheads and other artifacts such as stone tools and potsherds in his *Journal* but, disappointingly, did not catalogue his collection so that it now has little scientific value. When an artifact is removed from its context in the ground it loses most of its meaning unless that context is carefully recorded. On the other hand Thoreau's detailed description of the Concord Shell Heap site, the only known large inland shell midden in New England, has provided invaluable information no longer available through excavation since the site has effectively been destroyed.

Collecting artifacts became a popular form of weekend entertainment in the last decades of the 19th century. Thoreau was followed by some others who were careful enough to number their finds and keep notebooks of where they were found. As a result archeologists can now use their material to make at least a partial reconstruction of subsistence and settlement patterns in different periods. Ideally, archeologists prefer undisturbed sites where they can plot the fine details of the interrelationships of artifacts to features such as fireplaces so that the patterns of activity that shed light on lifestyles may be reconstructed. The artifacts in

Concord collections were usually found in fields turned over by the plow so that the conditions that made their discovery easy also disturbed the contexts to some extent. While less than ideal, if it were not for those collections made in the past, most of that information would now be totally lost because land that was chosen by ancient Native people is also desirable to the present human population now and much of it has been built on. In consequence preservation of Walden Woods also preserves a part of the ancient human heritage.

Benjamin L. Smith, an active collector and amateur archeologist in the 1930s and 1940s, estimated that there were thirty collections in the town, and my own survey in 1980 identified the same number (Blancke, 1981). Three outstanding collections with respect to the number of artifacts and their detailed cataloguing are in the Concord Museum: those of Benjamin Smith, Adams Tolman, and Alfred Hosmer, the two last made at the end of the 19th century. A few large and important collections are still in private hands, and there are many more small collections of no less value coming from single sites that usually belong to those who own or once owned the land. Some material from surveys conducted by the Institute of Conservation Archaeology (no longer in existence) is in the Peabody Museum, Harvard University. Several collections from the Concord Shell Heap made in the 19th century are also in the Peabody Museum, notably that made by Jeffries Wyman with which he founded the museum. (It is the first collection in the Peabody catalogue). A number of these sources have provided the material described here.

In order to present a coherent context by which the Walden Woods sites may be better understood, it is necessary to provide an overview of the sequence of changes that took place in the ecosystem and the human cultures that adapted to it from the end of the Ice Age to the European arrival in the 17th century. Changes in forest composition are known mainly through the study of palynology, and while varying in detail in different places, the overall pattern is similar throughout the northeast. As far as is known, the pollen profile from Cedar Swamp in Westborough is the closest to Concord that covers the whole span from the end of the Pleistocene to the present (Sneddon and Kaplan, 1987). Cedar Swamp is at the headwaters of the Sudbury River about twenty miles from Concord. The Sudbury and Assabet rivers join in Concord to form the Concord River, which flows north into the Merrimack, and they are in the southern portion of the Merrimack drainage area.

The last Pleistocene glaciation had retreated from the Northeast sometime before 12,000 years ago, leaving glacial lakes around which a tundra environment of sedges and bog species developed. Most of Walden Woods soils were deposited in Glacial Lake Sudbury (Walden Woods map; Koteff, 1964). In the Cedar Swamp profile a sparse and open woodland dominated by spruce began to supplant the tundra before 12,000 and became established by 11,000 years ago. Species such as larch, fir, alder, and later oak, hornbeam, and traces of temperate genera moved north from southern refuges. Approximately 11,000 B.P. (before present) marked the transition from a late-glacial to a postglacial rapidly warming climate that caused the spruce woodland to be quickly replaced by a denser pine-oak forest, which included other temperate genera such as oak, elm, ash, and hemlock. After 10,000 years the pine was overtaken by deciduous species, especially oak and hemlock, as the climate reached a warm maximum in 7,300 B.P., to be followed by maple, ash, elm, and birch, and hickory close to 5,000 B.P. The arrival of hickory was followed by a decline in hemlock which eventually rebounded to its original levels about 2,000 years ago, followed by the advent of chestnut. Marjorie Winkler suggested that because of the sandy soils, the incidence of pine in Walden Woods may always have been higher than the Cedar Swamp profile and other profiles in Massachusetts would suggest, and in that respect be more like profiles from Cape Cod (M. Winkler, personal communication).

## The Archeological Context

At what point in this forest progression did people arrive? A rough chronological framework is provided archeologists by changes in the manufacture of projectile points. Over history hunters changed the way in which they made their spear and dart points and later arrowheads, and this together with carefully excavated sites in the region which provide radiocarbon dates is the basis of the following reconstruction.

Concord has two sites where a very few Palaeoindian points were found, representing the caribou and mastodon hunters of the late Pleistocene who ranged the spruce woodland. Almost as rare are the spear points of the Early Archaic hunters who followed them in the pine-oak forest following deer and turkey. After 8000 B.P., approaching the time of the warm climatic maximum, occupation of the area began in earnest with perhaps a third of the sites in Concord showing points from the Middle Archaic time frame. This suggests a greater permanence of settlements lasting probably from two to four months of the year. The artifacts of Archaic peoples show similarities over a wide range of the East Coast from Tennessee to Maine. These peoples are thought to have been involved in communication networks, perhaps even marriage networks (Dincauze, 1985).

After 6,000 years ago the cultural picture became very much more complex. The population increased and cemeteries constructed between 4500 and 2000 B.P. indicate a greater degree of territoriality. It is rare for a site in Concord not to contain Late Archaic material. A greater ability to harvest seasonally available foods is demonstrated by the construction of large fish weirs such as that found under Boylston Street in Boston (Dincauze, 1985).

In Concord the Shell Heap site (also known as Clam Shell Bluff), on a bank overlooking the Sudbury River, has shown that at a date of 4500 B.P. river mussels were being collected as well as seven species of turtles, one of them the redbelly, now restricted in its range to the Plymouth area (Rhodin and Largy, 1984). Other species in the midden were pickerel, fall-fish (but not salmon), deer, muskrat, beaver, woodchuck, squirrel, water snake, and large birds such as turkey. The Shell Heap was a midden for what appears to have been a summer base camp of several months' duration in the adjacent field. It would have been reoccupied many times not only during the Late Archaic but also in the later Woodland periods. (Thoreau noted an engraved pot emerging from the midden profile.) A summer season is indicated by the growth rings on the mussel shells supported by the lack of spotted turtle remains, an estivating species now common in Concord.

The range of tools found in the field included axes, adzes, and gouges for woodworking, stone bowl fragments and pestles for cooking and food processing, scrapers and perforators for skin-dressing, in addition to points and plummets for hunting and fishing (Blancke, 1985; Smith, 1940). Women and children and some men would have stayed in the base camp while the men ranged out on hunting and fishing expeditions. The sites picked for large camps were usually high, well-drained, sandy banks overlooking a river or pond, and preferably near a large swamp. A variety of ecological niches no doubt provided an increased variety of plants and animals that could be foraged at close range.

There are four other areas in Concord in addition to Shell Heap Field whose tools indicate long-term campsites, but the faunal data retrieved from the shell midden are unique. A large winter camp of approximately the same date, 4500 B.P., was excavated at Flagg Swamp near the Assabet River, Marlborough, which suggests the river was used as a highway for seasonal harvesting strategies. Hickory nuts were favored over hazels and acorns at Flagg Swamp by a ratio of ten to one, which shows that the arrival of hickory at about 5,000 years was of importance to the human population (Huntington, 1982).

The great bulk of archeological sites in Concord represent short-term hunting or fishing camps, situated on well-drained sandy knolls, with a small number and range of types of artifact: usually a variety of projectile points indicating reuse of the location over an extended period of time, a number of different edge tools (knives and scrapers), occasionally perforators, and stone chipping waste left from making those tools. It is evident that the hunter carried his stone with him to be worked as needed. The pattern of removal of flakes to be worked into small artifacts produced characteristic shapes in the stones from which they were struck, referred to as cores. Over time the range of types of stone used was similar, but preference was shown for one kind over another at times or by particular traditions.

The complex volcanic history of the Boston Basin provided many fine-grained igneous rocks that were relatively easy to flake. Quartz cobbles could be collected in Concord from glacial moraines, but felsites were brought or traded from quarries further afield: black, red, and purple porphyritic felsites from Marblehead, Lynn, and the Mattapan areas; gray felsites probably from the Westwood dyke; red rhyolite from Saugus; tan quartzite from Westborough; rare green metaquartz from Sudbury; and even New York State cherts.

The appearance in the Late Archaic period of three different traditions of making projectile points indicates an increased cultural complexity. These points are usually found mixed together, but the result of a lack of stratigraphy on most New England sites is that one is looking at a palimpsest of remains from different periods that only appear to occur together chronologically. Several interpretations have been proffered to explain these traditions. The most common is to make a connection between styles of point manufacture and different peoples with different origins; indeed this is the basic assumption on which New England archeology rests (Dincauze, 1974, 1975, 1976; Dincauze and Mulholland, 1977).

By this theory the people of the Small Point tradition were indigenous, their points (most often made of white quartz) having developed out of the earlier Middle Archaic tradition. But they were joined by or else shared the same territory with infiltrating groups from the Laurentian or New York State area (who in Concord preferred the black and gray porphyritic felsites) and other groups whose origins were to the south on the Susquehanna River. The Susquehanna tradition was associated with mortuary ceremonialism (Dincauze, 1968). Another interpretation views the appearance of Susquehanna artifacts as the result of technological innovation and the adoption of new ideas throughout the East Coast area (Cook, 1976). It has also been suggested that they might represent a broad trade network (Cole, 1981).

During the third millennium before the present the picture radically changed. The rich Late Archaic culture disappeared from the record, and the evidence of succeeding Woodland cultures returns virtually to the sparsity of the Early Archaic. Whether because of deteriorating climate or other factors such as changing subsistence strategies or artifacts made usually of perishable materials which have not survived is not clear. There was a slight increase by the end of the second millennium (the late Middle Woodland period), but only three sites in Concord provide a few potsherds, and pottery is typical of Woodland cultures. The farming period (Late Woodland), which began some time after 1000 B.P. and lasted until the European arrival, is poorly represented and known. One of the sites with pottery is close to the area that the English started to farm when they arrived, the Great Fields, and so is assumed to have been the location of the aboriginal planting fields mentioned at the founding of the town.

## Archeological Sites in Walden Woods

There are nine archeological sites in Walden Woods, five in Concord and four in Lincoln, and two more just north of the northern boundary in Concord. All of the sites in Walden Woods belong in the category of short-term hunting or fishing camps, and range in date from the Middle Archaic period through the Late Archaic, with the late Middle Woodland also represented. They are best understood in the wider context of their relationship to long-term base camps such as the Shell Heap Field site. Only generalized descriptions of their locations are provided since there is a need to protect these sites from being further denuded by collectors; archeological sites are nonrenewable resources. The site numbers refer to the site files in the Massachusetts Historical Commission, and the terminology follows the Commission's *Guide to Prehistoric Site Files and Artifact Classification System* (1984).

To start in the northeastern corner of the Woods, two sites are located near a small stream that rises under Smith's Hill, east of Brister's Hill, and provides water for Crosby's Pond, a man-made pond in an area that probably was once a swamp. Their appearance in 1938 is described in Benjamin Smith's unpublished notebook. The larger area (No. 19-MD-118, -399) produced the most material of any of the known sites in the Woods. The projectile points indicated three time periods: Middle Archaic, Late Archaic, and late Middle Woodland (Plate 1; Figure 1). The Middle Archaic is represented by a Stark-Like point of gray-green felsite that is typical of these points in the Concord area, and another probable Stark-Like point of gray quartz with damaged base. The Late Archaic period is represented by two traditions: the Laurentian is indicated by three points, two Archaic Notched (Brewerton) points and a Norman skill-style point all of distinctive Marblehead black felsite with white phenocrysts; the Small Stemmed Point tradition is indicated by a narrow leaf-shaped point (Small Stemmed III) of white quartz and a Small Triangle of Marblehead felsite. Two broad leaf-shaped points also of Marblehead felsite and similar to the New York State Greene type, represent the late Middle Woodland. There were in addition three point fragments.

Found with these projectile points were a range of tools for cutting and processing meat and skins. In the category of edge tools were small two leaf-shaped knives, one made from a primary flake, a trianguloid end-scraper partly broken by a thermal fracture, a worked-out core used as

**PLATE 1**

Legend:  1 ......... *Stark-like point, site 118*
         2, 3 ..... *Archaic notched points, site 118*
         4 ......... *Small triangle point, site 118*
         5 ......... *Normanskill-style point, site 118*
         6, 7 ..... *Greene-like points, site 118*
         8 ......... *Greene-like point, site 117*
         9, 10 .. *Knives, site 118*

a side-scraper, a piece of a large oval biface, and part of a leaf-shaped knife. In addition there was an unfinished perforator with base similar to an Archaic Triangle and two perforator fragments.

These artifacts indicate an unknown number of small camps of perhaps one or two hunters over three time periods covering several thousand years. The skin-working tools suggest the presence of women: perhaps a man and his wife traveled together, he catching game and she processing skins.

East of this site on a small ridge is an area (No. 19-MD-117) where a late Middle Woodland leaf-shaped Greene-Like point was found with a broken perforator and chipping waste all of Marblehead felsite (Plate 1). The chipping waste consisted of a large core and seven trimming flakes. There was also a fragment of smoothed gray slate. Benjamin Smith reports in addition two points and a scraper which are not now in his collection. A rare feature was uncovered by deep plowing: a small fire-pit of charcoal and burned rock left from a campfire. This may have been the equipment of one Middle Woodland hunter camping for one night.

A little to the north of these sites on the boundary of the Woods was found an ulu, or woman's semicircular knife, of Late Archaic date (No. 19-MD-398).

Near the boundary in the northwestern area of Walden Woods in the vicinity of Bear Garden Hill is a site now divided by Route 2 (No. 19-MD-402, –401). Joseph Bartolomeo, a collector, found some material there but could only identify two projectile points in his collection as having come from that location: a Middle Archaic Stark-Like gray felsite point, and a Late Archaic Small Stemmed I point of black felsite.

Just north of the boundary a site of about a half acre in extent (No. 19-MD-113) was documented by Benjamin Smith on a sandy knoll in the vicinity of Thoreau's Clintonia Swamp, north of Fairyland Pond. The finds comprised four points with some fragments, chipping waste, a hammerstone, and an adze bit (Figure 1). The points were Late Archaic of the Small Stemmed Point tradition: one Small Stemmed I point; two Small Stemmed III points, one broken and two Small Triangles, one broken; all of white quartz. There was in addition a Fishtail point of the very late Late Archaic. With respect to the chipping waste, half of 39 trimming flakes were of Marblehead felsite and the rest were of gray felsites and white quartz.

Some other interesting artifacts are included with this material but are numbered in a system other than Smith's and are not listed by him, which makes their attribution uncertain. He mentions, however, material found by Adams Tolman and a Mrs. Thomas Sanborn that may have been given to him. They are a leaf-shaped, unifacial knife of gray-green chert, two thumbnail scrapers, one broken, of light-gray chert, and a drilled fragment of black chert. All of the chert probably comes from New York State. There is in addition a tiny piece of red slate.

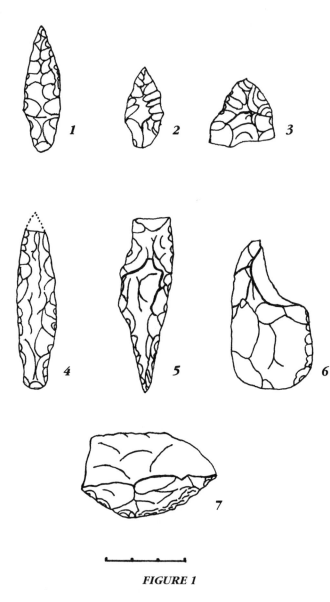

**FIGURE 1**

Legend:  1 ......... *Small stemmed III point, site 118*
2 ......... *Small stemmed I point, site 113*
3 ......... *Small triangle point, site 113*
4 ......... *Fishtail point, site 113*
5 ......... *Unfinished perforator, site 118*
6 ......... *Core-scraper, site 118*
7 ......... *Trianguloid scraper, site 118*

Also north of the boundary was a site reported by Joseph Bartolomeo in the vicinity of the Concord–Carlisle High School, formerly the Lendelius farm, but about which nothing is known (No. 19-MD-400).

In the southerly part of Walden Woods are two sites that were investigated by the Institute of Conservation Archaeology at Harvard University. One (No. 19-MD-331) in a sandy meadow in the Baker Farm area northeast of Fairhaven Bay was found through excavation to consist of three "loci," clusters of artifacts, on rises in the meadow (Gramly 1979). Some evidence of reddened burned soil and fire-cracked rocks was found, but its relevance to aboriginal fires was questioned. The locus farthest from the bay contained a quartzite Small Stemmed II (Lamoka) point of the Late Archaic Small Stemmed Point tradition; and 32 pieces of chipping waste of numerous stones: primarily quartz, but also quartzite, felsites from Marblehead and Braintree, Saugus rhyolite, hornfels, and argillite. The intermediate locus contained 72 pieces of chipping waste with a similar distribution of lithic materials but mainly Marblehead felsite, and no artifacts.

The locus nearest the bay and adjacent to a swampy area was not excavated because it was in the middle of the owner's garden, but he had a collection of artifacts from it: a Middle or Late Archaic point; two triangular points, one identified as Late Archaic; a Susquehanna Broad point of the Late Archaic Susquehanna tradition; a Fishtail point belonging to the end of the Late Archaic; and a pecked shale object perhaps part of a pestle or adze or gouge. There were also point fragments and a small quantity of chipping waste. Again at this site may be seen the pattern of small short-term fishing or hunting camps occupied in widely different periods, where artifacts were being manufactured.

Northeast of site 19-MD-331, also in the Baker Farm area, is site 19-MD-440 in a large sandy field (Barber, 1981). A surface survey identified two rises on the northwestern edge of the field which had concentrations of material. There were three artifact fragments: a blade base of black felsite, a point tip of brown quartzite, and part of an ovate biface of black felsite. The blade base belonged to a Mansion Inn blade of the Late Archaic Susquehanna tradition. The chipping waste consisted of 164 trimming flakes and one core, which were 90 percent felsite with tiny amounts of rhyolite, phyllite, argillite, quartzite, quartz, and chert. A small amount of bone, charcoal, and fire-cracked rock was also represented. Artifacts found in the general vicinity by a collector, Heather McCune, included, as well as Mansion Inn blade fragments, a part of a steatite pot (Late Archaic), and Late Archaic Laurentian tradition points of rhyolite and gray quartzite.

The three remaining sites in the list have essentially no data pertaining to them. No. 19-MD-468 on the southern boundary near Mount Misery is reported to have produced chipping waste and an untyped point. A few artifacts were reported by the collector, Gilbert Lawrence, to have been found on the south side of Walden Pond (No. 19-MD-408) but not by himself. Site No. l9-MD-125 on the southeast side of Fairhaven Bay is said to have produced a Susquehanna Broad point, but is of questionable existence since it could not be located by Benjamin Smith.

## Summary

The evidence from six out of nine sites within Walden Woods and one of two just north of the Woods demonstrates a pattern of small short-term hunting or fishing camps, situated on well-drained sandy rises, and used perhaps for a few nights by one or two hunters, who manufactured artifacts there and who, at the end of their hunting expedition, would return to a long-term base camp of several months' duration such as the one at Shell Heap Field on the Sudbury River. This pattern of foraging existed over thousands of years from approximately the time of the warm climatic maximum between 7,000 and 8,000 years ago when Middle Archaic settlers moved into the area, through the Late Archaic population increase after 6,000 years and its decline in the third millennium before the present. All three Late Archaic traditions are represented in Walden Woods, occasionally isolated in separate locations, which suggests that the Susquehanna tradition like the other two was a tradition of people on the move, and did not merely represent the spread of new ideas whether ceremonial or functional, or through trade. After a gap in the record from the end of the third millennium through most of the second millennium, the same pattern is exhibited again for the late Middle Woodland period just before the spread of agriculture into the area at approximately 1000 B.P. from its origins in Central America.

# Bibliography

Barber, Russell J. 1981. *Report on a Surface Survey of the McCune Site (#l9-MD-440)*. Harvard University, Cambridge, Mass.

Blancke, Shirley. 1981. *Survey of Pre-Contact Sites and Collections in Concord*. Manuscript on file, Massachusetts Historical Commission, Boston, Mass.

Blancke, Shirley. 1985. "Musketaquid: the Native Experience," in *From Musketaquid to Concord*, Concord Museum, Concord, Mass.

Cole, Stephen. 1981. *The McCune Site, Lincoln, Massachusetts*. National Register of Historic Places Inventory—Nomination Form. Manuscript on file, Massachusetts Historical Commission, Boston, Mass.

Cook, Thomas G. 1976. "Broadpoint, Culture, Phase, Tradition or Knife?" *Journal of Anthropological Research* 31(1): 51-68.

Dincauze, Dena F. 1968. "Cremation Cemeteries in Eastern Massachusetts," *Papers of the Peabody Museum of Archaeology and Ethnology* 59 (1). Harvard University, Cambridge, Mass.

Dincauze, Dena F. 1974. An Introduction to Archaeology in the Greater Boston Area. *Archaeology of Eastern North America* 2 (1).

Dincauze, Dena F. 1975. "The Late Archaic Period in Southern New England," *Arctic Anthropology* 12 (2): 23-34.

Dincauze, Dena F. 1976. *The Neville Site.* (Peabody Museum Monographs) 4. Harvard University, Cambridge, Mass.

Dincauze, Dena F. 1985. Introduction, in *From Musketaquid to Concord*, Concord Museum, Concord, Mass.

Dincauze, Dena F., and Mulholland, M. T., 1977. "Early and Middle Archaic Site Distributions and Habitats in Southern New England" in *Amerinds and Their Paleoenvironments in Northeastern North America.* Annals of the New York Academy of Sciences, 288:439–456.

Gramly, Richard M. 1979. Field Notes of the Concord Project. In Laurel Casjens, *Archaeological Site Catchments and Settlement Patterns in the Concord River Watershed, Northeastern Massachusetts.* Institute of Conservation Archaeology, No. 51., Harvard University, Cambridge, Mass.

Huntington, Frederick W. 1982. *Preliminary report on the excavation of Flagg Swamp Rockshelter.* Institute of Conservation Archaeology, No. 214, Harvard University, Cambridge, Mass.

Koteff, Carl. 1964. *Surficial Geology of the Concord Quadrangle Massachusetts.* Department of the Interior, United States Geological Survey, No. 331, Washington.

Rhodin, Anders G. J., and Largy, Tonya. 1984. Prehistoric Occurrence of the Redbelly Turtle (*Pseudemys rubriventris*) at Concord, Middlesex County, Massachusetts. *Herpetological Review* 15 (4).

Smith, Benjamin L. 1940. A report on a fresh water shell heap at Concord, Massachusetts. *Bulletin of the Massachusetts Archaeological Society* 1(3):14-26.

Sneddon, Lesley, and Kaplan, Lawrence. 1987. Pollen analysis from Cedar Swamp Pond, Westborough, Massachusetts. *Archaeological Quarterly* 9 (2), Massachusetts Archaeological Society, Ekblaw Chapter, Worcester, Mass.

---

**SHIRLEY BLANCKE, PH.D.**, has been guest curator at the Concord Museum and is the author of *Musketaquid to Concord: The Native and European Experience.*

# Soils of the Walden Ecosystem

❖

## Thomas Peragallo

Soil maps illustrate the extent and distribution of different types of soil in relation to the landscape. Soils are classified into categories that have similar properties and limitations for land use and management.

Soils are formed from parent material, affected by variations in topography, acted upon by the climate and vegetation, over a certain period of time. These factors result in the formation of characteristic soil layers and profiles that can be observed and examined in an open hole or core sample. Soil scientists examine soil profiles to a depth of at least 60 inches. A landscape segment is delineated, assigned a map symbol and given a soil series name based on observed characteristics. Soil maps are made at various scales and levels of detail depending on the intended use.

Soil surveys of the Walden Woods area were published as early as 1924. During the 1940s and 1950s, more detailed soil maps were made for specific sites and used for forest management and farm planning. During the 1960s many towns in Middlesex County provided cost-sharing to the U.S. Department of Agriculture, Soil Conservation Service for town-wide soil maps designed for a greater array of interpretations, from agricultural production to sewage disposal. In 1984 an accelerated soil-mapping program, sponsored by the Massachusetts Division of Conservation Services and the USDA Soil Conservation Service, began. The mapping was completed in 1989, with publication planned for 1992. Interim information from this report was used to produce the Soil Map of Walden Woods.

About thirty different kinds of soils have been mapped in Walden Woods. On the western boundary, along the Sudbury River, the soils developed in recent alluvium deposited by floodwater. The soils have a high organic matter content and a high water table. Most of this zone is wetland, providing important habitat for wildlife, and flood storage during periods of peak river flow. The Freetown and Saco soil series represent most of this zone.

Walden Woods is dominated by very sandy soils developed in stratified glaciofluvial parent material, derived from the meltwater of retreating glaciers. A few exposures of bedrock with a thin veneer of glacial till protrude above the fluvial deposits. These soils extend from the floodplain of the Sudbury River eastward to the base of Pine Hill and Bear Hill, surrounding Walden Pond. The water table is typically many feet below the surface. The depth to the water table and the low water-holding capacity of these soils make them susceptible to drought. Historically, these soils have been used for vegetable crop production. They respond well to fertilization and additions of manure, but irrigation is required for maximum yields. They can be tilled early in the spring, promoting early harvest. Soils in this zone of Walden Woods favor the growth of trees that prefer dry sites, such as white oak, red oak, hickory, white pine, and pitch pine. These deep, sandy soils allow sewage effluent to pass through rapidly, creating a potential hazard for groundwater pollution. Waste disposal in this area should be closely managed to prevent contamination of the underlying aquifer, which is exposed in Walden Pond. The Merrimac and Windsor soil series represent most of this region.

From the western base of Pine Hill and Bear Hill to the eastern boundary of Walden Woods, the soils developed in sandy and loamy glacial till parent material.* The till is typically dense and compact, having subsurface layers that restrict downward percolation of water. The upper two or three feet consist of a blanket of silty aeolian material derived from winds immediately after deglaciation. These soils typically have a high seasonal water table that is "perched" on the dense glacial till. Their water-holding capacity is moderate to high, favoring the production of a mixed hardwood forest of maples and oaks. They are well suited to forage production or pasture, but an abundance of surface stones restricts tillage in many places. Many surface stones have been removed by farmers from the earliest settlements through the 1800s. These stones may be observed in the numerous stone walls or "stone fences" that meander over the landscape.

---

*Glacial till parent material is the initial unweathered deposit left by glacial activity which will go through a weathering process to create soil.

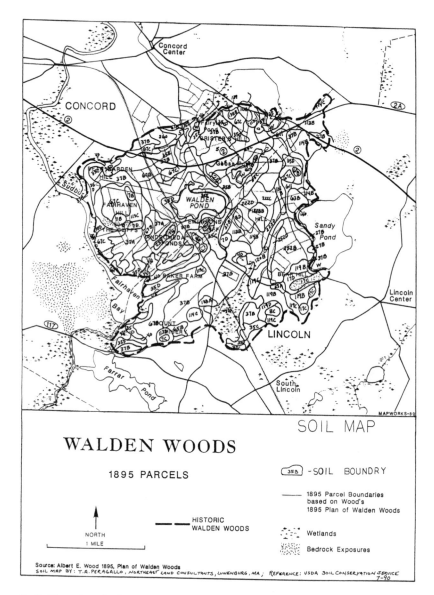

SOIL MAP

# WALDEN WOODS

### 1895 PARCELS

⬆ NORTH

1 MILE

—— HISTORIC WALDEN WOODS

⟨ 35B ⟩ – SOIL BOUNDRY

—— 1895 Parcel Boundaries based on Wood's 1895 Plan of Walden Woods

Wetlands

Bedrock Exposures

Source: Albert E. Wood 1895, Plan of Walden Woods
SOIL MAP BY: T.A. PERAGALLO, NORTHEAST LAND CONSULTANTS, LUNENBURG, MA; REFERENCE: USDA SOIL CONSERVATION SERVICE
7-90

Soil Map Symbols

Map Symbol
The numbers (e.g., "67") denote the type of soil, named for the area where it was first described. The letters (e.g., "B") denote the average slope of the land in percent. Map unit 67B is a Windsor soil with slopes of 3 percent to 8 percent.

Slope Classes
A = 0%–3%; B = 3%–8%; C = 8%–15%; D = 15%–25%; E = >25%

256

# Definition of Terms

## Soil Texture Classes

sandy = texture is dominated by sand-size particles (2.0–0.05 mm diameter), e.g..,
  sands, loamy sands
loamy = soil textures that have a distribution of particles including sand, silt, and
  clay (2.0–0.002 mm dia.), e.g., sandy loams
silty = texture dominated by silt-size particles (0.05-0.002 mm dia.)
organic = decomposed wood and herbaceous material

## Soil drainage class: depth to the seasonal high water table from the ground surface:

(1) excessively drained = water table at 6 feet or more, sandy/droughty
(2) well drained = water table at 4 feet or more
(3) moderately well drained = water table at 1.5 to 4 feet
(4) poorly drained = water table at 0 to 1.5 feet (wetland)
(5) very poorly drained = water table at or above the surface most of the year
  (wetland)

## Parent material is the original geologic material from which the soil has developed:

(1) glacial till = unsorted, nonstratified glacial drift consisting of clay, silt, sand,
  gravel, stones, and boulders, transported and deposited by glacial ice
(2) glaciofluvial material = stratified glacial drift dominated by sands and gravels
  deposited by streams flowing from melting glaciers. For the purpose of this
  report, this includes material deposited into glacial lakes (Sudbury)
(3) aeolian material = mostly silt and fine sand transported by postglacial wind
  action and deposited over other parent material
(4) alluvium = stratified mineral and organic material deposited by steams in
  floodplains

# Soil Map Legend

LF: Sanitary landfills, buried solid waste

5: Udorthents
Soils altered by man, including areas that have been cut, filled, or regraded

7, 8, 9: Charlton, Chatfield, and Hollis soil series and bedrock outcrops
A complex of well drained, loamy glacial-till soils and rock outcrops with soil depths
  varying from less than 20 inches (Hollis) to more than 60 inches (Charlton),
  and with the occurrence of rock outcrops increasing from unit 7 to unit 9

17: Narragansett–Hollis rock outcrop complex
Similar to unit 7 but with a 2- to 3-foot-thick mantle of silty aeolian material
  overlaying the glacial till and bedrock

27: Scituate series
Moderately well-drained, loamy glacial till having a restrictive layer (hardpan)
  within 40 inches of the soil surface

35: Hinckley series
Excessively drained, sandy and gravely glaciofluvial material

37: Merrimac series
Excessively drained, loamy material overlying sandy glaciofluvial material

38: Sudbury series
Moderately well-drained, loamy material overlying sandy glaciofluvial material

39: Walpole series
Poorly drained, loamy material overlying sandy glaciofluvial material

40: Scarboro series
Very poorly drained, shallow organic material overlying sandy glaciofluvial
   material

44: Saco series
Very poorly drained alluvium

45: Swansea series
Very poorly drained, organic material overlying sandy glaciofluvial material

46: Freetown series
Very poorly drained, deep organic material

63: Haven series
Well-drained silty aeolian material overlying sandy glaciofluvial material

65: Walpole variant
Poorly drained, sandy glaciofluvial material overlying silty material

67: Windsor series
Excessively drained sandy glaciofluvial material

113, 114: Canton series
Well-drained loamy and sandy glacial till

119: Narragansett series
Well-drained silty aeolian material overlying sandy glacial till

138: Deerfield series
Moderately well-drained sandy glaciofluvial material

139: Wareham series
Poorly drained sandy glaciofluvial material

222, 223: Montauk series
Well-drained sandy and loamy dense glacial till having a restrictive layer
   (hardpan) within 40 inches of the soil surface

252, 253: Broadbrook silt loam
Well-drained silty aeolian material overlying dense glacial till having a restrictive
   layer (hardpan) within 40 inches of the soil surface

260: Urban land
Areas where more than 85 percent of the land surface is covered with pavement
or buildings.

591: Scio series
Moderately well-drained, silty glaciofluvial material.

611: Birdsall series
Very poorly drained, silty glaciofluvial material.

---

**THOMAS PERAGALLO** is the Principal Soil Scientist with Northeast Land Consultants in Lunenburg, Massachusetts. His professional experience is in soil classification and soil mapping in both the public and private sectors. He has spent years in the Walden area and has authored numerous technical reports on soil types and quality.

# Renewal and Imagination
## Thoreau's Thought and the Restoration
## of Walden Pond

❖

### William R. Jordan, III

"Renew thyself completely each day; do it again and again,
and forever again."[1]

In June of 1939, essayist E. B. White paid a visit to Walden Pond. White
was an ardent admirer of the writings of Henry Thoreau, and the year before
had himself left a position at *The New Yorker* magazine to pursue a
Thoreauvian life on a small farm in Maine. He was still sending dispatches
back to the city, however, and his account of his visit, which appeared in
*Harper's* magazine and was subsequently anthologized in a collection of
White's essays entitled *One Man's Meat,* provided my first introduction to
the Walden Pond of our own day—(give or take a few decades)—a century
after Thoreau explored it, inhabited it, and finally made it one of the most
powerful images in American environmental literature.

White's short essay is filled with melancholy and regret over the
condition of the pond, which he found so much unlike the wilderness
retreat Thoreau's writing had led him to expect. It is characterized by
numerous ironic allusions to modern intrusions on the pastoral seclusion
of an imagined 19th century Concord and Walden: "Amos 'n Andy"
overheard on a car radio in town, ice cream on sale in the shops instead
of Indian meal and molasses, the freshly paved highway on which White
drives to Concord, and so on.

Reaching the pond itself, White continues his litany of regrets,
which reach a kind of lugubrious climax at the cabin site.

"It is a rather ugly little heap of stones, Henry," he writes. "In fact,
the hillside itself seems faded, browbeaten; a few tall skinny pines, bare
of lower limbs, a smattering of young maples in suitable green, some
birches and oaks and a number of trees felled by the last big wind."[2] In

the old foundation he notes trash: two beer bottles, a page from a magazine and—perhaps an ironic reference to Thoreau's habit of bringing his own lunch to the pond wrapped in a newspaper—"some crusts in wax paper." He also sees a young oak and some ferns growing up in the foundation of the cabin, but fails to see in them any sign of hope for renewal.

White's essay is certainly disheartening. It is also, despite the tribute it offers Thoreau, curiously at odds with the spirit of his thought. It is, one might say, precisely the sort of ode to dejection Thoreau himself promised not to produce when he sat down to write *Walden*.

Fortunately—no doubt in part because White's report had so lowered my expectations—my own feelings when I visited the pond for the first time on an October afternoon some forty years later was altogether different. Unlike White, I found the pond—admittedly without the usual crowd of bathers and fishermen on that drizzly autumn day—exquisitely beautiful, perhaps, with its opalescent water and fringe of flaming maples, the loveliest place I had ever seen. Lines from Thoreau's writings came into my mind, as they had to White's. But these were not ironic and sad, but exuberant and hopeful. "Why here is Walden," I remembered, "the same woodland lake that I discovered so many years ago ... ."[3]

Today, most of us agree that Walden Pond and the area around it is in need of renewal, of what at a purely technical level we have come to call ecological restoration. Beautiful as the pond and its surroundings may be to my Midwestern eyes, it has changed over the years, and in some ways the changes are regrettable. A persistent problem, for example, is erosion caused by heavy use around the pond's edge. The stones placed there to deal with this problem are ineffective and unsightly. And no doubt the biota could stand some restoration, some judicious removal of exotics, perhaps some reintroduction of native species to nudge it back toward the condition it was in at the time of Emerson and Thoreau. This is true, as Mary Sherwood has made clear, of the vegetation around the pond, and I suspect also of some of the animals in the surrounding forest and in the pond itself. In fact, Ms. Sherwood has already taken the first steps in the process. The state officials who are responsible for the pond and the area immediately surrounding it have already made some progress in regulating public use, and are currently developing plans for even more extensive work, including some real ecological restoration in the preserve. And musician Don Henley has made a valuable contribution through his moral backing and through financial support that will help protect the area from development, an obvious requisite to any hope for renewal.

What this means is that those of us who care about Walden Pond and what it stands for can look forward to a new era of restoration and

261

renewal of the pond and its surroundings. The purpose of this symposium to develop a set of guidelines for this effort. To this end, some reflections on the significance of this work and on the spirit in which it should be carried out are in order. We might regard the restoration of the pond as a mere process, a task, a way of cleaning up a mess. I think that would be a mistake. I say this because I think the experience of restoration is closely allied to the experience Thoreau sought at Walden, and actually offers an opportunity to continue his experiment at Walden while extending it to a wider circle of participants. In fact I believe that it is precisely the restoration of Walden Pond, far more than the pond itself, preserved as a cherished historic shrine, that will best express the spirit and carry out the ideas expressed in the book named after it. With this in mind we should regard this project not as a mere task to be completed, but, in the spirit of Walden, as a chance to renew ourselves and our relationship with nature.

Ecological restoration is a relatively new form of applied ecology that has gained widespread attention as a discipline and a strategy for environmental conservation only during the past decade. Though the term itself has many shades of meaning, and is used in different ways in various contexts, its meaning is quite straightforward. If restoration means bringing something back to an earlier condition, generally regarded, for whatever reason, as preferable to its present condition, ecological restoration means doing that to an ecological system—a prairie, a forest, a lake or a pond. The period chosen as the model or "target" for the restoration is ultimately arbitrary. In North America, restorationists often take the landscape at the time of European contact as a model. But this is obviously no hard-and-fast rule. Ultimately we choose a period that interests us, or that we consider important for some reason. At Walden, the period is pretty much defined by the terms of the agreement by which the pond was turned over to the state, according to which the pond is to be maintained "in the condition of the time of Emerson and Thoreau."

Of course even this allows for some latitude. For one thing, it covers nearly a half-century during which the pond underwent extensive changes, some of which were chronicled by Thoreau himself. Moreover, no landscape is ever static, and the restorationist, taking that into account, aims to reproduce not only the historic landscape but also its dynamics. The idea is not merely to produce an object, but also to set it in motion.

At the same time, it is important to keep in mind that the terms of the transfer of Walden Pond to the State of Massachusetts do demand restoration to the 19th-century condition, and restoration means just that—not making a place nice, or making it match our notions of its earlier condition, but bringing it back as best we can back into the condition it was actually in that period. At Walden this might mean including the occasional felling of trees, as described by Thoreau himself in his account of the pond ("The Ponds"), and it might certainly include restoration of Thoreau's famous beanfield.

But these are questions for those who will actually plan and carry out the restoration and renewal of Walden Pond and the surrounding forest. My purpose here, having defined restoration, is to explore the relationship between restoration and Thoreau's thought, to consider how this project offers a way for us all—spectator as well as participant—to continue Thoreau's experiment at Walden, and finally to comment on some of the implications of all this for the actual restoration effort itself.

Exactly what, then, is the relationship between this business of ecological restoration and what Henry Thoreau was doing and writing about at Walden Pond a century and a half ago? As it happens Thoreau did occasionally make references to restoration of the forests around Concord. In his *Journal* for September 4, 1851, for example, he wrote:

> A few oaks stand in the pastures still, great ornaments. I do not see any young ones springing up to supply their places. Will there be any a hundred years hence? We are a young people, and have not learned by experience the consequences of cutting off the forest. One day they will be planted, methinks, and nature reinstated to some extent.[4]

This passage is interesting because it actually fulfills the two essential criteria for restoration in the modern sense: it suggests an active effort (not mere natural recovery), and it is directed explicitly at the recreation of an entire community—not merely a plantation of trees, but "nature reinstated," at least, as he notes, "to some extent."

In addition, Thoreau's essay on the succession of forest trees bears directly on the subject of restoration. Now widely read, it is also to a considerable extent a kind of manual of ecological horticulture, a study of the dynamics of forests from the point of view of one keenly interested in their management, renewal and perpetuation.

Yet another piece of the restoration agenda emerges from the chapter on the beanfield in *Walden*. Here Thoreau, experimenting with agriculture, questions the "invidious distinctions" he finds himself making with his hoe in behalf of beans. He wonders why he should prefer beans to wormwood and piper and millet grass, refers to the surrounding wild and derelict lands as "fields," designates his own plot as "half cultivated," and in every way tries to break down the distinction between wild and cultivated.

I see him here on the very verge of restoration. If he had only followed up this thought as he did so many others, he might have taken to cultivating wormwood and millet grass. Then he would have become the first restorationist, anticipating Olmsted and Jensen and the work at the University of Wisconsin-Madison Arboretum by half a century and more. In the end, in fact, he did plant trees—putting white pines back on the site of his beanfield some years after leaving the pond.[5] Those pines grew up into a pine grove, which blew down in the hurricane of 1938. It must have been these trees that E. B. White referred to in the report of his visit to the pond eight decades later.

This, however, is merely skimming the surface of Thoreau's thought and its relationship to the business of ecological restoration. If Thoreau noted a few comments that suggest more or less what we call restoration today, this is interesting to us as we face the prospect of restoring Walden pond to a condition that might be familiar to him. But it hardly links this effort intimately with Thoreau's thought, which is what I propose to do here. To do this we must look below the surface of Thoreau's thought to the underlying themes. Of these, I think at least three are especially relevant to the business of restoration. These are: Thoreau's experiment in the reentry and reinhabitation of nature; the theme of renewal, which is at the core of *Walden*; and the discovery that the key to renewal is the imagination expressed through a performative relationship with the world—actually a kind of deadly serious, highly playful make-believe. Actually, each of these themes will be familiar to anyone acquainted with Thoreau's writing. Here I will only summarize them, drawing attention to their relevance to the restoration effort.

To begin with, Thoreau's experiment at Walden was an experiment in the reinhabitation of nature. Leo Marx, in his *The Machine in the Garden,* places *Walden* in the Arcadian tradition in American thought— an expression of the vision of America as Arcadia, where humans live in harmony with the rest of nature.[6] Like a succession of fictional figures in English and American literature, from Prospero in Shakespeare's *The Tempest* to Mark Twain's Huckleberry Finn and Fitzgerald's Jay Gatsby, Thoreau is a seeker after this mythic landscape. What distinguished Thoreau's search, however, was precisely the fact that it is not fiction. We tend to think of the Arcadian experience as an essentially literary one, and as reflecting a mere appreciation or attentiveness to nature, a sort of basking in it or yearning after it.

What marked Thoreau's Arcadian quest, however, was his insistence on reducing the fantasy to practice, actually trying it out rather than just thinking and writing about it. Unlike the backpacker who scrupulously avoids leaving any mark on the landscape through which he moves, Thoreau did not idealize the role of the observer. Instead he sought participation in nature, and insisted on having what—partly seriously, partly in ironic reference to his Puritan neighbors—he called "business" in nature. In other words, he insisted on being an active member of what Aldo Leopold nearly a century later would call the land community. He didn't want merely to observe what was going on in the pond and the woods around him, he wanted to participate in it. Hence his fishing, his huckleberrying, his half-comic attempt at agriculture, even his impulse— reported but not acted upon—to seize a woodchuck crossing his path and eat it raw ("Higher Laws").

In this way Thoreau sought an intimacy with nature that went beyond observation to actual participation, a truly ecological relationship that involved, as ecological relationships do, a genuine exchange of goods and services. Of course this strategy has at least one defect, at least for people living in densely settled areas. The limitation is that it involves an essentially consumptive relationship with the natural landscape. Face it: Thoreau's project at Walden was in this purely practical, ecological sense, actually consumptive. His cabin was the forerunner of the A-frames and condominiums we are now trying to keep out of Walden Woods. Moreover, even huckleberrying and fishing, so harmless when carried out by one or a few, become destructive when pursued by hundreds or thousands. (Think only of the matter of bathing in the pond—for Thoreau, alone in the woods, a ritual of renewal, but for us in our thousands, a serious threat to the pond.)

In his account of Thoreau's contribution to environmental thinking in *Nature's Economy,* Donald Worster notes this limitation: "It might be impossible," he notes, "for today's millions to pick huckleberries and otherwise pursue Thoreau's style of ecological intimacy."[7] What Worster does not fully acknowledge is the tragic implications this has for the relationship between nature and culture in a postindustrial democratic society. What it means, in effect, is that this way—Thoreau's way, which is also in many respects the classic way—of achieving intimacy with nature, is obsolete, or at least not accessible to most of us. If it is accessible, it may be only to an environmental elite who own land or otherwise have the use of ecosystems as expensive, exclusive toys.

This brings us directly to the subject of restoration as a way of carrying out Thoreau's agenda, as it were, and in fact popularizing it, while avoiding the undesirable consequences this might have for the environment. The solution is very neatly to continue the work, continue with your "business" with nature, but shift its purpose from consumption to creation. As I have pointed out elsewhere, restoration entails essentially all the interactions with nature Thoreau pursued at Walden.[8] Thus the restorationist may gather huckleberries not to eat them but to obtain their seed, to propagate them, and to enlarge their populations. He or she hunts or fishes, not to obtain food or for mere sport, but to remove exotics, to adjust populations (restoratively), or to obtain stock for reintroduction to habitats from which species have been extirpated. And at the same time the restorationist is a gardener and even a scientist, as Thoreau was at Walden.

Thus restoration provides a way of reentering nature in practical terms. It does so constructively and, as restorationists have found, it can feed one's genius as surely as Thoreau's activities fed his. (Beyond this, such a program, linking the work of restoration with the science of ecology, might rescue the practitioner from the loss of intimacy with nature Thoreau felt late in life, which some believe may have resulted from his increasing preoccupation with the science available to him, which was almost entirely descriptive.)

The second of Thoreau's themes relevant to restoration is the theme of renewal, a theme that runs through *Walden,* is reflected in much of its imagery, and reaches a climax in the penultimate chapter, "Spring." Again, this theme is evident everywhere in *Walden,* and has been explored in detail by others.[9] Consider by way of example only a few images: Thoreau's ritual bathing in the pond, the coming of spring at the climax of the book, the ecstatic concluding sentences, "There is more day to dawn. The sun is but a morning star." And, most pertinent for us, the joyful recognition that the forest of Walden, cut down years after Thoreau's sojourn there, is "springing up by its shore as lustily as ever" ("The Ponds").

Altogether, as Austin Meredith suggested to me during the symposium, whatever else it may be, *Walden* is essentially a manual for spiritual self-renewal. And the faith in renewal of the self is accompanied by a deep and explicit faith in the regenerative power of nature. If some of the trees have been blown down, he notes, he has cooked his supper over their stumps, and new trees are growing up to take their places. Ecological restoration is, of course, nothing less than taking this process of renewal seriously, reducing it to practice, and participating in it.

Taking these first two themes together, we have two principles—faith in the possibility of true intimacy with nature, and hope in its regenerative power—that are at the heart of the experience of restoration. Beyond this, however, a third theme in Thoreau's thought is equally relevant, and even more significant when we come to the matter of identifying what was really distinctive about it and how it differs from the thought of others, notably John Muir, who have contributed to modern environmental thinking. This is the theme of what I will call the performative relationship with nature—the idea, essentially, that symbolic acts are efficacious, that they are in fact the key to fashioning relationships that may be problematic or even impossible to achieve in the purely literal dimension of experience. This interpretation owes much to the ideas of Frederick Turner.[10]

*Walden* is permeated with this sense of meaning in everything. To Thoreau objects and events are not merely effective, they are expressive, significant. He reads these meanings in the surface of the pond, the fish in it, the trees leaning over it, and the events of daily life, hoeing beans, baking bread, or building a house.

This sense of the performative nature of experience is conveyed appropriately through theatrical images. The pond, for example, "has the appearance of an amphitheater for some kind of sylvan spectacle." And the motions of a squirrel "imply spectators," as much as do those of a dancing girl. Most significantly, the reader gradually realizes, the entire

Walden experiment is really a performance—Thoreau is literally playing house in the woods. And he also acts out his other pursuits, his farming, and fishing and huckleberrying in the same way. What he is doing is reliving the experience of the race performatively, acting it out—actually doing it (as Emerson did not), but also doing it actually—that is, deliberately acting it out for his own benefit.

Hence the consistently symbolic texture of the book. Everything in it is real, but it is also really a prop for the performance. The beanfield represents the experience of 10,000 years of agriculture. The cabin is an occasion for acting out the role of architect and builder. Perhaps most significantly for us, the "wilderness" of Walden is no wilderness at all, but a rural setting on the outskirts of a town that is itself virtually a suburb of Boston. The irony of this is heightened when we remember that Thoreau's life coincided with the expansion of the frontier beyond the Appalachians and into the Midwest. Thousands of young people of his generation— including, a bit later, the youthful John Muir—went west to encounter real wilderness on the frontier. Thoreau stayed at home, on land long since altered by European settlers and even then in the process of being abandoned. And it was, as Lewis Mumford has pointed out from his experience with this landscape, this make believe wilderness that he wrote what some consider the best account of the American experience of the wilderness in our literature.

We tend to forget this, and are surprised and perhaps a bit displeased when reminded of it. But we should not be. Because it is just here, in this derelict landscape, reclaimed as wilderness in the imagination that Thoreau found and we may hope to find the preservation of the world. The point is that the wilderness is where you imagine it to be. It may be beyond the Mississippi—or in Concord. Thoreau himself said that if he were confined to living alone in a garret he could still be content with his thoughts. If, as Thoreau insists, the preservation of the world lies in wildness, the real seat of wildness, the true frontier, is in the undiscovered country of the imagination.

An example of this approach to nature that is almost uncannily pertinent to the subject of restoration appears in *Walden* in, appropriately, the chapter on "Spring," where it serves as an ecstatic climax to the development of the theme of renewal. This is the famous passage on the thawing of the sand bank along the stretch of railroad between Concord and the pond. Consider this passage—and consider especially how E. B. White might have handled the same situation. Here we have a vast scar in the landscape, a disturbance of a new kind and on an unprecedented scale—actually the 19th-century equivalent of strip mining or a major oil spill. The railroad bank, moreover, is washing away. This is erosion on a vast scale, with sand and silt washing down the bank into, among other places, Walden Pond itself. This is, in other words, an environmental catastrophe by almost any standard. Yet what does Thoreau make of it?

Out of this thawing and eroding mass of sand and clay he fashions a long and ecstatic passage, almost hallucinatory in intensity, celebrating the organic shapes of the sand deposits as incontrovertible evidence of the creative (and we may say restorative) power of nature.

"Few phenomena gave me more delight," he writes. Then, after describing the myriad organic forms the sand assumes—in which he sees premonitions, as it were, of "leopard's paws, or birds' feet, of brains or lungs or bowels," he notes. "I am affected as if in a peculiar sense I stood in the laboratory of the Artist who made the world and me."[11] And he goes on in this way for several pages, without adding a syllable of regret for the environmental ruin going on around him.

What we see here is a reflection of the element of the imaginative and performative element in Thoreau's thought that is directly related to the business of ecological restoration and to the spirit and manner in which we carry it out. In fact, the same idea may be conveyed by any number of passages, but this one is ideal for our purposes because of the precise circumstances Thoreau has chosen to construct his symbol. What Thoreau is describing here is the revegetation (or restoration) of the railroad bank, but it is, as Marx points out, entirely and relentlessly figurative. There is no literal revegetation going on here. Only the emergence of shapes in flowing sand, an event that, if anything, has more to do with the denuding of the bank than with its recovery in a literal, ecological sense.

This is no formula for ecological restoration—certainly not in any literal sense. What it is a plea in behalf of the imagination and its role at the center of all insight, knowledge, healing and the formation of relationships. Many things are impossible in the literal here and now, Thoreau is saying. But the imagination is without limit and ultimately leads events. It is in the imagination that waste—the noise of a hoe tilling beans—becomes music, and work is transformed into art. (His description of this is actually a consecration, with, as Frederick Turner has pointed out, the tinkling of the hoe serving the role of the bell at Mass.) And it is in the imagination that an eroding sandbank can become a luxuriant bank of flowers. The imaginative experience is itself somehow efficacious. It matters, if only because it leads to recognition of the limitless capacity of nature for creation and self-renewal.

This may not be a prescription for restoration, but it does have important implications for the way restoration might actually be carried out at Walden. In the matter of goals, for example, it will be important to keep in mind that the Walden Thoreau knew was not a pristine wilderness at all, but really a make-believe wilderness. This is important because it is important to make it clear that Thoreau found the salvation of the world not in a Muir- like search for unspoiled nature, but precisely near his own home, in a partly despoiled landscape redeemed by the imagination. For the same reason, the work of restoration itself should be regarded not only as a task but also as a performance and a celebration. It should not merely be accomplished, it should be performed for the pleasure and instruction of the participants, but also of the entire nation and the world. And as it proceeds it should serve as a model for the development of restoration as a performing art.

All of this brings me to the subject of Earthkeeping and its possible contribution to the restoration effort at Walden Pond. For some years I worked with my colleague Brock Woods at the Arboretum and with Steve Packard of The Nature Conservancy and the Society for Ecological Restoration to create a program we call Earthkeeping. This is a program that will provide opportunities for people—students, administrators, and the general public—to participate in restoration projects as a way of learning about and developing an intimate relationship with the natural landscape. Each project will be carried out in behalf of the restoration of a particular ecosystem and will serve as the basis for a program of study of the ecosystem and its history. A pilot project was developed in the watershed of Lake Wingra, which adjoins the University of Wisconsin Arboretum on the west side of Madison. A second project could be set up to support the restoration effort at Walden Pond.

Exactly how would this work? Organizationally, Earthkeeping is modeled on Earthwatch, the highly successful program that turns tourists into part-time field researchers. Like Earthwatch, Earthkeeping projects will be supported by participants' fees. One advantage of this is that it will enable us to carry out restoration projects as they should be carried out, with ambitious goals on a large scale and over a long period of time. At Walden, this might make it possible to undertake long-term, labor-intensive projects such as high-quality forest restoration—or the restoration of Thoreau's beanfield—that would otherwise be impossible. Presumably a project at Walden would be carried out on a modest scale, with groups in the field for several months each year. If successful it could continue indefinitely, and would provide ongoing public education about the pond and a constantly growing constituency for its preservation.

In this way we believe that we can help make Walden Pond a model for a new way of "using" nature. And we believe this model has important implications both for the natural environment and for our relationship with it. For one thing, it offers a solution to the dilemma of overuse of places like Walden Pond or our national parks. The solution, we feel, is not to discourage or limit use, but to provide a way to make it constructive, restorative. Then two things can happen that cannot happen so long as we regard people—ourselves, the public, everybody—as essentially users and consumers of nature. The first is that people visiting natural areas will have at least the option of contributing in some way, however modest or even symbolic, to its improvement—to making it more natural. The second is that people will discover that this is more rewarding than just staring at scenery, however spectacular. Then they can abandon the fruitless quest for unspoiled wilderness in favor of a more practical and realistic, Thoreauvian participation in nature. They will learn that some of the best opportunities for this kind of experience are not in far away "pristine" natural areas, but at home, in the parks and derelict land around their own towns and cities. They will begin spending their free time restoring these areas—traveling at home, as Thoreau did at Concord, and as thousands of volunteer restorationists are doing today in places like Chicago and Austin and San Francisco. In this way, consumptive use of areas such as national parks and wilderness areas actually will be reduced, even as it is replaced by something better and more rewarding.

In this I begin to see some crucial part of the preservation of the world—not in wildness but in the experience of wildness carried out imaginatively and performatively, and not by an elite few but by millions. In this way we can turn every neighborhood park, every schoolyard, vacant lot, abandoned field or right-of-way into a Walden Pond, an arena for experimentation in the art of living with nature. Out of this we may expect the same kinds of discovery and increase in wisdom in our society that Thoreau achieved at Walden. The experience could have a profound effect on our environmentalism, our ideas about nature, and our ways of interacting with the natural environment. Indeed it could lead our society, as similar, practical experiences led Thoreau beyond pessimism and paralysis to a new intimacy with nature, and at the same time a deeper wisdom regarding our relationship with it.

Consider just one example of the value of such experience, borrowed from Professor Marx's discussion of Emerson and Thoreau.[12] Emerson, Thoreau's friend and mentor, shared the pastoral vision, and imagined an America of the future in which Americans would live "in the bowers of paradise." Emerson, however, only imagined and wrote about this vision. Thoreau, like Columbus, made the bold experiment. He moved into the woods, in search of it. Like Columbus he failed to find what he was looking for, but like Columbus he found something different, and even more interesting: what he brought back was a report of a sandy bank washing out in a spring thaw. Paradise, he is telling us, is real. But it is not a real place. Rather it is the product of the imagination in contact with nature—the imagination working on the experience of nature as a raw material.

In this way, Marx points out, Thoreau went beyond the abstract and sentimental pastoralism of Emerson. The key was his interaction with nature, which was always both practical and literal and figurative— always, to use his own word, sacramental. A similar project—restoration carried out as a performing art—can do the same thing for America. It can provide us all with a way of participating in the pastoral experiment, giving us a chance at least, by trying it out, to transform fantasy into wisdom. What better place to begin than Walden Pond.

# Notes

[1]From Confucius, The Great Learning, in The Commentary of the Philosopher Tsang, quoted by Thoreau in "Where I Lived and What I Lived for" in *Walden.*

[2]E.B. White, *One Man's Meat,* (New York: Harper and Row), p.86.

[3]Thoreau, "The Ponds," in *Walden,* pp. 173–174.

[4]Thoreau, *The Journal of Henry D. Thoreau,* vol. II, Bradford Torrey and Frances H. Allen, eds. (New York: Dover Publications), 1962, p. 259.

[5]*Walden,* pp. 140–150.

[6]Leo Marx, *The Machine in the Garden: Technology and the Pastoral Ideal in America,* (New York: Oxford University Press, 1964).

[7]Donald Worster, *Nature's Economy: The Roots of Ecology* (Garden City, NJ: Anchor Press, 1979) p. 111.

[8]William R. Jordan, III, "The Reentry of Nature," *Chronicles* (August 1990): pp. 19–22.

[9]Lauriat Lane, Jr., "On the Organic Structure of Walden," in *Approaches to Walden,* Lauriat Lane, Jr., ed. (San Francisco: Wadsworth, 1961).

[10]Frederick Turner, "Reflexivity as Evolution in Thoreau's *Walden* in *Natural Classicism: Essays of Literature and Science* (New York: Paragon House, 1985), pp. 171–203.

[11]*Walden,* p. 271 ff.

[12]*The Machine in the Garden,* p. 262.

**WILLIAM R. JORDAN, III**, received his Ph.D. in botany from the University of Wisconsin. He has been at the university Arboretum since 1971 and is presently the officer in charge of outreach. He is the founding editor of *Restoration and Management Notes* and a founding member of the Society for Ecological Restoration.

# Walden Restoration:
# Legal and Policy Issues

❖

## Cindy Hill Couture

## Introduction

Through the diligent work of ecologists, historians, and citizens' organizations who have embraced the environmental philosophies of Thoreau and Emerson, a Walden ecosystem of roughly 2,600 acres has been identified. Much of the research done on the Walden ecosystem has involved the identification and mapping of scientific and literary, or historic, sites. This research will be important in any attempt to restore and maintain Walden as a viable, functioning ecosystem. An additional layer of legal and policy issues must be surmounted, however, before the scientific and scholarly information can lead to environmental sanctity for the region. Chief among these additional issues is the basic tenet of our legal and economic system—that of private property.

Most people have heard it said that "possession is nine-tenths of the law." One common example of this maxim is that the person who owns a parcel of real property also owns the right to do as he or she pleases to do with that parcel. The full exercise of this rule is tempered by the requirement that actions remain within the bounds of laws that protect the health and safety of neighbors, such as zoning, wetlands, sanitation, and building code regulations (which are evidently the remaining one-tenth of the law).

Where a concerned person wishes to restrict the actions that occur on land owned by someone else—or, even more difficult, prescribe that a certain course of action, such as ecological restoration, be undertaken— that concerned person must find some way to surmount the obstacle of private ownership. One cannot simply walk onto another's land with shovel and seeds in hand and start routing out alien species and replacing them with native biota (or rather, one can, but not without violating criminal and civil laws and risking jail, fines, and lawsuits, thus creating more work for lawyers while espousing the principles of yet another great Thoreau essay, "On the Duty of Civil Disobedience.") The good news is that there are a variety of legal methods to achieve one's environmental goals. The bad news is that none of them are easy, quick, or inexpensive.

Which of the many approaches to take depends, first, upon who owns the parcel of interest. In the Walden ecosystem, we find the two major forms of land ownership: public ownership in the form of a state reservation surrounding Walden Pond, and private ownership, in the form of a multitude of residential and commercial parcels. Influencing the activities on land under these two forms of ownership warrants different tactics. As a general rule, the odds of changing actions taken on publicly owned land beat, by a small margin, the odds of doing so on privately owned land.

## Walden Pond State Reservation
## Legal Status, Agency Management

The state-owned lands in Lincoln and Concord have been designated Walden Pond State Reservation (WPSR). Surprisingly, Massachusetts law contains no definition of a reservation (as, for example, distinct from a state forest, park, or recreation area) and directs no particular course of action for the care and management of a reservation's land.

The original eighty-odd acres of WPSR were deeded to the Commonwealth of Massachusetts in 1922 by the Emerson family and was at first managed by the Middlesex County Commissioners. Management of a reservation's land by another party is not unusual in Massachusetts. For example, the Mount Tom State Reservation along the Connecticut River in western Massachusetts was managed jointly by a board of the Hampshire and Hampden County Commissioners until financial circumstances in 1990 led the state to assume management responsibilities. Other reservation lands have been managed by private organizations, such as Blue Hill Reservation, which is under the watchful eye of the Massachusetts Audubon Society.

After many years of county management, the Commonwealth took over WPSR, placing it under the control of the Massachusetts Department of Environmental Management (DEM).

DEM staff and administrators interpret the DEM mandate as the management of lands for human recreation, with access limited only at the point where recreational activities would damage fragile natural areas, threaten endangered species, or interfere with economically "desirable" programs such as logging. When I was a member of the Mount Tom Reservation Citizens Advisory Committee I heard a DEM administrator describe his draft "facilities assessment" for the reservation (a "facilities assessment" is supposed to be an inventory of existing facilities and accommodations on the property). The assessment couched its inventory data in terms of the reservation's potential for substantial increases in developed recreation. I asked him at what point and by whom the decision had been made to manage Mount Tom for intensive recreation. He responded with an expression of incredulity and stated, "We're DEM. That's what we *do*."

DEM is authorized to develop a variety of assessments, plans, and programs for state lands under its control. It is, theoretically, required to follow these plans, as well as other state laws, such as the Wetlands Protection Act, but in reality it has broad discretion in its duties and is rarely challenged on the efficacy of its decisions.

Absent other legal requirements, an attempt to require DEM to manage state lands in a way other than that in which it is doing so would most likely fail. Luckily, several legal circumstances converge at Walden that enable concerned citizens to seek alteration of DEM's management programs and policies.

One such circumstance is that Massachusetts law allows citizens to sue the state and its agencies to stop environmental degradation. Normally, under the legal doctrine of sovereign immunity, neither the state nor the federal government may be sued unless it consents to be sued; even then, it can be sued only under conditions and circumstances specifically delineated by statute.

Citizens of Massachusetts have the benefit of a special Environmental Citizens' Suit statute. This law permits any ten residents of Massachusetts to sue a state agency to prevent environmental harm when the agency's activities violate any state statute designed for environmental protection. This means that if any of DEM's management activities at WPSR violate the state's environmental statutes, interested citizens may sue to block those activities.

Walden Forever Wild (WFW), a citizens' group seeking the ecological restoration of WPSR, contacted my law firm and the activist network with whom we are associated, Preserve Appalachian Wilderness Network, Inc. (PAW), regarding the bringing of a lawsuit of this nature. WFW pursued numerous alternative courses over the years, including submission of several pieces of legislation to the state legislature seeking a declaration that WPSR is a sanctuary. None, however, received a favorable report.

PAW and WFW took the first step toward initiating litigation against DEM, which was to find ten individual residents of Massachusetts to send a notice of intent to file suit. Key to this citizens' environmental litigation is identification of the precise statutes that DEM may be violating in the course of its management of WPSR. We identified several such statutes in the course of our initial research. Primary among them is the state's Wetlands Protection Act, which requires environmental review by a local conservation commission before actions such as the annual filling of a portion of the pond shore with beach sand may be undertaken.

Yet a citizens' suit limited to strict statutory violations does not seem to satisfy all of the circumstances at WPSR. A more fundamental difference of philosophy underlies the contentions of the concerned citizens. Without more direct instructions than that the Reservation ought to be managed according to the philosophies and ethics of Thoreau and Emerson, an environmental citizens' suit would most likely result only in small changes in a few management techniques, but would otherwise be destined to fall under the weight of another legal doctrine that works as a companion to sovereign immunity: the doctrine of judicial deference to administrative agencies.

But just as Walden is unique in being a confluence of geologic, biologic, and cultural events, so too is it unique in having been given to the state with very particular restrictions on its management. Even better for those concerned about the condition of Walden, the restrictions were incorporated into the legislation that accepted Walden as a state reservation. They are thus part of a statute under which citizens are entitled to bring suit. The deeds to the Commonwealth from the Emerson family state that Walden Pond was granted to be maintained as the "Walden of Thoreau and Emerson." Examples of acceptable activities, such as bathing or fishing in the pond, are given in the deeds. These examples are tempered by a reference to Revere Beach, ordering that Walden not be converted to the type of developed playground found there at that time.

Much has been made of the fact that the deeds do not restrict all human presence or recreation at Walden. While this is true, there is obviously an unsubtle difference between a few individuals' walking from town to bathe in the Pond, as was the case in Thoreau's day, and thousands of people's flocking to a clear-cut beach loaded with trucked-in sand, their radios blasting, their litter and lotions floating on the surface of the Pond, as is the case today.

Much has also been made of the fact that the deeds seem to indicate a desire to "freeze" the natural condition of Walden as it was when Thoreau lived by the Pond's shores. Yet it is the consensus of both Thoreau and Emerson scholars, as well as of those whose concern is primarily ecological rather than literary, that the Walden of Emerson and Thoreau would be a dynamic, self-sustaining ecosystem characterized by balanced populations of indigenous species occupying natural, unaltered landscape features, not the Walden that happened to exist at one particular moment in time. This means that the Walden sought is one with the modern human interferences removed or reduced to an absolute minimum, and perhaps containing examples of the human presence prior to the European influence, as well as of the time of Emerson and Thoreau.

The first obstacle to overcome in reaching this goal is to convince a judge that the Walden Pond area of today is not the Walden of Emerson and Thoreau. It is not likely that any judge who receives this citizens' suit will be versed in either ecology or the related literature. To a person of citified sensibility, a drive by Walden Pond may not be sufficient to make obvious the problems due to present management practices. The average resident of Boston, or of any comparable metropolis, will see at Walden some clearish water, a wide beach, and a surrounding woodland of trees not yet flattened by shopping malls or highways. To most eyes, the mere absence of concrete and asphalt seems enough to make a site "natural," or even "wild."

The existing ecological disruption of Walden Pond is less obvious than buildings on its shores would be, but it is not inobvious to people knowledgeable in ecology and related disciplines. Aquatic weeds are spreading out from the base of the boat-launch ramp, clearly imported on hulls and propellers from other waters. The beach is the antithesis of the wooded shores of the pond, and its sand is washing into the water; because there is no outlet to Walden, the sand is slowly filling the Pond. As the water adjacent to the beach grows shallower, its waters warm and its chemistry is altered. High fecal and urine counts here add to the ecological disruption. The indigenous fish about which Thoreau once waxed eloquent have been chemically removed from the waters to make way for more "sportsman-like," alien varieties.

Around the shores and throughout the woodland are a hodgepodge of half-hearted, ill-conceived landscaping attempts, including several feet of Coney Island-style boardwalk, a double row of white boulders dug in by backhoe, and erosion-containment walls of stacked railroad ties. Destruction caused by the overwhelming numbers of visitors is also evident. The woodland soils have been compacted by daily trampling and no longer support an understory of shrubs and herbs; a widening, eroding trail rims the Pond, preventing trees and shrubs from naturally retaining its shores; and shoes, "poptops," and cigarette butts are found at every footfall.

It will take the collective testimony, scientific data, photographs, and historic and literary research of each of the organizations and individuals who have such information to persuade a court that the Walden which is, is not the Walden that ought to be. Only through unprecedented cooperation and coordination among those concerned with the condition and future of Walden Pond and its surrounding woodlands can the damage to Walden be undone and its natural state returned and preserved.

Circumstances conspire once again to assist those pursuing the cause of ecological sanctity at Walden. In 1960, while the Middlesex County Commissioners were still managing WPSR, a citizens' suit was brought charging mismanagement under the deed restrictions. The citizens won, and an order was entered directing the Commissioners to take certain specific actions, including the removal of a concrete pier that had been built into the Pond. More to the point of present efforts, the Commissioners were also ordered, in more general terms, to abide by the deed restrictions, taking notice of Thoreau's celebrated work *Walden* as a guide to the Reservation's proper management. The Commissioners were directed to limit the number of visitors to the Pond and to repair the ecological damage done by erosion and excessive human presence.

The Commissioners did take several steps that were specifically required by the Court. But in the years that followed, the state DEM took over management, and erosion and other ecological damage began to increase rather than abate. When criticized for this, DEM pointed to budget restrictions as their constraint, yet a few million dollars was spent on some of the "Band-Aid" projects described above, which have actually worsened the situation. Drastically restricting public access, coupled with a program of restoration (the removal of physical intrusions such as alien species, beach sand, and constructed retaining walls), followed by a long-term commitment to ecological self-recovery (simply put, leaving the woodlands alone to proceed at nature's will) would cost substantially less than present operations.

## The Dangers of Litigation

Citizens' suits are not without their dangers and pitfalls. Expense is one such problem. Expert-witness testimony, scientific testing, mapping, and even such basics as travel and telephone costs can quickly surpass the budgets of not-for-profit organizations. More than one citizens' suit has failed midstream when finances ran out and critical evidence was not available as a result. A lack of coordination among concerned parties can lead to a similar result. Those considering entering into litigation for the restoration of Walden would be wise to give due consideration to these practical constraints.

Of even greater concern is the danger of losing the lawsuit. Based on the ecological conditions of Walden and the guidelines for its management spelled out by statute, deed, and previous court suits, it seems likely the litigation will be a success. However, there is always the possibility of failure, the possibility that a court may choose to defer to the administering agency regardless of other directives, or that a judge may, even in the face of detailed expert testimony to the contrary, find that the management of Walden meets the legal restrictions. Losing citizens' suit litigation over the management of Walden would be bad enough if it were restricted to WPSR itself. But lawsuits create "precedent," the legal rule that courts are constrained to follow the rules set by prior decisions. A court order that the management of WPSR be left to the discretion of DEM might have negative ramifications for other state lands. This risk may be remote, but it cannot be discounted: courts have been known to do strange and unpredictable things. It is for the parties interested in pursuing litigation to decide whether the probability of success outweighs the risk of creating "bad law."

## Private Lands Within the
## Walden Ecosystem

Outside of WPSR, most of the Walden ecosystem is made up of a multitude of privately owned residential and business parcels. Unlike the publicly owned lands, there is no law that enables concerned citizens to impose a particular management scheme on the ecosystem. This is not to say that those concerned are without recourse, however.

The first step toward the protection of the privately held portion of the Walden ecosystem would be to supplement the existing scientific data with ownership and regulatory information. Accurate zoning maps could provide a helpful underlay. Tax maps from the tax assessors' offices and plot plans from the Registry of Deeds would add parcel boundaries and ownership over the zoning districts. The town conservation commissions could identify areas that come under the aegis of the state's Wetlands Protection Act.

Land-use maps or aerial photographs, probably available at town offices, in local libraries, or from the University of Massachusetts or the Tufts University geology department, would help to pinpoint development patterns and "hot spots." This could be enhanced quite efficiently by an organized door-to-door survey within the region to inquire as to landowners' plans for the future of their parcels. This would be especially important for large, potentially developable parcels because single residential lots can rarely be further developed or divided. This type of inquiry could also work as an educational tool if the citizens involved hand out maps and information on the region and on landowners' options.

There are "high-tech" capabilities that could assist in this type of endeavor, but they tend to be very expensive—and essentially unnecessary. It has been my experience in the land-use planning field that people who are dazzled by high technology tend to forget that the basic information still has to be gathered through on-the-ground collection of data. Once they have the basic information, citizens' groups need only raise enough to buy felt-tip markers for making hand-colored maps, which are quite satisfactory for most purposes. And, of course, the most complex computer-generated imagery cannot tell one what to do with the information they convey.

Once the ownership and use of land are identified, there is a laundry list of options for influencing the area's future. Only one—outright purchase of the property within the defined area—gives complete control. For at least some parcels in the Walden ecosystem, purchase is not out of the question, especially if concerned citizens work together with local land trusts and their town governments to raise money and to target priority purchases. If the state lacks funds for such purchases, the federal government, given its interest in Walden and the Concord–Lexington area, may be a likely buyer.

Many residential landowners may not wish to part with their land. A number of options short of complete purchase might be appropriate in this situation, such as buying conservation easements or development rights. Some landowners may wish to donate these rights, as they can get a tax deduction for the donation; doing so lowers property taxes by reducing the assessed value of the property, helpful both in the short term and in estate planning. Other landowners may wish to enter into contracts to have concerned groups manage their land without giving up any of the rights of ownership.

Each of these options has to be explored on a parcel-by-parcel, owner-by-owner basis. What is right for one piece of land and one owner may not be the best option for another. It is a long process, and frequently a costly one. The concerned organizations may wish to band together to hire a staff planner to oversee such efforts and establish a pool of volunteer labor in the legal and policy fields, perhaps relying on some of the Boston area's law school and graduate university programs.

Besides this list of options for dealing directly with landowners, there is another range of approaches through regulation on the state and local level. These would include zoning and subdivision regulations, creation of historic districts, and applying for designation of the area as a state Area of Critical Environmental Concern. Each of these options requires a fair amount of community knowledge and support, and thus would do best on the heels of a public-education campaign coupled with a good deal of factual information.

## Conclusion

There is remarkable hope for the restoration of the Walden ecosystem, despite its fragmented land ownership and its location in the midst of the sprawl of one of our nation's great cities. The affection of New England for its history and its natural environment creates a favorable climate for ecological protection, but this climate is not without its problems. Walden is choked by the very ties of bureaucracy, politics, and speculatory land ownership that Thoreau and Emerson deplored. A concerted, cooperative, long-term effort, including litigation, land purchases, public education, and regulatory management, can bring ecological peace and wholeness to the public and private lands of the Walden ecosystem.

———————

**CINDY HILL COUTURE** is a partner at Couture and Hill Law Firm in Northampton, Massachusetts.

# Thoreau's Poetic Vision and the Concord Landscape

❖

## J. Walter Brain

### The Poetic Vision

"I think I could write a poem to be called 'Concord,'" Thoreau had entered as early as 1841 in his *Journal*. "For argument I should have the River, the Woods, the Ponds, the Hills, the Fields, the Swamps and Meadows, the Streets and Buildings, and the Villagers. Then Morning, Noon and Evening, Spring, Summer, Autumn and Winter, Night, Indian Summer, and the Mountains in the Horizon." That poem to be called "Concord" proved to be the *Journal* itself, the bulk of which is but a poetic record of all that he had set out for 'argument' in that early entry. No secluded dale, secret grove or solitary spring in that landscape has been left unsung.

Thoreau's Concord spilled beyond the bounds of his native town to the surrounding country, largely into Lincoln and Carlisle, and stretched for miles along the river corridors to their sources and to the junction of the Concord with the Merrimack. For argument in that poem to be called "Concord," Thoreau's vision had reached to the "Mountains in the Horizon" to Wachusett "under the eaves of heaven" and to Monadnock and Uncannunuc. "Those hills extend our plot of earth," he asserted roundly, "they make our native valley or indentation in the earth so much the larger."

This Concord of the mind, Thoreau's home soil, a landscape that we may refer to as the Concord Region, or Thoreau Country, is this vast mosaic of tens of miles of winding rivers and of meadows, woods and hills, ponds and springs, with the prospect of distant mountains; a landscape that Thoreau made the abode of body and mind in his daily walks, for the "privilege of beholding it, as an ornament, a suggestion, a provocation, a heaven on earth," seeking at every turn "to stand on the eminence of the hour," and to translate the reality of nature and of his life in it into a life of reflection and poetic truth. In an early essay, "A Walk to Wachusett," he wrote: "In the spaces of thought are the reaches of land and water, where men go and come. The landscape lies far and fair within, and the deepest thinker is the farthest traveled."

This process of translation, a transmutation of matter into spirit, moving from the perception of nature to thought and reflection and to the revelation of "higher truths," was essentially a poetic one, arrived at, in the *Journal* and in his other writings, by means that were necessarily those of poetry: imagery, symbol and simile, trope and metaphor. As is often the case in the *Journal,* the natural object itself served as its own metaphor, as when he writes, "As I was stalking over the surface of this planet in the dark tonight I started a plover resting on the ground and heard him go off with whistling wings," a poetic device that distilled the sense of cosmic harmony that he lived in. We come full circle when this dispensation with metaphor propels thought and nature into what Thoreau perceived to be the essential oneness and harmony of all that is. On an autumn afternoon, contemplating the scenery of Fair Haven Pond and admitting to himself that [he] "did not see how it could be improved," he asks, without expecting an answer, "What are these things?," only to observe with unquestioning submission to that essential oneness that "we are made to love the river and the meadow as the wind is made to ripple the water."

In his poetic vision Thoreau had, on one plane, made of the Concord landscape, on one plane, a personal cosmology in which every aspect of his life and of reality was imbued with symbolic meaning. On another plane, Concord answered to perfection his need for an "Arcady" in which he could lead a life of simplicity and contentment in the beauty of nature, and in honest relation to other men, or, in his own words, "a life of simplicity, of independence, of magnanimity and trust such as all men should live," a feat that he, more than most men, brought nearest to consummation. He proved remarkably modern on both counts, far ahead of the "confusion and turmoil" of his time and of the pretensions of our own.

Thoreau had placed Concord at the very center of his universe and all the gyrations of the heavens and of earth, the days, the seasons, and the points of the compass he saw as revolving about his native place and his personal life. Even his daily walks, whither would he go on a particular afternoon, he saw as a function of some heavenly influence. He believed that he had been born in the most estimable place in the world, "and in the nick of time too," by which he meant to bring together the coordinates of time and space, of existence itself, to the very center of his own life, projecting a vision in which his life, as paradigm of the life of man, was in complete harmony with the cosmos, and he felt at home in it. There was an implied projection of this universality on the life of every man. "Be native to the universe. I too love Concord best," he had said, "But I am glad when I discover in oceans and wildernesses far away the materials out of which a million Concords can be made. Indeed unless I discover them I am lost myself. That there too I am at home." Emerson understood this well when in his biographical sketch of Thoreau he thought "his fancy for referring everything to the meridian of Concord" to be but a "playful expression of his conviction of the indifference of all places, and that the best place for each is where he stands." Except that Thoreau, for all his playfulness, was a serious thinker. "My trade is mainly with the celestial empire," Thoreau had said in an early *Journal* entry, and repeated it in various forms throughout his life, but Emerson seems to have understood less well the nature of his erstwhile disciple's trade.

And Concord was Arcadia. Once, passing through the "vale of Brown and Tarbell," in the Old Marborough Road Country, "a sunshiny mead pastured by cattle and sparkling with dew." in the morning freshness, Thoreau reflects: "The vale of Tempe and of Arcady is not farther off than are the conscious lives of men from their opportunities. Our life is far from corresponding to its scenery as we are distant from Tempe and Arcadia; that is to say, they are far away because we are far from living natural lives. How absurd it would be to insist on the vale of Tempe in particular when we have such vales as we have!"

## The Concord Landscape

How do we look at this Concord landscape that lies on our lap today? What does it consist of, what are its character and attributes? How do we attempt a classification of its riches, an assessment of its spatial and scenic values? Not for the purpose of some utilitarian enterprise. "Beauty," after all, Thoreau had prescribed, "is a finer utility whose end we do not see," but to know and understand the better that beauty before our eyes for the sheer enjoyment of it and that we may project intelligent actions toward its protection. Thoreau himself was fond of inventorying his nature trove for his own pleasure: "For brooks we have ... . For hills ... . For ponds ... ," he would exult and list his beloved haunts with the spell of an incantation.

For definitions and descriptions of the character of the Concord landscape, we have not only the observations that Thoreau left in his *Journal* and in his other writings, but also those of his fellow transcendentalists and of other writers of the local scenery who were inspired by its simple rusticity. For an analysis of this same landscape we may also take a cue from Thoreau's own promptings, in the *Journal,* at the identification of large units of the Concord landscape: the "great wild tracts," and of landscape types within or outside the great wild tracts, defined by a common physiography, such as the hills, the springs, the rivers, and other types, which he often tallied or studied together as a group.

Thoreau never undertook a systematic study or a complete classification of his native landscape, although the thrust of the *Journal,* the late essays, and of drafts left unfinished at the end of his life, appeared to move toward a sense of totality, in which all things, physical and spiritual, fact and thought, came together into a harmonious whole, and in which nature and the urgent plea to spare and preserve the local landscape and scenery intensified as the core of his vision.

With a push from Thoreau himself, but staying within the mainstream of his thought and vision, we may embark upon an analysis of the Concord landscape, complementing that vision with modern techniques of landscape analysis and assessment. Since our interest is his poetic vision on his native landscape, we will not expand in this text on the theoretical underpinnings of modern techniques of landscape analysis, but will apply them, only to complement or to more clearly define Thoreau's own notions on the Concord landscape.

## General Character

The landscape of Concord is characterized by homely and intimate scenes of subtle, placid, and demure beauty. Its rivers, meadows, ponds, woods, and hills weave a tapestry of no sumptuous design but of exquisite homespun finery. "No better place for his business," wrote the poet William Ellery Channing of his friend and walking companion Henry Thoreau, on noting this absence of grand scenery in Concord and the fitness of the land for "daily talk." Thoreau himself had described the local landscape, in one of his earliest *Journal* entries, as a "humble working day valley." He walked its woods and hills with the ease and content of a man ambling about his own house. Concord's is essentially a domestic landscape, and the homely and self-effacing scenery of its hills and meadows has also been remarked upon by other writers of the local prospect. Its native scenes are sustaining of the spirit, but do not overwhelm. As Nathaniel Hawthorne's Septimius Felton, the title character of that romance with the title by the same name, observed of the Concord scenery: "It is a landscape that never tires, though it has nothing striking about it; and I am glad that there are no great hills to be thrusting themselves into my thoughts."

"A scene of great rural beauty," Hawthorne had also observed of this landscape in a journal entry in 1842, as he had viewed it from the top of Ripley's Hill.

The scenery of Concord as I beheld it from the summit of the hill, has
no very marked characteristics, but has a great deal of quiet beauty, in
keeping with the river. There are broad and peaceful meadows, which,
I think, are among the most satisfying objects in natural scenery... a
meadow stretches out like a small infinity, yet with a secure homeli-
ness... The hills which border these meadows are wide swells of land...
The white village, at a distance on the left, appears to be embossed
among wooded hills.

Emerson shared this outlook on the local scenery, as we are reminded on
the first verses of "Musketaquid," his paean on the valley of the Concord:

Because I was content with these poor fields,
Low open meads, slender ad sluggish streams,
And found a home in haunts which others scorned,
The partial wood-gods overpaid my love,
And granted me the freedom of their state.

This was the valley whose "luxuriant simplicity" Bronson Alcott saw as
a source of inspiration: "The rural muse has traversed these fields,
meadows, woodlands, the brook-sides, the river; caught the harmony
of its changing skies ... "And Thoreau took the valley as his own
"garden" for his afternoon walks: "I have a garden, larger than any
artificial garden that I have read of, and far more attractive to me, mile
after mile of imbowered walks, with animals running free and wild
therein as from the first, varied with land and water prospect, and above
all so retired ... . You may wander away to solitary bowers and brooks
and hills, which never failed to inspire him." Once, while contemplating
the beauty of a stately pine grove at White Pond, "the western sun falling
in golden streams through its aisles," he asks himself: "What is this
beauty in the Landscape but a certain fertility in me? I look in vain to see
it realized but in my own life."

## Historic and Literary Character

For all its modest scale and humble semblance, Concord's is
preeminently a historic and literary landscape, home to momentous
events in history and to the first flowering of letters in the new ascendant
nation. Its rivers and meadows bespeak such events and our first and most
original letters are indelibly imprinted on them. These woods and hills
inspired Emerson, Thoreau, Hawthorne, and other thinkers, poets, and
artists who have left an unmatched lyrical testimony to the beauty and
simple nobility of this landscape. There is not one hill or meadow or
retired haunt in this valley that has not been accounted for in history or
in literature.

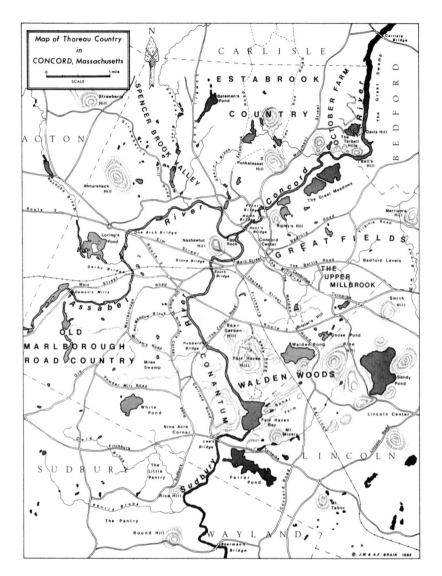

**Map of the Concord region**

There is only one Concord, and there is but one Walden. And what they signify to this country and to the world at large extends beyond the confines of time and space and of petty concerns that rule the fate of many a town or of entire nations. It was at Concord that tillers of the soil stood up in heroic defiance of tyranny; and it was at Concord too, that the new nation sought to sound the depth of the spirit. Nowhere did it fathom deeper than at Walden Pond and its surrounding woods.

## The Great Wild Tracts

Thoreau identified, in the *Journal,* four "great wild tracts" or "great uninhabited tracts" as the major units of landscape in Concord. These were the "Easterbrooks Country," the tract "on the Marlborough Road," the "Walden Woods," and "A fourth, the Great Fields." Ellery Channing, in his recollections of his friend, *Thoreau, The Poet-Naturalist,* remembers only three of these great wild tracts: "Three spacious tracts, uncultivated, where the patches of scrub-oak, wild apples, barberries, and other plants grew, which Thoreau admired, were Walden Woods, the Easterbrook Country, and the old Marlboro road." We may advance here a definition of a Great Wild Tract as a large and relatively unbroken, undeveloped, and uncultivated swath of country in a more or less primitive state of nature, composed of diverse physiographic elements, and with a scenic character and spell of its own that is readily recognizable.

Of the four great wild tracts identified by Thoreau, only two have come down to us in their relative entirety and integrity, with only limited development encroaching on them at the edges or even deeper: the Easterbrook Country and Walden Woods, each extending over a swath of country about two miles square. These two great wild tracts, one in the north of the town, the other in the south, and extending into the neighboring towns, constitute the core, in the form of two scenic poles, of the landscape of the Concord region.

The integrity of these great tracts must not be taken for granted, for large parcels within them remain unprotected and vulnerable to development or to substantial land alteration. The permanent protection of these tracts and of other endangered sites, intimately associated with what is perhaps the noblest contribution that this country has yet made to civilization, we cannot afford to forfeit.

The other two original wild tracts, the Old Marlborough Road, to the southwest of the town, and the Great Fields, to the east, somewhat larger than the former two, no longer constitute relatively unbroken and undeveloped tracts of land with a character of their own. Large sections of these two tracts have been suburbanized, although equally large undeveloped areas remain, however scattered or with a much reduced primitive core, about which the remaining parcels of open space could perhaps be made contiguous or linked up in a future protection plan aiming at the partial but effective restoration of these former great wild tracts.

These great wild tracts represented for Thoreau the wilderness he longed for, "a nature which I cannot put my foot through, woods where the wood thrush forever sings, where the hours are early morning ones," and which he foresaw and feared, in the projection of his own spirit across the ages and out of a transcendent sense of solidarity with all men "the wilderness is near, as well as dear, to every man"—being laid waste.

"Thank God they cannot yet fly," he cried prophetically in his lecture on "Huckleberries" toward the end of his life, "and lay waste the sky as well as the earth. We are safe on that side for the present." What he meant by "wildness" and his dictum that "in Wildness is the preservation of the World" he defined best perhaps when he had equated earlier in the *Journal*: "How important is a constant intercourse with nature and the contemplation of natural phenomenon to the preservation of Moral and intellectual health." In pursuit of this nature and wildness he "would go after the cows, I would watch the flocks of Admetus there forever, only for my board and clothes."

Thoreau was thinking of the great wild tracts at Walden and at the Easterbrook Country when he entered in the *Journal*, and then repeated in more or less the same words in his lecture "Huckleberries," that "each town should have a park, or rather primitive forest of five hundred or a thousand acres, where a stick should never be cut for fuel, a common possession forever for instruction and recreation. All Walden wood might have been reserved for our park forever, with Walden in its midst, and the Easterbrooks Country, an unoccupied area of some four square miles, might have been our huckleberry-field."

In his essay "Walking," published posthumously the year of his death, in 1862, Thoreau had again made emphatic the equation between primitive nature and man's higher nature, perhaps suspecting little that he was speaking of himself as much as he was of future regenerative thinkers, when he wrote:

> A town is saved, not more by the righteous men in it than by the woods and swamps that surround it. A township where one primitive forest waves above while another primitive forest rots below, -such a town is fitted to raise not only corn and potatoes, but poets and philosophers for the coming ages... and out of such a wilderness comes the Reformer eating locust and wild honey.

Concord stands, thus, not only at the dawn of this country's spiritual flowering but also at the very dawn of a conservation ethic that has awakened the conscience of the world. Thoreau not only was the first to articulate and plead eloquently for conservation in his writings, but that he set the example of in the conduct of his own life, of which he demanded that it "warrant the expense of nature" in the least of its acts.

## Walden Woods

The great wild tract at Walden Woods, in the south of the town and in Lincoln, consists also of a continuous, almost unbroken web of woods and ponds, bogs and meadows, brooks and springs, and prominent hills and cliffs. While the Estabrook Country is made up of "great rocky and moist tracts" not fit for cultivation, Walden Woods is defined by welldrained, droughty soils that support forest growth but not agriculture. One is too low and wet, the other too high and dry, each of the two great tracts affording distinct scenic attributes that reflect the particulars of their very different geology and physiography. If the Estabrook Country is Concord's moorland, Walden Woods is its hill and wold country of forested prominences and ridges, glens and hollows, stretched out and strewn among large glacial ponds.

Walden Woods is the tract that Thoreau made much his own and frequented the most, and which provided the physical structure for his great classic on nature and philosophy, economy, the conduct of life and the art of living- *Walden*. This book ripples across from the waters of the pond to the surrounding woods, to Concord, to the world, and to the starry sky, in a succession of expanding rings, like the pickerel makes when it nibbles the evening air at the surface of the pond.

This great tract, also two miles square, or roughly four square miles, ranges north to south from Hubbard's Close and Brister's Hill, in Concord, to Mount Misery, in Lincoln; and east to west, from the western shore of Sandy or Flint's Pond and the wooded dale of Saw Mill Run, both in Lincoln, to the shores of Fair Haven Bay and of the lower Sudbury River, in Lincoln and Concord. The tract includes many locales that Thoreau held close to his heart and that were the scenes of moments of reverie and of expansive thought, like the Cliffs at Fair Haven Hill; Walden Pond, where he lived for two years and two months; and Bear Garden Hill, which he roamed often by moonlight. Other significant or singular haunts in this tract include his Thrush Alley, Pine Hill, the Andromeda Ponds or Bogs, Orchis Swamp, the Boiling Spring and Hubbard's Brook; Brister's Hill and Brister's Spring, which take up much of the *Walden* chapter on "Former Inhabitants; and Winter Visitors;" Heywood's Meadow, Pleasant Meadow, and O Baker Farm!, to which he also dedicated a chapter in *Walden*. Places in Walden Woods that Thoreau loved and had frequent recourse to but that no longer exist were Trillium Wood and Laurel Glen. Both sites were bulldozed into athletic fields when the local high school was built many years ago.

Walden had also caught the imagination of Emerson. He had often resorted to it in his country walks after he moved to the Concord of his ancestors in 1834 "Hail to the quiet fields of my fathers! Not wholly unattended by supernatural friendship and favor, let me come hither. Bless my purposes as they are simple and virtuous ... "—and sought there inspiration in nature. Walden, where Emerson had, again in the words of his son, "bought house and land on the Boston Road, on the edge of the village towards Walden woods," made a decisive impression on the young philosopher and was a likely source of inspiration in the composition of his seminal essay *Nature,* published in 1836, though written for the most part while Emerson resided temporarily at his ancestors' home at the Old Manse on the banks of the Concord. The book, in turn, had a decisive influence on the young Thoreau and on an entire generation of Americans. The message in that essay, which Thoreau took to heart and made the cornerstone of his personal universe, and which Emerson had posed as a query, "Why should not we also enjoy an original relation to the universe?," is as provocative today, and will be in ages to come, as when it was first penned, "The sun shines to-day also."

## The River Corridors

The rivers define to the greatest extent the physiography, character, and scenery of the Concord region, and constitute, with their riparian landscapes, the most complex and richest and the most scenic features of the land, "where the animal and vegetable kingdoms attain their greatest perfection," as we are reminded of in a *A Week*. The river corridors are continuous, unbroken, linear landscapes consisting of the stream proper and of all other land features that come into view from its liquid lapse, as a seemingly endless sequence of scenic compositions. As such, rivers project a dynamic or cinematic prospect that informs the active mind, while at the same time make the ideal vessel for reflection and contemplation and the sublime. "A river" as Thoreau observes in the *Journal* "is superior to a lake in its liberating influence. It has motion and indefinite length … . A river touching the back of a town is like a wing … ready to waft it over the world." Yet the river scene can also have that "singularly ethereal, celestial, or elysian look … more gloriously and heavenly fair and pure than the sky itself," and be seen at once with the "placid" attributes of a lake and the fortunes of a stream, "to behold as a lake, but know it as a river, tempting the beholder to explore it and his own destiny at once."

Contemplating the river from Fair Haven Hill on an overcast evening, Thoreau observes in the *Journal:*

> The river at such an hour, seen half a mile away, perfectly smooth and lighter than the sky, reflecting the clouds, is a paradisaical scene. What are the rivers around Damascus to this river sleeping around Concord? Are not the Musketaquid and the Assabet, rivers of Concord, fairer than the rivers of the plain?

The river corridors thus knit together all the elements of the landscape —the meadows, the brooks, the fields, the wooded hills, the great tracts of woods, the abode of man in the shelter of more intimate settings—the rivers flowing among them in slow bends as though with a mind to lacing them together, including the mountains "on the verge of the horizon," when gazed upon from the tops of the river hills.

In his impassioned plea, in the lecture on "Huckleberries" for the preservation of his native landscape, or of nature anywhere, Thoreau singles out the river, which the town should have made "available as a common possession forever." In his words, "I think of no natural feature which is a greater ornament and treasure to this town than the river. It is one of the things which determines whether a man will live here or in another place ... . In this respect we enjoy a great advantage over those neighboring towns which have no river. Yet the town ... has never turned any but the most purely utilitarian eyes upon it—and has done nothing to preserve its natural beauty."

## The Great River Nodes and Meadows

The various scenic attributes of the rivers reach a scenic climax, within Concord proper, at two great scenic nodes, where the rivers, the hills, the meadows, and the great wild tracts come together to make up the setting for two outstanding landscapes: the Great Meadows, in the north, and Fair Haven, in the south. Geographically, these two great water nodes coincide with the two great wild tracts we have identified as the *scenic poles* of the Concord landscape: the Estabrook Country, in the north, and Walden Woods in the south. Extending imaginatively the polar analogy, we may conceive of the Great River Nodes, lying each beside one of the Great Wild Tracts, with their retinues of river hills and spectacular setting, as the *magnetic scenic poles* of the Concord landscape.

In Thoreau's own day, the Great Meadows were true river meadows which yielded a rich crop of native meadow grasses to local farmers, harvested in late summer, after the flood had receded. The meadows also yielded a wild crop of sedges, rushes, and "pipes" or horsetails, in the lowest spots. To Thoreau, the Great Meadows were a "grassy sea," with "often a foot of water amid the grass," which he waded across to flush snipe, bitterns, ducks, and other waterfowl. Today, the Great Meadows have been impounded for freshwater habitat and marshland, consisting of permanent large shallow pools, and extensive cattail and reed marshes that provide cover for a great variety of wildlife.

The scenic beauty of the Great Meadows was not lost in Thoreau, for all the distraction of the wildlife. He rejoiced in the beauty of both this "sea of grass," as he refers to it more than once, and of its splendid setting. Noticing, on a cool summer morning, as he relates in the *Journal* a "hoary sheen-like a fine downiness—inconceivably fine and silvery far away—the light reflected from the grass blades—a sea of grass hoary with light" over the broad prospect of the meadows as seen from across the river, he elevates the scenery before him to "miles of waving grass adorning the surface of the earth." On an overcast and serene April afternoon, "the water now beautifully smooth," Thoreau writes in the *Journal* of the beauty of the reflections on the watery meadows of the hills and woods which define them spatially and make up their scenic setting: "As we advanced into the Great Meadows, making the only ripples in their broad expanse, there being still not a ray of sunshine, only a subdued light. ... the reflections of the maples, of Ponkawtasset and the poplar hill, and the whole township in the southwest, were as perfect as I ever saw."

The beauty of this great river node is thus composed of the vast watery realm of the meadows themselves, and the panorama of the river hills that trend with the tight bends and short reaches of the Concord, and which together with the stream's course and the riparian woods, provide the setting for, define, and delineate the "broad moccasin print" of the Great Meadows, as Thoreau had likened them with.

The other Great River Node, at Fair Haven, consists also of primarily a large expansion of the river at the bay or pond of the same name, and of a set of river hills that do not cluster nor trend with the river, but stand to encircle the watery expanse in a great panoramic setting and shape the large bowl from which they rise steeply. Anchoring the entire scene, there rises a "pine covered island," as Thoreau knew it, on the west side of the bay, and which he called Witchhazel Island, or Birch Island, still pine-clad today and with a rich understory of witchhazel. This small island, like other retired places along the rivers, provides nesting habitat for the warbling vireo!

The scenic effect at this node is quite different from that of the Great Meadows. Though not as grand in its compass, but more intimate and more exquisite; more picturesque, while at the same time characterized by natural forms and lines that lend it a great sense of repose and tranquillity, and with many of those ethereal or heavenly attributes in the way light is received and reflected that Thoreau always had an eye for. "I saw Fair Haven pond," he writes in the *Journal,* of an autumn day in 1850, "with its Island and meadow between the island and the shore— and a strip of perfectly still and smooth water in the lee of the island and two hawks ... sailing over it. I did not see how it could be improved." In the spring of the same year, Thoreau had entered in the *Journal* in a moment of rapture: "In all my rambles I have seen no landscape which can make me forget Fair Haven," as he gazed upon that landscape from the Cliffs at Fair Haven Hill on "a new spring day and look over the awakening woods and the river and hear the new birds sing with the same delight as ever—it is as sweet a mystery to me as ever what this world is."

# The Lake Country

"This is our lake country," Thoreau sets down for the first time in a journal entry preparatory to the writing of *Walden,* during his sojourn at Walden Woods. This notion of a lake country of our own, at a village level, at our doorstep, he expands in *Walden.* Thoreau's lake country, in the chapter in that book entitled "The Ponds", defines a geography of ponds spread out along the southern tier of Concord and in Lincoln, across woods, hills, meadows, and the river; and encompassing, from east to west, Flint's or Sandy Pond, Goose Pond, Walden Pond, Fair Haven Bay or Pond, and White Pond. "This is my lake country," Thoreau writes in that chapter, taking possession of the ponds in his Walden house neighborhood, "These, with Concord River, are my water privileges; and night and day, year in year out, they grind such grist as I carry to them."

Walden Pond, whose scenery "is on a humble scale ... though very beautiful," Thoreau claims in that same *Walden* chapter, has "obtained a patent of Heaven to be the only Walden Pond in the world and distiller of celestial dews ... . It is a gem of the first water which Concord wears in her coronet." Writing still of Walden Pond, he says, "A lake is the landscape's most beautiful and expressive feature. It is earth's eye; looking into which the beholder measures the depth of his own nature."

The waters at Walden are still transparent, and the pond's patent as a "distiller of celestial dews" has not run out. The beauty is there still for one who wants to see it. However, the casual eye may miss it for the marring damage done to the pond by abuse from hordes of leisure consumers and the want of care, the mismanagement, and ill-conceived pond restoration work that has disfigured its banks, altered the appearance and integrity of the pond's geology, and introduced gardenesque improvements much offensive to a sense of aesthetics for the wild or natural.

Thoreau likens White Pond to Walden for the transparency of its waters, noting that, "though I am acquainted with most of the ponds within a dozen miles of this centre, I do not know a third of this pure and well-like character." White Pond and Walden are "great crystals on the surface of the earth, Lakes of Light," and, "since the woodcutters, and the railroad, and I myself have profaned Walden, perhaps the most attractive, if not the most beautiful, of all our lakes, the gem of the woods, is White Pond." Many passages in *Walden* and in the *Journal* describe lovingly the charm and beauty of the scenery of White Pond: "The blue flag (*Iris versicolor*) grows thinly in the pure water, rising from the stony bottom all around the shore, where it is visited by humming birds in June, and the color both of its bluish blades and its flowers and especially their reflections, are in singular harmony with the glaucous water."

Flint's, or Sandy Pond, in Lincoln, is the largest of the ponds, which in winter, sealed in ice, Thoreau had regarded, in an early *Journal* entry, as "our Davis straits or Baffin's Bay ... a somewhat novel scenery ..." In "The Ponds" chapter, he calls it an "inland sea" and observes that it is "comparatively shallow, and not remarkably pure," with a sandy bottom, as borne in its name: "I used to admire the ripple marks on the sandy bottom ... made firm and hard to the feet of the wader by the pressure of the water, and the rushes which grew in Indian file, in waving lines, corresponding to these marks, rank by rank, as if the waves had planted them."

Goose Pond, "of small extent, is on my way to Flint's," Thoreau writes of the smallest of the ponds that, in *Walden,* compose his lake country. This pond, and the smaller Little Goose Pond in a hollow next to it, he frequented when, in spring and summer, he set out along his Thrush Alley on the lookout and with an ear for the "genius of the wood," the hermit thrush; and on windy days, particularly in the very early spring, when, as he relates in the *Journal,* "watching the ripples fall and dash across the surface of low-lying and small woodland lakes is one of the amusements of these windy March and April days. It is only on small lakes deep sunk in hollows in the woods that you can see or study them these days, for the winds sweep over the whole breadth of larger lakes incessantly, but they only touch these sheltered lakelets by fine points and edges from time to time." Channing, he tells us in the same entry, called Little Goose Pond, "Ripple Lake or Pool," on account of that effect produced by the wind when it "stoops from a considerable height to dally with this fair pool which it discerns beneath."

"I see Fair Haven Pond from the Cliffs," Thoreau enters in the *Journal* for August 5, 1851, "as it were through a slight mist. It is the wildest scenery imaginable—a Lake of the Woods." Thoreau's lake country is still relatively unspoiled, and parts of it have reverted to a nearly pristine condition. The Ponds, the waters of this lake country, Thoreau holds up as a mirror to our elevated nature, as the cope of heaven itself is mirrored on them. "Perfect sincerity and transparency," he writes in the *Journal,* "make a great part of beauty as in dew drops, lakes, and diamonds ... and the ripples cast their shadows flickeringly on the white sand, as clouds flit across the landscape." Thus, we meet in the transparency of our lakes that of our nobler nature there, I believe, lies the beauty of nature in all its depth and elusive utility.

Thoreau discerned a moral order woven into natural law that molds and fashions the human spirit. We need our lake country, our ponds, woods and meadows at our doorstep for our own trying times a place that we may also come to plumb and sound our own nature and let it rise and fall to its just level.

# The Indian Hills

"Thoreau visited more than once the principal mountains in his prospect," Channing tells us in the biography of his friend and walking companion, mountains which, he reminds us in another text, "belong to Concord as much as elsewhere. First Wachusett, next Watatic, next Monadnoc, next the Peterboro Hills, and next Uncannoonuk," as they appear on Concord's horizon from due west to northwest. Channing then describes the outlines of these mountains: "Watatic is distinguished by its peculiarly rounded summit, Wachusett is low and long, Monadnoc is sharp and pointed, the Peterboro hills are graceful, convenient ranges."

Thoreau not only visited and climbed many of these mountains, and others beyond the visual boundaries of his native town, but he walked once from Concord to Mount Wachusett, climbed it, camped at its barren top, and walked back home, a journey that he relates in an early essay full of youthful vigor and high poetic expectation, "A Walk to Wachusett." For Thoreau, visiting these mountains in the horizon was, as Channing put it, "like looking off on a series of old homes. He went in the choice August or September days, and picked berries on Monadnoc's stony plateau, took his roomy walk over the Mason Hills, or explored the great Wachusett pasture, the fairest sight eye ever saw." Thoreau looked to "that blue rim of the earth" not only as the visible boundary of his own home ground, but as an expanded Concord of the mind.

It is that Concord of Elysian expansion, of transcendental thought, of an elevated preoccupation, that he means to report to his fellowmen. What the blue mountains in the horizon meant to Thoreau, and what they must mean to all men, he set down clearly, in "A Walk to Wachusett," upon his descent from that mountain.

> And now that we have returned to the desultory life of the plain, let us endeavor to import a little of that mountain grandeur into it ... and understand that this level life too has its summit, and why from the mountain-top the deepest valleys have a tinge of blue; that there is elevation in every hour, as no part of the earth is so low that the heavens may not be seen from, and we have only to stand on the summit of our hour to command an uninterrupted horizon.

There is a connection to be made between the blue mountains in the horizon and Thoreau's fascination with "uninhabited roads," which, as intimated above, he realized fully in his walk to Wachusett. The thought thrusts itself, from that Wachusett journey, from his yearning for abandoned or dusty roads, from his Old Marlborough Road, and the lure of those blue mountains, to try a pilgrim's trails from Concord to the outermost confines of its prospects, a trail that may take us from Walden to Wachusett, or another one to Monadnock or to Uncannunuc through uninhabited corridors. Thoreau enters in the *Journal* for July 21, 1851:

Now I yearn for one of those old, meandering, dry, uninhabited roads, which lead away from towns ... which conduct to the outside of the earth ... along which you may travel like a pilgrim ... where earth is cheap enough by being public; where you can walk and think with least obstruction ... where you are not in false relations with men ... by which you may go to the uttermost parts of the earth ... to a Sudbury and Marlborough in the skies.

## The Old Scenic Roads and Paths

Many of Concord's old roads and paths still remain, however modified in themselves or their surroundings changed, such as the old Miles Road, today the paved and busy Old Road to Nine Acre Corner; or the old Corner Road, today's Sudbury Road; or the Walden Road, leading from the center of the town to Walden Pond, which has lost some of its former steeper grade. There were paths in Thoreau's Concorde, alluring by their very names, that no longer exist or that have been improved into roads, or only segments of which remain. "For roads," Thoreau wrote in the *Journal,* "I think that a poet cannot tolerate more than a footpath through the fields; that is wide enough, and for purposes of winged poesy suffices. It is not for the muse to speak of cart-paths. I would fain travel by a footpath round the world ... . What more suggestive to the pensive walker?"

## Concluding Remarks

The intent of this study has been, in part, to point by way of Thoreau's vision to ways of looking at the landscape: how to perceive it, understand it, reflect on it, how to come to a poetic symbiosis with one's own home landscape, or with any parcel of this planet for that matter; earth is home.

This vision also points to ways of looking at the landscape for the purpose of analyzing and classifying its scenery, and perhaps other sensory attributes, within the compass of a total and harmonic view of it. The idea here is to allow the scenic resource itself, its physical constitution as physiography, and its abstract attributes of form, line, scale, texture, and its "spell," to suggest formal categories of scenic classification, rather than to impose arbitrarily on any specific landscape a predetermined system of classification and assessment with set scenic value scores. The analysis of landscape and scenery is an analysis of the beautiful. Attention should be paid universally to writers and artists of the past and present who have addressed the beauty of a particular landscape, as we have done here. Nature writers, artists, and gifted scholars may look at landscape and scenery—and beyond seeing, may smell, taste, touch, and listen to what they may have to whisper to our soul.

We trust that this approach may also serve as the basis for a blueprint for the preservation and protection of the totality of the Concord landscape, including not only the great tracts, the scenic rivers, the hills, and the ponds, but also the brooks and springs, the river bridges, and the old scenic roads and paths. This vision and this blueprint may also serve as a model for other home landscapes or regional landscapes, the "million Concords" that Thoreau spoke of and and that may be considered far more critical for the daily bread of the spirit than the vast and remote national parks and national forests such a paradigm suggests that each landscape must be looked at afresh for what may inherently be its own, its unique character or composition, its spell, and for what it may suggest of itself as ways of classifying and assessing its scenery, and projecting a blueprint for its protection.

———————

**J. WALTER BRAIN** is a man of many interests. He is a landscape architect, Thoreau scholar, nature photographer, and poet. He also consults in urban design and site development, as well as being a faculty member of Boston Architectural Center and leading architectural study tours. Mr. Brain was born in Lima, Peru, and studied at San Marcos University. He holds degrees from Harvard University and the University of Massachusetts, Amherst.

# Part VII

# THOREAU AND THE
# TRADITION OF AMERICAN
# NATURE WRITING

# Some Thoughts of
# Henry David Thoreau

❖

When I detect a beauty in any of the recesses of nature, I am reminded, by the serene and retired spirit in which it requires to be contemplated, of the inexpressible privacy of a life,—how silent and unambitious it is. The beauty there is in mosses must be considered from the holiest, quietest nook.

— *"Natural History of Massachusetts"*

All nature is classic and akin to art. The sumac and pine and hickory which surround my house remind me of the most graceful sculpture. Sometimes their tops, or a single limb or leaf, seems to have grown to a distinct expression as if it were a symbol for me to interpret. Poetry, painting, and sculpture claim at once and associate with themselves those perfect specimens of the art of nature,—leaves, vines, acorns, pine cones, etc. The critic must at last stand as mute though contented before a true poem as before an acorn or a vine leaf. The perfect work of art is received again into the bosom of nature whence its material proceeded, and that criticism which can only detect its unnaturalness has no longer any office to fulfill. The choicest maxims that have come down to us are more beautiful or integrally wise than they are wise to our understandings. This wisdom which we are inclined to pluck from their stalk is the point only of a single association. Every natural form—palm leaves and acorns, oak leaves and sumac and dodder—are untranslatable aphorisms.

—*August 1845*

I fear only lest my expressions may not be extravagant enough,— may not wander far enough beyond the narrow limits of our ordinary insight and faith, so as to be adequate to the truth of which I have been convinced. I desire to speak somewhere without bounds, in order that I may attain to an expression in some degree adequate to truth of which I have been convinced. From a man in a waking moment, to men in their waking moments. Wandering toward the more distant boundaries of a wider pasture. Nothing is so truly bounded and obedient to law as music, yet nothing so surely breaks all petty and narrow bonds. Whenever I hear any music I fear that I may have spoken tamely and within bounds. And I am convinced that I cannot exaggerate enough even to lay the foundation of a true expression. As for books and the adequateness of their statements to the truth, they are as the tower of Babel to the sky.

*—1854*

Write often, write upon a thousand themes, rather than long at a time, not trying to turn too many feeble somersets in the air,—and so come down upon your head at last. Antaeus-like, be not long absent from the ground. Those sentences are good and well discharged which are like so many little resiliencies from the spring floor of our life,—a distinct fruit and kernel itself, springing from terra firma. Let there be as many distinct plants as the soil and the light can sustain. Take as many bounds in a day as possible. Sentences uttered with your back to the wall.

*—November 12, 185__*

In literature it is only the wild that attracts us. Dullness is only another name for tameness. It is the untamed, uncivilized, free, and wild thinking in Hamlet, in the Iliad, and in all the scriptures and mythologies that delights us—not learned in the schools, not refined and polished by art. A truly good book is something as wildly natural and primitive, mysterious and marvelous, ambrosial and fertile, as a fungus or a lichen.

My Journal should be the record of my love. I would write in it only of the things I love, my affection for any aspect of the world, what I love to think of. I have no more distinctness or pointedness in my yearnings than an expanding bud, which does indeed point to flower and fruit, to summer and autumn, but is aware of the warm sun and spring influence only. I feel ripe for something, yet do nothing, can't discover what that thing is. I feel fertile merely. It is seedtime with me. I have lain fallow long enough.

Notwithstanding a sense of unworthiness which possesses me, not without reason, notwithstanding that I regard myself as a good deal of a scamp, yet for the most part of the universe is unaccountably kind to me, and I enjoy perhaps an unusual share of happiness.

*—November 16, 1850*

The earth I tread on is not a dead, inert mass. It is a body, has a spirit, is organic, and fluid to the influence of its spirit, and to whatever particle of that spirit is in me .... It is more cheering than the fertility and luxuriance of vineyards, this fundamental fertility near to the principle of growth

—*December 30, 1851*

As it is important to consider Nature from the point of view of science, remembering the nomenclature and system of men, and so, if possible, go a step further in that direction, so it is equally important often to ignore or forget all that men presume that they know, and take an original and unprejudiced view of Nature, letting her make what impression she will on you, as the first men, and all children and natural men still do. For our science, so called, is always more barren and mixed up with error than our sympathies are.

—*February 28, 1860*

Where is the literature which gives expression to Nature? He would be a poet who could impress the winds and streams into his service, to speak for him; who nailed words to their primitive senses, as farmers drive down stakes in the spring, which the frost has heaved; who derived his words as often as he used them—transplanted them to his page with earth adhering to their roots; whose words were so true and fresh and natural that they would appear to expand like the buds at the approach of spring, though they lay half-smothered between two musty leaves in a library— ay, faithful reader, in sympathy with surrounding Nature.

— *"Walking"*

# Better Mythology
## Perception and Emergence
## in Thoreau's *Journal*

### H. Daniel Peck

[T]ime for Thoreau revival, not on his Rousseau but on his
perception of better mythology.

*—Ezra Pound*

If, as Barry Lopez believes, nature writing will "one day produce
a major and lasting body of American literature," then Henry Thoreau
surely will occupy a central place in the development of that literature.[1]
No one in American letters has been more dedicated both to nature and
to writing than Thoreau; nature was his "bride," as he said in an 1857
*Journal* entry, and the *Journal* itself—a two-million-word composition
largely about nature—testifies to the extraordinary range of his ambition
as a nature *writer*.[2]

Once we move beyond these central and obvious facts about
Thoreau, however, his contribution to the development of American
nature writing becomes more difficult to define. This difficulty comes, in
part, from the work of contemporary critics, who have stressed the 19th-
century contexts of Romanticism and natural science in describing
Thoreau's ideas about nature. Such critics implicitly caution against
unrefined application of these ideas to contemporary issues.[3] Their
caution is, I think, salutary. Potentially, it drives us deeper into Thoreau's
work as we search for his contemporary relevance and his influence on
20th-century nature writing.

Ezra Pound, late in his life, hinted in this direction when he made
the following remark in a letter: "Time for Thoreau revival, not on his
Rousseau but on his perception of better mythology." Pound provided
little context for his cryptic remark, and thus can not help us with its
meaning.[4] But it serves nevertheless to suggest an important distinction:

between Thoreau's legacy of specific ideas about nature and some fundamental shift in "perception," which he enacted for his time and which, in providing the basis for a new "myth," a new way of thinking about the world, may have relevance for ours. As a way of considering that possible relevance, I want to examine the following passage describing Thoreau's response to a row of willows; it begins his *Journal* entry for March 2, 1860:

> Notice the brightness of a row of osiers this morning. This phenomenon, whether referable to a change in the condition of the twig or to the spring air and light, or even to our imaginations, is not the less a real phenomenon, affecting us annually at this season (*J*, 13:171).

If Thoreau's assertion of the "realness" of the osiers' brightness sounds strange to late 20th-century ears—why should he have had to make it?—this is because the issue underlying his claim is no longer at issue for us. That issue is the ontological status of what Thoreau here (and in hundreds of other instances in his *Journal*) calls a "phenomenon."

The word itself, in 19th-century philosophical thought, carried most prominently the sense of an "appearance," as in Kant's distinction between phenomena and noumena. That distinction, as understood in America, was closely related to philosophical idealism (which Thoreau had absorbed in his Harvard studies), and to the dualism between spirit and matter that characterized much of American artistic and philosophical thought in the 19th century. For Thoreau, then, to assert the "realness" of a phenomenon is, on the face of it, contradictory. Yet, over and over again in his *Journal*, he uses this term to describe sights and events in nature that were, for him, not merely apparent but profoundly "real."

In Thoreau's usage the term "phenomenon" never entirely relinquishes the implications of philosophical idealism. But, as I have pointed out elsewhere, it more prominently came to signify for him the relation among elements in a natural scene.[5] In this case, the observed phenomenon involves not one osier but a "row" of them, as perceived in the morning, at a particular time of year, and flooded by a special cast of the sun's "brightness." Lacking any one of these elements, it would not be this phenomenon at all. Its integral, composite nature is the thing that makes it a phenomenon. Though the phenomenon's emergence to the senses is thus entirely contextual, Thoreau insists upon its more or less empirical standing. That it emerges for "us" testifies to its public, as opposed to purely private or subjective, standing.

But while the shining osiers have some kind of empirical reality, this clearly is not the reality apprehensible through the focused, analytical view of nature that Thoreau associated with science. As he put it in a *Journal* entry of May 1, 1859, the "prying instruments [of science] … disturb the balance and harmony of nature" (*J*, 12: 171).[6] Much earlier, in an entry of August 5, 1851, he had written: "The astronomer is as blind to the significant phenomena—or the *significance of phenomena* as the wood-sawyer who wears glasses to defend his eyes from sawdust—The question is not what you look at—but how you look & whether you see" (*PJ*, 3: 354–55; emphasis added). Thoreau's defense of the integrity of phenomena in the osier passage can thus be viewed as an implicit objection to science's atomistic way of "looking at" things. To witness a "phenomenon" is to "see" things—to see them whole, in their relations.

The composite and unified nature of phenomena would seem to make them a fitting subject for poetry. (Thoreau often contrasted "poetry" and "science" as opposing modes of apprehension.)[7] Yet, as the osier passage demonstrates, the Thoreauvian phenomenon does not quite open itself to poetic apprehension either, whether we are thinking in terms of 19th-century polite verse ("poesy") or of the higher, "symbolic" form of poetry that Emerson called for in his essay "The Poet." Poetry, for Thoreau, had everything to do with the transforming power of imagination, which could, as Emerson had taught, elevate the *merely* phenomenal to the realm of the spiritual.

But Thoreau's osiers resist transformation; they are "things," even though, as the passage suggests, imagination may play a role in their composition. Indeed, their integral recognizable form, emerging in the same way every spring, is an essential aspect of their being. They belong undeniably to the world as well as to the imagination. Any response that does not take account of their palpable reality in nature, as well as their aesthetic suggestibility, fails really to see them.

Osiers shining in the spring's morning sun were, then, too contextual an "object" for the analytical gaze of 19th-century science, even the "natural science" (dominated by classification) practiced by Thoreau himself. Yet their undeniable "realness" and their organic, emergent form made them inaccessible to 19th-century "poesy," which gave itself to static idealizations of nature, and to Emerson's "symbolic" mode of poetry. Here was something whose mobile, contextual reality neither 19th-century science nor art could fully account for.

There is another possible category of response for the bright osiers, however. Their mediate position (between art and nature) would seem to make them a fitting subject for the landscape aesthetics propounded in the writings of William Gilpin and John Ruskin, both of whom Thoreau studied with care. Yet we know that Thoreau was chronically restless with the formulations of these thinkers, eventually casting them off as emphatically as he (initially) had taken them up.

This restlessness has sometimes been associated with habitual crankiness, or with a lack of sophistication, on Thoreau's part. But while he was harshly unfair in some of his judgments, especially of Ruskin, these judgments do have a consistent theme. Gilpin's work, which was based on (Lockean) 18th-century perceptual theory, failed, for Thoreau, to provide anything more than a distanced, "appreciative" view of nature.[8]

And Ruskin's work, though it engaged nature at a deeper, "moral" level, was still too removed from its object. As Thoreau wrote in a Journal entry of 1857, "[Ruskin] does not describe Nature as Nature, but as Turner painted her, and though the work [*Modern Painters*] betrays that he has given a close attention to Nature, it appears to have been with an artist's and critic's design" (*J*, 10: 69).

Thoreau's rejection of Gilpin and Ruskin belongs, at its heart, to a profound restlessness with all the conceptions of natural beauty that dominated 19th-century thinking in America. Thoreau *knew,* from his daily walks in the fields and hills and swamps around Concord, that there was an emergent reality in nature that did not answer alone to "poesy," or to scientific investigation, or to Ruskinian paradigms of natural beauty. There was this something else, this set of "phenomena," which compelled his imagination utterly, yet for which he had no philosophical rationale adequate to explain its ontological status or its evocative power over him—its power, in the language of the osier passage, to "affect" him.

That is, the twin legacies of philosophical idealism and dualism inherited by Thoreau offered him no coherent way in which to honor, at once, the integrity of the phenomenon (its "realness") and its emergent, processual nature. Osiers shining in the spring's morning sun were, on the one hand, a transitory, even evanescent, occurrence. No sooner had this phenomenon emerged into being than it disappeared. Yet its appearance was entirely regular and predictable; when it occurred in its "turn," every spring, its integral being and form became undeniable. The issue, then, was the paradox of change, of being and becoming. Several decades after Thoreau's death, process philosophers such as William James and Alfred North Whitehead would address this issue in ways that would have spoken directly to his concerns. James would argue that the relations between things are as "real" as the things themselves, and Whitehead would explain the paradox of change by calling forth his conception of the "event"—an emergence of form out of the flux of experience.[9]

In Thoreau, unlike James and Whitehead, these philosophical issues remain inchoate. Yet, as Loren Eiseley has written, Thoreau resembles Whitehead and other 20th-century process philosophers in his search for the mysterious force that holds "the thing called nature together, [gives] it duration in the midst of change."[10] Indeed, the "realness" of the osiers' brightness that compels and perplexes Thoreau has precisely to do with the phenomenon's duration—with its power of "affecting us *annually* at this season." Like Whitehead, Thoreau is concerned with the way things get established in a world characterized by continuous change.

As I have said, these concerns and preoccupations rarely come forward *as* philosophical issues, for, as Eiseley wrote, Thoreau "never resolved his philosophical difficulties."[11] And lacking such resolution, all he can do—as in the above passage—is to *assert* the reality and integrity passage is the ease, and self-confidence, with which he has done so. Four years earlier, in March 1856, Thoreau had written in a more defensive tone when reflecting on another row of willows: "There is, at any rate, such a phenomenon as the willows shining in the spring sun, however it is to be accounted for" (*J*, 8: 209). And the *Journal* as a whole, during the early and middle 1850s, exhibits a good deal of confusion about the meaning and status of natural phenomena.

But Thoreau's late *Journal*—from about 1858 through its close in 1861—shows a marked impetus toward consolidating his conceptions of nature's meaning, and a diminishment of earlier doubts. This consolidation may owe, in part, to his deepening sense of mortality, as the effects of tuberculosis became increasingly debilitating. But, as Joan Burbick has recently shown, it also owes to his deepening commitment to a method of "extracting from sequences of perceived natural events a law or demonstrable pattern of redemptive growth," a method that characterizes the late Journal and Thoreau's late natural history essays.[12] That is, Thoreau's late writings, especially the *Journal,* work toward confirmation of natural law *as* demonstrable, manifest, and constant.

Thus, the 1860 *Journal* passage we have examined reveals more than Thoreau's failure to have developed a philosophical rationale for validating the reality of phenomena. It also reflects his implicit decision, made gradually through many years, to move beyond this impasse, and to accept what a lifetime of intimate observation of nature had taught him: that nature's phenomena were indeed "real," as real as anything might be.

It is hard to overestimate the importance of this decision for the future of American nature writing. It represents a major departure from the idealism, abstraction, and sentimentality that characterized many literary representations of nature in the 19th century. In finding his way toward a viable response to nature's reality, Thoreau was opening a space for the brightness of his osiers to be real, and thus opening a (literary) space for a new kind of discourse about nature. Such a discourse would be factual without being narrowly scientific, and it would be artistic without being artful. What was at stake here was nothing less than a new conception of natural beauty; Thoreau was implicitly acknowledging that any authentic response to nature was in some mysterious way, as yet unarticulated by 19th-century thought, "aesthetic." Almost a century after Thoreau, Aldo Leopold—perhaps reacting to his own scientific training—evokes the same mystery in observing that "our ability to perceive quality in nature *begins,* as in art, with the pretty. It expands through successive stages of the beautiful to values as yet uncaptured by language" (emphasis added).[13]

In resolving that his bright osiers had their being in the world as well as in human perception, Thoreau was describing a reciprocity between nature's emergent reality and the perceiving mind. In doing this he was following out Emerson's insight that the human soul could find something "connate" in nature, some answering "correspondence." But for Emerson, at least in his early essays, the balance always lay with human consciousness, with the mind's transforming powers. Without the "ray of relation" connecting the human soul to everything around it, the world lies blank and inert.[14] This cannot be said about Thoreau, for whom the most vital aspect of his osiers' realness is their capacity to "affect" us. He is centrally concerned with the power of natural phenomena to move us and, in turn, with the depth and authenticity of our response to them. That is, they are "real" to the extent that they engender in us a vivid sense of their presence. Barry Lopez makes the same point, in late 20th-century terms, when he argues that the "interior landscape [of consciousness] responds to the character and subtlety of an exterior landscape; the shape of the individual mind is *affected* by land as it is by genes" (emphasis added).[15]

Thoreau's great achievement was to take Emerson's (centrally Romantic) insight on the crucial role of perception—that everything begins with individual perception—and to test it with great exactitude and thoroughness against the world itself. The Walden experiment may be considered a concentrated form of this test—an experiment in living intentionally, and intensively, within nature. While Thoreau never relinquished his Emersonian dream of translating natural facts into spiritual truths, he could not leave facts behind. They had, for him, a resonant being of their own. If Emerson's ideal poet would illuminate the world through perception, Thoreau's poet would engage the world's own luminous presence (a process also suggested by the work of 19th-century landscape painters such as Fitz Hugh Lane and Martin Johnson Heade).[16] The resulting reciprocity between perception and emergence was, potentially, an even more radical conception than Emerson's "correspondence."

All of Thoreau's individual works about nature—his books, essays, and lectures—dramatize an encounter with the world in which the possibility for the reciprocity I have described is tested. His first book, A *Week on the Concord and Merrimack Rivers* (1849), exhibits such reciprocity through the perspective of a voyager engaging the sights and sounds of the New England landscape. *Walden* (1854) has a more static setting, yet its engagement with nature is even more fully reciprocal, as shown beautifully in Thoreau's lyric pursuit of the loon (a symbol of wildness); *Walden* performs a dance between the self and nature.[17] Other landscapes, such as Mount Katahdin as represented in *The Maine Woods* or the barren shores depicted in *Cape Cod,* resisted Thoreau's attempts at engagement, though they provided the opportunity for dramatic encounter.

But the "work" in Thoreau's canon that most fully dramatizes this encounter, in its very procedures, is his great *Journal.* This document's meditative, provisional form opened the largest possible space for his complex involvement with nature. In this space, Thoreau's act of perceiving the bright osiers could itself be replicated in the act of composition. Indeed, part of the phenomenon's realness is the authentication it receives from his activity of "writing" it, as he re-creates in language the experience of perception. Thoreau was a probing and sophisticated student of his own perceptions, and "composing" these perceptions provided, for him a further level of engagement with the world.[18] A *Journal* passage such as the one about osiers *enacts* the reciprocity between perception and emergence that it describes.

Thoreau's *Journal* may thus be likened to the "sketch" of Renaissance artists, as described by E. H. Gombrich:

> To the Middle Ages, the schema is the image; to the postmedieval artist, it is the starting point for corrections, adjustments, adaptations, the means to probe reality and to wrestle with the particular. [Postmedieval art's] symptom is the sketch, or rather the many sketches which precede the finished work and, for all the skill of hand and eye that marks the master, a constant readiness to learn, to make and match and remake till the portrayal ceases to be a secondhand formula and reflects the unique and unrepeatable experience the artist wishes to seize and hold.[19]

Gombrich calls "this constant search" a process of "sacred discontent," a phrase that serves well at many levels to describe the enterprise of Thoreau's *Journal.*[20] Unlike the Renaissance sketch, however, the *Journal* never becomes a "finished work"; its provisionality is endless, and in this sense it is an endless document—an ongoing dialogue of the self with itself and with nature

> But if the *Journal* was the place where Thoreau could best express his restlessness, his sacred discontent, it was more it was more importantly the literary space where he could most authentically meet the world-where he could onder at the beauty of his bright osiers and respond to their emergent reality. The composition of the *Journal*, especially as it occurred after 1850, lent itself to this process. Typically, Thoreau would walk in the afternoons, taking field notes (the word "field" resonating with a sense of contextuality), and then the next morning, or several mornings later, he would work from these notes in describing to his *Journal* his observaations of and encounters with nature.

Often, these descriptions were rendered in the present tense—a tactic less artful than it might seem, for it serves to dramatize Thoreau's struggle to reenact experience. What he was trying to do was capture, in a more immediate sense than the writing of books or essays would allow, the *recent* and periodic manifestations of nature. He was attempting to keep the experience of perception alive in himself, in order to recognize nature's phenomena. A particularly dramatic encounter with nature's emergent reality is recorded in Thoreau's *Journal* entry for June 11, 1851:

> I now descend round the corner of the grain field through the pitch-pine
> wood in to a lower field, more inclosed by woods—& find my self in
> a colder damp & misty atmosphere, with much dew on the grass—I
> seem to be nearer to the origin of things— There is something creative
> & primal in the cool mist—this dewy mist does not fail to suggest music
> to me—unaccountably—fertility the origin of things— (*PJ*, 3: 251).

The "music" evoked here is the music of encounter, which makes
itself heard, as Carlyle wrote, when the "mind … has penetrated into the
inmost heart of the thing; detected the inmost mystery of it, namely the
*melody* that lies hidden in it; the inward harmony of coherence which is
its soul, whereby it exists, and has a right to be, here in this world."[21]

The very process of keeping a journal validated nature's "right to be"
by reenacting the moment of encounter between human perception and
nature's emergence, its "origins." This process called for the writer
repeatedly to walk forth into the world, to bring the fruits of observation
back home into his book, and then to go forth again. In this way, the
*Journal* dramatized a primary activity of the self, of reading nature and
writing it, of continuously mapping the world and locating the self.
Thoreau's osiers, after all, did not come to him; he had to find them—to
position himself for encountering them. And this "position" existed in
both space and time: in a particular field adjacent to Concord, and during
a particular moment in the duration of spring. Their location was a
coordinate of space and time, and only the disciplined observation of
years could teach him how to find it.

Nature, of course, was always displaying its emergent phenomena—
in all their infinite variety and beauty—and was, in this sense, always
reaching out to meet the human perceiver. But the perceiver would be
blind to these phenomena without alertness and patience. As Thoreau
wrote in a *Journal* entry of 1858: "You will not see these splendors,
whether you stand on the hilltop or in the hollow, unless you are prepared
to see them. The beauty of the earth answers exactly to your demand and
appreciation" (*J*, 11: 278). This process of "answering," of full reciprocity,
is the *desideratum* of Thoreau's *Journal* and of the lifelong engagement
with nature that it records.

As we have seen, the reciprocity between perception and emergence dramatized in Thoreau's *Journal* adumbrates certain ideas central
to 20th-century philosophical thought; potentially, it anticipates contemporary ecological thought as well. For to understand natural phenomena
as fully "real" and emergent is to grant them standing on their own terms,
and to see them, in Henry Beston's words, as the "other nations" of the
earth.[22] American nature writers from the time of John Muir and John
Burroughs to that of Barry Lopez and Gary Snyder have reflected in their
writings this view of nature's autonomy and independence.

But, for all the efficacy and contemporary applicability of Thoreau's
ideas about nature, his *Journal* comes forward vitally into our time not

so much for these ideas as for the process that it enacts. That is, the indebtedness of later nature writers to Thoreau is, in a certain sense, more formal than ideological. By this I do not mean, necessarily, that these writers have imitated the form of Thoreau's *Journal* (though the fact that it was published in 1906, and has been available as a model for close to a century, is suggestive). Rather, I mean that the most serious nature writers of twentieth-century America have understood the necessity of finding a literary form that somehow could enact the *process* of the self engaging the natural world. In several cases—Leopold's *Sand County Almanac* or Gary Snyder's "Lookout's Journal," for example—that form has literally been a journal.[23]

But the specific form is less important than the challenge these writers—like Thoreau himself—have felt to break down, through style, the traditional Western dualism of self and world; all of them have sought a style that would dramatize their engagement with nature. Just as important, they have understood that the space for that engagement has to be created in language, that language serves as the vehicle for reenacting perception. This requisite surely underlies Lopez's call for the development of a major body of American nature writing; indeed, his own recent work on the Arctic—surely the equivalent of Thoreau's "wild"—is eloquent testimony to his own Thoreauvian legacy.[24] Lopez's work, along with the work of other contemporary nature writers, can be said to occupy the space that Thoreau opened in struggling to authenticate the reality of his bright osiers.

This returns us to Ezra Pound and his elusive distinction, made late in his life, between Thoreau's "Rousseau" and his "perception of better mythology." Pound's failure to explain his distinction need not confound us, for the explanation lies in his own early writings about poetry. In a footnote he appended to Ernest Fenollosa's essay "The Chinese Written Character as a Medium for Poetry" (1919), he distinguished between "true metaphor ... or image" and "untrue, or ornamental metaphor." This distinction was confirmed for Pound by Fenollosa, who in his essay argued that "primitive [natural] metaphors do not spring from arbitrary subjective processes. They are possible only because they follow objective lines of relations in nature herself."[25]

The objectivist poetics that Pound worked out for his generation in the early 20th century grew centrally out of his position, stated in "A Retrospect" (1918), that "the natural object is always the *adequate* symbol." His affirmation of nature's "adequacy" evokes for us, as it must later have evoked for Pound himself, Thoreau's hard-won conviction in nature's luminous reality—a conviction that does, indeed, provide the basis for "better mythology."

# Notes

¹See Lopez's entry in "Natural History: An Annotated Booklist," in the special issue on nature writing in *Antæus*, ed. Daniel Halpern 57 (Autumn 1986): 297.

²*The Journal of Henry David Thoreau*, ed. Bradford Torrey and Francis H. Allen (Boston: Houghton Mifflin, 1906), Vol. 9, p. 337 (April 23, 1857). All subsequent citations of this edition, appearing parenthetically in the text, will be identified by *J*, with volume and page numbers following. (Volume numbers of the above edition refer to the independently numbered fourteen volumes of the Journal rather than to the twenty-volume 1906 edition of Thoreau's complete works.) The Princeton University Press edition of Thoreau's Journal presently runs to three volumes, carrying the Journal from its beginning in 1837 to August 1851. Two Journal quotations in my essay fall within this period, specifically from Princeton's *Journal 3: 1848–1851,* ed. Robert Sattelmeyer, Mark R. Patterson, and William Rossi (1990); they are identified parenthetically in the text by *PJ*, 3.

³For example, William Rossi's recent analysis of Thoreau's "Walking" challenges the common perception of that essay as a "position paper on the need to preserve wild lands" (94). Instead, he places "Walking" in the context of Coleridgean Romanticism: "'The Limits of an Afternoon Walk': Coleridgean Polarity in Thoreau's 'Walking,'" *ESQ: A Journal of the American Renaissance,* 33 (2nd Quarter, 1987): 94109. For book-length studies of Thoreau's relation to nineteenth-century Romanticism, see Frederick Garber, *Thoreau's Redemptive Imagination* (New York: New York University Press, 1977) and James McIntosh, *Thoreau as Romantic Naturalist: His Shifting Stance toward Nature* (Ithaca: Cornell University Press, 1974). For Thoreau's relation to the natural science of his day, see works cited in note 6.

⁴Pound made this remark in a letter to John Theobald, written on September 5, 1957. See *Pound/Theobald Letters,* ed. Donald Pearce and Herbert Schneidau (Redding Ridge, Conn.: Black Swan, 1984), p. 79. The context of the remark is a discussion of the relative worth of various writers (favoring Henry over William James, T. S. Eliot over Karl Shapiro, and Ford Maddox Ford over William Faulkner), in which Herman Melville suffers by implicit comparison with Thoreau: "to hell / and to Mel with Hellville."

⁵See my *Thoreau's Morning Work: Memory and Perception in A Week on the Concord and Merrimack Rivers, the Journal, and Walden* (New Haven: Yale University Press, 1990), pp. 67–69.

⁶As Nina Baym has shown, Thoreau's distrust of science as an avenue to truth becomes pronounced around 1850, even though, paradoxically, his empirical investigations of nature intensify in this period ("Thoreau's View of Science," *Journal of the History of Ideas* 26 [1965]: 233–34).

⁷In a Journal entry of February 18, 1852, Thoreau wrote: "It is impossible for the same person to see things from the poet's point of view and that of the man of science" (*J*, 3: 311).

⁸Six months after first reading Gilpin, Thoreau says of him: "I wish he would look at scenery sometimes not with the eye of an artist. It is all side screens and

fore screens and near distances and broken grounds with him" (*J*, 4: 283: August 6, 1852).

[9]See esp. James, "A World of Pure Experience," in *Essays in Radical Empiricism* (Cambridge, Mass.: Harvard University Press, 1976; first published, posthumously, in 1912); and Whitehead, *Science and the Modern World: Lowell Lectures, 1925* (New York: Macmillan, 1925), pp. 95, 121 and *passim*. See my *Thoreau's Morning Work*, pp. 69, 74, 106–07, for further discussion of Thoreau's relation to the thought of James and Whitehead.

[10]Eiseley, "Thoreau's Vision of the Natural World," in *The Star Thrower*, intro. W. H. Auden (New York: Harcourt Brace Jovanovich, 1978), p. 229.

[11]Eiseley 229–30.

[12]Burbick, *Thoreau's Alternative History: Changing Perspectives on Nature, Culture, and Language* (Philadelphia: University of Pennsylvania Press, 1987), p. 124.

[13]Leopold, *A Sand County Almanac and Sketches Here and There* (New York: Oxford University Press, 1949), p. 96.

[14]See Emerson's *Nature*, in *The Collected Works of Ralph Waldo Emerson*, ed. Alfred R. Ferguson *et al.* (Cambridge, Mass.: Harvard University Press, 1971), Vol. 1, pp. 10, 19, and *passim*.

[15]Lopez, *Crossing Open Ground* (New York: Vintage, 1989), p. 65. For a compelling discussion of Lopez's relation to Thoreau, and of Lopez's work generally, see Sherman Paul, *Hewing to Experience: Essays and Reviews on Recent American Poetry and Poetics, Nature and Culture* (Iowa City: University of Iowa Press, 1989), esp. pp. 357–58, 361, 380, 382.

[16]See my discussion of the "horizontal" framework of Thoreau's landscapes, in relation to the works of luminist painters such as Lane and Heade: *Thoreau's Morning Work*, pp. 55–58.

[17]Peck 120–23.

[18]Cf. Burbick, p. 134, on how, for Thoreau in his later years, "the mind must structure perception before correct observation can occur."

[19]Gombrich, *Art and Illusion: A Study in the Psychology of Pictorial Representation*, 4th ed. (Princeton: Princeton Univ. Press, 1972), p. 173.

[20]Gombrich, 173. For an interesting application of Gombrich's notion of "sacred discontent" to western literature, see Herbert N. Schneidau, *Sacred Discontent: The Bible and Western Tradition* (Berkeley: University Press, 1976), pp. 265 and *passim*.

[21]Thomas Carlyle, *On Heroes, Hero-Worship, and the Heroic in History*, ed. Archibald MacMechan (Boston: Ginn, 1901), pp. 94–95.

[22]Beston, *The Outermost House: A Year of Life on the Great Beach of Cape Cod* (New York: Viking, 1962), p. 25.

[23]Snyder, "Lookout's Journal," in *Earth House Hold: Technical Notes and Queries to Fellow Dharma Revolutionaries* (New York: New Directions, 1969), pp. 1–24.

[24]Lopez, *Arctic Dreams: Imagination and Desire in a Northern Landscape* (New York: Scribner, 1986).

[25]Fenollosa's essay was first published, with Pound's notations, in *Little Magazine* in 1919, and is reprinted in Karl Shapiro, ed., *Prose Keys to Modern Poetry* (Evanston, Ill.: Row, Peterson, 1962), where the relevant quotations appear on pp. 148, 149*n*. For an illuminating discussion of Fenollosa's influence on Pound, see Herbert N. Schneidau, *Ezra Pound: The Image and the Real* (Baton Rouge: Louisiana State University Press 1969), pp. 56–73.

---

**H. DANIEL PECK** is director, American Culture Program, Vassar College.

# Gentleman Amateur or "Fellow-Creature"?
## Thoreau's Maine Woods Flight from Contemporary Natural History

❖

### Phillip Round

"It is difficult to begin without borrowing."
—*Walden*[1]

Henry Thoreau's impatience with the natural history of his day is well-documented. As early as 1842, he lamented that an amateur naturalist "cannot go into any field or wood, but it will seem as if every stone had been turned, and the bark on every tree ripped up."[2] In Thoreau's view, not only was there very little fresh ground to botanize, but those facts that had already been gathered had been rendered by his culture's vigorous pursuit of the Baconian method just so many dead letters. The Baconians "inspected" rather than beheld nature's offerings. Their natural history reduced nature to "grammars and dictionaries."[3] And in the process, their natural facts seemed to ooze gentility. State geologists like Edward Hitchcock of Massachusetts, Charles Jackson of Maine, James Percival of Connecticut, and John Lesley of Pennsylvania could often sound downright magisterial in their pronouncements on nature's grandeur. For even though their geological surveys were conceived of by state legislatures in utilitarian terms, these "official" documents salt their compendious lists of empirical facts with gentlemanly sentiments.[4]

Witness Edward Hitchcock's description of the state geologist's role in the "Topographical Geology" section of his *Report* (1833):

> [He is] to direct the attention of the man of taste to those places in the State, where he will find natural objects particularly calculated to gratify his love of novelty, beauty, and sublimity ... by sketching their obvious features, I would hope to induce gentlemen of leisure and intelligence, who are lovers of the beautiful, the sublime, and the picturesque in nature, to visit and more minutely describe them. [5]

Encapsulated in Hitchcock's phrases are the two poles of the Baconian method that so vexed young Henry. Hitchcock will "minutely describe" geological features for "gentlemen of leisure."

Hitchcock's Baconianism reaches its pompous peak when he climbs to the top of the Massachusetts State House to gain a view of the picturesque settlements which "present[s] the observer, a most forcible example of human skill and industry, vying with, and almost eclipsing nature."[6] Looking down on the countryside below, he sees "the happy influence of our free institutions," and is swept up in "the pleasure with which every true American heart contemplates this scene."[7] At this point, Hitchcock's geology disappears and Yankee regionalism triumphs:

> From this elevation the whole of Boston, with its wharves, shipping, and public edifices; all the islands in its harbor; the shores of the harbor lined with villages and cultivated fields; and within the circle of ten miles, not less than 20 villages, containing, with Boston, more than 120,000 inhabitants, are here surveyed at a glance. ... So richly cultivated is the vicinity of Boston, that it has the appearance of a vast garden. Yet we do not see here a trace of the vandal spirit, which, in so many parts of our land, is making sad havoc with our groves and shade trees; but enough have been spared or planted in this vicinity to give a refreshing and luxuriant aspect to the scenery. [8]

The Trinitarian minister-cum-geologist envisions a progressive New England that encourages industry and agriculture without succumbing to the "vandal spirit" of rampant capitalism. In its picturesque qualities, balancing homestead and interval with the occasional shaggy wood, New England (and her best representative, the gentleman-amateur) has achieved a political equilibrium between communalism and entrepreneurialism.

Hitchcock's own sentiments are elevated to

> political and moral considerations which irresistibly force themselves on the mind when contemplating such a scene. How refreshing to the benevolent spirit, [he declares] to survey from this eminence the dwellings of 120,000 human beings, to be assured that there is not a slave among them all. ... The traveler of a benevolent heart ... need not fear being detained in the wildest and most secluded parts of the State. For scarcely will he find the hut, where if really needing shelter, he will not find a welcome, and all that a temperate man needs to make him comfortable. A man who has frequently been thrown into such situations, or in other words, has had the opportunity to learn the character and circumstances of the lowest as well as the highest classes in our community, will find his pleasure greatly heightened in surveying our scenery. [9]

Never mind that there are slaves aplenty to be found in 1830s America, should the gentleman turn his gaze more sharply toward the south. Hitchcock prefers to focus on the common man in his hut, the epitome and triumph of a common sense born in Yankee industry and tutored by the cultural elite's benevolent heart.

As Hitchcock's own ascent of the Statehouse makes clear, New England's moral center (composed of genuine benevolence and a convenient disregard of Irish poverty and African-American degradation) resides in gentlemen like himself "who [have] frequently ... had the opportunity to learn the character of the lowest as well as the highest classes in our community."[10] The entire *Report* along with its actual scientific and economic uses, chronicles the progress of just such a man, who in his tour of the Massachusetts landscape has likewise tutored his readers in the proper pursuit of a common sensical and well-balanced natural world. By mediating between the low and the high, and between professional and amateur, Hitchcock gives voice to his culture's complacent aspirations and sketches a landscape in which they could flourish.

In 1846 Thoreau embarked upon an ascent of his own, determined to transcend the patent absurdities found in Hitchcock's vision of nature. He would go in search of "the wild" on Mount Ktaadn, rallying to Emerson's admonition to the disaffected sons of a retrospective age: "Why should not we also enjoy an original relation to the universe?"[11] But his climb of Maine's most impressive peak is hauntingly similar to Hitchcock's, revealing the daunting fact that even "wilderness" had already been "foreclosed and monopolized" (to borrow Emerson's phrase) by the scientific language of the dominant culture. Having come to the Maine woods to experience nature in its pristine form, he finds instead an institutional text and language already in place, duly noting in the very first page of his narrative that Ktaadn had already been "placed" by Charles T. Jackson in an 1837 report, a work very much like Hitchcock's *Report,* and one that would accompany Thoreau on all of his Maine woods journeys.[12]

From the start, Thoreau's excursion into the wild is borne back ceaselessly into his own anxious past. Even his initial boat ride toward Ktaadn is faintly retrospective. It contains echoes of his voyage with his brother on the Concord and Merrimack rivers, but this time he is not in command of the craft, nor in control of his narrative's flow of events. Unlike the previous expedition's humble, homemade boat (a vessel that was "in form, like a fisherman's dory"), the bateau he rides in Maine reminds him of his own marginality in New England culture. Like the surname Thoreau, *bateau* brings to mind a foreign element of the American experience that Yankees like Hitchcock preferred to ignore. Haunted, even in this simple mode of conveyance, by the blue-blood natural world upon which all the dominant culture's assumptions were founded, Thoreau tries to make the best of his anxiety by saying:

> There is something refreshing and wildly musical to my ears in the very name of the white man's canoe, reminding me of Charlevoix and

Canadian Voyageurs. the bateau is a sort of mongrel between the canoe and the boat, a fur-traders boat.[13]

But he is whistling in the dark. Instead of providing an insouciant freedom as it would in *Walden,* this recognition of his own marginality only causes him discomfort. For riding the "mongrel" craft toward his encounter with the wild, he finds his transcendental goals increasingly in opposition to those of his companions. His own quest is hemmed in by lumbermen whose work, he laments, will bring down the great Maine woods to the will of the New England FrictionMatch Company. Although in *Walden* he celebrates the woodcutter's familiarity with nature, and sets up Alex Therien as a model for living, he cannot find solace in these men who leave trash at every campsite and set forest fires.

Disenchanted with the lumberman's gross relationship with the forest, Thoreau turns to the boat pilots for a model of the "wild" identity. He cites with justifiable admiration both their stamina in the arduous portages and their skill in shooting the white water. In contrast, he details his own clumsy handling of the bateau during those few times he is given the chance to pilot the craft upriver. The boatmen, at least, are admirable as Yankees whose business will in the long run yield their countrymen an "intellectual culture of independence." Like the Yankee husbandman in Edward Hitchcock's *Report,* the pilots symbolize a positive side of entrepreneurialism, rendering the sublime picturesque without actually succumbing to the lumberman's "vandal spirit" of capitalism.

However, they too eventually fail as models for the naturalist in the wild. Even though their skillful piloting suggests an understanding of nature that might serve as a proper foundation for a translated natural history of the Maine woods, they, like the lumberman, have changed the face of nature and reduced to common-sense a wilderness once full of mythic and poetic promise: "The Indians say that the river once ran both ways, one half up and the other half down, but that, since the white man came, it all runs down, and now they must laboriously pole their canoes against the stream, and carry them over numerous portages."[14] The synchronous, the primitive, even the "mongrel" he seeks in the wilderness is simply no longer there. The Yankees have forced the rivers to bend to their common sense expectations (water runs downhill). Even the stories that nature may tell are now reduced to mere picturesques. The "narrative flow" of the rivers—once synchronic (running both upstream and down simultaneously)—has been reduced to a linear and single-minded stream of events.

Thus, even before reaching Ktaadn, Thoreau has pondered a variety of possible social and linguistic identities for a white man in the wilderness. Although he clearly disapproves of the lumberman's relationship to nature, he is also incapable of wholly embracing the batteau pilots' linear and normative approach to the wild. Unable to pilot the boats and disgusted with cutting timber, Thoreau finds himself without a role in the microcosm of New England society that his fellow travelers reflect. By the time he arrives at the mountain, Thoreau's identity crisis has reached a corresponding height. Unable to fit in among his comrades, he turns to the peak for solace. But even on Ktaadn's wind-swept face he finds none. By reenacting previous expeditions to the mountain's summit, he is driven to reexperience nature in a borrowed language of scientific description. Instead of transcendental nature, he discovers himself amid the chaotically jumbled scree that guards against the mountaineer's approach: "The mountain seemed a vast aggregation of loose rocks, as if at some time it had rained rocks, and they lay as they fell on the mountainsides, nowhere fairly at rest, but leaning on each other, all rocking-stones, with cavities beneath, but scarcely any soil or smoother shelf." [15]

Although the rocks perform a conventional literary function, representing in their confusion his own psychological anxiety, Thoreau presents them in the geologist's language, thus highlighting the special kind of disorder they evoke. The boulders suggest a "time it had rained rocks," echoing the "deluge theory" of mountain formation propounded in Charles Jackson's *Report*. Jackson had also mentioned the slide, noting an abundance of diluvial boulders of grauwacke, and compact limestone, filled with impressions of marine shells, showing that the diluvial current once passed over the summit of this lofty mountain.[16] Along with this Noachian imagery, the boulders are described as "rocking-stones"—a reflection not only of the precarious balance that Thoreau has so far achieved between the wild and the civilized, but also of the picturesque geology that most appealed to the popular imagination. Even professional geological surveys spent time analyzing these strange phenomena that had caught many a traveler's fancy.[17] On Ktaadn the "wild" has come to Thoreau cloaked in a text that repels him as much as the lumbermen.

It was not until 1859 that Thoreau was able to articulate how a transcendentalist should approach wilderness. That year, in a rather cryptic aside typical of his later journals, he noted that "the lake or the bay is not an institution, but a phenomenon. ... "[18] On Ktaadn's boulderstrewn face, Thoreau has indeed come face to face with an institution, not a mountain. He experiences the peak as a jumble of observations that might have been culled from popular scientific journal descriptions or lyceum lectures on geology. And instead of the promising views that the survey geologists advertise, Thoreau enjoys only "occasional vistas." In fact, in the ultimate blow to the traditional climbing narrative, Thoreau never reaches the top and has to turn back in order to adhere to his companions' schedule. Like Charles Jackson's companions who "became discouraged" and returned to camp, Thoreau comes away from the wilderness profoundly alienated.

But, unlike them, Henry Thoreau is alienated more by his own descriptive language than by inclement weather. In Thoreau's narrative, the mountain threatens something more ominous than a good soaking—it is a "factory" for clouds. Faced with his old adversary, the city, he strains to "conceive" of a region uninhabited by man. Yet it is only after he has experienced the geologist's "rocking stones" and the city dweller's "factory" that Thoreau can enter such a place—the "Burnt Lands ... that Earth of which we have heard, made out of Chaos and Old Night."[19] Some readers would point to Thoreau's inability to conceive (read: "imagine") of "the wild" on Ktaadn as a failure of his transcendental vision of nature. In this reading, Thoreau is daunted by forces larger than the imagination, by that "Titan" whose presence casts into question Emerson's assertion that evil was merely the privation of good. And even in his later discovery of a landscape "exceedingly wild and desolate," the naturalist seems disoriented by the language that the scene unleashes: "And yet we have not seen pure Nature, unless we have seen her thus vast and drear and inhuman, though in the midst of cities. Nature was here something savage and awful, though beautiful."[20] If Thoreau had just moments before portrayed the mountain as a factory, he now defines even its sublimity in terms of the city, a location that he himself had repeatedly vilified as "unnatural." Why point to the "midst of cities" as a place where we might have seen "pure Nature?"

The answer may lie in the fact that the Maine woods, like the urban landscape of New York, which upset him a few years earlier, seems so overdetermined by received discourse that it is no longer "natural". Rather than blame Nature herself, he vaguely connects the failure of his transcendental vision to cities and factories. In his subsequent analysis of the scene, he lays the blame directly at the feet of the gentleman amateur:

> What is it to be admitted to a museum, to see a myriad of particular things, compared with being shown some star's surface, some hard matter in its home! I stand in awe of my body, this matter to which I am bound has become so strange to me. I fear not spirits, ghosts, of which I am one,—*that* my body might,—but I fear bodies, I tremble to meet them. What is this Titan that has possession of me? Talk of mysteries!—Think of our life in Nature,—daily to be shown matter, to come in contact with it,—rocks, trees, wind on our cheeks! the *solid* earth! the *actual* world! the *common sense! Contact! Contact! Who* are we? *where* are we?[21]

The Baconian's facts (the "myriad of particular things") have solidified into an institution—they are museum pieces. Thoreau must somehow experience them as "phenomena" again. It is with this in mind that he invokes "spirits" and "ghosts." Perhaps by exploring the phenomenology of his fear he can recover his transcendental vision.

Although Thoreau's terror makes him acutely aware of his body, it does not remind him of the "liver lights and bowels"—the organic bodily processes—that redeem him in *Walden*. Nor does it make him feel much like Emerson's transparent eye-ball. It returns him, rather, to the solid material body that troubles Emerson in his essay "Experience." From this vantage point, from the point of view of the material body, Emerson notes that "from the mountain you see the mountain." And it is with no little irony that this passage ends with an echo of Emerson's "Experience" ("Who are we? Where are we?"). Thoreau answers that we are gentlemen of *common* sense, living in a world of brute matter.

In an effort to transcend (or, in *Walden*'s formulation, "overcome") this hard, material body of the dominant culture, Thoreau tries on "the red face of man." The "true Indian wisdom," which in "The Natural History of Massachusetts" takes the place of a science that left "no stone unturned" pressed him to adopt a different narrative point of view, a stance adequate to a wilderness "inhabited by men more kin to the rocks and wild animals than we."[22] Unlike Emerson's "bodies that never come in contact," the Native American straddles the materiality of common sense, and the irrationality of Chaos and Old Night.

In 1858, Thoreau would insist that the Natives' understanding existed prior to the gentleman amateur's scientific method, arguing with John Langdon Sibley that "the Indian stands between the men of science and the subjects they study."[23]

In the boatmen who guided him up the rivers and streams of Maine, Thoreau had found one sort of hardihood that appealed to him. But in the Native American he felt that he had finally found a vantage point—a position from which to view nature and society—that gained him entrance to a past where both mythology and natural history were still possible:

> Can you well go further back in history than this? Ay! ay!—for there turns up but now into the mouth of Millinocket stream a still more ancient and primitive man, whose history is not brought down even to the former. In a bark vessel sewn with the roots of the spruce, with hornbeam paddles, he dips his way along. He is but dim and misty to me, obscured by the aeons that lie between the bark canoe and the batteau.[23]

Pointing out that "an Indian is still necessary to guide … scientific men to headwaters in the Adirondac country,"[25] Thoreau attempts to realize a position similar to that of the Native American. By the end of "Ktaadn," Thoreau has clearly formulated the belief that this perspective can "unrealize" the gentleman amateur's vision of the natural world. And although he admits that civilization has substantially encroached on the wild, striving to erect telegraph poles and lay railroad lines across Maine, he maintains that " … the Indian still looks out from her interior mountains *over all* these to the sea."[26]

The Indian's perspective is higher than anything Edward Hitchcock can imagine. In "Ktaadn," however, Thoreau is not yet willing to acknowledge his own Indian guides as the potential saviors for the transcendental science of nature. Although he will determine by the chapter's end that the Native's perspective is the most appropriate "business" he can aspire to, he omits the Indians' role in the ascent of "Ktaadn" itself. Louis Neptune and his party arrive too late to guide the adventurers, having been drunk and incapacitated the night before. Like the mountain's summit and the untamed Burnt land below, these wild men have suffered from the encroachment of civilization: Met face to face, these Indians in their native woods looked like the sinister and slouching fellows whom you meet picking up strings and paper in the streets of a city. There is, in fact, a remarkable and unexpected resemblance between the degraded savages and the lowest classes in a great city. The one is no more a child of nature than the other.[27] Neither mythical figures of romantic wisdom nor savages of uncivilized barbarity, the Native Americans are subject to the same social and economic forces that have driven others in the industrial age to the periphery of urban life. And, like Thoreau on Ktaadn, they are consigned to "picking up strings and paper," the offal of the rapidly growing progressive institutions that Edward Hitchcock praised from his perch high atop the Massachusetts State House.

In the face of a co-opted wilderness, and a degraded "native" voice, Thoreau attempts throughout the remaining chapters of *The Maine Woods* to salvage the Native American, making him his methodological model, in much the same way that he would attempt to redeem "the mass of men" in *Walden*. "Chesuncook's" Joe Aitteon represents a stage in Thoreau's progress from the debased Indians of "Ktaadn" to the book's final image of native "genius," Joe Polis. Although Aitteon's "job" is ostensibly to guide Thoreau's companions on a moose hunt, Thoreau claims he "employed an Indian mainly that [he] might have the opportunity to study his ways."[28] And yet, as in his investigation of "wilderness" at Ktaadn seven years before, Thoreau's study of this so-called primitive man exposes a great deal of "debris" left over from white society.

First, like the lumberjacks whom Thoreau disdains in "Ktaadn," Aitteon is attired in "a red flannel shirt, woolen pants, and a black Kossuth hat." Thoreau notes that Joe "appeared to identify himself with that class."[29] He also shares some of their more quaint personal characteristics, "whistling O Susanna," and chiming in with an occasional "Yes, Siree." Thoreau seems eager to point out just how far Joe has slipped away from the traditional ways of the Penobscot people so that the reader never mistakes this "savage" for the primitive identity he himself will seek. When, for example, Thoreau suggests that they try living off the land, off "game, fish, and berries," like the early Native peoples, Aitteon replies, "Yes, ... that's the way they got a living, like wild fellows, wild as bears. By George, I shan't go into the woods without provision,—hard bread, pork, etc."[30] In a final, eerie echo of the previous chapter, Thoreau's inquiry into Aitteon's method of making fire raises the spectre of the dreaded New England Friction Match Company when Joe produces wooden matches from a "little cylindrical box."

Yet Joe Aitteon's role as "hunter" best exemplifies where Thoreau's search for a voice apart from his culture's gentleman amateur stood in 1853. Although he carries the aforementioned traces of white culture, he is a true woodsman in ways that the lumbermen could never dream of. As Thoreau assiduously records how he painstakingly stalks the moose, the reader is led toward viewing the killing as the cathartic event that will cleanse the transcendental naturalist of his borrowed guilt and alienation. In the capable hands of an Indian guide, Thoreau finds himself much closer to the primitive that he was in 1846. In language refreshingly wild and patently un-genteel, he plucks plants and navigates his canoe so that he "might see what was primitive about [his] native river."[31] In effect, Joe has guided him away from the shadow of the State House and all of the linguistic and political complacency that it entails.

But in a variation of the Ktaadn ascent, the moose hunt concludes as "a tragical business." Watching the "warm milk stream" from the pierced udder of the slain moose cow Joe butchers, Thoreau is smitten, and exclaims: "The afternoon's tragedy, and my share in it, as it affected my innocence, destroyed the pleasure of my adventure."[32] Although Thoreau relishes the thought that he came ... near to being a hunter," he must finally discard even this dearly bought primitivism. He must conclude of Aitteon and his people: "What a coarse and imperfect use Indians and hunters make of nature!"[33]

While Thoreau has escaped Edward Hitchcock's gentility—"Chesuncook's" nature is full of blood letting and lumbermen who brag about "which man could handle' any man on the carry"—his transcendental philosophy chastises him, cautioning "that our life should be lived as tenderly and daintily as one would pluck a flower."[34] He has gotten closer to the primal, but not to its poetry. He remains trapped in "tender" and "dainty" diction. Only briefly does this chapter move beyond Ktaadn's disillusionment. In the Penobscot and Abnaki's fireside conversation Thoreau glimpse a "wild" that the poet might finally put to use:

> While lying there listening to the Indians, I amused myself with trying to guess at their subject by their gestures, or some proper name introduced. There can be no more startling evidence of their being a distinct and comparatively aboriginal race, than to hear this unaltered Indian language, which the white man cannot speak nor understand. We may suspect change and alteration in every other particular, but the language which is so wholly unintelligible to us. [35]

Finally, a voice without the taint of civilization! The language here is not borrowed from the state survey or the botanical guide. Much more frequently than in the opening chapter of *The Maine Woods* words like *wighiggin* (writing), *ebeeme* (rock), and *medawisla* (loon) swirl up out of the deepest woods.

Sadly, Thoreau's narrative of 1853 does not pick up on this submerged source of power. Instead, in a move that sounds painfully like Edward Hitchcock, Thoreau recants on his ringing declaration of the power of wilderness that he has written only a few pages earlier, paying homage to "our smooth, but still varied landscape."

Thankfully, such is not the case in "The Allegash and East Branch," the final chapter of *The Maine Woods* represents the culmination of Thoreau's search for a narrative voice that began in "Ktaadn" in both its choice of Native American hero, Joe Polis, and in the narrative style which Thoreau uses to describe his final excursion north in 1857. By shifting his narrative focus almost completely to the Native American in this final chapter, he replaces the failed quest story in "Ktaadn" with a chronicle of tutelage in the wild, and its hesitant transcendental method with Joe Polis' effective melding of myth and practical skills as a model for the transcendental naturalist.

First of all, Polis represents a substantial "improvement" over Louis Neptune and Joe Aitteon. Unlike the other two men, he exemplifies the mediating position between the wild and the civilized that Thoreau himself is desperate to achieve. From the beginning, Thoreau presents him as a gentleman among his sadly degraded countrymen:

> He was stoutly built, perhaps a little above the middle height, with a broad face and as others said perfect Indian features and complexion. His house was a 2-story white one with blinds, the best looking one I noticed there, and as good as an average one on a New England village street. It was surrounded by a garden of fruit trees, single corn stalks standing thinly amid the beans. [36]

From his "perfect Indian features" to his 2-story house and fruit trees, Polis' identity spans the gap between the wild and the civilized that Thoreau himself is seeking to bridge. Even though it might seem that Polis is redeemed only through the visible evidence of economic success and Yankee industry, it becomes clear as the narrative progresses that Thoreau wishes to focus upon Joe Polis' *method* rather than on any fleeting material "improvement" that he may seem to have made over his culture's previous "savage" existence. Others have observed that Joe Polis is Thoreau's most well-rounded portrait of a Native American. Where Louis Neptune hints of urban degradation and really only exists in "Ktaadn" as a mythological spirit of primitivism, Polis seems to deserve the title that Philip Gura has given him—a representative man. [37] But perhaps most interesting is his role in Thoreau's own "translation" of the dominant culture's natural historians. Significantly, Joe Polis instructs Thoreau not so much as a hunter, but rather as a "natural philosopher" of the wild. At one point, having discovered a stump of phosphorescent wood which the Indian shrugs off as a "common" occurrence, Thoreau concludes that this Native American indeed embodies a wholly alternative epistemology:

I did not regret my not having seen this before, since I now saw it under circumstances so favorable. I was in just the frame of mind to see something wonderful, and this was a phenomenon adequate to my circumstances and my expectation, and it put me on the alert to see more like it. I exulted like "a pagan suckled in a creed" that had never been worn at all, but was bran new and adequate to the occasion. I let science slide, and rejoiced in that light as if it had been a fellow-creature. I saw that it was excellent, and was very glad to know that it was so cheap. A scientific *explanation*, as it is called, would have been altogether out of place there. That is for pale daylight. Science with its retorts would have put me to sleep; it was the opportunity to be ignorant that I improved. It suggested that there was something to be seen if one had eyes. ... One revelation has been made to the Indian, another to the white man. I have much to learn of the Indian, nothing of the missionary. [38]

A true Baconian—an Edward Hitchcock—would do much more than "regret" not having seen such a fact before. A stone unturned? Heaven forbid! Yet Thoreau relishes "the frame of mind" this discovery puts him in. Better prepared by the Native American's perspective to take advantage of this moment, he descends from the "objective" point of view afforded by the State House to become a "fellow-creature" with phenomena. Alienation gone, scientific detachment on the slide, Thoreau focuses on the imaginative potential of nature that was so often lacking in Baconian "reports." Polis exemplifies a fact gatherer whose method subsumes the whole being, rather than merely the intellectual side of a man. Watching him navigate the seemingly trackless wood, Thoreau notes:

It appeared that the sources of information were so various that he did not give a distinct, conscious attention to any one, and so could not readily refer to any when questioned about it, but he found his way as an animal does. Perhaps what is called instinct in the animal, in this case is merely a sharpened and educated sense. ... Not having experienced the need of the other sort of knowledge, all labelled and arranged, he has not acquired it. [39]

No longer "labelled and arranged," the same phenomena that make up the Baconian scientist's natural-history cabinet or his geological survey, become in the Native American's experience a continual *process* of integrating himself with the natural world. Both Edward Hitchcock's self-imposed distance from the landscape achieved in his ascent of the State House and Henry Thoreau's own alienation from nature on Ktaadn's summit might in this way be avoided. By gaining the unifying perspective of the Indian, the poet/naturalist might master a method whereby "he might live and die and never hear of the United States, which make such a noise in the world,—never hear of America, so called from the name of a European gentleman."[40]

Had we time, we might explore the expert way Thoreau's seemingly objective account of Joe Polis' apparent "blind obedience to a blundering oracle"—to the white man's economics and to the white man's religion—is more often than not undercut by observations like "such was the Indian's pretense always."[41] Because of Joe Polis, we feel better about Native America and better about Thoreau himself. Polis is a gentleman with a difference, and Thoreau can finally paddle a canoe "just like anybody." But there is no mistaking the residual anxiety that remains at this chapter's conclusion.

Although Thoreau has come down from the Baconian's summit to mingle with phenomena, and although his facts have gained some poetic valence, the Native Americans themselves have become a "sign" in the larger body of scientific and travel literature they inhabit. Tragically, the Native American has become a "thing" and his bricolage and primitive science are ultimately victimized by the political economy that Edward Hitchcock celebrates in his *Report.* The little Indian boys who meet white travellers now cry, "put up a cent," and offer to demonstrate their forest skills only to supply the "vandal spirit" of capitalism. As Thoreau puts it:

> Verily the Indian has but feeble hold on his bow now; but the curiosity of the white man is insatiable … . That elastic piece of wood with its feathered dart, so sure to be unstrung by contact with civilization, will serve for the type, for the coat of arms of the savage. Alas for the Hunter race. The white man has driven off their game and substituted a cent in its place. [42]

And so *The Maine Woods* ends with Thoreau's dying thoughts—the gentleman will triumph and never enter the woods as a fellow traveller with Nature herself. His concluding words resonate with loss: "This was the *last* I saw of Joe Polis. We took the *last* train and reached Bangor that night."

# Notes

[1] Henry D. Thoreau, *Walden,* ed. J. Lyndon Shanley (Princeton: Princeton University Press, 1975), p. 40

[2] Henry D. Thoreau, *Journal,* "The National History of Massachusetts," in *Henry David Thoreau: The Natural History Essays,* ed. Robert Sattelmeyer (Layton, UT: Peregrine Smith, 1984).

[3] Henry D. Thoreau, *Journal, Henry Thoreau,* ed. Bradford Torrey and Francis H. Allen (Boston: Houghton Mifflin, 1906). Vol. 7, p. 103.

[4] Whether it was termed Topographical Geology, as it is in this version of the *Report,* or "Scenographical Geology," as it is in Hitchcock's *Final Report*

on *The Geology of Massachusetts,* (Amherst: Press of J.S. and C. Adams, 1841), the pursuit of gentlemanly sentiments proved worthy of taxpayer dollars. See also, James G. Percival, *Report on the Geology of the State of Connecticut,* (New Haven: Osborn and Baldwin, 1842) and Rev. Elias Cornelius's "On the Geology, Mineralogy, Scenery and Curiosities of parts of Virginia ... " In *The American Journal of Science,* vol. 1, ed. Benjamin Silliman (1818).

[5]Edward Hitchcock, *Report. On the Geology, Mineralogy, Botany and Zoology of Massachusetts* (Amherst: J. S. and C. Adams, 1833), p. 73.

[6]*Ibid.,* p. 84

[7]*Ibid.,* p. 84

[8]*Ibid.,* p. 93

[9]*Ibid.,* p. 93

[10]*Ibid.,* p. 93

[11]Emerson, "Nature," in *The Collected Works of R. W. Emerson,* ed. Robert Spiller and Alfred Ferguson, Vol. 1 (Cambridge: Harvard Univ. Press, 1971), p. 1.

[12]Charles T. Jackson, *First Report in the Geology of Public Lands in the State of Maine.* Boston: Dutton and Wentworth, 1837).

[13]Thoreau, *The Maine Woods,* ed. Joseph J. Moldenhauer (Princeton: Princeton Univ. Press, 1972), p. 6.

[14]*Ibid.,* p. 32–33

[15]*Ibid.,* p. 63

[16]Jackson, *First Report* (1837), p. 17.

[17]The presence of "diluvial" rocks in geological description indicates how much theology remained an important part of natural history.

[18]Journal, Vol. 12, p. 52.

[19]*The Maine Woods, p. 71.*

[20]*Ibid.,* p. 71.

[21]*Ibid.,* p. 71.

[22]*Ibid.,* p. 79.

[23]Quoted in Richardson, *Henry Thoreau: A Life of the Mind* (Berkeley and Los Angeles: Univ. of California Press, 1986), p. 356.

[24]*The Maine Woods,* p. 79.

[25]*Ibid.,* p. 82.

[26] *Ibid.*, p. 82

[27] *Ibid.*, p. 78

[28] *Ibid.*,p. 95

[29] *Ibid.*, p. 90

[30] *Ibid.*, p. 107

[31] *Ibid.*, p. 106

[32] *Ibid.*, p. 119

[33] *Ibid.*, p. 120

[34] *Ibid.*, p. 120

[35] *Ibid.*, p. 136

[36] *Ibid.*, p. 157

[37] Philip Gura, "Thoreau's Maine Woods Indians: Representative Men," *American Literature* XLIX (November, 1977) #3, pp. 366–384.

[38] *The Maine Woods*, p. 181

[39] *Ibid.*, p. 185

[40] *Ibid.*, p. 775

[41] *Ibid.*, p. 294

[42] *Ibid.*, p. 146

----------

**PHILLIP ROUND** is an Assistant Professor of English at Tufts University, Medford, Massachusetts.

# Thoreau in Yellowstone?
# Natural History Writing About
# America's First National Park

❖

## Bruce A. Richardson

My subject is natural-history writing about Yellowstone by writers more or less influenced by Thoreau—John Muir, John Burroughs, Gretel Ehrlich, Peter Matthiessen—and how their essays on Yellowstone fit into its textual tradition. I will argue that Yellowstone is a difficult subject for nature writers working the Thoreau vein especially because it was shaped by cultural habits inimical to Thoreau's approach to nature. The cultural Yellowstone raised questions about the intrinsic value of wilderness, the role of process and renewal in nature and the interconnectedness of humans and nature Although many preservationists and ecologists today think of Yellowstone in Thoreau's words—"this vast, savage, howling mother of ours, Nature"—it was not generally presented this way in the 19th century. As Richard Bartlett, Aubrey Haines, Alfred Runte, Katherine Early, and others have argued, Yellowstone was preserved not for its wildness, but for its curiosities—the geysers—and scenery, especially the Grand Canyon and Lake. The wilderness was, in fact, an obstacle to creating a pleasuring ground, a park where humans could enjoy the wonders.[1] Naturalists of the 19th and 20th centuries looking for wilderness first find tourist nature, a cultural construction that dominates texts about Yellowstone.

Tourist nature emerges first from the language of discovery and then recovery. Discovery, the "first" sight of something, and the second-sight confirmation visit, depend on the status of the object as potentially valuable, something worth revisiting. One does not discover the banal or useless, but "treasures" and "wonders." Early Yellowstone texts are often quest stories with the Canyon and the geysers sitting in for the Holy Grail. The pattern reflects a central cultural fact about the West; stories of discovery are part of the pattern of conquest (Limerick, *Legacy of*

*Conquest*, p. 26). Discovery and the drama of appropriation of the unknown have a special logic which appears in many examples including Spanish literature about the Americas. Financed by would-be owners and developers, the explorers gave the patrons what they wanted: reports of amazing wonders and abundant riches (Bryant, *Yellowstone*, p. 207). The pattern of Coronado and DeVaca's reports recurs in the English writings about Virginia which also function as advertising to lure colonists to the sensual lushness of the place. The enumeration of wonders becomes a standard feature of the American literature of conquest. This for Jefferson, Thomas Cole, and many others was part of the defense of America against European condescension. William Bartram's account of Florida, filled with references to Romantic poetry and Marco Polo, shows the multiple purposes of such scenic inflation.

The textual Yellowstone easily called forth this language. Trapper tales from the early 19th century spoke of the smoking ground where the Indians feared to go. The great entrepreneur and spinner of tall tales Jim Bridger described geysers and, along with other trappers, spoke of a forest where petrified birds sat in petrified trees and sang petrified songs (Haines, *The Yellowstone Story*, pp. 53–59). Written reports from Warren Ferris and Osborne Russell were somewhat calmer, but still comment on the geysers in tones of wonder. The report of the 1870 Washburn expedition, written by Nathaniel Langford, is a journal of hyperbole where marvel tops marvel. The temptation for the writer about Yellowstone is to succumb to open-mouth awe and fall into a catalogue of the stupendous. Langford's widely read book set a pattern repeated in tourist guidebooks.[2]

These books and the narratives of early visitors generally follow the form and ideology of the picturesque tour, popularized in England by William Gilpin. His tour books identified, in great detail, the most visually pleasing spots. Rather than treating land as a continuous flow of perception, the picturesque traveler segments the whole into a collection of discretely framed spaces—those places that had the pleasing mix of variety and order of landscape paintings. The individual scenes were separated not only from each other but from history, both human and natural. Nothing about the pictures counted except for their ability to give pleasure to the visual consumer—the tourist who desires that potentially disturbing elements disappear into a purely visual experience.[3]

Picturesque touring became popular in the United States after the Revolutionary War and gained in favor through the 19th century (see citations by Robertson, Sears). Crucial to the tour was the development of a set of cultural practices that guided and validated the practice of touring. The tourist is a second-sight visitor. Led by guidebooks, traveling in some comfort, and staying at hotels, the tourist seeks out the places already discovered and designated as significant. In his study *The Tourist*, Dean MacCannell acknowledges that there may be things "so spectacular in themselves that no institutional support is required to mark them off as attractions," but most "wonders" are the result of "sight sacralization" (*The Tourist* pp. 44–45). This proceeds through institutions that name, frame, elevate, enshrine, and mechanically reproduce the sight. Connected to the process is the development of roads, hotels, transportation, lunch stops and the like which enhance sacralization. They provide access, translate the sights into commodities, and create spatial systems that frame and dramatize the sacred object.

Even before 1885 when John Muir first saw Yellowstone, it offered a nature filtered and processed by the economic and perceptual imperatives of tourism. *Picturesque America*, a highly popular collection of engravings published first in 1872 had a chapter on "Our Great National Park (Yellowstone)" with images of the prominent wonders (Moritz, *America the Picturesque,* p. 36). Wylie guidebooks and works such as Langford's Journal and James Richardson's *Wonders of the Yellowstone Region* publicized the place and gave it shape by designating the prominent sights. On the ground, Yellowstone had roads, hotels, lunch stations, stagecoach tours, and a tourist circuit that featured stops at the well-known wonders or scenic attractions. Rudyard Kipling, a visitor in 1889, neatly defined the situation:

> The Park is just a howling wilderness of three thousand square miles, full of all imaginable freaks of a fiery nature. An hotel company, assisted by the Secretary of State for the Interior, appears to control it; there are hotels at all the points of interest, guide-books, stalls for the sale of minerals, and so forth, after the model of Swiss summer places (*From Sea to Sea,* pp. 88–89).

Kipling's Yellowstone is wildness shaped by the imperatives of tourist nature. Rather than existing as a continuous whole, the land is segmented into "points of interest" that can be experienced during the structured sequence of a tour. Travel from the 1880s until the introduction of automobiles in 1917 was by stagecoaches, which hauled the visitor from sight to sight and hotel to hotel, each placed by prominent wonders: Mammoth Hot Springs, the Lower Geyser Basin, the Upper Geyser Basin, Yellowstone Lake, and the Grand Canyon. The Canyon, generally considered the best of the sights and celebrated in Moran's large painting which hung in the Capitol, provided the appropriately visual conclusion to the tour. The result was, as Kipling wrote, "a howling wilderness" tamed into tourist nature. Dean MacCannell argues that

> The modern touristic version of nature treats it not as a force opposing man ... but as a common source of thrills, something we must try to preserve. Tours of natural wonders organize the thrills nature provides into discrete experiences guaranteeing results for those who would take in the approved sights (*The Tourist,* p. 81).

The tourist moves from picture to picture, collecting the framed spots, as it were, in a search for the authentic. It is the translation of nature into scenery and dividing it into views that creates for the tourist the possibility of possessing the sacred commodity, here the immediate experience of the thing itself—the geyser, the Grand Canyon, the hot springs, and so on. These "wonders" divided out from their context become the objects of desire in the tourist exchange economy. Tourists are willing to spend money for true contact with these curiosities. In an essay on souvenirs, Susan Stewart argues that "under an exchange economy, the search for authentic experience and, correlatively, the search for the authentic object become critical. As experience is increasingly mediated and abstracted, the lived relation of the body to the phenomenological world is replaced by a nostalgic myth of contact and presence" (*Loaning*, p. 133). The abstracting of value onto money and mass produced commodities creates a strong need for what is felt to be real experience possible through direct contact with the unique, singular object—the original. Tourists buy souvenirs as a reminder of their encounter with the real, but also to mark the difference between the substitute and the authentic. On a quest for the real, tourists are drawn to Yellowstone, the site of originality.

Muir was bothered by this situation, but made good use of it. The essay done after his 1885 tour of the park shows a persistent struggle against the structure of tourist nature. He plays with the expectations of the reader who expects a catalogue of hyperbole. Take, for example, a section near the opening:

> Besides the treasures common to most mountain regions that are wild and blessed with a kind climate, the Park is full of exciting wonders. The wildest geysers in the world, in bright, triumphant bands, are dancing and singing in it amid thousands of boiling springs, beautiful and awful, their basins arrayed in gorgeous colors like gigantic flowers; and hot paint-pots, mud springs, mud volcanoes, mush and broth caldrons whose contents are of every color and consistency, plash and heave and roar in bewildering abundance. In the adjacent mountains, beneath the living trees the edges of petrified forests are exposed to view, like specimens on the shelves of a museum, standing on ledges tier above tier where they grew, solemnly silent in rigid crystalline beauty after swaying in the winds thousands of centuries ago, opening marvelous views back into the years and climates and life of the past (*Our National Parks* p. 38).

Muir initially seems to fall into the traditions of tourist nature. He praises Yellowstone as a sort of "treasure" chest, "full of exciting wonders" valuable to the visitor and then calls the petrified forest "shelves of a museum." Nonetheless, things are not that stable, but threaten to explode outward as the "thousands of boiling springs ... plash and heave and roar in bewildering abundance." He also seems to evoke the picturesque by stressing vision: the trees "exposed to view" and "opening marvelous views" into the deep past. Nonetheless, here we can see Muir shifting away from picturesque assumptions, which takes the scene out of time, and reinstating the view into deep time. Similarly the flower metaphor and the process language (dancing, singing, boiling, plash, heave, roar, swaying) suggests the interconnectedness of the features through their common growth. The move from the action of the second sentence to the solemn stillness of the third implies that change is omnipresent, if we expand our sense of time. The process has been going on through deep time, which Muir implicitly compares to the speedy round of tourist travel. He urges that the "rushing tourist" slow down.

> The regular trips—from three to five days—are too short. Nothing can be done well at a speed of forty miles a day. The multitude of mixed, novel impressions rapidly piled on one another make only a dreamy, bewildering, swirling blur, most of which is unrememberable. Far more time should be taken. Walk away quietly in any direction and taste the freedom of the mountaineer. Camp out among the grass ... of glacier meadows, in craggy garden nooks full of Nature's darlings. Climb the mountains and get their good tidings. Nature's peace will flow into you as sunshine flows into trees (*Our National Parks,* p. 56).

Muir understood the tourist condition very well. He had a short time for a visit and was worried that he might end up with only blurry impressions. Ill from bad railroad food and a horrid lunch at the Mammoth Hotel, he traveled not by himself but with a honeymooning couple and their cook and guide. They went on the standard roads and saw the standard sights—Tower Falls, the Grand Canyon, the Lake, Old Faithful Geyser, and so on. At last arriving at Old Faithful, Muir saw the geyser erupt and promptly vomited. He found sleeping among the geysers disturbing; in fact he did not like many of the scenic attractions in the tourist circuit, including the Grand Canyon.

Here Muir addresses the epistemological and ontological conditions of tourist nature. Nature segmented into views and points of interests is intelligible and unrememberable since it is treated as a collection, not a continuous process. In addition, the tourist is fundamentally separated from the thing itself and regards her experience as distinct from the vital processes. The way back is to slow down, move through the frame and into the picture, camp in a meadow. Or expand the view. Muir did climb Mount Washburn. There he saw larger patterns, the movement of the trees, the connection between geysers and rivers, the work of the animals, the sliding of glaciers as part of nature the artist "ever working toward beauty, higher and higher" (*Our National Parks,* p. 74).

Tourist institutions then help Muir define "wilderness." It is the other, the real Yellowstone, which lies "beyond the wagon roads and hotels." Wilderness functions here, as it does for Thoreau in "Walking," as a relative term—what's out of town. The tourist institutions provide a hierarchy of authenticity. Muir describes the stagecoach "in showy style" leaving the hotel while the passengers prattle on until the mountains come into view and "all become natural and silent" (pp. 52–53). The next stage, the geysers leave viewers "awe-stricken and silent, in devout, worshipping wonder" (p. 54). Muir then presses the traveler to go further: "walk away quietly" (p. 56), "camp … on mountaintops above the timberline" (p. 59), "climb Electric Peak" (p. 59), or, at least take a "saunter" up Mount Washburn (p. 66). After "you will remember these fine, wild views, and look back with joy to your wanderings in the blessed old Yellowstone Wonderland" (p. 75).

"Wanderings" are not what one gets on the tourist circuit, but it is that structure that gives spatial reality to the wild, the place beyond the boundaries.[4] Muir, presses the traveler toward what he sees as the real Yellowstone beyond the preformed tourist circuit. In so doing Muir recommends a touristic trope: get off the beaten track. This argues Jonathan Culler (following MacCannell) is an essential part of tourist behavior and discourse. Tourists seek to transcend their condition by going one step further toward the authentic so they can then look back with some disdain at those following the standard routine ("The Semiotics of Tourism," p. 158). But, as Culler says, getting off the beaten path may be the most beaten path of all (p.162). Muir's climb up Mount Washburn, in fact, followed a good horse trail that many took and was soon improved into a wagon and then an auto road. It has since been reclassified a trail, though cars could and sometimes do go up. The authentic, since it is established by difference, is wonderfully available to the tourist, since there is always someone who has not seen or experienced what you have. Many have not seen Old Faithful, but fewer have climbed Mount Washburn, though soon it would be a standard part of the tour, Muir could count it as a true experience of Yellowstone apart from the tourist circuit.

Here we see the significance of this cultural construction of space. Stephen Greenblatt describes Yosemite as a series of zones through which you pass in order to reach the "wilderness," but the structuring of the zones through signs and such assure that the "wilderness is at once secured and obliterated" and the distinction between nature and culture is rendered meaningless *(Towards a Poetics of Culture,* p. 9). Greenblatt, describing an extremely well-traveled path (the trail to Nevada Falls), might find the distinction clearer if he went further, but his general point— that wilderness is a cultural term and defined by institutional markers certainly applies to Yellowstone. Its roads, trails and boardwalks through geyser basins create movement systems that define the wonders and the wilderness, just off the boardwalk. Muir does not transcend these institutional constraints, but uses them to argue for the superior value, the greater authenticity of the other over the conventional authentic, the institutionally sanctioned wonders. Go a little further—it is just beyond the spaces on which you travel.

In his 1903 essay, John Burroughs plays another standard part, the disillusioned tourist. Bombarded by guidebooks and the other apparatus of secralization, the visitor comes to compare text and object and finds the latter wanting and the whole institution of tourist nature suspect. Burroughs was particularly disappointed by Yellowstone's most famous features:

> The novelty of the geyser region soon wears off. Steam and hot water are steam and hot water the world over, and the exhibition of them here did not differ, except in volume, from what one sees by his own fireside … . To be sure, boiling lakes and steaming rivers are not common, but the new features seemed, somehow, out of place, and as if nature had made a mistake. One disliked to see so much good steam and hot water going to waste; whole towns might be warmed by them, and big wheels made to go round. I wondered that they had not piped them into the big hotels which they opened for us, and which were warmed by wood fires (224).

Here is tourist nature with a vengeance. Burroughs sees the geysers as segmented features that are under an obligation to interest him. One is reminded, unfortunately, of Ronald Reagan's comment about Redwood trees: when you've seen one you've seen them all. If the objects exist for utility—here visual pleasure—we need no infinity of them, but just one or two examples. Burroughs picks up also on the common association with industry, but here to the geyser's detriment. Like railroads and manufactures they have immense energy, but unlike the others, wasted to no end. Burroughs fully adapts the values of the picturesque traveler: everything has a use, aesthetic or otherwise. Since the geysers and hot springs did not please, they might be pressed into other service. He does find other scenery to interest him, particularly the Canyon, which he rates as the "grandest spectacle in the Park" (*Camping and Tramping with Roosevelt*, p. 227), but the reasoning of the essay here still turns on the tourist habit of segmentation and enumeration.

Burroughs is concerned less with the scenery and more with the wildlife, but most of all with his friend and traveling companion, President Theodore Roosevelt. In Burroughs' account, Yellowstone is an place of odd geysers, a space to see wildlife, but most importantly, an arena for Roosevelt to strut his stuff. "Evidently, hungry for the wild and aboriginal," the President leaps into the scene with a gusto that impresses the sixty-five year old Burroughs. During their 1903 trip we see Roosevelt display his vast knowledge and enthusiasm for wildlife, tell stories, chase birds, ride and hike vigorously, and, in a remarkable episode, chase and corner a herd of elk who are left in gasping submission, while Roosevelt laughs with glee. Burroughs concludes that the President is "doubtless the most vital man on the continent, if not on the planet, to-day. He is many-sided, and every side throbs with his tremendous life and energy; the pressure is equal all around" (*Camping and Tramping with Roosevelt,* p. 223).

Roosevelt is quintessentially American and a model for the nation because of his energy and industry, which he shares with manufacturing, railroads, and geyser basins. Implicit in Burroughs' essay is support for dynamic individualism, the driving spirit of enterprise. The President, though, uses his energy to bust trusts, tame runaway capitalism. and preserve wild land from development. For Roosevelt, preservation of wild lands essentially meant keeping the game alive for the delight of the nature-lover, but also for the hunter who can exercise his manly virtues and keep the nation strong *(Outdoor Pastimes* p. 186) Yellowstone for Roosevelt was an arena to practice, if not hunting, the vigorous equivalent which keeps the nation strong. Burroughs reports episodes showing Roosevelt's energy as "glimpses of the great, optimistic, sunshiney West" to show there is no separation from the vital spirit in nature and the roaring energy opishing the nation forward. *(Camping and Tramping with Roosevelt* p. 228.)

The optimism and belief in control that were part of Roosevelt's energy received a severe testing in 1988 when large and well-publicized fires raced through Yellowstone. These fires have generated a lot of writing, which is worthy of careful study. The essays about the fire have fallen into narratives of fierce conflict: the firefighters against the flames, the National Park Service against local businesses, the press, politicians, and the explanatory gesture toward ecology and the benefits of wildfire. The event has tested national mettle and the skill of writers and filmmakers to recast what seemed an apocalypse into a resurrection. The event raised such profound questions about tourist nature and the purposes of the park that writers inevitably are forced to rethink the values at the heart of our vision of the land. The 1988 fires provided a significant opportunity for nature writers. Besides the basic interest in essays about the fire, the subject provided a chance to redefine Yellowstone in terms more Thoreauvian than allowed by tourist nature. Here is a chance to assert the value of wilderness and natural process over human preferences and comfort.

Many writers on the fire stick with the traditions of Yellowstone literature. Peter Matthiessen's essay in *The New York Times* and reprinted as the introduction to *Yellowstone's Red Summer* narrates his trip through the park during the fires recording the condition of various spots, now blackened, charred, apparently destroyed. He also recounts tales of firefighting and fire behavior. But deeper lies what Matthiessen presents as a powerful truth about rebirth told by Park officials Don Despain, John Varley, Bob Barbee, and others. Their premises are resolutely Thoreauvian and suggest how thoroughly the rhetoric of natural process and the Romantic ideas behind it have become institutionalized. Despain, a Park research biologist, focuses on the land with language familiar from Thoreau and Muir: "This black ground absorbs more sunlight and it warms up faster, and now it's fertilized with ash.' He expected a quick return of grasses and heartleaf arnica, firewood, and other deep-rooted plants ("A Case for Burning," p. 14). The fire was similarly defended as an agent of renewal, and associated continuously with growth—a value in a wide range of popular publications—*Life, National Geographic, Sunset, Outside, Smithsonian,* and many books, almost all of which cite Despain, Varley, and Barbee. Equally revealing are the commercial videos sold in park stores. One moves from luscious images of harrowing flames underscored by military language and threatening music to scenes of chirping birds, pastoral music, and a soothing text that promises fresh growth and a green park.

The rhetoric of renewal serves an educational function, but also is part of a very practical effort to preserve not just wilderness but the National Park Service and the Yellowstone Administration. Matthiessen participates in the effort to naturalize the much attacked institution. The result is a redefinition of tourist nature, which now incorporates nonpicturesque elements, indeed process itself, as part of the traveler's interest. Boardwalks through burned areas, interpretative signs about the fire, and a fire museum institutionalize the maneuver supported by the articles, books, and videotapes. Despite fears that visitor numbers would fall in the post-fire years, Yellowstone set records for visitation in 1989, 1990, and 1991. The reason seems simple: the Park became a focus of media attention, and thus a lure for visitors seeking the authentic, that which appears on television. One can see the "disaster" close-up and report back how things really are. Tee-shirts, bumper stickers and postcards provide totems that the visitor was there. The fire became a part of tourist nature, swept up into the processes that seek to turn everything into a commodity.

Gretel Ehrlich writes against those processes. Her essay on the fire resolutely avoids enshrining the event. In fact, "Summer" (originally published as "A Season of Portents" in *Harper's*) undermines the premises of picturesque travel and tourist nature. The picturesque depends on vision as the source of information, order, and pleasure. And equally it assumes the ability to replicate the sight in photos, paintings, words, and the like. Desire—or longing, to use Susan Stewart's term—should be obliterated by the moment of seeing, of fulfillment in the scene. Desire can be satisfied again by signs, souvenirs, descriptions, images of the authentic. Ehrlich's subject, though, is desire, frustration, the unseen, and the inability of words to be things. She writes a meditation that undermines the culture of acquisition essential to tourist nature.

Ehrlich's essay, structured as a journal, tells of the fire, but interweaves it with a summer away from her husband, reading of Dante, meditations on blood, thoughts on the end of the world, on fire above and below. All is pulled in, made part of the self. The erotics of flame fill her body, and the gaiety of last things delight and horrify her. This summer of smoke is filled with unanswered questions and unseen things. She searches for summer and finds nothing ("Summer," p. 38). The heat of the season is "an answerless question" (p. 39). Suffering an accident, she dreams of blindness and thinks of the divining powers of the sightless (p. 46). Hearing from a geologist who maps the landscapes of the earth's molten core, she tries to see through the smoke, "to sense the ghosts and the landscapes it hides, the shape and weight of desire" (p. 47).

The personal story carries a larger cultural weight. Frustration and longing were a theme of that summer. Dan Sholley, head ranger in 1988, nicely describes the anger of nearby residents; who feared the destruction of their property; the tension of park concessioners who faced a vast loss of visitors, the rage of politicians who warned of heads rolling; the visitors, fascinated and annoyed as the scenery disappeared in smoke; and the choking, wheezing locals. More than that, newspaper headlines proclaiming the destruction of America's first national park, speak of national insecurities and frustrations, that the glorious symbol of the nation was so vulnerable. The fire, writes Ehrlich, leaves "behind ideas about what a national park should be, and even those are charred" (p. 51).

The park as a collection of wonders framed by beautiful scenery had been gradually replaced by ideas less amenable to tourist nature. The decision in 1972 to let naturally started fires burn was part of a systematic attempt to let the wilderness alone, rather than structuring it to suit the pleasures of visitors. We see this process, for example, in the closing of the Mount Washburn car road, as well as the others through the Lower Geyser Basin and to Lone Star Geyser and, most significantly, the closing of garbage dumps where bears gathered to feed and be observed. But the choice to leave things alone exists in uneasy tension with the picturesque tour, and its institutional apparatus. Ehrlich notes how fire suppression was done "to preserve natural beauty, because under 'beauty' there is no slot for burned ground" (p. 49). But what is lost is, for Ehrlich, a "thick … monocultural … screen" of "unnaturally preserved timber" (p. 49). The fire has though revealed how problematic is the idea of beauty and the priority of vision by rearranging "light the way light reorders landscape" (p. 51). And the fire tells her something about language:

Walking back to camp I realize I'm lost. Smoke has swallowed all landmarks. But why must I see to know something? I let my feet take me. At sunset the gray flannel sky turns red. It's a thick broth made of rubies and plasma—comet tails, plant seeds, human and animal blood rising up from fire … . Night is the backdrop against which desire for what is not has been thrown like a dart. Against night, against all progress toward morning, the sparks that drop from my forehead are not the eloquent words I'd once hoped for but only pieces of thought—what is left after grammar and syntax are burned away (p. 56).

The fire shows the inadequacy of words to be the land, to represent it, to name desire and quench it, to show anything eloquently and clearly. Ehrlich writes darkly through a darkling land. The views are now obscured, rendered temporary and cultural by the fire. The search for the authentic, Stewart's "nostalgic myth of contact and presence" is seen to be myth, "desire for what is not." Ehrlich, though, makes the darkness and the longing the point of contact between her and the earth, both on fire, both dark, both yearning. At the end of the piece, she and her husband kill a doe. Hauling the carcass out, Ehrlich sees aspen trees looking "like spires of light—spirit streamers or torches carrying the wild soul of a dead deer and lifting it to a place over the roof of my head onto which my voice climbs, calling. ..." (p. 59). In the longing, the call, she feels a union with something that transcends order.

Tourist nature is an ordered thing—comfortably there for the consumer/traveler to see and acquire. It provides a nicely mapped universe through which we walk with delight and comfort toward an appointed end. The fire, as Ehrlich points out, disrupted the idea of nature as a safe array of thrills that could be divided, framed, and consumed. By internalizing the threat of disorder, Ehrlich advances a Thoreauvian language adequate to her difficult subject. Matthiessen, using a journal-istic approach, shows how the wild and the promise of rebirth can become part of institutional discourse that tries to reshape tourist nature. Burroughs raises questions about the structured tour of wonders, seeing instead a massive energy that breaks boundaries. Muir uses the bound-aries, the spaces of Yellowstone's tourist infrastructure to define the nature of an authentic meeting with the wild. The four essays considered here then use and question the traditions of travel and acquisition that dominate the language of Yellowstone, while struggling toward forms and language adequate to the subject of wilderness.

## Notes

[1]Nathaniel Pitt Langford describes the glories of Yellowstone Lake in terms of future development: "It possesses adaptabilities for the highest display of artificial culture, amid the greatest wonders of Nature that the world affords, and is beautified by the grandeur of the most extensive mountain scenery, and not many years can elapse before the march of civil improvement will reclaim this delightful solitude, and garnish it with all the attractions of cultivated taste and refinement" (*Discovery of Yellowstone Park* , p. 96).

[2]Langford, in his first report as superintendent wrote: "In the catalogue of earthly wonders it [Yellowstone Park] is the greatest ... here, the grandest, most wonderful, and most unique elements of nature are combined, seemingly

to produce upon the most stupendous scale an exhibition unlike any other upon the globe" (9).

[3]See, for example, *Landscape* in *Britain c.1750–1850*, p. 58. "Picturesque theory was not simply, as its protagonists claimed, the attempt to introduce a new aesthetic category to fill the gap between the Sublime and the Beautiful, but the building into experience of the countryside of a comfortable myth, imposing upon the more troublesome aspects of that experience a set of rules which quickly bred its own scholasticism. The Picturesque tourists trained themselves to see the world about them not only *via* pictorial models but, with willful editing, actually as pictures: the gypsy could then be an interesting piece of local colour rather than a peripatetic threat to the *status quo*, the decaying cottage and the neglected wood textual variations of an 'abstract' theme: for all the praise of 'roughness' as against 'smoothness' edges were blurred, centres softened. It was a holding operation, by and for the squirearchy which had lost ground and continued to lose ground in the dynamic of country life." This political account of the picturesque has been elaborated and applied to painting by David Solkin, John Barrell, and Michael Rosenthal.

[4]As Hans Huth points out, though Burroughs was the most popular nature writer of his time, he always claimed "that he did not owe much to Thoreau." Although they shared an interest in close observation of the natural world, Burroughs did not have a transcendental purpose and did not especially like the wilderness. He was also bored by John Muir's obsession with the wild (Huth, *Nature and the American*, p. 103).

# Bibliography

Bartlett, Richard A. *Yellowstone: A Wilderness Besieged.* Tucson: Univ. of Arizona Press, 1985.

Bryant, Paul. "Nature Writing and the American Frontier." *The Frontier Experience and the American Dream,* Eds. David Mogen, Mark Busby, and Paul Bryant. College Station: Texas A & M Univ. Press, 1989. pp. 205–216.

Burroughs, John. *Camping and Tramping with Roosevelt.* Boston: Houghton Mifflin, 1907.

Culler, Jonathan. "The Semiotics of Tourism." *Framing the Sign: Criticism and Its Institutions.* Oklahoma Project for Discourse and Theory 3. Norman: Univ. of Oklahoma Press, 1988.

Early, Katherine E. *"For the Benefit and Enjoyment of the People": Cultural Attitudes and the Establishment of Yellowstone Park.* Georgetown Monographs in American Studies 1. Washington D.C.: Georgetown Univ. Press, 1984.

Ehrlich, Gretel. "Summer." *Islands, the Universe, Home.* New York: Viking, 1991. pp. 35–59.

341

Greenblatt, Stephen. "Towards a Poetics of Culture." *The New Historicism*, ed. H. Aram Veeser. London: Routledge, 1989. pp. 1–14.

Gowans, Fred. R. *A Fur Trade History of Yellowstone Park: Notes, Documents, Maps*. Orem, Utah: Mountain Grizzly, 1989.

Haines, Aubrey L. *The Yellowstone Story*. Vol. 1. Yellowstone National Park: Yellowstone Library and Museum Association, 1977.

Huth, Hans. *Nature and the American: Three Centuries of Changing Attitudes*. Lincoln: Univ. of Nebraska Press, 1957.

Kipling, Rudyard. *From Sea to Sea: Letters of Travel*. New York: Scribners, 1910.

Langford, Nathaniel Pitt. *The Discovery of Yellowstone Park*. Report Lincoln: Univ. of Nebraska Press, 1972.

Report of the Superintendent of Yellowstone National Park *for the Year 1872*. Senate Executive Document No. 35, 42nd Congress, 3rd session.

Limerick, Patricia Nelson. *The Legacy of Conquest: The Unbroken Past of the American West*. New York: Norton, 1987.

MacCannell, Dean. *The Tourist: A New Theory of the Leisure Class*. New York: Schocken Books, 1976.

Matthiessen, Peter. "Introduction: A Case for Burning." By Alan and Sandy Carey. *Yellowstone's Red Summer*. Flagstaff, AZ: Northland Publishing, 1989.

Moritz, Alfred F. *America the Picturesque in Nineteenth Century Enqraving*. New York: New Trend, 1983.

Muir, John. *Our National Parks*. Boston: Houghton Mifflin, 1901.

Parris, Leslie. *Landscape in Britain c.1750–1850*. London: Tate Gallery, 1973.

Pomeroy, Earl. *In Search of the Golden West: The Tourist in Western America*. Lincoln: Univ. of Nebraska Press, 1957.

Richardson, James, ed. *Wonders of the Yellowstone Reqion*. London: Blackie, 1874.

Robertson, Bruce. "The Picturesque Traveler in America." *Views and Visions: American Landscape before 1830*. Ed. Edward J. Nygren. Washington D.C.: Corcoran Gallery of Art, 1986. 187–210.

Roosevelt, Theodore. *Outdoor Pastimes of an American Hunter*. New York: Scribner's, 1923.

Runte, Alfred. *National Parks: The American Experience*. Lincoln: Univ. of Nebraska Press, 1979.

Sears, John F. *Sacred Places: American Tourist Attractions in the Nineteenth Century*. Oxford: Oxford Univ. Press, 1989.

Sholley, Dan R. *Guardians of Yellowstone.* New York: Morrow, 1991.

Stewart, Susan. *On Loaning: Narratives of the Miniature, the Gigantic, the Souvenir, the Collection.* Baltimore: Johns Hopkins, 1984.

Wylie, W. W. *Yellowstone Park or the Great American Wonderland. A Complete Hand, or Guide Book for Tourists.* Kansas City, MO.: Ramsey, Millet & Hudson, 1882.

*Yellowstone Aflame: Before, Durina & After the Great Yellowstone Fires of '88.* Videocassette. Finley-Holiday Films, 1989. 30 min.

---

**BRUCE A. RICHARDSON** obtained his doctorate in English from the University of California at Los Angeles. He is now an assistant professor at the University of Wyoming and has published a variety of articles on western landscapes. He regards Thoreau as the principal starting point in understanding American landscapes.

# Joseph Wood Krutch
## The Unlikeliest of Thoreauvian Nature Essayists

❖

### Paul O. Williams

In 1930, when he first read *Walden,* Joseph Wood Krutch was a prominent drama critic in New York. Born in Knoxville, Tennessee, in 1893, he grew up there and attained his bachelor's degree at the University of Tennessee. Then he immediately went to New York to study English at Columbia. He received his Ph.D. in 1924 as a specialist in 17th century British theater. His first academic job was at the Brooklyn Polytechnic Institute. He worked there from 1920 to 1924, and, as his biographer, John D. Margolis, put it, did not gain a sterling reputation as a teacher (35). Following that experience, he left academics for thirteen years, aside from part-time teaching, to work as a writer and editor for *The Nation,* and to produce his famous, pessimistic book, *The Modern Temper*, published in 1929.

He was as urban a person as one could find, it would seem. He and his wife, Marcelle, lived in Greenwich Village. They worked in the city. In *The Modern Temper* Krutch displayed none of his later conservationist or conservative views on what passes for progress in the United States.

Perhaps two influences brought about a change in Krutch. The first and more important was allergies and the attempts of Marcelle to preserve his health. This caused her to convince him to rent a house in Cornwall, Connecticut, in 1925, largely as a week-end and summer house, and three years later to purchase a house in Redding as a place of longer stays, and as the beginning of the point of view from which he wrote his first natural history essays, collected in *The Twelve Seasons* (1949). Clearly, to Marcelle, he was healthier in Connecticut than in the befouled air of New York. His increasing allergies later caused him, again urged by Marcelle, to summer in the Southwest, and later to move there and begin his new career as a nature essayist and writer about the beauties of the desert.

The second influence was his reading of *Walden*. This did not bring about any immediate conversion experience, surely, but Thoreau slowly grew on Krutch, both before and after his biography of 1948, until he became the most often mentioned author of the large number that Krutch quoted and cited in his writings.

It should be stressed that Krutch himself states in his autobiography, *More Lives Than One*, that he did not become interested in nature because of Thoreau, but became interested in Thoreau because he had become interested in nature from his life in Connecticut (292).

Krutch had been strongly influenced in his early attitudes toward Thoreau by his great friend Mark van Doren, whose master's thesis, *Thoreau: A Critical Study*, was published by Houghton Mifflin in 1916. Van Doren's study focuses on the *Journals*. He notes in his preface that "if now and then unwelcome conclusions are arrived at, the Journal is to blame." But in part van Doren's own preconceptions are responsible, and in part Robert Louis Stevenson's essay, on which he relies quite heavily. For his own part, he writes, "It is easy enough to point out that Thoreau's main effort came to nothing, but the likelihood remains that Thoreau will always count for something among sophisticated persons who take him with the sufficient allowance of salt" (123).

Marcelle recounted to me how van Doren and Krutch would make jokes about Thoreau, about whom van Doren had some strongly disparaging opinions. It seems likely that such views, held by Krutch's best friend and roommate, significantly postponed his early appreciation of Thoreau.

It is interesting that among the Krutch manuscripts in the Library of Congress is a single sheet, in pen, of marginal vituperations taken from a copy of van Doren's book and written by Franklin Benjamin Sanborn, of Concord fame, who thought the book uninformed and at least in part stupid. Walter Harding has told me that this annotated book is in the Thoreau Society Archives.

While Krutch to my knowledge never said he would not have written nature essays if it had not been for Thoreau, both the chronology and the discursive literary method of his early nature essays is strongly suggestive. Krutch claimed that after 1930, Thoreau and Samuel Johnson were the two chief influences on him (*More Lives,* pp. 292–293). It is also suggestive that Krutch's 1948 biography of Thoreau immediately precedes his nature writing. His own account of the matter is: "One winter night shortly after I had finished *Thoreau* I was reading a nature essay which pleased me greatly and it suddenly occurred to me for the first time to wonder if I could do something of the sort. I cast about for a subject and decided on the most conventional of all, namely Spring" (*More Lives,* p. 293).

A book in the American Men of Letters series, Krutch's *Henry David Thoreau* is still a fine biography. It is insightful, more compactly written than any of his nature writing, as comprehensive as possible in its small compass of 287 pages, and full of shrewd judgments.

For Krutch, the complete Thoreau had three basic aspects: the mystic, the lover of the primitive, and the critic of society. Krutch's discussion of these aspects reflects in part his own attitudes toward them. Krutch was already a social critic. He was becoming if not a lover of the primitive, at least of the natural. He was more troubled about the mysticism.

One feels, without real evidence, that he would have liked an admixture of mysticism or transcendentalism himself, but it was not part of his makeup. His account of Thoreau's mysticism is not wholly consistent. He says of Thoreau:

> One catches some very significant glimpses of several never quite resolved conflicts, including a conflict between the transcendental moralist and a kind of scientific pantheism which threatens to undermine the serene mysticism of the orthodox transcendentalist as alarmingly as that transcendentalism had undermined orthodox Christian faith (148).

Perhaps he is right, but I believe the problem of consistency is at least as much Krutch's, as I hope to show in a discussion below of *The Great Chain of Life*. At any rate, Krutch, though aware of the noumenal and phenomenal aspects of nature in transcendental thought, seems usually not to have regarded the noumenal as real. Hence he saw Thoreau as a pantheist, with nature as an end, and not a means to insight of something beyond it.

This is a natural conclusion for a rationalist and humanist, but not wholly reflective of Thoreau's thought. It also reflects the fact that he saw in himself "a kind of pantheism which was gradually coming to be an essential part of the faith—if you can call it that—which would form the basis of an escape from the pessimism of *The Modern Temper* upon which I had turned my back without ever conquering it" (*More Lives,* p. 295).

On the other hand, Krutch does acknowledge that though Thoreau's late *Journals* reflect a growing tendency to view nature objectively, he remained a mystic (*Thoreau,* p. 178). Krutch saw him "moving, in conviction as well as technique, away from the transcendental assumption that the meaning of nature can be reached by intuition and toward what is the fundamental scientific assumption—namely, that only through observation may one ultimately reach not merely dead facts but also those which understanding can make them live (175). But he adds, " ... there seems no reason to suppose that his sense of intimate communion ever left him completely" (175). He concludes that "the intuitionist and the observer, the humanist and the pantheist persist, if not side by side, then at least alternately, as the mood of the thinker changes from day to day"(179–180).

But of course this is true of everyone, and it is hard to avoid the notion that Krutch is discussing his own presumptions as well as

Thoreau's, trying in part to explain the to him somewhat embarrassing fact that Thoreau had such a strong intuitionist, transcendentalist aspect.

I hope to show, at least in part, that Krutch's own nature writing, which notably omits the mystical, not only reflects the two other aspects of thought he saw in Thoreau, the social critic and the lover of the natural, but is influenced by the organic assumption so typical of Romanticism, and so rich in Thoreau, and by making that assumption, Krutch has given a rational, but feeling, conclusion a hint of the mystical—but no more than a hint or gesture.

A hinge book, beginning the natural-history period of Krutch's life, was *The Twelve Seasons*, published only a year after his biography of Thoreau. Late in life, Krutch told Edward Abbey that *The Twelve Seasons* was his favorite book, calling it "the most deeply felt thing I've done" (Abbey, p. 190). The book is indeed different from his early literary criticism, and even his later work on the desert, in part perhaps because it is more personal, while the later books are more academic, reserved, and reportorial.

And yet the first of the essays, "The Day of the Peepers," especially, is pretty thin gruel. It is a testing of the water before plunging in. In places it verges on the sentimental. In it, as in all the essays of this first volume, Krutch discusses a number of subjects discursively, perhaps because he knows so little about his central subject. The difference between it and his later study of an amphibian, the spadefoot toad, in *The Voice of the Desert*, in terms of knowledge and observation, is strong.

The peepers essay is graceful, urbane, and entertaining. And while it is a mere peep first announcing the eventual harvest of his mass of later work, it does end with a statement which is extremely important in Krutch's development. Krutch sees himself whispering to the peepers, "Don't forget, we are all in this together" (13).

While this remark may seem not of great importance, nonetheless it is the first of many in which Krutch operates from an organic assumption, of the oneness of all being, and while no one would ever call him a mystic, as Thoreau often is, still there is an alliance in their attitudes. From that point on one can say Krutch is on the side of the natural world.

*The Twelve Seasons* is laid out as twelve essays, one for each month; the first, the peeper essay, being assigned to April, the last, March, finding Krutch looking forward to spring again. The first sentence of the book is repeated as the last. It seems clear that this cyclical structure owes something to *Walden*.

Each of the essays is about a philosophical subject rather than its ostensible subject. The beetle, Meloe, the subject of the May essay, is only a springboard to a general discussion of the method of nature and its connectedness. Krutch's knowledge of the insect is taken largely from the study of Henri Fabre. In the essay he develops further the concept of organicism, writing, "Even the most ardent of humanists will have to admit that in some respects and to some degree we are a part of a contingent natural universe" (27). Clearly he is addressing this modest claim to an urban audience. He is almost shamefaced. He adds that the modern mental life may possibly be withering "because its roots no longer go down to nature"(28).

As the essays develop, they are entertaining, thin in substance, generally ordinary in knowledge, often wordy to a fault, at times inaccurate or inadequate in coverage, and very charming. Krutch cites Thoreau eight times, and, perhaps most important, persistently makes statements that bear on the above mentioned organic attitude, which one never would have expected from early Krutch.

In the January essay, he explains his attitude of mind as clearly as I have seen it anywhere in his writings with relation to the possible mystical meanings the natural scene may convey. The passage is a little long, and probably most or all of it deserves quotation. But I will abbreviate it to keep it manageable Krutch writes:

> I am, I think, rather less a transcendentalist than even the average man is. No voice has ever spoken to me in unmistakable, unambiguous terms. I have never simply "felt" that anything was and must be absolutely true. Neither have I ever believed in the authenticity of the communications which others are convinced that they have received from beyond humanity and beyond Nature. A stubborn rationality has always had for me the last word. There are, I say, far too many instances when the mechanism is obvious to me not to suspect that some all-too-human mental quirks responsible for what I tend to regard as only less gross examples of self-deception. Awake or asleep I insist, you dreamed. ...

Krutch goes on to say that silence, solitude, and snow seem to be the best settings, for him, in which he feels "open to transcendental communication." He insists that the sense of "intimacy with living things" or a "fellowship with them," is not transcendental but "merely an extension of that solidarity with one's own kind" which is commonly felt. This he sees as "either purely rational or but little beyond rationality." He goes on to say:

> What I do mean is the half conviction that one has been spoken to by, or that one has to some extent penetrated into the meaning of, something which is neither the self nor anything like the self. And there is no time when one seems so surrounded by or so immersed in that which is not even remotely like the self as when one is out alone in a night of snow (pp. 152–153).

Krutch goes on to recount an incident, rather like that in Emerson's *Nature*, in which the "currents of universal being" pulsed through him. But in Krutch's case they didn't make it. "Suddenly," he writes, "I was alone with the universe. The realest things besides myself in all existence were not either human beings nor any other living things. I seemed about to grasp what the earth, the suns, and the stars mean to themselves as distinguished from what they mean to any of us creatures ... who live and grow and then die ... " (154). At that point, though, an owl hooted, and shattered the moment for him. Krutch remarks, "Sometimes I wonder whether God, the only time He ever began to speak to me, was interrupted by one of His own owls" (154). He verges on denying his own rationalism. It is a fine moment. But nothing happens. Nor is there a real feeling of disappointment in Krutch's tone. In his later work, he ceased to speculate on the reality of Thoreauvian mystical insight and quoted Thoreau for his wit, his observations of nature, and his political and philosophical views.

And yet he was not merely a rationalist in his regard for the natural world. He absolutely delighted in it. In fact, the final essay in *The Great Chain of Life*, the "Epilogue," focuses on the joy in life, especially in bird song as he observed it. He notes, "Nature's ways are described as one of the richest subjects for the exercise of intellectual curiosity; knowledge of the miscalled indispensable for survival. All these reasons are valid. But none of them seems to me so persuasive as the simple fact that the lives of creatures other than man remind us compellingly of the fact that joy is real and instinctive" (227). His concept of the widespread joy in natural life also echoes his feeling, expressed several times in his biography of Thoreau, that the Concord naturalist felt the exhilaration of nature and was basically satisfied with his life (247). He accepts Thoreau's affirmations. For Krutch there is a hint of a dark Thoreau, but only a hint. He takes Thoreau's upwelling pleasure, as so often recount edit his *Journals* and essays, as an accurate reflection of his feelings. He also notes that one of the basic criticisms Thoreau had of his society was of its joylessness (12).

But this is to leap too far ahead. Marcelle Krutch, who had gotten her husband to rent a house in Lornwall, Connecticut, and later to buy one in Redding, also convinced him to take a summer vacation in the American Southwest in 1938. She was concerned with his health. He found great relief from his allergies there, but also an exhilaration in the desert scene, to which he immediately responded. They returned yearly to the area until the war interrupted them. After the war, they resumed their visits, finding Tucson in 1948. Two years later, the Krutches returned to Tucson when Joe Krutch had a sabbatical. This resulted in his first desert book, *The Desert Year* (1952). He returned to Columbia University the next year, but resigned from his professorship, as well as from his longtime connection with the *Nation,* and returned to build a house in Tucson, well out of town until the city expanded, and to resume his writing career.

*The Voice of the Desert* appeared in 1955, *The Great Chain of Life* in 1956. *Grand Canyon, Today and All Its Yesterdays,* was published in 1958, and *The Forgotten Peninsula: A Naturalist in Baja* California in 1961. A collection, *The Best Nature Writing of Joseph Wood Krutch,* was printed in 1964, shortly before his death in 1970. This constitutes the core of his nature writing, though one must point out that he did other nature essays, gave lectures, and even, with the help of a former student, Gerald Green, who had become a network executive, three television programs on the nature of the Southwest. He also wrote and edited a number of other things during this period, both literary and critical . He was a disciplined and busy man intent on earning his living and leaving Marcelle with an adequate legacy.

In fact, though one could never accuse Krutch of simply making a career change to nature writing because it was a reasonable conclusion that he could earn a living by writing in the desert while maintaining his health, still this common-sense choice and possibility did have much, one feels, to do with his nature writing career. Yes, he did become a naturalist, though a gifted amateur. He was an active conservationist, a thorough-going organicist. The perception with which he ended "The Day of the Peepers," that we are all in this together, is something he truly believed. But his move to the Southwest seems not to have been so much a conversion so much as an opportunity to remain productive.

Because of the limits of this paper, I would like to move ahead to a discussion of *The Great Chain of Life,* which, as I mentioned above, I feel has strong implications for Krutch's position on the nature of things, especially with relation to the possible influence of Thoreau.

A good portion of *The Great Chain of Life* is taken up with a complex argument about evolution. His questioning the absolute doctrine of evolution, which he calls mechanistic, is all the more surprising when we recall that as a young man he had returned to Tennessee to cover the Scopes trial for the *Nation* in 1925 and he heaped scorn on the prosecution.

This is not to say that he opted in favor of a biblical view of the matter, but rather that he presents a curious set of notions that is both humanistic and teleological .

Krutch, in spite of his keen awareness of the pitfalls of his position, and the fact that he typically offered his views as possibilities or rhetorical questions, nonetheless maintained that life forms seem to be fulfilling a purpose, and that the end point of evolution was not mere successful adaptation, or survival, but the production of greater awareness.

He begins by confessing that he is not a scientist but a "mere nature lover" (xiv). He tends to unify man and other animals in his suggestion that if man has a soul, so do all other creatures that die" (35–36). Thoreau would have been comfortable with this concept as his remarks on the pine tree in *The Maine Woods* indicate (122). What Krutch chiefly explores, though, is man's similarity to other creatures. He sees evolution as a rising to higher levels with man at its summit (44). This direction he sees as toward intelligencel 19v. After noting that Julian Huxley posits greater complexity as an end of evolution, because this has survival value, Krutch writes:

> If Nature has advanced from the inanimate to the animate; if she "prefers" the living to the lifeless and the forms of life which survive rather to [sic.] those that perish; then there is nothing which forbids the assumption that she also "prefers conscious intelligence to blind instinct; that just as complex organization was developed even though it had no obvious survival value for the species, so also the awareness of itself which complex organization made possible is also one of her goals (123).

But Krutch has here made a huge leap, and in a Thoreauvian direction. That is, he has posited something his calling "Nature," something that has a preference, something overall, if not an Oversoul, then an overall intention, and an intention that has something like an altruistic or at least an abstract end. After all, he has already acknowledged in his text that the ant is probably a more effective survivor than man, all through instinct, not intellect. Krutch has carefully omitted the divine, even the transcendental, but he has let the ideal in by the back door, and so he is in the transcendental camp, even though nodding and bobbing, being tentative and rhetorical, to avoid the attribution.

Perhaps I am taking this too far. Perhaps it is all a part of an elaborate set of arguments designed to put his own inclinations, which are intellectual, Western, and white, at the top of things. After all, he does suggest that children playing Indian are perhaps in a stage of social evolution they will grow out of as they become civilized (90). He does propose that both animals and men are capable of being civilized "and that a civilized man or a civilized animal reveals capacities and traits which one would never have suspected in the savage" (139). Civilization, he says, offers the greatest encouragement of potentialities. Thoreau, of course, would never confess to such an attitude, though in some part he had it.

Clearly, what Krutch would like to be so is that "intelligence, beauty, and everything which goes to make up the vivid consciousness of being alive goes on surviving and increasing—whether these characteristics have any 'survival value' or not" (186).

Later in his volume, Krutch suggests,

> If the universe really is alive, then one is free to believe also that living creatures were from the beginning endowed with some power to intervene in the evolutionary process; that it was not exclusively an external force which moved them upward toward greater complexity; that their own dim minds, dim wills, and dim preferences helped them along the way (196).

Again, the notion that they were "endowed" makes one ask what endowed them, and some sort of careful closet transcendentalism seems to stand in the background. Being is all at once collective, purposeful, directed, familiar, and perhaps leading toward the literary and even the urbane.

I am not suggesting that Krutch was unaware of the possible self-contradiction in his position, because he offered it so tentatively. He didn't push it. In a sense he retreated from it in his later work by limiting himself either to the literary journalism of *Grand Canyon* or *The Forgotten Peninsula*, or writing of other matters altogether. Nor am I suggesting that he wanted to place himself in the basically theistic position that Thoreau often does. But he verged on it. He toyed with it. He did not, ultimately, reject it in *The Voice of the Desert* he explicitly discusses the fact that his position might be taken to be teleological.

In sum, Krutch does a lot of philosophical prestidigitation. His consistency, and the solidity of his contribution lie not in any brilliant new insights into a philosophy of nature, but simply in his obvious love of and amusement by it, as well as his hard hitting conservation writing. The discursive, literary style he uses, comfortable to the urban and educated, entertaining, instructive but not demanding, has introduced millions of readers to a fascinating natural area of the United States and Mexico. He makes a strong case for not forgetting nature in one's calculations. His nature writing has a tendency to be bookish, as one might expect, but he was on the scene and made many trips and observations.

Ultimately, I believe one can confidently say that even if he developed some interest in the natural scene in Connecticut, Thoreau lay close to its inception and helped Krutch with a method of developing it—the literary essay. What he did with it shows a tinge of Thoreau in method and in his grapplings with both organicism and the sense of a purpose or direction behind nature. But in his own charm, his own humor, and his comfortable exploration of a region often ignored, what he did was pure Krutch. The mass of his writing is impressive. His contribution, though, seems to be fading, perhaps because of the mass of it and its sense of daily output, of conscientious industry and professionalism. Crotchety Edward Abbey will be longer remembered, I feel. Still, we are grateful for Krutch, and the vitality of his shelf of books on the desert.

# Bibliography

Abbey, Edward. *One Life at a Time, Please.* New York: Holt, 1988.

Krutch, Joseph Wood. *Henry David Thoreau.* New York: Dell, 1965.

Krutch, Joseph Wood. *More Lives Than One.* New York: Sloane, 1964.

Krutch, Joseph Wood. *The Great Chain of Life.* Boston: Houghton Mifflin, 1956.

Krutch, Joseph Wood. *The Twelve Seasons*. New York: Sloan, 1948.

Margolis, John D. *Joseph Wood Krutch: A Writer's Life*. Knoxville: Univ. of Tennessee, 1980.

Thoreau, Henry David. *The Maine Woods*. ed. Joseph J. Moldenhauer. Princeton: Princeton University, 1972.

van Doren, Mark. *Henry David Thoreau: A Critical Study*. Boston: Houghton-Mifflin, 1916.

---

**PAUL O. WILLIAMS** is Professor Emeritus, Principia College, Elsah, Illinois. He is a former president of The Thoreau Society and has written extensively on Thoreau. He is now a full-time author.

# The Striped Snake at the Bottom of a Shrinking Pond

## Water and its Scarcity in Mary Austin

❖

**Reuben J. Ellis**

I

They are "pleasant spring days" as Thoreau swings his borrowed axe, days when "the life that had lain torpid began to stretch itself." But the serpent of analogy slides into Walden Pond. Thoreau writes:

> I saw a striped snake run into the water, and he lay on the bottom, apparently without inconvenience, as long as I stayed there, for more than a quarter of an hour; perhaps because he had not yet fairly come out of the torpid state. It appeared to me that for a like reason men remain in their present low and primitive condition; but if they should feel the influence of the spring of springs arousing them, they would of necessity rise to a higher and more ethereal life. (*Walden*, p. 33)

The function of Thoreau's trope is linked intimately to the cool and moist New England spring, and it would be unfair to ask the analogy to work so honestly beyond that locale. Yet if Ed Abbey can transport Thoreau to the muddy rivers of the western American desert, I would like to claim a similar privilege, that of transporting Thoreau's striped snake to the same arid region. If the primitive, reptilian impulses of humanity lie in their spiritual torpidity at the bottom of a cool New England pond, how will they respond as the water level drops? If the striped snake lies instead at the clammy bottom of a shrinking desert water hole, or in the cracking mud of a failed irrigation ditch, how does the human analog behave when the water rights to the pond have already been sold?

With the shift to the arid West that they imply, these questions bring us through Thoreau, to another voice, that of western American nature

354

writer, novelist, and regional theorist Mary Hunter Austin. Austin's forty-year relationship with the deserts of the American West expresses itself vividly in her non-fictional prose, most notably in that part of her large oeuvre usually considered "nature writing." In focusing on the desert West, Austin incorporates water and its scarcity as the central elements in both her natural history and philosophy. Dryness defines the character of place and experience in the landscape that Austin saw as she looked across the Mojave and Sonoran deserts. For Austin, the scarcity of water in the desert is at once a limiting and an enabling agent. The harsh environment of the arid West imposes the necessity of adaptation, a function Austin elevates to the level of value, as an essential mode of accommodation and harmony that registers on three indices: biological evolution, spiritual growth, and finally, most problematically, the political economy of Western water use and how it divides rural from urban development. Adaptation in Austin's work reflects liberation and surfaces in her notion of the significance of ideologies and symbols, central among them the snake.

## II

Of Mary Austin, Larry Evers rightly maintains that "it is in the tradition of Thoreau, Burroughs, and Muir that her achievement is most secure" (xxiii–xxiv) and posits Austin in the continuum of nature writers that for him includes Aldo Leopold, Joseph Wood Krutch, Edward Abbey, Annie Dillard, Frank Waters, and Barry Lopez. Marjorie Pryse suggests that, "like Thoreau in *Walden*, she creates analogies between nature and human life and yet remains faithful to literal accuracy in her natural description" (*Country of Lost Bordeis*, xiv). Yet as a girl at least, any familiarity Austin may have had with Thoreau, for example, must have been largely covert. Austin's mother discouraged her from taking a too ardent interest in nature. In her 1932 autobiography, Austin remembers:

> Especially you must not talk appreciatively about landscapes and flowers and the habits of little animals and birds to boys; they didn't like it. If one of them took you walking, your interest should be in your companion, and not exceed a ladylike appreciation of the surroundings, in so far as the boy, as the author of the walk, might feel himself complimented by your appreciation of it. (*Earth Horizons*, p. 112)

The social dangers of a love for the natural world extended to literature as well. Austin continues: "You must not quote; especially poetry and Thoreau. An occasional light reference to Burroughs was permissible, but not Thoreau" (112). Not willing to confine herself even to extensive, improper reference, Austin eventually developed as one of the most unique voices in western American nature writing. Beginning with the short story "The Mother of Felipe," prepared under the tutelage of Ina Coolbrith and published in the *Overland Monthly* in 1892, Austin's work spanned four decades. In the American West, it was an era when twentieth century technology and demographics convulsively changed both the geophysical and human landscape of the region and the terms by which nature writing could legitimately describe them.

Mary Austin's work is roughly bounded at its beginning with Frederick Jackson Turner's still controversial "Frontier Hypothesis" and at its end with the impoundment of the Colorado River behind Hoover Dam, the first great icon of the fierce struggle over appropriation and use of natural resources that has characterized the history of the west in the 20th century. Her writing is an important regional index to the change represented by these two events. Most remembered today for her collections of autobiographical essays: *The Land of Little Rain* (1903), *Lost Borders* (1909), and *The Land of Journeys' Ending* (1924). Austin also articulated feminist positions in such works as the drama *The Arrow-Maker* (1911), the novel *A Woman of Genius* (1912), and the non-fiction *The Young Woman Citizen* (1918). Her *The American Rhythm* (1923) is an attempt to define and exemplify a uniquely American poetics based on Native American oral tradition. Her essay "Regionalism in American Fiction" (1932) is an intelligent and still useful study of western American regional identity and its signification that defines it in contrast to the then largely denigrated category of "local color" to which experimental modernism and its theoreticians showed a tendency to confine such writers as Sarah Orne Jewett, Mary Wilkins Freeman, and Austin herself. Among her fiction, Austin's California novels, *Isidro* (1905), *The Flock* (1906), and *The Ford* (1917), stand out today as the most important.

As a child, Austin developed an intriguing sense of self as what she calls the "I-Mary," a liberated, private observer "associated with the pages of books" as Austin explains (*Earth* p.46), who first read around the fringes of, then wrote into clearer existence, the world that she perceived. It was this inner I-Mary that first encountered a sense of spiritual presence in the natural world. Standing at a walnut tree at the bottom of the orchard near her family home, "God happened to Mary under the walnut tree" (*Earth* p. 51). In a 1928 essay Austin explains more fully:

> To this day I can recall the swift inclusive awareness of each for the whole—I in them and they in me and all of us enclosed in a warm, lucent bubble of livingness. I remember the child looking everywhere for the sources of this happy wonder, and at last she questioned—"God?"—because it was the only awesome word she knew. Deep inside, like the murmurous swinging of a bell, she heard the answer, "God, God?" ("Experience Facing Death," p. 763)

That this Voice speaking somehow through her, but not of her, seemed confused at being called by name did not detract for Austin from the powerful personal experience of divinity. Throughout her life and writing career she called upon this Presence. As she grew older and as she developed a more clearly geographical and regional perspective, her understanding of this Presence became more consistently spatial in nature. Influenced by Native American cosmology, she began to see her experience as operating within what she called the "Earth Horizon," a term she explains in her autobiography:

> In the Rain Song of the Sia, Earth Horizon is the incalculable blue ring of sky meeting earth, which is the source of experience. It is pictured as felt, rays of earth energy running together from the horizon to the middle place where the heart of man, the recipient of experience is established, and there treasured. (*Earth*, p. 33)

It was this Sacred Middle that was enacted for Austin most poignantly in the desert of California, and later New Mexico and Arizona. In *Earth Horizon*, Austin describes the spirit of the lower San Jaoquin Valley as:

> a lurking, evasive Something, wistful, cruel, ardent; something that rustled and ran, that hung half-remotely, insistent on being noticed, fled from pursuit, and when you turned from it, leaped suddenly and fastened on your vitals. This is no mere figure of speech, but the true movement of experience. (*Earth*, p. 187)

As she came to know it better, this, what she calls, "beauty-in-the-wild, yearning to be made human" (p. 187) became for Austin the all-encompassing life principle of the desert, and the desire to communicate and participate in its shaping power became the motive force behind her most powerful work. The primary assumption controlling Austin's thinking is this intense connection between the natural world and human life. For Austin, the emotional engagement of the individual in the environment provides the basis for a gradual spiritual merger between human and place. Austin seems to have felt that writing could embody, in an almost performative sense, this experience of union. In 1932 she writes: "I have seen America emerging; the America which is the expression of the life activities of the environment, aesthetics as a natural mode of expression" (*Earth,* p. 368). Of her own writing she observes: "my books have no sequence other than the continuity of the search for the norm of moral and spiritual adjustments which I have tried herein to describe" (*Earth,* p. 367).

Most of her work seems, however, styled by the assumption that her audience does not precisely share the author's search. Even if she does not write programatically, she does write instructionally—for outsiders, not liturgically—for participants. Her message is observation. Pay close attention to the plants and animals of a desert locale; see how place exerts its power over life, how it shapes behavior and morphogenesis. When you have that down, concentrate on the aboriginal and indigenous peoples of the desert—Paiutes, prospectors, sheepherders, Hopi—notice how their adaptations to the environment create the basis for a material and finally psychic harmony with the land. By the time you truly understand all this, the distinction between observer and observed will have broken down; you will have become a part of it.


III


As explorers and observers from John Wesley Powell to Wallace Stegner have pointed out, aridity in varying degrees is the principal shaping force of almost the whole of the American west. Mary Austin focused her attention on how the deserts of California and the Southwest exemplify this in extreme. In *The Land of Little Rain,* Austin defines that land as the country "east away from the Sierras, south from Panamint and Amargosa, east and south many an uncounted mile" (p. 3). Here the inherent "nature of the land" (p. 3) is distinguished by the scarcity of water. In Austin's *The Land of Journeys' Ending* (1924) in which the author extends her examination of the desert environment to the arid regions of Arizona and New Mexico, an area she explored at length when she settled in Santa Fe in 1924, definition is similarly a matter of dryness. The Little Colorado River is a "true desert river" (p.415), one that either floods or runs underground. The vast Sonoran Desert is also marked geophysically by limited water and biologically by adaptation to that limitation, what Austin calls the experiments of the Vegetative Spirit (p.139).

"The choice of habitat among arid-region plants," she observes, "is governed by the nature of the adjustments they have learned to make to the restricted watersupply" (p. 49). Desert plants respond dramatically to available water. During the short rainy season, Austin writes, "the processes of foliation and floration are pushed almost to explosion; followed by a long quiescence in which life merely persists" (pp. 37–8). But this unpretentious persistence counts largely for Austin. Praising the adaptation of the "saguaro" cactus, she concludes "I salute it in the name of the exhaustless Powers of Life" (p. 140). Austin finally sees environmental limitation in terms of the necessity of *human* psychic and spiritual response. "Not the law, but the land sets the limit," she writes (p. 3) in *The Land of Little Rain,* her comparison positioning the notion of human restriction prominently within her understanding of the desert environment. Suggesting the same sense of limitation in terms of its mode of expression, Austin notes "that one falls into the tragic key in writing of desertness" (p. 12). Thoreauvian in her gesture, Austin allows the flora of the desert to overlap with human experience, observing how the "dwarfing effect" (p. 6) imposed by a dry environment on plants can have a comparable effect on the human heart. She writes:

> It is recorded in the report of the Death Valley expedition that after a year of abundant rains, on the Colorado desert was found a specimen of Amaranthus ten feet high. A year later the same species in the same place matured in the drought at four inches. One hopes the land may breed like qualities in her human offspring, not tritely to "try," but to do. (*The Land of Little Rain*, p. 5)

Movement, too, in the desert is determined by the availability of water. Small animals make "water trails," white ribbons in the leaning grass" (p. 17) to the brackish pools of drying riverbeds. The coyote, the traditional *trickster* figure of southwestern Native America, for Austin is a "true water-witch" (p. 18). In the desert mountain ranges the glyphic water signs left both by historical Shoshones and by "an older, forgotten people" (p. 27) point the human way to lifesaving springs and water holes. The desert region of Arizona and New Mexico that Austin details as the "Land of Journeys' Ending" is for her defined in part by what she calls the "limits of habitableness" (*Journeys'* p. 3). During the dry season, Austin writes, "the land assumes … that aspect of life defeated which is the accepted note of desertness" (*Journeys'* p. 56). Like plants in the desert that "merely persist" (*Journeys'* p. 38) during the long dry season, the region's human occupants in Austin's view make the same adjustment.

Coping with a scarcity of water for Austin is finally a measure of human achievement; the infinitely valuable dynamics of human adjustment and response are inscribed by this limitation. In *The Land of Little Rain* subjectivity is grounded in the refinement of spiritual union with place. "The earth is no wanton to give up all her best to every comer," she warns in her Preface (p. xiv). The wilderness, she advises, is not for "the ordinary traveler" (*Little Rain*, p. 115). It is dryness that is the geophysical basis for this qualitative exclusivity. Spiritual merger with place in the desert means adaptation to aridity, and thereby Austin's insistence on limitation associated with dryness gives way to liberation. A true regional thinker, Austin repeatedly employs the metaphor of "borders" to delimit and describe the Western landscape, yet it is instructive to notice that the borders she establishes are consistently distinguished by water—"water borders," "stream borders," "lake borders." The bone dry Mojave Desert, on the other hand, extends to the east "illimitably" (*Little* p. xiv) and is therefore in Austin's lexicon the "Country of Lost Borders" (*Little* p. 3).

IV

Although it surfaces prominently in the registers of biological evolution and spiritual growth, Austin's understanding of the relationship between humans and water in the west is not fully described without reference to how it also surfaces in terms of political and economic constraint and potential. In her essay "Water Borders" Austin writes that a stream "knows its purpose and reflects the sky" (*Little* p. 135), yet in the larger scheme of Austin's thinking its purpose is more *functional* than this. In the next essay, "Other Water Borders," Austin explains: "It is the proper destiny of every considerable stream in the west to become an irrigating ditch" (*Little* p. 139). There exists a point in Austin's understanding of the desert at which spirituality must be regrounded in the economy of human material survival. "The manner of the country makes the usage of life there, and the land will not be lived in except in its own fashion," she writes (p. 59). The Indians of the desert, the Paiutes and the Shoshone, provide Austin with a model of successful human adaptation to its harsh, spare environment, a people who understood the desert's "own fashion" of life. The model is bound up with adaptation to the scarce availability of water. "The Shoshones live like their trees," she writes, "with great spaces between, and in pairs and in family groups they set up wattled huts by the infrequent springs" (*Little* p. 59).

Yet Austin is rarely romantically uncritical in her observation of indigenous Americans. For her, Native Americans also provide a disturbingly ambiguous archetype of cultural evolution. Although Austin writes in *The Land of Journeys' Ending* that the "secret charm of the desert is the secret of life triumphant" (p. 56), the metaphor of conquest is inconsistent with her larger view. The ancient Anasazis, the probable ancestors of today's Pueblo Indians—the case of whose "disappearance" from their great stone cities at places like Chaco or Aztec or Mesa Verde continues to be debated today—suggest to Austin a model to test the limitations of the notion of human environmental adaptation. For Austin they crossed "that hesitating line on the hither side of which we begin to speak of cultures as civilized. It is the line at which peoples cease merely to accommodate themselves to their environment, and attempt its mastery" (*Journeys'* p. 86). She defines that Rubicon in terms of water use, noting that "the line at which our Ancients crossed over from snuggling themselves into the environment as the wild bee into the hiving rocks, and began to control it, is the line of *acequia madre*" (*Journeys'* p. 89), the irrigation ditch.

By the time she wrote *The Land of Journeys' Ending* these attempts at control by the Ancients seem to anticipate for Austin the actions of Euro-Americans, often trying to ride roughshod over the inherence of the desert environment as if it were green New England or Ohio. In *The Land of Little Rain,* when she asserts that "desert is a loose term to indicate land that supports no man; whether the land can be bitted and broken to that purpose is not proven" (p. 3), the notion of "support" clearly takes its meaning within a context of 19th century agrarian practices of European origin, not the hunting/gathering or marginal agrarian economies of Native Americans. In *Earth Horizon,* Austin makes this explicit:

> It is the restraining condition of Beauty in the arid West that man cannot simply appropriate individual holdings of it; he cannot, in a country where there is an average rainfall of an inch a year and eleven cloudy days, make any quarter-section of it bear. (pp. 270–271)

Yet there is a persistent strain of thought in Austin that seems to accept and even value the attempt to make the land bear. Falling almost precisely at the center of *The Land of Little Rain,* the brief essay "My Neighbor's Field" is one of Austin's most consistent arguments for the human economic necessity of water in the desert. A small and "not greatly esteemed" pasture beside a stream on the edge of Kearsarge, California, the field is for Austin "one of those places God must have meant for a field from all time" (p. 81). The remark summarizes the thesis of this short essay. *Field,* after all, is an economic term. Not akin to the open and inhospitable desert nor the barren, strange, and mystical mountains, Austin's field, is an environment defined by its human mediation. Like all watercourses in the desert, it is the stream beside the field that gives the place value and significance and draws human attention.

Accordingly, Austin traces a brief economic history, or as she calls it, a "human occupancy of greed and mischief" (*Little,* p. 82) for the field. Here a watercourse is a function of its human utility, diverted for irrigation and domestic water use. Its headgates and supply pipes are as much a part of its "natural" history as its flora and fauna. The water that flows across the low-lying field is merely "waste water" (p. 83) from irrigation ditches, and Austin writes that it is its "little touch of humanness" that gives the field its variety and pleasantness" (p. 87). This environment, as Austin describes it, is largely characterized by the tussle between the domestic and the wild, between Midwestern-like gardens and orchards and the "wild plants, banished by human use" (p. 84). In this essay, desert water is portrayed in the avatar by which the 20th century has most commonly known it, as a resource harnessed for one scheme or another to make the desert bloom.

Similarly, in her essay "The Little Town of the Grape Vines," Austin draws irrigation into a romantic portrait of Hispanic rustics, anticipating the later southwestern work of Frank Waters and John Nichols. Again it is scarcity that determines value. In a later essay Austin worries that "it is difficult to come into intimate relations with appropriated waters; like very busy people they have no time to reveal themselves. One needs to have known an irrigating ditch when it was a brook," but at the same time, to get into what she calls the "mood of the waterways" (*Little*, p. 139), Austin suggests that it is necessary to understand the nature of "water right difficulties" (p. 141). She suggests the image of a homesteader guarding his headgate with a rifle as an emblem of water and its scarcity in the West. Disputes and conflicts over limited supplies of water characterize the experience of the West. "Unless you have known them," Austin suggests, "you cannot very well know what the water thinks as it slips past the gardens in the long slow sweeps of the canal. You get that sense of brooding from the confined and sober floods, not all at once but by degrees" (p. 141).

Compared to the Mojave of *The Land of Little Rain*, the Sonoran Desert of *The Land of Journeys' Ending*, as Austin portrays it, is even more full with human history and in complicity with the function of water as the determining environmental toggle. Human settlements are oriented by their *acequias*; the line of the "history maker" (*Journeys'*, p. 202), the Rio Grande, is intersected by the lines of "crops in long narrow fields running down to the river's edge" (p. 183); Indians dance the corn dance to bring rain (p. 250); the Havasu take their name from the their river, the People of the Blue Water, and the irrigated peach orchards are the best that the Pueblos kept of the European culture of the *Conquistadores* (p. 276). In a long chapter on the Colorado River, Austin sees the river as the heart of the southwest, a view more true economically and politically today than it was in 1924. Austin correctly predicts that the Colorado will be the "foundation of cities and rich orchards" (p. 433).

If Austin's perspective on water use in the West seems unresolved, it is in part because she wrote of this attempted biting and breaking of the land with an insider's perspective. Austin's own life experiences, as a starving homesteader, as a partner in a disastrous marriage pinning its economic hopes to a pie-in-the-sky irrigation project, and as a participant in political battles over natural resources, were her primer in the material actualities of water in the American West. Austin's family came west in 1888 to begin homesteading the Tejon country at the extreme southern end of California's San Joaquin Valley, the first year of a disastrous three year drought. She later described her first view of the family's homestead as "a narrow strip of waterless and therefore unprofitable country" (*Journeys'*, p. 190). The connection between water and success was predictive. The would-be desert farmers from the lush midwest who had "only a speaking acquaintance" with techniques of irrigation (p. 190) were unprepared for the realities of farming in the desert. Austin writes that they were "prey for all manner of half-formulated and often rankly dishonest schemes for inducing their participation in irrigation canals that never were intended to be built, that never could have been built in the regions for which they were advertised" (p. 190).

Paradoxically, the economic catastrophe of the homestead for a time gave Austin the time to travel the Tejon on horseback, to become acquainted with the mirages of the open space, the wild flowers of the hollows. She visited with vaqueros and sheepherders and observed, as she puts it, "how Indians live off a land upon which more sophisticated races would starve" (*Earth*, p. 198). She writes that "the whole basis of her social philosophy and economy altered beyond the capacity of books to keep pace with it," that she began to experience the desert as what she calls "ultimate reality, the reality first encountered so long ago under the walnut tree" (*Earth,* p. 198).

But Austin's spiritual apotheosis and growing awareness of the intricacies of the desert continued to be complicated by the exigencies of economic reality. In 1891 she married Stafford Wallace Austin, at least in part to escape the desperation of the homestead and the drudgery of the schoolteaching to which she had been forced by the need to help support her family. Again Austin's life fell under the control of the politics and economics of water, this time in the Owens Valley, wedged between the Sierra Nevada on the west and Death Valley on the east. Here Austin and her husband moved in 1892, to the fledgling agricultural community of Lone Pine. Like the desolate Tejon country had been in the 1880s, during the early 1890s the high desert Owens Valley was being settled by homesteaders whose hopes hinged on tapping the snowmelt of the Owens River for irrigated agriculture. Wallace Austin's career in the valley was a series of water-related debacles. After failing as a vinyardist, he took a position as an engineer for a large-scale irrigation project then being promoted by the Bureau of Reclamation. How the project was undermined makes one of the central moments in the history of water use in the West.

When Austin visited Los Angeles in 1888, she describes it as "daunted by the wrack of the lately 'busted' boom" (*Earth,* p. 186), a city many of whose streets were only marked out by surveyors' stakes and lined with dying palm trees. By 1900, however, the city had a population of 100,000, and by 1904 that figure had doubled. In that year the Los Angeles Department of Water and Power under the visionary but predatory control of William Mulholland made the announcement that changed forever the destiny of the Owens Valley, reporting that it would seek to supplement the city's water supply "from some other source" (quoted. in Reisner, *Cadillac Desert*, p. 64). The Owens River as it turned out. Pursuing a series of intrigues—lies, bribery, and divisiveness—the Water Department quickly gained control of a sufficient number of water rights to dry up the valley's agriculture at will and to forestall the Reclamation Service's irrigation project. When Mulholland began the construction of the huge Los Angeles Aqueduct to transport water across the desert to the city, the fundamental script for the film *Chinatown* had been written.

Mary Austin opposed the machinations of Los Angeles almost from the beginning. In this resource conflict be ween city and valley, she saw that the valley and its agrarian way of life were set up as the losers. Already in 1904 something of a minor literary celebrity after the publication of *The Land of Little Rain*, Austin even gained an audience with Mulholland in Los Angeles to voice her resentment. After the interview, Mulholland is said to have remarked "By God, that woman is the only one who has brains enough to see where this is going" (quoted in Reiser, p. 82). In spite of her understanding, Austin soon abandoned the fight and the valley. In *Earth Horizon,* Austin explains the end of her involvement in the controversy in terms of an ominous encounter with the Voice. She writes:

> She walked in the field and considered what could be done. She called upon the Voice, and the Voice answered her—Nothing. She was told to go away. And suddenly there was an answer; a terrifying answer, pushed off, deferred, delayed; an answer impossible to be repeated; answer still impending; which I might not live to see confirmed, but hangs suspended over the Southern country (308).

As it turned out, Austin—or perhaps the Voice—was correct in anticipating an ongoing struggle over water that would continue to shape the character of life in the West. Later in her life Austin would take her positions on water squarely into the political arena, serving as a delegate for the state of New Mexico at the Seven States Conference debating the then proposed Hoover Dam project. Austin was against the project, primarily because it was weighted in favor of the urban needs of Los Angeles. Her other experience with the city had led to the destruction of the agrarian potential of the Owens Valley. "The place is given over to desolation," she concludes in *Earth Horizon* (p. 363). What I call here the notion of the "shrinking pond," the register of political and economic constraint that completes Austin's understanding of how the relationship between humans and the land is mediated by the limitation of water in the West surfaces, clearly in her better-known works of nonfiction nature writing.

Austin's nonfiction, however, tells only part of what she has to say here. Her many novels, now usually dismissed, are important correlatives to her much recognized nature writing. In particular with regard to water issues, the novel *The Ford* (1917) acts as a useful cross-reference to the role of water and its scarcity that she describes in her nonfiction. This intertextuality shows Austin's understanding of water in her nature writing to be grounded in ideological and political issues, issues more openly expressed in *The Ford*. Austin thought a novel should be a "social document" (Pearce, *Mary Hunter Austin*, p. 74), a clear reflection of the author's experience in a larger public context. Although presented as fiction, *The Ford* dramatizes Austin's own direct experience both as an unwilling homesteader in the Tejon and facing the disastrous effects on the Owens Valley of the unscrupulous appropriation of water by Los Angeles.

The novel focuses on the Brents, a family of homesteaders in the Tierra Longa Valley of California, a thinly fictionalized version of Austin's own Owens Valley. Like Austin had twice herself, the Brents gave over their hopes for economic survival to water from an elaborate irrigation project planned for the valley. The river in *The Ford* begins its course "with the happiest possibilities of watering fields and nursing orchards" (p. 34). Although the Reclamation Service conducts surveys for a dam in the valley, real estate agents representing San Francisco gain control of valley land and water rights. Although the urban evil in the novel is San Francisco rather than Mulholland's Los Angeles and although Austin crafts a wish-fulfilling happy ending for her fiction by which city and agrarian valley share the water, the parallel to Austin's life is clear. Steven Brent nostalgically recalls his image of the valley's past and in so doing also announces Austin's pastoral view of water and its appropriate use: "Water," he says, "water and power ... and farms, not cities" (p. 361).

Commodity is at the heart of *The Ford*. Its story is shaped by the presence of natural resources up for grabs—land, oil, water. The scramble over resources is dramatized in a broad social and political context that develops dichotomies along lines of class, region, and gender and includes the labor movement, the Marxist critique of capitalism, populism, and the growing momentum of feminist awareness and activism leading to the extension of the franchise. Accordingly, the character Virginia Grant turns her back on her affluent "capitalist" upbringing to become a radical labor organizer; Anne Brent, on the other hand, becomes a real estate agent and investor who opposes the valley's most powerful land owner, for whom resources, "lands, waters, and minerals," are merely something that "he took ... up and laid ... down again" (p. 176). Water is made the centerpiece of Austin's display of power and acquisition, the "great scheme of things" (p. 182) that is business, a scheme that Austin compares to a bubbling pot that occasionally "boiled over" to the disastrous detriment of small farmers and other marginal dependents of the region's limited water.

As *The Ford* makes plain, for Austin, on balance, the ideal environment is less an untouched wilderness than it is a balanced, well-cared-for agrarian paradise. Even with the images of the ancient Anasazis and their now dry irrigation ditches alive in her imagination, Austin still inclines toward a kind of attempted agrarian "mastery" of the environment, but in all cases a mastery where intent and scale and even spiritual involvement are tempered by accommodation and adaptation. In Austin's history, when this sparingly watered paradise is endangered or destroyed, the agent is invariably the city. In *Earth Horizon*, Austin describes the Tejon desert degraded by activities clearly associated with urban and industrial development. "The mystery," she writes, "was eaten up, it was made into building lots, cannery sites; it receded before the preemptions of rock crushers and city dumps" (pp. 187–188).

## V

"Man is not himself only," Austin writes. "He is all he sees; all that flows to him from a thousand source. ... He is the land" (*Journeys'* p. 437). Place, in Austins view, must be the "determining factor" (p. 438) if there is to be a new design of the human heart and mind. Perhaps the most controversial element of Austin's thought today remains her commitment to the truths and determinations of a regional perspective. Art, for Austin, is an extension of this idea. "The profoundest implications of human experience are never stated rationally, never with explicitness, but indirectly in what we agree to call art forms ... symbolic substitutions" (*Journeys'* p. 440). In her essay "Regionalism in American Fiction," Austin explores the notion that place must be a theoretical premise for writing. The regional environment, according to Austin, "must enter constructively into the story, as another character, as the instigator of plot" ("Regionalism" p. 105). The mechanism for this, she writes, is that the narrative must "come up through the land, shaped by the author's own adjustment to it" ("Regionalism" p. 101). She sought to make her own writing, in form as well as content, a reflection of or cognate to place. In *Earth Horizon* she explains that in writing *The Land of Little Rain* she found the pattern for her prose in the "rhythm of the lonely lives blown across the trails" by the twenty-mule team borax wagons of the California desert (*Earth,* p. 296). To cultivate a new and constructive sense of human relation with place, according to Austin, we require a new set of symbolic language encoding adaptation to the environment, what she calls the "rhythm of acceptance" (*Journeys'*, p. 440). Writing of the Southwest, she calls for the "realization and general adoption of native symbols for experiences intimate and peculiar to that land" (*Journeys'*, p. 440). She writes: "We can no more produce, in any section of the United States, a quick and characteristic culture with the worn currency of classicism and Christianity, than we can do business with the coinage of imperial Rome" (*Journeys'*, p. 441)

Austin's notion of "symbolic substitution" brings us back to Concord. In Walden Pond the striped water snake is a vehicle for lost human potential. When we make the long trip west to the American deserts by way of the work of Mary Austin, however, the snake assumes a very different symbolic role. "Look for native festivals," she suggests, "look for signs on garages and shops, signs of the stepped horizon, the altar-line of the mesas, signs of the four great winds of the world, of the fructifying cloud" (*Journeys'*, p. 443). And finally, she suggests, "signs of the plumed serpent, Guardian of the Water Sources" (*Journeys'*, p. 443), a creature Austin observes in *The Land of Journeys' Ending*, "being found always in proximity to indispensable water-holes" (p. 47). For the Pueblo Indians of the Southwest whom Austin studied and emulated, the snake lives in the iconography of ceremony and art. It is the waving line at the top of the black San Ildephonso pot, the writhing wall leading to the kiva entrance. Far from nature affording an emblem of human sloth, the snake in indigenous Southwestern culture is associated with the life-giving power that allows careful subsistence in the desert. The sacrality of the snake is understood because of, not in spite of, its association with water, and the snake image resonates in a complex signification of devotion and perpetuation. Austin writes:

> Springs are sacred, and under the protection of a symbolic concept made out of the analogy of snakes to the zigzag lightning and the sinuous course of rivers, and the use of plumes to symbolize the bird-flight of prayers on their way to Those Above. Thus, a cleverly constructed effigy of a great snake having feathers growing out of his head has become the chief fetish of a desert people. (*Journeys'*, p. 252).

It is a signification available to non-Native Americans as well, and characteristically for Austin it surfaces in the language of material survival. Austin extends the snake to a further level of symbolic remove, noting that "lost cattlemen in the San Juan country look for the kiva pits and the sage-brush-covered house mounds, as index of a possible water-supply in some ancient artificial reservoir" (*Journeys'*, p. 69). This signification of water translated between cultures is alive in the work of Mary Austin. She begins with the Biblical symbol of sin, disobedience, and primal evil, the image that has rallied a Western mythology of human environmental subjugation and gives it new life instead as an icon of careful observation and adaptation to that environment. In the desert Southwest it carries the message that the human heart must be shaped by scarcity, that the "development" that Edward Abbey sees as the product of the "ideology of the cancer cell" cannot forever fly in the face of the salutary limitations of water.

Austin's snake is not the snake of unlimited suburban development in Los Angeles or Phoenix; it is not the snake of the well-watered lawn, nor of Lake Powell and its drowned, torpid canyons. Instead it is the vital snake of what Austin saw, and what many continue to see, as an immediately necessary and new era for the dry American west, when humans must, as Thoreau said, "feel the influence of the spring of springs arousing them" and learn the lessons and the language of honest and unselfish adaptation to the environment.

# Notes

Austin also has a few things to say about John Muir. In "Nurslings of the Sky" in *The Land of Little Rain*, Austin argues that a mountain storm is "a visible manifestation of the Spirit moving itself in the void" (152). In support of this, she remarks that "hardly anybody takes account of the fact that "John

Muir, who knows more of mountain storms than any other, is a devout man" ( 152) .

Frank Waters' *The People of the Valley* and Nichols' *New Mexico Trilogy* both focus their plots around the conflict between traditional rural water use and modern, technological and commercial development. In both works, morality is on the side of tradition, although Waters' view is more complex, suggesting adaptability as a universal value.

More broadly, Austin sees her husband's failings as a symptom of what she regards as the potentially destructive side of human relations to the land, "the spell of the land over all the men who had in any degree given themselves to it," a spell she associates with "the desire to master and make it fruitful" (*Earth,* p. 270), as opposed to being shaped by its constraints. For Austin this spell is mostly associated with men rather than women.

It is an interesting coincidence (perhaps nothing more useful in this case) that in *Land of Journeys' Ending* Austin narrates how a roadrunner, a "sleek cock of the choyital" kills a rather rigorously non-torpid "small striped snake" (p. 131) during a primal desert encounter.

# Bibliography

Austin, Mary. *Earth Horizon: Autobiography.* New York: Literary Guild, 1932.

Austin, Mary. "Experiences Facing Death." *Forum,* vol. 80 (1928): 763.

Austin, Mary. *The Ford.* Boston: Houghton, 1917.

Austin, Mary. *The Land of Journeys' Ending.* 1924. Tucson: Univ. of Arizona Press, 1983.

Austin, Mary. *The Land of Little Rain.* 1903. Garden City, N.Y.: Natural History Library, 1962.

Austin, Mary. "Regionalism in American Fiction." *English Journal* vol. 21 (Feb. 1932): 97–107.

Fink, Augusta. *I—Mary: A Biography of Mary Austin.* Tucson: University of Arizona Press, 1983.

Hall, Jacqueline D. "Mary Austin," in *A Literary History of the American West,* ed. Thomas J. Lyon. Fort Worth: Texas Christian Univ. Press, 1987. pp. 359–366.

Pearce, T. M. *Mary Hunter Austin.* New York: Twayne, 1965.

Pryse, Marjorie. "Introduction," *Stories from the Country of Lost Borders,* ed. Marjorie Pryse. New Brunswick: Rutgers Univ. Press, 1987.

Reisner, Marc. *Cadillac Desert: The American West and Its Disappearing Water.* 1986. New York: Penguin, 1987.

Thoreau, Henry David. *Walden, or Life in the Woods* and *On the Duty of Civil Disobedience.* New York: Signet-NAL, 1960, p. 33.

Waters, Frank. *Book of the Hopi.* 1963. New York: Penguin, 1977.

**REUBEN J. ELLIS** has a Ph.D. in English from the University of Colorado. He is an assistant professor at Teikyo Loretto Heights University in Denver and has a special interest in the works of Mary Austin.

# A Backyard Marco Polo
## Edwin Way Teale's Literary Adventures
## in the Insect World

❖

## David S. Miller

After Edwin Way Teale died in 1980, at the age of 81, Walter Harding delivered a moving tribute to his memory at the next annual meeting of The Thoreau Society. Harding recalled that Teale had belonged to The Thoreau Society for nearly four decades, and had missed no more than two or three meetings—when he had unbreakable appointments in distant places. Teale called the annual gatherings here in Concord "the only ones where each meeting was better than the one before. They never failed expectations."[1] Teale did more than attend meetings, of course. He served on the Executive Committee and the Save Walden Committee, and he was president of the society for the 1957-1958 term. In closing his tribute, Harding said that Teale himself "never failed expectations. Each time I met him, he seemed more wonderful than before."[2]

I feel unfortunate not to have met the man who inspired such affection. I know Edwin Way Teale only through his books, which were the subject of my doctoral dissertation in American Studies. But even a strictly literary acquaintance with Teale inspires affection and admiration. He was the sort of writer who received letters and personal visits from his readers. After several years away from Teale's books, I've been rereading him to prepare this article, and I have found that, like the man, the writing "seems more wonderful than before." I have marveled again at the combined scope and detail of his knowledge of nature; the effortless grace of his descriptions and explanations; his intense, though carefully understated, passion for his subject. I had not forgotten his gift for storytelling, but I was surprised at the extent of his wit, often self-deprecating. I gained renewed respect for his ability to spot the philosophically relevant image amid the chaos of experience or the overwhelming plenitude of scientific literature. And I found reinforced my respect for the complexity of perception encoded in his beautifully crafted imagery.

My purpose here is to discuss the way Teale's writing works—what sort of picture it paints of nature and of the author, how it communicates information and emotion. There has been a general predisposition, even among sophisticated readers, to approach nonfiction mainly as a conduit for fact and argument, overlaid, in some cases, by the author's sentiments. In the case of nature writing, these sentiments are often rejected as simplistic and artificially heightened. Even so sophisticated and generous a reader as Joyce Carol Oates, for example, has written that nature writing is "painfully limited" to such emotions as "REVERENCE, AWE, PIETY, MYSTICAL ONENESS."[3] Only a few works of nonfiction, Thoreau's *Walden* among them, have infiltrated the canon of books assigned in English classes (though the idea of such a canon has come under siege). These canonical works are thought to contain imagery that suggests as well as states, so they can be read on levels beyond the merely factual. They are assumed to speak to our deeper and more complex thoughts and feelings.

Although Teale's works do not have the literary status of *Walden,* I believe they can be read for something deeper, more suggestive, more passionate, and more personal than a catalogue of natural-history facts embedded in a friendly narrative. His view of life in nature is assuredly too complex to be written off as limited to awe, reverence, and mystical oneness (though I myself have no quarrel with those responses). There is more humorous irony than solemnity in Teale, and overtones of paradox that defeat any simple interpretation of nature. Perhaps because of the general good humor in his books, we may have to look twice to notice the inherent Darwinian ferocity that makes Teale's worldview a tragic one. To make my case for reading Teale at several levels, I have chosen to concentrate here on his writing about insects. Though Teale took the whole of nature as his literary province, the insect world held a special fascination for him. When photographing or taking notes for essays on insects, he felt like "a backyard Marco Polo." The reference is humorously self-mocking, to be sure, but it also truly expresses his sense that visits to the insect world were adventures as exotic and significant as Marco Polo's. Like the explorer of distant lands, he brought back stories of strange customs in a place at once like Lewis Carroll's Wonderland and Darwin's terrifying "tangled bank."

I grant at the outset that Teale is probably not best known as a writer on insects. If you visit your bookstore in search of Teale's works, as I was reminded in my tour of Concord's bookstores, you are most likely to find a volume or two from his quartet of travel writings—*North with the Spring, Autumn Across America, Journey Into Summer,* and *Wandering Through Winter,* leisurely chronicles of his automobile trips with wife Nellie through each of the American seasons. You may also find *A Naturalist Buys an Old Farm* and *A Walk Through the Year,* two books about life on the 130-acre

Connecticut farm that the Teales bought in 1959 and treated as a combination home and nature reserve. In these six volumes, Teale writes about all the natural phenomena that measure the passage of time across the continent, or through the woods and meadows of his old farm. After publication of *Wandering Through Winter,* the final book of the American seasons' quartet, Teale received the 1966 Pulitzer Prize for general nonfiction—the first such prize given to the author of a nature book.

Clearly, it is easier to make your reputation, and your living, writing about long vacations or bucolic solitude than chronicling the lives of insects. Many of us find it easy and pleasant to identify with the Teales as they travel or enjoy their rustic retreat. We are a nation of restless migrants and immigrants who cherish movement and, perhaps paradoxically, also hold the family farm in mythic esteem. We dream of taking long trips by car, even as we entertain the pastoral urge to escape the city and settle into that middle landscape between urban jungle and actual wilderness. In this vision, insects are generally the annoying or downright destructive pests that inhibit our enjoyment of nature. The general attitude is well expressed in a story Teale used to tell about himself, and which Walter Harding recounted in his tribute. When Teale was once invited to speak in Baltimore in place of a lecturer who canceled at the last minute, the moderator informed the audience that Mr. So-and-So had been scheduled to give a *very interesting* lecture on such-and-such a topic, but instead they were going to hear Mr. Teale talk about *bugs*—the last word spit our with great distaste.[4] As a devout contrarian, I have developed a special affection for Teale's books on bugs. And *bugs* is probably a better description of the topic in some ways than *insects,* for Teale did not hesitate to cross the boundaries of the six-legged world to include the daddy-long-legs in *Grassroots Jungles,* a book devoted to insects. His affection also extended to creatures with more legs than eight. He writes, for instance, of his attempt to rescue a common household centipede that was trapped on the wet surface of his kitchen sink. As he tried to free the creature, which many of us would shiveringly name a thousand-legger as we shriveled it up with a blast of poison from a spray can, its legs came off one by one in his fingers.[5] (It did eventually escape, unhampered by its loss of several legs). I'm reminded that one of Teale's favorite books was *Don Quixote.* Surely there is something charmingly quixotic not only in the attempted liberation of the thousand-legger, but in the general project of studying, writing about, and giving public lectures on those bugs that most of us would happily spray into oblivion. Teale expressed the problem this way in a book published in 1942:

> For many years, I have been interested in observing and photographing the beauty and strangeness of insect life. I soon learned, however, that a full-grown man peering into a grass clump, or stretched out prone to watch an ant-lion at work is inevitably an object of curiosity and concern. If a man beats his wife, squanders his fortune, or jumps off a bridge and

commits suicide, the world will understand, if it doesn't condone. But if he begins to spend his leisure time associating with insects, watching the minute dramas of their little world, people may condone, but they rarely understand.[6]

To be able to observe insects without being observed in the process, he rented—or, as he put it, purchased the insect rights to—a small portion of an unused apple orchard near his house. For ten dollars a summer, he was allowed to plant what he called an insect garden, where the vegetation was supposed to become infested. He began this project in 1936, before he was a well-known author of nature books. In those days, he worked as a writer and photographer for *Popular Science* magazine in New York City, and lived on Long Island with Nellie and their only child, David.

Leasing an insect garden may not seem to have the philosophical scope or monastic purity of living by Walden Pond, but it served some of the same purposes. The secluded orchard gave Teale a place to observe nature—not only insects, but the bushes, flowers, and trees they lived in (and on). It provided the uninterrupted solitude necessary for taking photographs and making the careful, copious notes about insect behavior that soon became his first successful nature books: *Grassroots Jungles* (1937); *The Golden Throng* (1940), a book about bees; and *Near Horizons: The Story of an Insect Garden* (1942). Soon his books were so successful that Teale was able to make what he called his own personal declaration of independence. In 1941, the year The Thoreau Society was founded, he became a free-lance writer.

But here is a puzzle. How does an author find an audience for books about a subject that the general reader finds disgusting? One answer is to write about insects as pests that your books will help people avoid or destroy. Another answer is to humanize your subjects—the method that made Disney wealthy. (Jiminy Cricket is no more an insect than Mickey Mouse is a rodent.) Teale's solution was to turn an apparent liability to his advantage by *emphasizing* the strangeness, the otherness, of insects:

> My orchard hillside can be crossed in a few hundred strides; yet its miniature forests are filled with interest. This close-to-home stretch of grass and weeds, set among moldering trees, has been my veldt, my tundra, my Amazon jungle. And what explorer, returning from the most outlandish corners of the earth, has encountered stranger forms of life than those which dwell amid the tiny thickets and Lilliputian mountains of my hillside? What jungle has a more fantastic inhabitant than the doodle-bug that always walks backward? Or the monarch butterfly that tastes with its legs? … Even the commonest insects, once we enter the Alice-in-Wonderland realm they inhabit, become engrossingly interesting. Their ways, their surroundings, their food, their abilities are so foreign to our own that imagining ourselves in their places becomes an exciting adventure of the mind.[7]

One could object that Teale is rationalizing. Elsewhere, he complains about being confined to near horizons. In *The Golden Throng*, he even displaces his frustration onto his subjects:

> During the earliest days of my acquaintance with the bees, I must confess there were moments of rebellion against the ordered routine of their lives. To me, the adventurous, free-lance existence of solitary insects appealed far more than the machinelike life of the social bees.[8]

Now *that* is a declaration hammered out on the anvil of quiet desperation. Most of the time, however, Teale so clearly enjoys his discoveries, and is so wholly engaged by his "adventures of the mind," that he forgets any resentment at being unable to pursue more distant adventures. "It was Victor Hugo," he writes, "who once remarked that the most interesting thing in the world is something occurring on the other side of a high wall."[9] Nothing on the other side of the wall between humans and insects was more fascinating to Teale than the praying mantis:

> I have watched hundreds of these creatures lying in wait or stalking their prey. I have marvelled at their patience as they remained, minute after minute, motionless as the plant to which they clung, forelegs raised as though in silent prayer. Then, as surprising as lightning from a cloudless sky, comes that split-second strike. ... Faster than the eye can follow, the forelegs dart out and, like the jaws of a toothed steel trap, the blades snap shut over the body of the victim.[10]

According to Edward Dodd, who was Teale's friend, publisher, and biographer, the naturalist was especially pleased to have established the territoriality of the mantis.[11] In his nature writing, however, Teale does not narrow his focus to one aspect of mantis life, described in the dispassionate prose of the scientific journal article. His approach is personal, inclusive, and ecological. He shows us not only mantises, but himself watching mantises—hundreds of them. We can, it is true, amuse ourselves by skimming off astounding trivia. "From the making of that curious ball of solidifying froth which forms its egg case, to the weird cannibal feast, which ends the mating season, the story of the mantis is a succession of surprising events."[12] But this is not primarily a *Teale's Believe It or Not*. It is the personal narrative of a natural philosopher testing his worldview against the challenge of this "strange and fearsome insect." What sort of world is it, Teale asks in effect, that includes this cannibal with toothed traps in its jaws? Teale shows us this world first hand by abruptly adopting the perspective of an insect:

> If you enlarged a bee to the size of a man and magnified a praying mantis proportionately, you would produce a monster stretching sixty feet from spiked forelegs to spread tail. It would rear fully two stories into the air and its great compound eyes would be bigger than windowpanes. Far

larger than Tyrannosaurus Rex ... it would have forelegs with folding blades longer than automobiles.[13]

Throughout this chapter, titled "A Garden Dinosaur," and elsewhere in the book, Teale emphasizes the mantis' predatory ferocity by referring to its carnivorous diet and fearless behavior in combat. But as soon as we are accustomed to viewing the mantis in the role of implacable villain, Teale introduces irony: "The only living creature the mantis seems to fear is, paradoxically enough, the tiny ant. When they meet, like an insect David and Goliath, it is the mantis that backs down." Teale assures us that he has seen the drama unfold "scores of times," and surmises, like an entomological Freud, that the fear can be traced back to childhood trauma: ants often attack helpless baby mantises.[14] Teale kept mantises as pets, and could come to their defense when provoked. "In spite of its fierce appearance and bloodthirsty habits," he notes, "(the mantis) is harmless to man." In fact, its "bloodthirsty habits," such as devouring "flies and beetles and the thousand and one pests a garden is heir to" are precisely what make it our friend, Teale claims.[15] But we sense an unintended contradiction here, because if mantises are "good" in their consumption of insect pests, then they must be "bad" in their consumption of one another.

Teale's healthy sense of irony quickly catches up with him, however, and he turns it against himself. "Like Mark Twain's aunt who warmed the water before she drowned the kittens, I often put crickets and grasshoppers in an ammonia jar to render them unconscious before I feed them to my mantis pets."[16] It is an insect-eat-insect world that Teale has led us into. Teale doesn't always soften the violence in his "insect Eden" with ironic humor. He struggles to maintain a balance between ethics and objectivity. In explaining mantis cannibalism, for instance, he looks beyond particular insect tragedies to general laws of evolution. If female mantises eat their male partners, perhaps some grand natural end justifies this ignoble means:

> Science suggests that [cannibalism] is a manifestation of the economy of nature. The male has satisfied his purpose in life when he fertilizes the female. If he dies when his mission is fulfilled, the food he would otherwise consume is saved. This cannibalistic instinct, it is believed, dates from some long-ago age of scarcity when food was at a premium.[17]

Perhaps Teale excuses the individual mantis, but only by shifting the burden of evil to nature itself, thereby making his economics a dismal science indeed. Teale closes his chapter with an image that embodies the conflicting feelings he has evoked. He is discussing the the way color helps camouflage a mantis while it hunts for its dinner. Then he cites an instance of a mantis hiding among flowers of a color similar to its own until an insect blunders by and is "snapped up in a flash." But that moment of brutality is merely a transition into a final image of natural harmony:

> The underplates of these mantises are sometimes pink, sometimes blue, white, mauve, or purple. Always they seek out blooms that just match their particular hue. In searching for a suitable resting place, they often climb up and down half a dozen branches. If they reach the tip and find no flowers, they retrace their steps and start up another limb or plant. They never take a position on a flowerless twig but always in the midst of blossoms.

> As soon as it is satisfied with its surroundings, such a mantis will settle down, turn the colored plates outward, and remain perfectly motionless, unless a breeze is blowing. Then it begins a gentle swaying from side to side which reproduces the movement of the wind-stirred blooms around it.[18]

At the factual level, Teale establishes that his descriptions are based on first-hand observation and his interpretations are buttressed by science. Yet his images are not merely factual; they also color our emotional reaction to the insect and the natural process that has created them. Initially described as an agent of death with machinelike attributes (jaws toothed like steel traps), the mantis undergoes literary evolution and, in the end, becomes akin to flowers swaying colorfully in the wind, a complex image of quiet beauty in the service of violence. The mantis is a fake flower, a sinister but beguiling bloom with jaws that bite and claws that catch. This passage is susceptible of several interpretations. It is reportage, telling us *what* happened, *when,* and to *whom.* It presents a series of surprising facts and dramatic incidents from the insect wonderland on the other side of the high wall. It is also interpretation; Teale tells us *why,* according to science, insect dramas take place as they do. And, if interpretation lies a layer below incident, one layer deeper still is an undercurrent of imagery that adds ambiguous power to overt messages. Read poetically, Teale's story is charged with deep and conflicting emotions that arise from disciplined reflection on the world we inhabit, a world from whose brutality we are not exempt, a world whose mysterious beauty draws us in—and threatens to pull us under. Among the tranquil flowers we find those lethal, folding forelegs. Finally, I would like to consider a passage from *A Naturalist Buys an Old Farm,* in which I believe we can see yet another level in Teale's writing on insects—a subtler, more personal level that merges with his passionate reflections on nature's evolving Wonderland. The passage appears in an apparently unassuming chapter devoted to Teale's writing cabin. If the old farm was a sort of Walden shared with Nellie, the writing cabin was a more solitary Walden within a Walden:

> Here, within five minutes' walk of the house, I am surrounded by a scene that appears from my cabin windows as wild as ... northern Maine. Here

I can read and write uninterrupted by ringing telephones, more or less disconnected from the world.[19]

He looks around inside the cabin and describes the objects he sees. *Walden is* there, of course, with *Alice in Wonderland, The Rubaiyat,* and *Robinson Crusoe,* books of strange adventures and exotic landscapes. Also present are "relics of past adventures" in the real world.[20] Among these are homely icons, such as rubber flippers and snowshoes, a cap worn on the occasion of Teale's first sighting of a rare marsh bird, a rapier dug from a swamp, a piece of driftwood, and the insect-collecting net that Teale's friend William T. Davis once used to ward off gun-carrying muggers:

Later a friend asked him, "But weren't you taking an awful chance?" "I suppose I was," he replied. "I didn't think of it at the time. But I might have injured them severely."[21]

Other objects, such as a piece of pottery discovered by John Muir on a trip with John Burroughs, recall Teale's literary lineage. Many relics are *memento mori:* a piece of petrified wood from Death Valley, a stomach stone from a dinosaur, a bone from an extinct bird (the great auk), the skull of a kit fox. The cabin is adorned with hard facts transformed into emotion-laden symbols of adventure, travel, discovery, literature, death, and the finality of extinction. The most affecting symbol is "the pack basket made long ago by our son, David. It rests on the floor beneath the rear window of the cabin, a window that looks toward the south into the heart of the aspen grove."[22] This, too, is a reminder of mortality, though Teale forebears to explain what faithful readers would know. David died in Italy during the last days of World War II.

Teale seems to digress, recalling a day when he lifted the basket and discovered what appeared to be a pile of black seeds underneath. On inspection, the apparent seeds, symbols of life, prove to be the severed heads of carpenter ants. How these heads came to be there, Teale declares, is an unsolved mystery. He advances several hypotheses: perhaps this was a battlefield where groups of ants waged war on one another. Since the heads are indigestible, they remain after the rest of the insect has been eaten. Or perhaps some predator of a different species discarded the inedible heads under the pack basket. Most likely, he surmises, he has uncovered an ants' kitchen midden, where the heads of deceased colony members are deposited after the bodies have been consumed. At this juncture, the reader accustomed to deciphering encoded fictional messages is likely to find a lump in his or her throat. Underneath the discursive bit of natural history (which may remind one of the battle of the ants in *Walden*) are a host of horrible symbolic correspondences: the heads, like the pack basket, are all that remain after the deaths of the soldiers to which they belonged. In a novel, of course, the images would have been invented to embroider death's universal inevitability. Here the images are accidentally discovered, not invented. Yet I cannot imagine that Teale overlooked the correspondences. What bereaved father could?

Teale stays close to the hard facts of his natural-history discoveries. He writes about ants, not—not ostensibly—about his son:

> The ways of the ants and the ways of insects that ants prey upon represent an especially fascinating area of natural-history investigation. Not long ago scientists studying a neotropical wasp, *Mischocythorus drewseni,* observed that the greatest hazards faced by these insects were raids made upon their nests by ants. But the wasps—or rather the long processes of evolution—had provided an effective safeguard against such forays. Within the bodies of the female, glands produce a viscous fluid. When this is applied in a heavy coating over the long stem of the nest, it tums the invaders away, for the glandular secretion contains an ant repellant.[23]

The pack basket and the memory of David seem to have been left behind as Teale, apparently by free association, takes us from ants to wasps that ants prey upon to the wonders of evolutionary chemistry. If we follow carefully, however, I think we will find that the theme of death's triumph has simply gone underground to re-emerge in a more philosophical form. Concerning the chemical that wasps use to repel ants, Teale asks an evolutionary question: "How did it take place that this particular chemical should be produced within the bodies of these particular wasps?"[24] Apparently free-associating again, Teale mentions a chemical in the mouths of leeches, an anticoagulant that increases blood flow; from there he proceeds to a chemical that deadly snakes inject to *stimulate* coagulation, thus locking poison in a victim's wounds. Finally, he refers to a secretion that helps water beetles navigate across the pond near his cabin. By reducing the surface tension of the water, the chemical helps speed the beetle on its way, while its pursuers drown in its wake:

> How did the little water beetle *Stenodus* ... evolve the glandular secretion that destroys the water film behind it? Such instances of glands appearing just where their specialized chemicals are needed most, where the lives and welfare of their possessors depend upon their presence, represent for me the most baffling aspect of evolution.[25]

As with his description of mantises imitating flowers, Teale seems to have transformed anecdotes of death into illustrations of more hopeful general principles. The gruesome mystery of the severed heads gives way to the more sanguine mystery of chemicals that help wasps and water beetles escape their enemies. In the most offhand manner, beginning with a simple survey of his cabin's furnishings, Teale serves up a catalog of nature's horrors—warfare, cannibalism, poisoning, and drowning, all suggested by the "seeds" under the dead son's pack basket. He incorporates these horrors into his sense of wonder at nature's intricate and apparently (but not really) purposeful design. He shows us that blind, stumbling, amoral, uncaring chance takes miraculously good care of wasps and water beetles.

On the surface, this is a mystery story with a happy ending. It also is a summary of nature's inherent cruelty. I think we must assume that Teale means to question the ethics as well as the mechanics of nature's design, for both are mysteries. How can it possibly happen that chance evolves these chemicals where they are needed? How can we accept the fact that slaughter is the engine powering the miraculous process? The rational mind and the ethical impulse both are stymied by these facts of nature. What does Teale conclude, whom death robbed of a son, about this Darwinian Wonderland? Would he have us marvel at nature's beautiful, intricate, mysterious design? Or do we draw back in revulsion?

I think that Teale's answer is in the arrangement of his images—and in his life. He turned from brooding over David's death to study nature. There he saw, with clear but not disinterested eyes, all the horror he turned from in his grief. Yet he also saw more hopeful literary possibilities. David's last mission required crossing a river running between Axis and Allied positions. He made it across and back once but, unlike the waterbug, failed the second time.[26] Teale's meditation on evolution and mortality seems in part to be a version of his son's death replayed in the microcosmic world of insects, where it culminates in a miraculous escape. The imagery is both tragic and triumphant. It is a water beetle's version of transcendence, to be sure, but it had to suffice for Edwin and Nellie Teale. It may have to suffice as well for the rest of us.

# Notes

[1] Walter Harding, The Thoreau Society Bulletin, New York: The Thoreau Society, Inc., #156, summer, 1981), p. 5.

[2] *Ibid.*

[3] Joyce Carol Oates, quoted in *This Incomperable Lande: A Book of American Nature Writing,* Thomas J. Lyon, ed. (Boston: Houghton, Mifflin, 1989), p. xiv. Capitalization in original.

[4] Walter Harding, op. cit., p. 4.

[5] Edwin Way Teale, *Circle of the Seasons* (New York: Dodd, Mead, 1953), p. 233.

[6] Edwin Way Teale, *Adventures in Nature* (New York: Dodd, Mead, 1959), p. 22.

[7] *Ibid.*, p. 26-27.

[8]Edwin Way Teale, *The Golden Throng,* (New York: Dodd, Mead, 1940), p. 20.

[9]*Ibid.,* p. 14.

[10]Edwin Way Teale, *Grassroots Jungles* (New York: Dodd, Mead, 1937), p. 47.

[11]Dodd, Edward H., *Of Nature, Time and Teale* (New York: Dodd, Mead, 1960), pp. 16–17.

[12]Edwin Way Teale, *Grassroots Jungles,* p. 50.

[13]*Ibid.,* p. 47.

[14]*Ibid.,* p. 52.

[15]*Ibid.,* p. 48.

[16]*Ibid.,* p. 49.

[17]*Ibid.,* p. 57.

[18]*Ibid.,* p. 58.

[19]Edwin Way Teale, *A Naturalist Buys an Old Farm* (New York, Dodd, Mead, 1974), p. 217.

[20]*Ibid.,* p. 220.

[21]*Ibid.,* p. 221.

[22]*Ibid.,* p. 219.

[23]*Ibid.,* p. 220.

[24]*Ibid.,* p. 220.

[25]*Ibid.*

[26]I owe this information to Tom Potter (Martinsville, Indiana), who is writing a biography of Teale for Indiana University Press.

---

**DAVID S. MILLER**, a freelance writer, received his Ph.D. in American Studies from the University of Minnesota and wrote his dissertation on Edwin Way Teale. His initial interest in Thoreau's writing has led him to a study of Thoreau's influence on other nature writers.

# Edward Abbey and Thoreau

❖

## Isaac P. Rodman

In 1944, Edward Abbey at 17, hitchhiking to see the country before being drafted, was stranded at the side of the road in Needles, California. Later he recalled:

> Nobody stopped. In fact, what with the war and gasoline rationing, almost nobody drove by. Squatting in the shade of a tree, I stared across the river at the porphyritic peaks of Arizona, crazy ruins of volcanic rock floating on heat waves. Purple crags, lavender cliffs, long blue slopes of cholla and agave—had never before even dreamed of such things (BW, pp. 51–52)

This was the beginning of Edward Abbey's experience of the desert. After discharge from the army he returned to the West to go to school, and on weekends he went to the desert. Later he wrote of an early trip to Comb Ridge, Utah; it was, he said, "a landscape that I had not only never seen before but that did not *resemble* anything I had seen before" (BW, p. 54).

> I hesitate, even now, to call that scene beautiful. To most Americans, to most Europeans, natural beauty means the sylvan—pastoral and green … But from Comb Ridge you don't see anything like that. What you see from Comb Ridge is mostly red rock, warped and folded and corroded and eroded in various ways, all eccentric, with a number of maroon buttes, purple mesas, blue plateaus and gray dome-shaped mountains in the far-off west. Except for the thin track of the road, switchbacking down into the wash a thousand feet below … ; we could see no sign of human life. Nor sign of any kind of life, except a few acid-green cottonwoods in the canyon below. In the silence and the heat and the glare we gazed upon a seared wasteland, a sinister and savage desolation. And found it … fascinating (BW, pp. 54–55).

Abbey's subject is the desert country of the American Southwest. He did write about other things—a moving essay on Hoboken and New York, an essay on rafting "the wavy green waters of Idaho's Salmon River" ("River of No Return," OL p. 107ff), and an informed, sympathetic essay on Emerson. But these are not the entrees. The desert is his main course.

He worked for years, part time, on the model of Thoreau, as a ranger for the National Park Service in Arches National Monument, organ Pipe Cactus National Monument, Petrified Forest, and Everglades National Park, and he served as a fire lookout for the Forest Service at the Grand Canyon. He published some eighteen books. He has been called by others and by himself a nature writer, a desert mystic, a novelist, a libertarian, an anarchist, a dedicated scofflaw, a confirmed desert rat, an environmental journalist, and an agrarian anarchist.

Abbey's nature writing often has a note of melancholy, of nostalgia, of retrospection. He is a writer of elegies, a voice crying in the wilderness. Abbey hated the Glen Canyon Dam, for instance, as an example of human arrogance destroying an irreplaceable natural resource. Of the Colorado River and the Glen Canyon dam he wrote:

> Centipedes crawled, flies buzzed, cows stumbled, vultures cruised, spiders crept, weeds grew where once ... not so long ago a living river flowed and sparkled, fish danced, herons stalked and falcons gyred and stooped, with a green fragrant forest, on either bank, sheltering the secret lives of deer and ocelot, jaguar and javelina, gray wolf and black bear, red fox and puma, armadillo and snapping turtle, anhinga, elegant trogon, ivory-billed woodpecker, kingfisher, bald eagle, marsh hawk ... (HL, pp. 221-222).

> Great blue herons once descended, light as mosquitoes, long legs dangling, to the sandbars. Wood ibis croaked in the cottonwood ... Snowy egrets in the tamarisk, plumes waving in the river breeze ... [ellipsis in original] (MWG, p. 12).

> "... the real Colorado, before damnation, when the river flowed unchained and unchanneled in the joyous floods of May and June, swollen with snow melt. Boulders crunching and clacking and grumbling, tumbling along on the river's bedrock ... the noise like ... grinding molars in a giant jaw."

> "That was a river" (MWG, p. 59).

> "Gone. A river no more" (HL, p. 222).

In another context Abbey happened to use these words. "My sole weapon was ... intelligence. Which functions, however, only in retrospection" (AR, p. 166 top).

Why compare someone who wrote about the Southwest deserts and canyons with Henry David Thoreau?

Abbey invites comparison by invoking the name of Thoreau more often than he mentions any other writer, Major John Wesley Powell being a close but different second. When Thoreau wrote, "The west of which I speak is but another name for the Wild; ... in Wildness is the preservation of the World" ("Walking"), he mapped out Edward Abbey's life's work.

Reading Abbey one encounters many little touches of Henry in the night, unidentified allusions. Some of Abbey's characters play the flute, often in the woods, and flute sounds are rather frequent comparisons.

Hayduke in *The Monkey Wrench Gang* says: "When I see somebody coming to do *me* good, I reach for my revolver" (p. 106).

After an interview, Abbey reports that he approves of the governor of Arizona because he governs not at all (JH, pp. 150–153).

During another interview, Joseph Wood Krutch gives an example of sportsmen not being allies of the conservationists. Abbey thinks, "I was once a sportsman myself—before I grew up" (OL, p. 184).

"Still we live meanly, like ants," Thoreau had said, "though the fable tells us that we were long ago changed into [human beings]" ("Where I Lived and What I Lived For"). An Abbey character muses, "Every [one] has [a] phobia. My pet phobia is the ant, the anthill, the formic way of life" (FP, p. 103), a speech that reflects Abbey's fears of a technocratic future in air-conditioned geodesic domes after human beings overpopulate their world and "develop" the last of their wilderness. One character thinks cars are the enemy of the canyonlands. "They're drivin' their tin cars into the holy land. They can't do that; it ain't legal. There's a law against it. A higher law" (MWG 32). A peculiar kind of volunteerism is central to the projected personae of both writers. Thoreau had written, "For many years I was self-appointed inspector of snow-storms and rain-storms, and did my duty faithfully" (Walden, p. 16). Abbey combined Thoreau and a little Robert Frost when he wrote, "One could do worse than be an inspector of volcanoes" (Walden, p. 212). Of a hike in Death Valley, Abbey wrote:

> Where the salt flats come closest to the base of the eastern mountains, at 278 feet below sea level, lies the clear and sparkling pool known as Badwater. A shallow body of water, surrounded by beds of snow-white alkali. According to Death Valley legend the water is poisonous, containing traces of arsenic. I scooped up a handful and sampled it in my mouth, since the testing of desert waterholes has always been one of my chores. (JH p. 81)

The spirit of Thoreau is present here: to be self-appointed *because* no one else cares, to push against the *common* sense with individual insight, and to make one's vision so compelling in writing that many people come to care. This comic element has larger proportions, which Abbey expressed in this way:

The task of the honest writer ... is to seek out, write down, and publish forth those truths which are ... self-evident, not universally agreed upon, not allowed to determine public feeling and official policy (OL, p. 166).

Thoreau and Abbey were both literary comic exaggerators. Thoreau wrote:

If you are ready to leave father and mother, and never see them again,— if you have paid your debts, and made your will, and settled all your affairs, and are a free [person], then you are ready [to go] for a walk. ("Walking," p. 598 [ML]).

A parable Abbey told to illustrate his perception of Thoreau's place contains much that is typical of Abbey's irascibility and impatience with domestication. A parable of coyotes.

Down near Tucson, where I sometimes live ... the suburban parts of the city are infested with pet dogs. ... Most evenings at twilight the wild coyotes come stealing in from the desert to penetrate the suburbs, raid garbage cans, catch and eat a few cats, dogs, and other domesticated beasts. When this occurs, the dogs raise a grim clamor, roaring like maniacs, and launch themselves in hot but tentative pursuit. ... The coyotes retreat into the brush and cactus, where they stop, facing the town, to wait and sit and laugh at the dogs. They yip, yap, yelp, howl, and holler, teasing the dogs, taunting them, enticing them with the old-time call of the wild. And the dogs stand and tremble, shaking with indecision, furious, hating themselves, tempted to join the coyotes, run off with them to the hills, but afraid. Afraid to give up the comfort, security, and safety of their housebound existence. Afraid of the unknown and dangerous. Thoreau was our suburban coyote. Town dwellers always found him exasperating (DR, pp. 38–39).

Surely "Our Spartan-Buddhist Henry" (Emerson, in a letter to Lidian; Harding, *Days of Henry David Thoreau*, (New York: Alfred A. Knopf, 1965, p. 222) would delight in being called a coyote. Besides being high praise for Henry, this parable describes a role Abbey defined for himself, that of gadfly. Abbey wrote, "It is my belief that the writer, the free-lance author, should be and must be a critic of the society in which he lives" (OL, p. 161).

It seems that often the person who creates an area also completes it. A hundred Hemingways and Joyces in their days wrote in shadows rather than discover their original relations. this must be a disconcerting proposition; it is easy to see how it leads to some animosity. I am not saying that Abbey was a Thoreau manqué. Abbey was a strong original writer. But Abbey did say, "Thoreau's mind has been haunting mine for most of my life" (DR, p. 13), and it seems there were some problems in this father-son-like relationship.

Abbey chose to attack Thoreau on the issue of purity, with sexuality and vegetarianism the subsets he focused on. Abbey overreacted. His stridency indicates that it came from something deep. It is as if Thoreau is so close to Abbey that Abbey had to kill off some parts of this father figure to clear out some territory for himself as a writer.

Abbey's defensiveness causes him to misread Thoreau. (Unfortunately these are often not *strong* misreadings—they are merely insufficient readings.) As one small example: In *Desert Solitaire,* which, like *Walden* puts the experience of a longer period into a one-year frame (actually a one-season frame), Abbey wrote, "Unlike Thoreau[,] who insisted on one world at a time[,] I am attempting to make the best of two. After six months in the desert I am volunteering for a winter of front-line combat duty—caseworker, public welfare department—in the howling streets of [New York]" (DS p. 265).

Here Abbey takes his Thoreau out of context and ignores "several more lives to live."

Abbey quotes Thoreau's section near the end of "Spring." Thoreau had written:

> There was a dead horse in the hollow by the path to my house, which compelled me sometimes to go out of my way, especially in the night when the air was heavy, but the assurance it gave me of the strong appetite and inviolable health of Nature was my compensation for this. I love to see that Nature is so rife with life that myriads can be afforded to be sacrificed and suffered to prey on one another ... [ellipsis in Abbey]. The impression made on a wise man is that of universal innocence. Poison is not poison after all, nor are any wounds fatal. Compassion is a very untenable ground. It must be expeditious. It will not bear to be stereotyped.

Abbey quotes Thoreau's paragraph and then asks, "Henry, I say, what the devil do you mean?" (DR, p. 30).

Here Thoreau, by taking a macrobiological, almost geological, view of death, has made sense of a generalization that modern readers have often found unfortunate in Emerson, about disagreeable things vanishing. The redneck Abbey claimed not to understand, but the Thoreauvian Abbey had written from the same place in "The Dead Man at Grandview Point" (DS), where the Abbey voice reflects about the death of a man in his sixties in the desert sun.

> Every man's death diminishes me? Not necessarily. Given this man's age, the inevitability and suitability of his death, and the essential nature of life on earth, there is in each of us the unspeakable conviction that we are well rid of him. His departure makes room for the living. Away with the old, in with the new ... The plow of mortality drives through the stubble, turns over rocks and sod and weeds to cover the old, the worn-out, the husks, shells, empty seedpods and sapless roots, clearing the field for the next crop. A ruthless, brutal process—but clean and beautiful (DS, p. 214).

In both examples, the scope is broader than human sympathy. The biological, geological, scope has something to do with the Greek idea of Fate overriding even the wishes of the gods.

Thoreau asked for a continuing evolution of boyhood hunter into adult vegetarian.

On this issue Abbey is terrifically ambivalent as his Thoreau side battles with his redneck side. He never misses an opportunity to make himself obnoxious to vegetarians (from Thoreau to river rafting partners), yet he has written many moving passages that argue for animal rights by implication although he himself does not.[1]

At one point Abbey says we need coyotes. There are too many people and too many dogs, but we need to encourage coyotes. We should grind up dogs to feed to coyotes (DS, p. 209). The point here is that for Abbey domestic animals are out of grace.

To save overgrazed, eroding rangeland throughout the West, Abbey says:

> I also suggest we open a hunting season on range cattle. I realize that beef cattle will not make sporting prey at first. Like most domesticated animals (including most human [beings]), beef cattle are slow, stupid, and awkward. But the breed will improve if hunted regularly.[2] And as the number of cattle is reduced, other and far more useful, beautiful, and interesting animals will return to the rangelands and will increase (OL, p. 16).

Abbey brings a new dimension to Thoreau's paradigm. Cattle have been bred by human beings until they no longer rate respect as part of nature. As, at the beginning of the industrial revolution in America, the railroad is animated in Thoreau's imagery to sound like a hawk; now cattle bred to stand and be pumped with hormones and antibiotics are machines to Abbey. The argument could be made that Abbey moved beyond the Thoreauvian paradigm to a place where he sees that man has devalued some animals and removed them from nature, from the pale of protection. Abbey fails Thoreau's test, does it consciously and deliberately, and part of his argument is that man's intervention in nature has changed the assumptions on which Thoreau proposed his model. But in many ways he shows he carries Thoreau's Higher Laws with him as a burden about which he is sometimes defensive, but which he sometimes does not mind carrying.

Late in his life Abbey wrote one thick novel that is in its entirety a problem in the Abbey-Thoreau relationship.[3] The protagonist of *The Fool's Progress* (1988) is named Henry, Henry Lightcap, and he bases his life on Thoreau's teachings and example. He insists on a life of what he calls "Voluntary Simplicity," and he works six months a year for the National Park Service to free himself for higher pursuits, reading and hiking, philosophy and nature. He says, "If as Henry Thoreau claimed a man could get by on six weeks' work a year, then Henry Lightcap—with the occasional odd wife and maybe a kid to support—should be able to manage on six months' work a year" (FP p. 246).

The problem is that Henry Lightcap's life is a mess. Henry speaks to one wife:

> Voluntary simplicity, Myra. Many professors of philosophy but no philosophers. I want to be a philosopher, goddamnit, ... There's two ways to be rich: (1) sweat and scheme and grovel for money and never get it anyhow; or (2) live the simple life, (FP, p. 181).

His wife has said, "What you mean is there *is* no bathroom in this dungeon, right? This mud tomb. That's what you mean, isn't it Henry? You bastard" (FP, p. 181). Divorce papers followed.

Henry writes to another wife, who has already left: "Darling Elaine, ... We must simplify our lives, my darling—simplify! simplify!" (FP, p. 70).

Is Abbey blaming the mess of Henry Lightcap's life on Thoreau? Henry Lightcap muses,

> There was a flaw in the program. The program did not appeal to women, especially married women, especially those married women married to Henry Lightcap. No, screamed Myra (for example), I will not spend my life drifting from park to park, scraping by on unemployment checks, living in a nomadic state. How about Utah, he'd suggested. No! Arizona? Impossible! Alaska? Never! Well, he said, there's Idaho. Why not Siberia? she said; at least then the misery would be permanent. I'll apply, he said (FP, p. 302).

The divorce papers followed soon after.

He tells his last wife, Claire: "I believe in working for my bread— six months a year ... we're going to live. In honest poverty. Voluntary simplicity, like Thoreau said" (FP, p. 367).

Having said "honest poverty" Henry Lightcap takes a part-time temporary job guarding a dope deal (FP, p. 366). He makes $500 (FP, p. 367ff), making a mess of Thoreauvian integrity. Claire burns up his $500 (FP, p. 369). (Claire has defended Thoreau personally and stylistically when Henry Lightcap has attacked him.)

Henry's brother Will, too, seems to regulate his pastoral life back on the Appalachian farm according to principles of Thoreauvian simplicity, and he measures expense in days of work (FP, p. 420), "the amount of *life* one has to pay for something," as Thoreau wrote.

The issues are not simple. At one point Henry Lightcap ascribes a quotation from Thoreau to Jesus. At another point, needing to disown Thoreau briefly to win an argument with his wife, Henry Lightcap calls Thoreau a pederast (FP, p. 367). Later when he cites Thoreau for authority to bolster another argument, his wife asks, "The pederast?" "Yes," he replies. This I think is where Abbey can laugh at his own ambivalence, but, especially because the novel presents its protagonist as a self-confirmed fool, there is no sure footing for analysis. There is just a sure indication of a deep and emotional relationship between the two writers.

Abbey's war with Thoreau, while occasionally venomous, was never very deep. He was always in deep basic agreement with Thoreau, especially on the need for wild(er)ness. Abbey wrote:

> [Thoreau] becomes more significant with each passing decade. The deeper the world] sinks into industrialism, urbanism, militarism ... the more poignant, strong, and appealing becomes Thoreau's demand for the right of every man, every woman, every child, every dog, every tree, every snail darter, every lousewort, every living thing, to live its own life in its own way at its own pace in its own square mile of home. Or in its own stretch of river (DR, p. 36).

For Wordsworth nature was a nurse; for Thoreau, a source of integrity. For Abbey, wilderness represents nothing less than the possibility of political freedom. As wilderness grows more scare, it becomes more *radically* necessary.

Something like a shadow has fallen between present and past, an abyss ... that cannot be bridged, ... so that memory is undermined and the image of our beginnings betrayed, ... rendered not mythical but illusory. We have connived in the murder of our own origins. ... A fanatical greed, an arrogant stupidity, has robbed us] of the past and transformed tour] future into a nightmare. (JH, pp. 225–226) Abbey has large answers, but they are especially problematic.

As with Thoreau's focus on the succession of forest trees, Abbey provides, within a larger philosophical context, specific suggestions for improvement. I will use one microcosm as an example: Abbey's suggestions for preserving our national parks, which now too often resemble drive-in theme parks, complete with motels, restaurants, and exhaust pollution. Abbey's plan is to ban automobiles; these are the three points: (1) no more cars in national parks (DS, p. 52), (2) no more new roads in national parks, (3) Put the park rangers to work. He saw a certain remoteness and difficulty of access as necessary to a wilderness experience. Abbey would supply shuttle buses to take hikers and campers into the parks, Park Service trucks to carry in their equipment, but people would be required to walk. This is Abbey's third point (and please remember he spent years as a park ranger).

> Put the park rangers to work. Lazy scheming loafers, they've wasted too many years selling tickets at toll booths and sitting behind desks filling out charts and tables .... Put them to work. They're supposed to be rangers—make the bums range; kick them out of those ... air-conditioned offices, yank them out of those overstuffed patrol cars ... .

They will be needed on the trail. Once we outlaw the motors and stop the road-builders and force the multitudes back on their feet, the people will need leaders. A venturesome minority will always be eager to set off on their own, and no obstacles should be placed in their path; let them take risks, for Godsake, let them get lost, sunburnt, stranded, drowned, eaten by bears, buried alive under avalanches—that is the right and privilege of any free American. But the rest, the majority, most of them new to the out-of-doors, will need and welcome assistance ... . Many will not know how to saddle a horse, read a topographic map, follow a trail over slickrock, memorize landmarks, build a fire in rain, treat snakebite, rappel down a cliff, glissade down a glacier, read a compass, find water under sand, load a burro, splint a broken bone, bury a body, patch a rubber boat, portage a waterfall, survive a blizzard, avoid lightning, cook a porcupine, ... predict the weather, dodge falling rock, climb out of a box canyon, or pour piss out of a boot. Park rangers know these things, or should know them, or used to know them and can relearn; they will be needed" (DS, p. 56).

Yes. This is it, Abbey's answer to the urban wasteland: every American's right to be eaten by a bear. And underlying the comic exaggeration is the seriousness of the enterprise. Abbey believed that "The only foreseeable alternative ... is the gradual destruction of our national park system" (DS, p. 57).

Edward Abbey, in the tradition of Henry Thoreau, was never quite serious, was always very serious.

## Works by Edward Abbey

AR: *Abbey's Road.* New York: Plume, 1991.

BC: *The Brave Cowboy: An Old Tale in a New Time.* 1956. Albuquerque: Univ. of New Mexico P, 1977.

BW: *Beyond the Wall: Essays from the Outside.* New York: Holt, 1984.

DR: *Down the River.* New York: Dutton, 1982.

DS: *Desert Solitaire: A Season in the Wilderness.* New York: Touchstone/Simon & Schuster, 1968.

FP: *The Fool's Progress: An Honest Novel.* New York: Holt, 1988.

HL: *Hayduke Lives!.* Boston, Toronto, London: Little, Brown and Company, 1990.

JH: *The Journey Home: Some Words in Defense of the American West.* New York: Dutton, 1977. Plume (Penguin group), 1977?

MWG: *The Monkey Wrench Gang.* Philadelphia and New York: J. B. Lippincott, 1975.

OL: *One life at a time, please.* New York: Holt, 1988.

# Notes

[1]In another paper I am focusing on this subject and on the specific differences over vegetarianism. This paper will now focus on the novel which all of Abbey's issues about Thoreau seemed to overflow.

[2]This is, of course, a fallacy. Human beings generally hunt for trophies. Even if we know better, our eyes are drawn to the biggest prey—weakening the gene pool of the hunted animals. Other predators take the easiest way and kill the old, the slow, the weak—improving the gene pool of the hunted animals.

[3]FP was published in 1988, HL posthumously in 1990.

---

**ISAAC P. RODMAN** is a scholar and writer now camping in the West.

# North by Northwest
# with John Muir

❖

**Richard F. Fleck**

Edward Abbey once wrote that he may never get to Alaska, but just knowing it was there was enough. John Muir knew it was there, but it was not enough. Alaska was for John Muir what the Maine woods were for Henry Thoreau. Alaska was the place where he learned to appreciate the wisdom of sound environmental living of Tlingit and Haida cultures where he observed the grinding process of huge living glaciers creating future Yosemites and where he was able to botanize to his heart's content.

Muir loved Thoreau's book *The Maine Woods* and carried a copy of it with him to Alaska in 1879 aboard the *Dakota*. Muir had begun reading Thoreau as early as the 1860s during his Wisconsin days and he quotes Thoreau frequently throughout his later writings. In 1906 he ordered a complete set of the writings of Henry Thoreau which he read cover to cover with underlinings and marginal commentary in all 20 volumes. Muir utilized Thoreau's works as a literary model for his own books which he began to write at the age of 54. It is interesting to note that both *The Maine Woods* and *Travels in Alaska* are composed of three essays based on separate excursions, and each book expresses a growing awareness and appreciation for Native American cultures. Muir writes of the Tlingits:

> I greatly enjoyed the Indians campfire talk this evening on their ancient customs, how they were taught by their parents when the whites came among them, their religion, ideas connected with the next world, the stars, plants, the behavior and language of animals under different circumstance, manner of getting a living, etc. When our talk was interrupted by the howling of a wolf on the opposite side of the strait, Kadachan puzzled the minister (the Reverend Samuel Hall Young) with the question, 'Have wolves souls?' The Indians believed that they have; giving a foundation to their belief that they are wise creatures who know

how to catch seals and salmon by swimming slyly upon them with their heads hidden in a mouthful of grass, hunt deer in company, and always bring forth their young at the same and most favorable time of the year. I inquired how it was that with enemies so wise and powerful the deer were not all killed. Kadachan replied that wolves knew better than to kill them all and thus cut off their most important food supply.

Muir respected the Indian's environmental awareness as opposed to the white man's lack of concern for Nature. In commenting on the deleterious effect of the white man's commercialism and the introduction of alcohol to native communities on Saint Lawrence Island in the Bering Sea, Muir writes forcefully in 1881:

> About two hundred perished here, and unless some aid be extended by our government which claims these people, in a few years at most every soul of them wall have vanished from the face of the earth; for, even where alcohol is left out of the count, the few articles of food, clothing, guns, etc., furnished by the traders, exert a degrading influence, making them less self-reliant, and less skillful as hunters. They seem easily susceptible of civilization, and well deserve the attention of our government."

The respected Muir's concern for Nature and communities living close to it. They called him "Glate Ankow" or Ice Chief. When Samuel Young preached the Christian word, they listed with interest, but they preferred listening to Moiré's ice sermons. One of them went like this:

> I spoke of the brotherhood of man—how we were all children of one father; sketched the characteristics of the different races of mankind, showing that no matter how they differed in color and no matter how various the ways in which they got a living, that the white man and all the people of the world were essentially alike; we all had ten fingers and ten toes and in general our bodies were the same whether white or brown or black. It is [as] though one family of Tlingit boys and girls should be sent abroad to different places and forget their own language and were so changed in habit of talking or color by the winds and sunshine of different climates."

A Chilcat elder responded to Muir by saying, "It has always seemed to me while speaking to fur traders that I have met and those seeking gold mines, that it was like speaking to a person across a broad stream that was running fast over stones and making so loud a noise that it was very hard to understand a single word that was said. But now for the first time the white man and the Indian are on the same side of the river, and understand each other." Thus Muir achieved a rapprochement in ways few others of that day had done.

Muir was to write two books about Alaska: *Travels in Alaska* and *The Cruise of the Corwin*, both posthumously published and the former available in many trade paperback editions. He was quite an artist and made many sketches of Alaskan glaciers, trees, and landscape. Muir adored the rugged coastal landscapes of panhandle Alaska, so much so that he dashed off in 1879 dragging his friend the Reverend Samuel Hall Young with him having the intention of climbing Glenora Peak in one quick day. Unfortunately, Young slipped and desperately clung to the edge of a cliff while Muir backtracked down and around to save the minister's life and reset his dislocated shoulders back in the safety of their ship. Not to be deterred, Muir set out once again to climb Glenora Peak by himself. Here is what he writes of the view from the summit:

> I reached the top of the highest peak and one of the greatest and most impressively sublime of all the mountain views I have ever enjoyed came in sight—more than three hundred miles of closely packed peaks of the great Coast Range, sculptured in the boldest manner imaginable, their naked tops dividing ridges dark in color, their sides and canyons, gorges, valleys between them loaded with glaciers and snow. From this standpoint I counted upwards of 200 glaciers, while dark-centered, luminous clouds with fringed edges hovered and crawled over them, now slowly descending, casting transparent shadows on the ice and snow now rising high above them, lingering like loving angels guarding the crystal gifts they had bestowed.

Alaska was a magnet for Muir that drew him back many times.

---

**RICHARD F. FLECK** is a professor of English at Teikyo Loretto Heights University, Denver.

# Appendix

## "The Artist of Kouroo" Project at the University of Minnesota

❖

### Austin Meredith

The present scholarly discovery apparatus is cumbersome and expensive. It is expensive to get a grant to fly to a distant city, live in a rented room for weeks or months, and venture daily into the bowels of a strange library to identify people in one-of-a-kind tintypes, trace genealogies, leaf through crumbling stacks of newsprint, etc. It is cumbersome to try to guess where, in seventeen rolls of eye-straining microfilm, is that one piece of information that may or may not be relative to a project.

At the University of Minnesota, we are building a hypertext multimedia textbase of the works of Henry David Thoreau not only to serve the needs of Thoreau scholars everywhere but to extend the research horizons of all humanities disciplines. The database is a gathering together of the public and private writings surrounding *Walden*, along with a significant body of criticism and scholarly commentary. We are enhancing texts with 19th century imagery and with small sound files. For example, you can "click" on an "icon" and listen to a performance of one of Thoreau's two or three minute poems in 19th century ballad form. We are setting up the compact disk so that, with a Thoreau paragraph on your computer screen, you will see, in a diagram, which of your colleagues have made commentaries on that particular text, and when these commentaries were made. Historians are essentially making these materials as useful as if they were fresh.

One of the things that makes this project possible is that Thoreau scholars are commenting on a completed corpus of texts: the works, letters, and poems of Henry David Thoreau, a man who isn't going to write any more words. Our prototype, *Walden*, even with its multiple drafts and wealth of commentary, is a nicely limited focus. Therefore, the corpus clearly needs to be within the same work space and search horizons as the commentaries, in a repository immediately available to all. When the technology has made internal references possible, it is merely shortsighted to continue to use external references.

The mainstay of such a project is its textbase. The selection of primary Thoreau texts is not controversial, since the standard editions are well defined. However, we are committed to a multimedia approach to Thoreau and his world, and will complement the text with visual and auditory materials. Black-and-white photographs, copies of daguerreo-types, and 19th century wood blocks will be included. Auditory material will begin with natural sounds, because these were Thoreau's focus, as well as the songs the Thoreau family sang, flute music, and the music-box melodies that Thoreau repeatedly played.

And so, humanities scholarship stands at the threshold of exciting new opportunities for research, and the best news is that we are not waiting for the technology, the technology is waiting for us. And we much prefer this situation!

---

**AUSTIN MEREDITH** is the creator and director of the "Artist of Kouroo" Project at the University of Minnesota. A graduate of Harvard, he has devoted his full time and effort to this project. Since the presentation of his paper at the Thoreau Jubilee, he has expanded the online chronology of Thoreau's life to a total of 1500 pages. Mr. Meredith is currently engaged in time-phasing the eight editions of *Walden* into this chronology, so that scholars can see how the revisions of the manuscript occurred within the framework of Thoreau's life. This provides the first diachronic, rather than synchronic, rendition of *Walden* that has ever been available to the general public.

# Index